# THE RELUCTANT

# COUNSELOR

## VOLUME 1 AND 2

BEYOND THE STARS, UFOs, TRAUMA AND

TRANSFORMATION

PILGRIMAGE TO THE MYSTERY OF PRESENCE

SELF-REGULATION. SKUBALON. SPACE DADDIES.

LOVE & ELVIS.

A Psychotherapeutic Practitioner's Story.

This Memoir is a work of non-fiction. While the publisher and the author have made every effort to ensure the accuracy of the information in this book at press time, please note that some aspects of the narrative have been modified for privacy, clarity, or creative purposes.

Unless otherwise indicated, all the names, characters, businesses, places, events and incidents in this book are based on the author's personal life experience. However, certain names, times and places have been altered to safeguard the privacy of individuals involved and to enhance the storytelling. Any resemblance to other persons, living or dead, or other actual events is purely coincidental.

This publication is the first edition of a true story designed to provide accurate information concerning the subject matter covered, but the publisher and the author assume no responsibility for errors. Readers are encouraged to enjoy the narrative while understanding that therapeutic practice is integrated to ensure an engaging and respectful presentation of true events.

THE RELUCTANT COUNSELOR: Vol 1: BEYOND THE STARS, UFOs, TRAUMA AND TRANSFORMATION: A PSYCHOTHERAPEUTIC PRACTITIONER'S STORY.

THE RELUCTANT COUNSELOR: Vol 2: PILGRIMAGE TO THE MYSTERY OF PRESENCE, SELF-REGULATION. SKUBALON. SPACE DADDIES. LOVE & ELVIS.
By JOE TAGLIARINI

OXFORD SERAPHIM WELLNESS PUBLICATIONS

This book is dedicated to *Flower*,

*Chubby Chops* and *Pumpkin.*


In the words of Rumi:

"Only from the heart can you touch the sky."

'Knowing your own darkness is the best method for dealing with the darkness of other people. One does not become enlightened by imagining figures of light, but by making the darkness conscious. The most terrifying thing is to accept oneself completely.'

— Carl Jung

'You are the light of the world. A city set on a hill cannot be hidden. Nor do people light a lamp and put it under a basket, but on a stand and it gives light to all in the house. In the same way, let your light shine before others.'

— Yeshua

# VOLUME 2

# FOREWORD

One of the most important things that I have learned in my twenty-seven years of performing proper and thorough UFO and Alien Abduction investigations (the Safety Accident Investigations I perform as a Safety Professional) is that you have to include observable data (witness or trace) from as many different perspectives as possible to obtain the most comprehensive conclusion of the event.

Looking at the UFO and Alien Abduction phenomenon researched and investigated for over seventy years by thousands of competent people, from lay researchers to our top scientists and government agencies, we have only more questions than answers.

In 2017, things started to change with the release of data from former U.S. Government sources, including evidence from Luis Elizondo, formerly of the Advanced Aerospace Threat Identification Program (AATIP). Some of the information that was released by the program included videos of military jets encountering something they couldn't identify and defying natural laws of physics. The release of those videos was part of a campaign by Luis Elizondo to shed light on the program he was now part of working with former Blink 182 Rocker, Tom DeLonge and To The Stars Academy of Arts & Science.

I have been closely following Mr. Elizondo and the information releases he has put out ever since. This was one that I felt was crucial for the UFO community to pay attention to.

"You have this infinitely huge universe that's beyond our reach and this infinitely small universe inside of us that we can't interact with. We're stuck in the middle and we're using five elementary senses to judge our environment: touch, taste, hearing, smelling and seeing. Therefore, if we are unable to interact with the universe with none of those five rudimentary senses then we'll never know it's there and yet, all around us, we know there's this reality that we will never perceive. At present, there are Wi-Fi signals, radio signals and GPS signals coursing through our bodies, but because we can't perceive them, we can't interact with them, thus we need a technological device to help us do that.

Whenever you look at the universe with human eyes, you see a bunch of little dotted sprinkles up in the sky and you may say, "Wow, how pretty." When you look at it through a radio telescope, microwave, infrared and ultraviolet projections, suddenly, the whole universe lights up and you see things that you've never seen before.

In conclusion, we tend to look at things in extremes. If it's not from here and if the congressional report says it's not from here and it's from outer space, now what?

Well, what if it doesn't say that? What if it says instead that these things are potentially interdimensional, which can be explained through quantum physics?

What if it says these things have always been here? In fact, what if they're more natural to Earth than we are? We've only arrived at the point where advancing technologically can help us interact with these things to some degree. But, what if they're more natural to Earth than us humans? If so, then maybe we are the aliens. I'm being speculative here and somewhat hyperbolic for a reason I want to encourage people to think beyond the terms of just either/or.

It is either from inner space or outer space (or off the world). That's one option, but there are other options there and I think to even begin to answer that question we need more data and we need to make this a comprehensive conversation with our top scientists, our best academics and even our most renowned and respected philosophers.

This is a conversation that involves every one of us, not just the Department of Defense and not just the intelligence community. From a national security perspective, they should be involved, but from all other perspectives, not so much.

Maybe the question of whether it is from off-world or not shouldn't even concern the U.S. Government. The only question that should concern the powers that be is if it is a threat or not and if it's not, then we're not going to worry about if indeed the origin doesn't matter.

I think it is essential that we go down just a little bit of that rabbit hole because I'm not sure it's a binary solution.

Imagine how inefficient it would be if to get to work there was no straight path and you could only get to work by taking a series of left or right turns. It would take you a long time to get to work. So, that binary way of thinking isn't necessary. It's helpful for us as humans because we are cardio-social animals, but Mother Nature ultimately has her vote. She doesn't have to abide by our rules and considering that, we may need to broaden our aperture a little bit about what these things could be."

Over the decades, after ruling out the misidentification of aerial phenomena as being man-made objects, atmospheric disturbances, prosaic natural phenomena, etc., the hypothesis that has gathered the most support has been the extra-terrestrial hypothesis (ETH), suggesting that the unexplained sighting reports are of alien spacecraft from far-off worlds or galaxies in our vast universe.

When Mr. Elizondo says, *'Maybe we just need to broaden our aperture a little bit about what these things could be...'* [1] - I believe he is speaking to that vast support and following of the ETH hypothesis because there has been an almost ignored group of different viewpoints that have tirelessly tried to bring their research findings to the UFO puzzle table in attempts to shed light on the TRUE picture of the source behind the phenomenon to no avail. Maybe now is the time for their perspectives to be respected and reviewed for their contribution to a comprehensive conclusion to this fascinating question.

Whether it be John Mack's viewpoint; *'the reported experience of the witness and our clinical assessment of the genuineness of that report, maybe the only means by which we can judge the reality of the experience.'* [2] Or, Jacques Vallee's viewpoint; *'the result of a shifting of our mythological structure, the learning curve bending toward a new cosmic behavior. When this irreversible learning is achieved, the UFO phenomenon may go away entirely. Or it may assume some suitable representation on a human scale. The angels may land downtown.'* [3] Or, Budd Hopkin's viewpoint; *'any feeling of uneasiness about a place, or any sense of lost time (that is often accounted for by daydreaming), could be attributed to alien abduction. He believed aliens were capable of blocking or submerging memories in the people they abducted.'* [4] Or, J Allen Hynek's viewpoint: *'I do believe',* he said, *'that the UFO phenomenon is real, but I do not mean necessarily that it's just one thing. We must ask whether the diversity of observed UFOs... all spring from the same basic source, as do weather phenomena, which all originate in the atmosphere,* or whether they differ *'as a rain shower differs from a meteor, which in turn differs from a cosmic-ray shower.'* We must not ask, Hynek said, simply which hypothesis can explain the most facts, but rather which hypothesis can explain the most puzzling facts. [5] *'I hypothesize an 'M&M' technology encompassing the Mental and Material realms. The psychic realms, so mysterious to us today, maybe an ordinary part of an advanced technology.'* [6]

Norio Hayakawa's viewpoint: *'The UFO phenomenon appears to me as a paraphysical intrusion into our physical dimension by an unknown intelligence or unknown sentient entities, Para physically materializing themselves to a "pre-selected" observer (or a group of observers, whether large or small) and presenting to the observer a physical extra-terrestrial phenomenon and visitations for reasons yet unknown.'* [7]

Gary Bates's viewpoint: *'They are both spiritual and physical. Humans also possess these two characteristics. I think the difference is that both good and bad angels can manifest in their realm and ours, whereas we are limited to our corporeal existence. And when they manifest in our realm, they seem to be able to alter our perceptions and even our physical environment somewhat.'* [8]

Or Ross Douthat; *'The UFO believers, most of the serious ones draw the line of the supernatural, but I don't. There are interesting parallels between descriptions of UFOs, UFO encounters, especially UFO abductions and stories associated with abductions by the Good People, supernatural beings that are neither angels nor demons throughout pre-modern human history. That's just a really interesting continuity and if you think it's all folklore if you think none of it real, then that makes sense, maybe there's like some union archetype of abductions that get interpreted as aliens in the space age and as other creatures, the secret Commonwealth in more supernaturally inclined ages, that totally could be, or they could be similar because they're the same beings who like to mess with us. I don't think you can rule out the possibility of a zone of the supernatural realm that messes with human beings without being demonic in the way we understand that term.'* [9]

Sundar Ganapathy states; *'Because, if these spirits are real, we do not know their true intentions and they may be far craftier than we can imagine. We should continue to explore and attempt to communicate in the altered state. However, we must approach such realms with caution and reserve. Data should be collected, hypotheses should be formed and tested and the scientific method should be applied as much as possible. At the end of the day, we should remain skeptical. We can only entrust the future of humanity to humanity itself.'* [10]

These are just a few of those other perspectives that have been seemingly ignored that we should have been looking at all along. Maybe, now is the time. I believe we needed to get to this point in time, as society needed to slowly be prepared to accept these other perspectives.

If that is the case and I am kind of thinking that it just might be, then it is the right time for THIS new perspective, by Joe Tagliarini, the author of this book, to bring it to you.

I have never come across such a compressive study of this magnitude into the UFO Phenomenon from a Psychotherapist viewpoint in my twenty-some years of UFO studies. He has brought a fresh new perspective that is much needed to the UFO Puzzle table.

From Joe Tagliarini's viewpoint, *'So what connection am I seeing here? My understanding is that the alien message 'the majority' of this purported, biological mixture of expressed technology, spirit and flesh bring is one of confusion, which in turn indicates how confused they may be. I am convinced, that these things are spooked by us, that they see an image of something that they want to be, that they know what we are, concerning identity, but that we as humans do not know who or what we represent.'* [11]

Joseph G. Jordan, Researcher, Investigator
President, CE4 Research Group
MUFON National Director, South Korea
MUFON CAG International Investigator
ROCKET COUNTY
State Section Director, BREVARD COUNTY, FLORIDA
+1 (321) 390-1025

# Preface

## The Times Journalist

Twenty years had passed since I last saw Bill Sebastian. Sebastian was a sharp-witted journalist I'd met on my early adventures who meticulously documented his own, having hiked hundreds of miles through enemy territory into a world of landmines, tanks, brutal weather and snakes. An urgent need to escape Ethiopia as quickly as possible for the safe and familiar comforts of Bethnal Green in the East End of London was one of many hilarious accounts of a man struggling to save himself from possible death and any form of exercise. Sebastian often attributed his sense of humor to Spike Milligan. He recounted how the Bald Twit Lion story [1] had managed to pull him back to consciousness from a coma in 1974. This awakening followed a visit from his mother, a WWII nurse, who ignored the nurse's caution about his brain activity. "Saying, 'Rebecca (my two-year-old sister) has been doing your piano practicing for you,' I laughed and the brain monitor flickered into life," Sebastian recounted with a chuckle.

During one autumn month in 2019, while making plans for my transition to Beijing, little did I know that the eventual invasion of COVID was on the horizon. In the midst of it all, I received a message from Bill, who had tracked me down through social media. I was surprised to hear his voice, he wanted to meet and catch up as he was writing a book, with a first draft entitled 'Fake News.' He wanted to include a chapter of my story. We arranged to meet at an IKEA in Tottenham, North London (a place I classed as 'Disneyland for grown-ups').

We had aged gracefully, although slightly weathered in some areas. Many late nights and the pace of London's city life had taken its toll on us. Bill handed me an A4 copy of the digital journal I'd typed back in 1996. It was the same journal I had purposefully burnt two years later, along with other memorabilia. Bill's retained copy marked its *twenty-third anniversary*. I flicked through its pages and laughed at the exploits of my younger self.

'Did I do this?' I asked myself.

I certainly am not the person I was then, or am I?

Comedy, media manipulation, spirituality and the seeking of a childhood mystery suddenly seeped back into my subconscious, reminding me of my mid-twenties.

Re-evaluating the larger-than-life characters from my younger and more creative imaginations, I could see why I had scorched the files, mainly when revisiting the memories and the feelings of the darker parts therein. Perhaps providence wanted me to look upon things with wiser and kinder eyes. Therapeutic, nonetheless. What was my intent all those years ago?

Amid Bill's collection of fabricated news stories amassed by my work with a maverick and cheeky British insurance broker, lay the gem of a story—a fictional larger-than-life personality. This character's tale would captivate, bewilder, and ignite the public's imagination, yet resonate deeply with them too. Appearing on the front page of the New York Journal of Commerce, the story garnered worldwide media attention until the mysterious figure purportedly retired to a remote island near the Bermuda Triangle.

Within minutes of meeting up with Bill for the first time in years, I'd asked him if he had any pain in his body. He immediately told me of a persistent, old shoulder injury. Placing my hand on his shoulder, I gently told the pain to leave. A total cynic when it comes to unconventional healing, Bill

15

told me he felt light and dizzy as a warm haze slipped through his shoulder. Then suddenly, he told me, beaming with relief, the discomfort departed.

Soon after, I dunked my Swedish gingerbread man headfirst into the foamy lava swirl of a dusted chocolate cappuccino and slowly bit its head off. I began to share with Bill a summary of twenty years in time, including a genuine encounter of love in 1998 (a story hidden until now). It was one I did not want to write and had long shied from. Bill's recovered files gave me that chance to explore my younger self therapeutically and evaluate things considering experience, dogma and evidence. Caffeine aided our utterance through laughter, empathy, mystery and existentialism as Sebastian and I held our cuddly IKEA polar bears.

I initially lacked the desire to write, reluctant to tread the path of pain down memory lane. However, the Beijing lockdown provided me with ample time to scale the great wall of my imagination. Despite my initial hesitation, I still hope that what I've written resonates with many readers.

Everyone has a story to tell. This is mine (so far). It is my witness. Though it is a candid testimony, it does not define me, for I am not the same person or version I once was. The following fast-paced chronicle you are about to read has remained buried since 1998 until now. I take responsibility for my choices. In some instances, I would do it all over again, but I would approach people differently in hindsight, lyrically and rhythmically. I pass no blame to anyone, for one could argue that pain seeks pleasure and vice versa. The characters are real and thanks to the Internet tracing movie release dates, news articles and the current music and pop hits of the time, the timeline is accurate. Particular names have been changed for legal reasons, which do not alter the authenticity of the actual stories.

I'm a child of the eighties—a child of TV and too many movies that perhaps inspired me to sprout the wrong sort of crop circles. I get goosebumps when I am missing the answers, but in the words of Michelangelo "Ancora Imparo" —*I'm still learning* that life is beautiful, full of wonder and love, that there is hope and grace and reason in mystery.

The search for identity commonly takes place during adolescence and early childhood. Therapy allowed me to release those trapped feelings and find the missing jigsaws of my authentic self. So, I guess my story is to give myself an understanding whilst on this rocky cradle of humanity and maybe it might help someone else too.

If I had read this story twenty years ago, I might get angry for several reasons. It has been said, *'And you shall know the truth and the truth shall set you free.'*

Be that as it may, *'but then it shall make you angry.'*

*'Since emotional regulation is the critical issue in managing the effects of trauma and neglect, it would make an enormous difference if teachers were thoroughly schooled in emotional regulation techniques. At the core of recovery is self-awareness.'*      *— Bessel Van Der Kolk.* [2]

The acknowledgment of trauma marks the initial step toward resilience, as it prevents emotional denial and unconscious avoidance. Resilience emerges from fostering self-awareness and embracing the wounded aspects of ourselves. There are numerous paths to navigate this journey, but it invariably commences with recognition and acceptance.

From birth, we are inherently attuned to our gut instincts, our innate and essential mode of existence. Yet, in the face of overwhelming trauma and lacking support, individuals may resort to emotional detachment as a means of self-preservation. This disconnect leads to a diminished sense of authenticity and wholeness.

Using free association, a process for discovering my genuine thoughts, memories and feelings by freely sharing seemingly random thoughts that pass through my mind, I will traverse through the past, present and future to create connections that reveal how my brain equates ideas. I revisited this journal to analyze my behavior, finding it painful to clarify my thoughts and to revisit the darker aspects, yet cathartic in other respects.

There are hidden treasures in the darkness of our past to explore — the reasons and motivations behind our life's choices. Memories contain feelings and patterned thoughts. Each chapter reopened Pandora's box of emotions and learned or inherited behaviors, such as confusion, pain, joy, shame, embarrassment, cognitive dissonance, emotional wounds and ultimately healing. Every generation blames the one before and the earth is spinning at over 1,670 miles per hour. If it weren't for gravity, we would all be floating and squished up against one another, pointing fingers. Yet, we are all impacted by the gravity of trauma, even in a world where we have the power of free will.

Our early experience is the template for our lifelong view of the world (an unconscious window through which we see and understand our environment). If the early domain is unreliable or hurtful, we may develop a limited view of the world where we perceive threat even when there isn't any. However, we may defensively deny or misperceive danger when it is present. In short, our view of the world is skewed away from actual reality.

I was told by one of my therapy clients, a former air cadet, that during training they were placed in a forest with a compass, Swiss knife and tent. They might find themselves lost and begin to panic. However, they would remind themselves, *'We are not lost, but temporarily unaware of our location.'*

Feeling lost indicates that we have a home to return to. The journey of discovering our authentic selves shapes the way that home looks and feels. It's alright to lose our way at times. My story stands as a testament to the strength of imagination, hope and renewed joy. Everyone has a story to share and this is mine so far. Now, before I enjoy another gingerbread man, where would *you* like to begin?

# Chapter One

## Communication that comes from a Wound

*'I suppose that since most of our hurts come through relationships, so will our healing and I know that grace rarely makes sense for those looking in from the outside.' — Paul Young.* [1]

September 2015. NLM University, London. Counseling Degree Course: Year 2

PROF. BEATRICE: "What can you see Joe?"

The morning air was alive with the flutter of pigeons, their wings tracing patterns against the sky. As I made my way to class, a distinct aroma permeated the surroundings, unmistakable and lingering. The scent of marijuana hung in the air, drifting outside from the café where students gathered, indulging in moments of leisure. Against this backdrop, an adventurous pigeon had managed to slip past security, finding itself an unexpected haven within the university canteen. Its daring presence added a whimsical touch to the scene. I am not sure if jerk pigeon was on the menu, but this rock dove looked baked already. Undeterred by the potent fragrance, I resumed my journey, the late afternoon sun casting a warm embrace. It is the second year of my course and as I return to class, NLM University beckons—a place where academia and the vibrant spirit of campus life intertwine seamlessly.

Within the hallowed halls of the university stands a bastion of knowledge and academia. Sunlight filters through the grand arched windows, casting a warm glow upon the worn blue carpet that covers the classroom floor. The atmosphere is one of quiet anticipation, as students and faculty go about their daily routines.

## The Lion

In a corner of the bustling hallway, a figure stands apart, commanding both respect and attention. This figure is none other than Professor Bernard Clairvaux, a venerable presence in the realm of psychology. At the age of 65, his countenance carries the weight of decades of study and contemplation, having been tutored by the likes of Rogers and Bowlby.

Perched upon the bridge of his nose, a pair of spectacles adds an intellectual touch to his appearance, acting as windows to a mind brimming with insights. His eyes, a warm shade of brown, provide a gentle contrast to his overall presence reminiscent of the rich hues of his Caribbean heritage. His softly spoken words create ripples of hushed reverence as he imparts his knowledge to attentive students and colleagues alike. Each syllable is carefully chosen and delivered with a gentleness that belies a hidden strength.

A subtle sternness underlies his interactions, ensuring a delicate balance between guidance and distance. Professor Bernard possesses an artful ability to avoid offending, his demeanor is a finely tuned instrument of diplomacy. His gentle approach encourages open dialogue, while his understated authority commands respect without imposing dominance, all the while never colluding with the client if they are blindsided by the elephants in the room that need addressing.

Dressed in a soft, light brown cotton suit, Professor Bernard walks the line between classic sophistication and contemporary ease. His tie, a symbol of formality, hangs loosely from his collar—a testament to his refusal to be confined by conventions. This seemingly nonchalant touch speaks volumes about his character: a man who acknowledges tradition while embracing individuality.

As he navigates the corridors, his steps are purposeful yet unhurried, as if time itself bows to his presence. A dash of British humor to downplay the stage —"If I am not inherently intelligent, at the very least I shall present myself as though I am"— captures his unwavering dedication to his craft. It echoes in the minds of those who cross his path, serving as a reminder of his commitment to excellence and the art of perception.

In his interactions with his cohorts and clients, Professor Bernard, like a gentle lion, often poses thought-provoking questions that encourage introspection. He has a particular penchant for asking probing questions that challenge his audience's assumptions and prompt deeper self-reflection. This combination of gentle guidance and unwavering strength fosters a nurturing yet transformative learning environment.

PROF. BERNARD: "Can you recall the last time someone showed you Unconditional Positive Regard?"

His question underscores his interest in the emotional and psychological well-being of those around him, as well as his belief in the value of unconditional support and empathy.

So, my story began. On the 28th of October 2015, I recalled being at war, or instead, I was passionately playing paintball a tad too seriously, jumping in the air and evading pellets. While vaulting high, I crashed heavily onto my right shoulder, causing the instant, clean break of my right collarbone. My squad wondered why I was sitting leaning with my back against a wall. When the medics arrived, I was given nitrous oxide (commonly known as laughing gas) to ease the immense pain and relax the tendons. It helped me breathe more easily and helped the broken bone to rest. When my gas canister was empty, I asked for more.

The nitrous oxide seemed to briefly remove inhibitions, providing me with an opportunity for things to surface that lay deeply buried in my subconscious. While being aware of the moment and cognizant that I would eventually come back to earth with a bump, the feelings of ecstasy and moments of calm made me ask the blonde medic, 'To mask the pain, to silence the hurt, is this why people lose themselves in alcohol?'

'If this is why people take drugs, I don't blame them,' I added.

It appears this insightful moment in the ambulance gave me a moment to step back, reflect and see things from a different perspective as to why emotionally hurting people may turn to pharmaceutical therapies.

I wasn't making a well-researched connection between my physical pain and my emotions. I gave a running commentary to myself and those around me about what I was experiencing as some things began to surface like kaleidoscope strata.

'How fragile we are? One moment the people we love are here and the next, they are gone forever.' It was like an onion layer of fear and distrust began to peel off when sharing these feelings with others, even in a euphoric state of mind.

Turning to my friend and loyal cohort, Patricia, who accompanied me in the ambulance, I said to her in response to the care from the paramedics, 'They have compassion for me.'

The blonde medic asked me, 'Have you broken anything else before?'

'Only my heart,' I replied.

I felt vulnerable to the medic's goodwill toward me at that moment. To feel their empathy for me allowed me to lower my defenses.

Why did I think this? I believe part of the answer lies in the fact that I had allowed my self-concept of how I perceive most people as untrusting and incapable of care to create a defense mechanism within. What had happened to me? Why did I think this of people? It is essential to link these reflections and studies so that when my future clients come in wounded, vulnerable, or wanting to self-harm, I hope I will be able to facilitate and relate to them. Suppose there was a disturbance between the primary caregiver and child (in the dyad). In that case, therapists can help to unlock the repression of the bad when the ideal object did something malevolent, but the client repressed it because of idealizing him/her.

Klonsky & Muehlekamp, two leading researchers in the field of self-harm, concluded in their Review for the practitioner on self-harm that the essential effective pathway to treating those presenting with self-harm is 'the clinician's ability to form an empathic, non-judgmental relationship with the client... and to be malleable in adapting the theoretical approach to the individual.' [2]

PROF. BERNARD: "Do we need love? What happens when you have no attachment or idealization?"

Research from Scottish Physician Ronald Fairbairn would answer our professor Bernard's question over time. The therapeutic key is to let go of the idealization for many others and me. I dare to release, feel and forgive, allowing the emotions to surface as I recall the wounds and the process of self-repair continues.

As a psychotherapist, I'm conscious of how unconditional positive regard affects my client. A process that I hope to be intentional about, to be consistent in its extension to others (mainly to myself) while exploring my client's inner world with my use of empathic understanding involves a fearless exploration of another's inner world to sense what meanings remain unspoken.

PROF. BERNARD: "As counselors, it is our duty to respond to our clients with authenticity and understanding. Some clients may be quick to detect insincerity and prefer organic counseling methods over mechanical ones. Therefore, counselors need to approach the client with empathy and actively engage in understanding their perspective."—He pauses, glancing at his cohort, emphasizing the importance of what he's about to say.—

"I learned a long time ago that we are not supposed to rescue our clients. This requires being fully present in the moment, without distractions or rushing. By truly empathizing with the client, the therapist can create an environment where the client feels valued and loved unconditionally."

## The Eagle.

Seated alongside Professor Bernard is Professor Beatrice Potter, a woman in her mid-50s with piercing blue eyes, who possesses an air of quiet intensity that immediately captures the attention of those around her. Her hair, a combination of blonde tones intermingled with threads of silver, cascades gracefully down her shoulders, exuding an aura of time-tested wisdom and experience. It carries with it the essence of the sky itself, with strands that shimmer and dance like rays of sunlight piercing through clouds. Each strand seems to possess a natural strength and resilience, as if infused with the spirit of a majestic creature that soars effortlessly through boundless skies. Hailing from the heartland of Kansas, her presence seems to embody the vast expanse of the prairie, hinting at hidden secrets and untold stories yearning to be unveiled. Yet, it was in the bustling cityscape of New York where she honed her skills and crafted her narrative.

Her eyes, deep and penetrating, hold a gaze that could rival the most observant of eagles. They scan and probe, peering beyond the mere words spoken, delving into the uncharted territories of thoughts and emotions that lie beneath the surface. Professor Beatrice possesses a unique ability to unravel the intricate tapestry of the human mind, laying bare the hidden corners that often remain untouched and unexpressed.

Much like her counterpart, Professor Bernard, she wears her wisdom with a sense of serenity that comes only from years of navigating the complexities of the human psyche. The lines etched on her face are not signs of weariness, but rather testaments to the countless journeys she has undertaken alongside her clients. Her presence exudes a quiet reassurance, enveloping those who seek her guidance in a comforting embrace.

In the realm of counseling, Professor Beatrice skillfully navigates the intricate landscape of emotions, guiding individuals through the labyrinth of past traumas and unhealed wounds. Her discerning gaze pierces through the surface layers of words and actions, revealing the profound truths that lie beneath. While she remains mostly silent, her silence is far from passive, it is a deliberate choice. She is the cradler of secrets who has been granted a clarifying lens through which to view the world – a view with less distortion, denial and illusion, a view of the way things truly are.

Oh, how I wish I had what she had, but to soar on thermals means you must go through a journey from which you sometimes wish you could retract.

A silent understanding passes between Beatrice and those she counsels—a mutual acknowledgment of the unspoken truths that reside within the edge of awareness and the felt sense. She knows that they know that she knows, creating a bond of trust and vulnerability that allows for profound transformations to take root. Her patience appears infinite, a wellspring of strength that flows from her journey through the struggles and triumphs of countless broken souls.

Professor Beatrice stands as a pillar of support, a guardian of emotional well-being who has traversed the winding road of human suffering and resilience.

PROF. BEATRICE: "The counselor understands what's goin' on in their client's world and treads carefully, like walkin' 'round in their mental garden, not wantin' to mess up anythin' with some plan to shift their space. They won't snap a bent reed, and they won't lose themselves in the client's story." Her voice, soft yet deliberate, conveys a profound respect for the intricacies of the therapeutic journey. She pauses, her gaze drifting as if lost in thought, before continuing. "The talker needs to tune into their own inner world—whether it's fear, comfort, sunshine, rain, or snow—not just the other person.

### August 1941—20<sup>th of</sup> January 1943

In the vast and freezing landscape of Siberian snow, a Sicilian soldier finds himself a world away from his modest hometown and pastoral life as a shepherd. Amidst the biting cold, he stands resolute, rifle gripped firmly, each exhales a puff of silver in the frigid air. The staccato reports of his luger rifle piercing the frosty horizon, targeting a Russian sniper methodically eliminating his fellow company members.

Amidst the chaos, a moment of dire consequence unfurls as the Sicilian bears witness to his comrade's fall, struck down by a well-aimed shot. Driven by a surge of courage, he charges towards his fallen friend, intent on offering aid. Yet, amid his valiant advance, his adversary takes aim and fires. A sharp, searing pain ripples through him as the bullet finds its mark, embedding itself in the Sicilian's buttocks. Despite his gallant effort, he is subdued and captured by the very foe he sought to vanquish.

During and after the tumult of World War II, numerous Italian soldiers found themselves in the clutches of Soviet forces, confined within a web of prisoner-of-war camps scattered across Russia. These captives were primarily ensnared during Italy's role in the Axis incursion, an operation known as Operation Barbarossa, as well as the bitter skirmishes of the Eastern Front.

Within these POW camps, conditions were often brutal, with Italian soldiers enduring the unforgiving elements, scarce sustenance, inadequate medical care and forced labor. While the exact tally of Italian prisoners in custody remains uncertain, estimates suggest that tens of thousands were swept into captivity.

Among the most notorious episodes involving Italian POWs was the "Tragedy of the Italian Hall," a terrible event that unfolded in April 1942. Thousands of Italian captives confined in a camp near Yelabuga, Tatarstan, staged a protest demanding improved treatment. The response of the guards was marked by brutality, resulting in the loss of many Italian lives.

As the echoes of conflict faded and the war's curtain drew to a close, some Italian POWs were eventually repatriated to their homeland, while others endured extended periods of confinement within the Soviet Union's borders. The experiences and fates of these captives varied widely, shaped by the specific circumstances of their internment. [3-7]

Giuseppe (Beppe) Frangiamore, my maternal grandfather, spent an undisclosed period as a POW during the war before returning to his village in Aqua Viva (Living Water), Sicily, to resume farming. He consistently avoided discussing his wartime memories whenever the topic arose. It was obvious the memory still troubled him.

At the age of twenty, he was illiterate, but eventually, a man skilled in secret arts and clairvoyance taught him how to read. According to the story, Giuseppe allegedly witnessed tables dancing and with further instruction, he developed the ability to make wolves appear in the shepherd fields by whispering to the ground, a clever trick. (Stories of shepherds who summon wolves by whispering to the ground are shared among the community, some speculate that thieves spread such tales to operate undetected, knowing people were too frightened to venture out at night).

However, my mother told me that he would direct his anger towards animals, a temper that seemed to stem from the hauntings of flashbacks of the war. Undoubtedly, his PTSD sought solace and healing.

*'Anyone who was tortured remains tortured ... anyone who has suffered torture never again will be able to be at ease in the world ... faith in humanity, already cracked by the first slap in the face, then demolished by torture, is never acquired again.' — Jean Améry.* [8]

Another soldier, also from Aqua Viva, Platani, Sicily, Giuseppe Tagliarini—my father's father—clings desperately to a piece of wood, his belt tied tightly around it. Incapable of swimming, he battles exhaustion, hunger and the biting cold. As his ship, ravaged by enemy fire, succumbs to the depths, his unwavering will to survive keeps him afloat for hours, awaiting rescue.

Tagliarini, a young railway worker, is conscripted into the nefarious machinations of a failed artist turned German dictator with a distinctive mustache. After a day adrift at sea, he is eventually taken captive aboard a

British vessel, only to find himself once again confronted by nautical peril as the ship comes under attack and begins to sink. Bound by the constraints of his inability to swim, he once again secures his belt to a fragment of floating debris, while memories of his mother's tearful farewells resurface—her somber words foretelling the loss of one of her beloved sons.

For three arduous days, Giuseppe clings tenaciously to the makeshift buoy, until rescue finally arrives in the form of an Italian vessel, sparing him and others from a watery grave. Thankfully, fate had intervened, sparing him from yet another tragic demise.

These experiences indelibly mark Giuseppe's second encounter with the horrors of war, their weight forever imprinted upon his soul. Yet, amid the chaotic tapestry of despair, glimmers of hope persist, showcasing the resilience and ingenuity of Giuseppe and his compatriots. Together, they navigate treacherous territory, seeking refuge in a macabre haven concealed beneath the lifeless bodies of fallen comrades—an eerie tableau where the boundaries between life and death blur.

Meanwhile, during World War II, Giuseppe's brother, Antonio, a courageous war courier, was not as fortunate. He exhibited remarkable bravery by infiltrating enemy camps and raining hand grenades into their bunkers, eliminating all who stood in his path. In a testament to his heroism, he was posthumously bestowed with a medal for valor, forever honored by the people of Acquaviva Platani. Nestled among natural springs, the town derived its name from the abundant water sources within its vicinity. Within the town's central square, a tall pillar stands as a symbol of remembrance for Antonio's sacrifice and the indomitable spirit of a community united by shared loss.

After the war, Giuseppe Tagliarini returned home, vowing never to eat fish again, *'The fish did not eat me, therefore, I won't eat them either.'*

He managed to maintain his sense of humor. Giuseppe Tagliarini was a hardworking, honest man who recounted Triskelion [9] stories to his son, Vincenzo, my father. These stories, no doubt passed down through generations, originated from the time when Sicily was part of Magna Graecia, the colonial extension of Greece beyond the Aegean. Myths, legends, and tales about hidden treasures revealed to people in dreams were common.

<u>Questa è la storia di uno di noi.</u>

This is the Story of one of us

Grandpa Tagliarini retired to the country, where he cultivated his gardens for the remainder of his days and kept a beehive producing honey. He liked to listen to Sicilian songs, including Adriano Celentano and the song *'Il Ragazzo Della via Gluck.'* [10] The song's lyrics nostalgically depict how the landscape of the singer's old neighborhood has changed. The mention of grass being replaced by a city signifies the urban development and growth that has taken place, altering the familiar surroundings of the singer's youth. A sentiment that captures the bittersweet feeling of seeing a beloved place undergo significant transformation. Grandpa, I am told, always kept the same folding box cutter with which he cut pieces of cheese for his Granddaughter, *Eleonora*, who liked sandwiches with tumazzo or Nutella.

His youngest son, Vincenzo, would also later recount stories to his three children of a villager chased by someone who has 'Mal di Luna' (moon sickness), which was caught when Sicilian shepherds took their young children out to the fields and left them alone with nothing to play with but the full white moon. In turn, this level of exposure to the moonlight triggered epilepsy in some, causing the child to run and scream in fear whenever the full moon rose.

*'I was like a boy playing on the seashore and diverting myself now and then finding a smoother pebble or a prettier shell than ordinary, whilst the great ocean of truth lay all undiscovered before me.'—Isaac Newton.* [11]

Vincenzo, with his rich black hair slicked back, could easily have been a surf dude if only surfboards had been available in Porto Empedcole (the Italian commune on the coast of the Strait of Sicily, a province of Agrigento, named after the Greek pre-Socratic philosopher and citizen of the City of Akragas, Empedocles). At school, dynamos and the inventions of Nikola Tesla, Marconi and Alessandro Volta fascinated Vincenzo, the youngest child of three. As a child, he also loved songbirds and as a teen, Vincenzo would go to the beach with his specially made headphones. He would astound my two younger brothers and me with the story of how he made his very own radio using galena (diode) as a teenager. Crystal minerals receptive enough to catch faint radio signals using a special headset with sensitive cat whisker needles enabled him to tune into local AM stations when hovered.

During our early years, dad used to share his hobbies and stories with us. He'd show us how to make magnets using batteries and metal forks. He often brought up Marconi, the ingenious inventor and how experts were curious about studying his brain after his death to understand his exceptional abilities. He'd also recount a memory from his past when he was at the beach hunting for minerals.

Back then, a preacher had gathered a crowd and talked about fallen angels corrupting the world during Noah's time, as well as falling stars. This childhood memory left a lasting mark on him and it had a vicarious impact on me too. In the stillness of that moment, the preacher's words echoed like whispers of ancient truths, painting vivid pictures of celestial battles and divine mysteries.

*1965 Soundtrack 'Le colline sono in fiore' – New Christy Minstrels, No 1*
*'The hills are in bloom'*

March 1965, Beppe Frangiamore and his wife, *Graziella,* took their two young daughters, *Maria* and *Lucia* and immigrate to England in the quest for work. This was a new chapter for her and her family as they moved to a little place in Hertfordshire called Waltham Cross. My Mother (born on December 12th, 1949) was named after the patroness *Saint Lucia of Syracuse,* who was persecuted for her faith and had her eyes removed which were then restored by God.

*Nonno Beppe* eventually worked for British Rail. It was only two days after arriving in their new home that mum began working in a shoe factory with her mother, who worked the machines and her sister Maria, who was also her best friend. They often laughed and cried together, sharing a unique bond with twin-like intuition. Lucia's strong work ethic was visible from an early age. Maria performed the finishing touches and mum put the shoes into boxes to be retailed. While Lucia had exciting hopes and dreams for a new future with her family, it was just eight months later that their world would be turned upside down.

One sad day in November 1965, sixteen-year-old Lucia and her mum, Grace Picone, crossed a road in Waltham Cross, where a lorry hit them both. Grace was killed and Lucia was in a coma for weeks. My mother would carry those emotional scars throughout her life.

PROF. BEATRICE: "Check your notes and let's see what Darwin's has written down."

*'The emotion of love, that of a Mother for her infant, is one of the strongest of which the mind is capable ... No doubt, as affection is a pleasurable sensation, it generally causes a gentle smile and some brightening of the eyes.'* [12]

PROF. BEATRICE: "How 'bout we go 'round and take turns readin' what the other Psychotherapists had to say. Joe, you up for readin' Sigmund Freud?"

JOE: *'... the mother-infant relationship is unique, without parallel, established unalterably for a whole lifetime as the first and strongest love-object and the prototype of all later love relations.'* [13]

PROF. BEATRICE: "Any of y'all got a taste of Melanie Klein's stuff? Who's up for sharin'? Much obliged, Patricia."

PATRICIA: *'The process of transferring love from a person to a love of life is of the greatest importance for the development of the personality and human relationships: indeed, one may say, for the development of culture and civilization as a whole.'* [14]

PROF. BEATRICE: "Dinah, reckon you can take the next bit and read it out loud for us?" *'John Bowlby's* (the pioneer of attachment theory) *major conclusion, grounded in the available empirical evidence, was that to grow up mentally healthy, the infant and young child...'"*

DINAH: *'...should experience a warm, intimate, continuous relationship with his Mother (or permanent Mother substitute) in which both find satisfaction and enjoyment.'* [15]

As a young teenager, mum carried on and persevered with life. With limited help and resources, Lucia was determined to make her life count and make her mum and dad proud by living an honorable life. When she became a young lady, my mum was incredibly beautiful and resembled a young Sophia Loren. Naturally, she would attract much interest through family introductions.

A year later, Nonno and his daughters moved to Standard Road. It didn't help that the place they now lived was a stone's throw away from the Royal Small Arms Factory, also known as RSAF Enfield. This factory produced firearms for the British Armed Forces, operating for over 200 years, from the early 19th century until its closure in the 1980s. It played a significant role in supplying firearms for various military conflicts, including both World Wars. Therefore, every now and then, it would be involved in testing firearms or conducting other manufacturing processes that could produce noise. This would no doubt exacerbate Nonno's condition, as well as fueling racist tendencies toward Italians among those who worked near the plant.

Amidst this backdrop, an unexpected family occasion brought an encounter with Vincenzo, a young man keen on mum. He eagerly requested to meet her the following week at the end of her working day. Despite mum's reservations, she agreed to the meeting, albeit setting the time half an hour after finishing work to minimize her presence.

Handsome Vincenzo came to the UK at age eighteen in 1966. Sporting his delightful Elvis quiff, he turned up day after day for about a week until he figured out that mum was playing hard-to-get and arrived early another time to surprise her.

Vincenzo and Lucia were married on the 7$^{th}$ $^{of}$ March 1970 and they moved to Paddington (the place where Prince William, Prince Harry, Prince George and Princess Charlotte were all born, not forgetting the middle-class Brown family who found Paddington Bear at Paddington railway station in London) to start their newly married life. After two years, they came back to live in Enfield. They had humble beginnings renting themselves a small bedroom to accommodate the whole family.

PROF. BEATRICE: "What can you see Joe?"

JOE: "My mother was remarkable—always caring, compassionate and full of love. Her actions spoke volumes, putting others before herself, even moving back to Sicily for six months to care for her ailing mother-in-law."

PROF. BERNARD: "Truly selfless and admirable. Providing care like that takes immense dedication."

JOE: "Absolutely and amidst her hard work, she never lost sight of spending quality time with her family. We embarked on small family adventures, ensuring they were enjoyable for all."

PROF. BERNARD: "She was the heart of your family, the glue that held everyone together."

JOE: "Like a nurturing hen, she shielded her chicks under her wings, fostering unity throughout her life. She stood by her children unwaveringly, even during challenging times."

PROF. BERNARD: "Unconditional love and unwavering support—an exceptional trait."

JOE: "I guess her love surpassed achievement, she believed in the goodness within everyone, nurturing hope through encouragement."

PROF. BERNARD: "It sounds like her positive approach undoubtedly left a lasting impact on those around her."

JOE: "Absolutely, whenever anyone faced pain or challenges, her natural ability for healing and offering light earned her immense affection. Interestingly, her name, Lucia, translates to 'Light.' "

PROF.BERNARD: "Very fitting indeed. Your mum radiated brightness, leaving an indelible and remarkable impact on all she encountered."

JOE: "Her sense of humor was a natural gift."

PROF. BEATRICE: "Appreciate you sharin' her story, Joe. It's a fine testament to the might of unconditional love and the deep impact one person can make on others' lives, sounds like she is the warmth of the sun on a snowy day."

# Chapter Two

## Nonna

*'Each human being is born with a brain that is not yet fully structured, it takes at least the first three years to complete this process. According to the early experiences of the child—whether he receives love or cruelty—his brain will be structured.'—Alice Miller.* [1]

My Grandfather remarried a few years later. I had a Nonna who was affectionately known to my brothers and me as 'Nonna Columba' meaning *Grandma Dove*. Together, they had a child in 1972, Calogero who was born with Down syndrome.

I was born on the day that *John Paul Getty III* (Grandson of oil tycoon, J. Paul Getty) was kidnapped in Rome by Italian gangsters wanting a ransom for his abduction.

For the first few years of my life, my Nonna looked after me while both my parents worked. I fondly treasure memories of being cared for by my Nan, including playing with newborn kittens in the shed, watching Elvis musicals, enjoying the joy of watching George Formby playing his banjo and comedian Norman Wisdom, who portrayed a lovable and clumsy individual getting into comical situations while working odd jobs. I also marveled at Evel Knievel's stunts and indulged in candy sweets. Later, I collected Superman the Movie stickers.

An entire allotted garden space of homegrown vegetables was there for me to explore, whilst catching white butterflies that hovered over the cabbages with a net. Nonna would make strips of pasta and let them dry on broom handles holding them high in place in the kitchen. I would get ice cream whenever the ice cream van came to Standard Road, with its American Roger Ramjet jingle playing, with *Mario*, the same ice cream man who would continue to serve Enfield into my adult life. Nonna was so kind that once when I dropped the ice cream, she didn't shout but bought me a new one.

However, memories of my Grandfather were not as consistently enriching. Picture a stern figure, one minute smiling, laughing and telling jokes, the next serious, moody and angry with a cigarette often in his hand. Yet, I loved him and I sensed that he could see that I loved him whilst he shared his stories in the Sicilian language.

I recall my Nonna, Columba, was very fond of me. She would look after me and Calogero, who was born a year before me. Nonna would proudly introduce me to everyone as her grandson. Mum seemed to resent her in some respects, as she never referred to her as 'Mum.'

Sometimes, growing up, my feelings became ambivalent, should I look upon her as a step-grandma or my real grandma? My mother's resentment soon projected onto me. Regardless, as I look back now, I see the love she had for my younger brothers and me.

*'Lovin' you is easy cause ...' – Minnie Riperton (1974)*

PROF. BERNARD: "What's the earliest memory you recall, Joe? I mean, the very first thing you recollect, Joe?"

JOE: "My *earliest* memory? My Mother dropped me off at my Grandparents. She held me in her arms and I remember being angry with her for leaving me. I did not want her to go. She sang me a song, 'Lovin' You', she rocked me, kissed me and I would fall asleep as she laughed and spoke in Sicilian."

Once I woke up, my Nonna would come and give me a bottle of water or milk and I would be placed on a sofa, watching TV musicals or playing with Calogero.

Calogero died at the age of four during a complex heart operation, I am told. I mourned and asked constantly for him, being told he went to Heaven.

Another memory from childhood is when, for no reason at all (not that you needed a reason), perhaps I squashed one of my grandfather's lettuces in the garden during the heat of the day while catching butterflies. I recalled waking up on the sofa from an afternoon siesta, my throat parched for a drink. As I cried, my grandfather came and slapped my face hard. I bit my lip and swallowed my tears. Upon reflection, I realized and felt my inner child: dazed, confused and sad. I could even hear the sound of the slap. 'Why did Grandad do this?' Nonna came to my defense, shouting in Sicilian, 'What are you doing? He's just a toddler!' I recalled her using the words 'Caro bambino' while she soothed me and gave me a drink, still scolding my Granddad.

PROF. BERNARD: "Do you know what happens to a kid's brain when they're hit, when kids are subjected to that?"

JOE: "No, I can only imagine."

PROF. BERNARD: "When kids are subjected to that, it shatters their regulatory system."

JOE: "Jesus!"

PROF. BERNARD: "They dissociate... when this was ever happening to you, did you ever feel like you were in a dream or watching from above?"

JOE: "Yes, I used to have these recurring dreams where I would walk in my sleep, it felt so real!"

PROF. BERNARD: "You felt good because you were disconnected from it, yeah? From distressing emotions, but it's not a healthy long-term coping mechanism."

JOE: "For sure, I wish I could dream walk now!"

PROF. BERNARD: "Well, that is a survival strategy that becomes a way of managing unpleasant emotions. That's pathological. It's not a good way to manage emotion, it's a good way to survive in that moment. But when it happens over and over, it just becomes the way you manage unpleasant feelings, which are left behind by all those experiences too, It's like a neglected plant that only gets watered during a drought—it survives, but it never truly thrives"

## The Potato plant

JOE: "Another time, I proudly grew a potato plant in my mum's Garden and one day my Nonno (Grandad), knowing that I had nurtured and watched the plant's growth, pretended that he was going to remove it with his fork hoe while he tilled the ground. I begged him not to, yet he seemed to enjoy laughing at my reaction. He did this three times before I snatched the fork from his hand and destroyed the plant myself."

PROF. BERNARD: "The incident you've shared reveals an intriguing psychological narrative. Your experience with your Grandfather (Nonno) and the potato plant touches upon themes of attachment, vulnerability and the complexities of human emotions. It seems to reflect a delicate dance between nurturing and loss, with your emotional investment in the plant symbolizing a sense of accomplishment and connection.

Your Nonno's actions, seemingly lighthearted in his mind, unveil layers of underlying dynamics. His actions could be viewed as playful teasing or mocking, yet they also emphasize the transient nature of things we care for. The interplay between your attachment to the plant and the potential threat of its removal raises questions about trust and the emotional impact of such experiences."

JOE: —*Speaking from a child's perspective, addressing Nonno in the empty chair* — "It's like I really loved that potato plant Nonno and I felt all happy and proud watching it grow. I loved you, I respected you and I didn't know why you were doing this. Then, you... you pretended to take it away and it made me feel super upset. I think you were teasing me, but it made me overly worried about losing my plant. I didn't understand why you'd do that, Nonno, it was like you were taking the piss."

PROF.BERNARD: "Joe, you feel as though Nonno really challenged the connection you had with him. It leaves you feeling vulnerable. How do you think this experience might be affecting your sense of trust in relationships now?"


## The Tricycle


When I was five years old, my parents bought me a red tricycle, with white tires and black trimmings on each side and a bell on the left handlebar. I loved the freedom and speed so much that one day, whilst at my Mother's house, I took it for a spin, cycling the two-mile journey from Albany Road through Albany Park and over the River Lea Bridge to Standard Road and finally to the back garden door of my Nonna. It was the same park that our mum used to take us through to visit our grandparents. She would place us all into one pram, with Mark in the central cot part, David near the foot pedals and me underneath the main frame that separated the frame from the gravel. It was such fun. However, as was often the case, we crossed the bridge and some children would taunt us, saying 'Pakis, go back to your own country.' I felt scared for my mum.

Needless to say, Nonna was shocked to see me and instantly said that my mum must be worried about me. I became scared as she picked up the black rotary phone and placed her finger in the corresponding finger hole, rotating the dial clockwise until it reached the finger stop. Half an hour later, mum came through the door, livid. She held me upside down by my feet and smacked my bottom in front of my Grandparents and their guests in their living room, while Nonna implored her to go easy on me."

September—December 2015 NLM University.

PROF. BERNARD: "Let's talk about working with clients who need to regress to early infant experiences to heal and continue their development and who Winnicott describes as those who must address *'the early stages of emotional development (that) are full of potential conflict and disruption... primitive love has a destructive aim and the small child has not yet learned to tolerate and cope with instincts.' He can come to manage these things ... if his surroundings are stable and personal. At the start, he absolutely needs to live in a circle of love and strength."* [2]

Shame.

JOE: "How do I let go of the shame?"

PROF. BERNARD: "The key is to recognize that your shame is a response to past pain, not a reflection of your true self. The first step is to bring compassionate awareness to these feelings. Understand that your shame is a response to unmet needs and unresolved pain from your past. By acknowledging this, you can start to separate your true self from the shameful feelings that were imposed on you."

PROF. BEATRICE: "Shame, you see, it's a kind of social tool. It's like a guide showin' us the ropes. When a mom, dad, or someone watchin' over ya says, 'No, don't get near that fire!' and you feel that shame deep down, it's your body sayin', 'Hold up, danger zone.' We learn from it, like, 'Ah, that's risky stuff,' or 'Not cool, better not have taken that two-mile bike ride when I was five.' "

PROF. BERNARD: "But when shame is chronic and unprocessed, it can lead to the development of a shame-based personality. This results in an uncoupling of the autonomic nervous system and a disconnection between the right brain and the body, leading to numbness or a pervasive negative sensation. This emotional state becomes both a mechanism and a cause of various issues later in life, including addiction, as it perpetuates itself. To overcome shame, we need to foster self-awareness, practice self-compassion, build a support system, challenge negative beliefs, embrace mindfulness, educate and forgive ourselves, adopt healthy coping mechanisms, and be patient in our healing journey." [3/4]

PROF. BEATRICE: "Seems like shame had a regular hold on you during your early days and teenage years, keeping you from fully letting loose in life. You know, we're often much kinder to others than we are to ourselves. So it's important to remind yourself that you are worthy and that the shame you feel is more about the hurt you've experienced than who you truly are. How 'bout we dig into your relationship with your dad?"

JOE: "*My dad?* He was often absent during the day due to his night shift work. I have memories of missing him, longing for his companionship, playtime and those trips to the park to play football that he'd occasionally take me on. His daytime sleep schedule made me hesitant to wake him, as it would often lead to irritability and occasional anger. As I reflect on my self-concept, I can't help but wonder if my instinctive quietness, which eventually morphed into a habit or coping mechanism, stemmed from a deep-seated desire for his love and acceptance. I remember the fear of upsetting him if I disrupted his sleep, and the sting of being labeled as a dreamer by him only deepened my sense of inadequacy. By the end, it seemed like my silence was not only misunderstood but also used against me, leaving me feeling not just overlooked, but outright mocked."

## Solipsism

During this introspection, I questioned whether this identity had become ingrained due to the circumstances. Did my lack of confidence lead me to become quiet and somewhat introverted as I grew up? Was this attitude reinforced by my limited interaction with my father and his response to a noisy child seeking to play? I want to emphasize that I'm not seeking to place blame on anyone for my thought patterns or negative perceptions of my upbringing. It's not my parents' fault for the world wars or the templates of the traumas of life. This is the world we live in, where the imprints of life affect us all. However, I do ponder whether my current 'self-concept'—the aspiration to express myself and communicate effectively—reflects a yearning for my true, authentic (organismic) self, entwined with perceptions formed during my childhood.

My conditions of self-worth were such that though both my parents loved me and my two younger brothers, their lives were hard and everyone had to work hard, study hard and look after one another because mum had long discovered, *'The world is a nasty place and people can be horrible. Trust no one.'*

This would seem to be a slow, self-fulfilling prophecy as I entered primary school to encounter some good friendships and pleasant memories apart from April to June 1982 when England went to war with Argentina. In addition, negative school reports and low grades were not received well by my mother, who would cry and shout at me in disappointment at her own unfortified hopes, yet all I wanted to do was make her happy.

My conditions of worth were shaping my self-concept and my confidence was affected for most (though not all) of my school life. I have fond memories of sitting at a table with *Enzo, Sam, Colin and Asif,* discussing how only the good people would be rescued from a world torn by a future World War 3.

Was this a form of escapism and a better world perspective that appealed to me, but one that I didn't know how to reconcile with my Catholic upbringing? Looking back now, did I subconsciously yearn for a better world with kinder individuals, a secure foundation, or a rescue-oriented outlook, fueled by a season of sci-fi movies I had watched at home on our second-hand color TV?

JOE: "Did I feel disconnected not only because my parents were foreigners in this country, entangled in some form of genealogical bewilderment, but also due to my cultural interactions with children my age and the echoes of my Grandfather's psychic pain? Did this make me feel like I couldn't quite fit into this world, as it seemed so violent and devoid of love? It just didn't seem to make sense why the world was the way it was, why children were so aggressive. Something was amiss, but I couldn't pinpoint what it was. Why were people like this? Coupled with the later rupture of my relationship with my Mother, I would go on to seek comfort and rescue."

PROF. BERNARD: (Pauses thoughtfully) "Comfort and rescue. Joe, your words echo a profound sense of introspection and self-discovery. You've grappled with complex emotions and experiences that have shaped your view of the world. Many of us struggle to find our place and understanding in this sometimes-tumultuous world. Comfort and rescue.. it sounds like you were seeking connection."

JOE: "There were happier times, of course, outnumbering the negative moments. We used to make wine together, every summer, mum and dad would order crates of grapes and craft their own wine, with my brothers and me providing the backdrop, imitating airplane bombing noises as we swatted away wasps drawn in by the sweet aroma."

PROF. BERNARD: "... but trauma keeps score and the body retains the sting of the memory."

JOE: "Yes, but there were also joyful memories of assemblies with my friends, where we would sing hymns and listen to a well-intentioned former Navy Headmaster deliver colorful presentations on morals and emotional intelligence."

# Chapter Three

## Colors of Day

On December 12th, 1901, *Guglielmo Marconi* made the first-ever transatlantic radio broadcast. This means that at 110 light-years away from Earth—the edge of a radio 'sphere' that contains many star systems—our very first radio broadcasts are beginning to arrive. At Signal Hill, Marconi and his young assistant, *George Kemp*, confirmed the reception of the first transatlantic radio signals. With a telephone receiver and a wire antenna kept aloft by a white kite in a slate gray sky, they heard Morse Code for the letter 'S' transmitted from Poldhu, Cornwall. Their experiments showed that radio signals extended far beyond the horizon, giving radio a new global dimension for communication in the Twentieth Century. Technically, the first astronaut was the letter 'S.' You can take your pick of S's, S for spirit, S for soul, S for salvation, or S for 'show me who I am in this time-space continuum of solace.'

S for star, S for a sailor, or, rather amusingly, the Ancient Greek ἄστρον (Astron), meaning 'star,' and ναύτης (Nautes), meaning 'sailor.' In Greek, 'astronaut' translates to 'Star Sailor.'

We live in what intellectuals consider a remarkable chance or a created universe of mystery and color. It's an understatement to say that this universe is immense, it's ever-expanding, with galaxies, stars and solar systems scattered like innumerable sand particles throughout the silent or noisy expanse of space. Scientists estimate that there are at least two trillion galaxies in the observable universe. That's about two hundred galaxies for every man, woman and child on Earth. But the reality is that this number is just a rough estimate, nobody truly knows.

Meanwhile, on a blue planet with nearly six thousand years of recorded history, I zoom down back in time to North London, England, in 1981, Chesterfield Junior School. Victorian, orange, oven-baked, brickwork and heavy-duty wooden parquet flooring surround an assembly of young children singing *'Give me oil in my lamp keep me burning'*, [1] followed by *'Colors of day dawn into the mind.'*

*'So light up the fire and let the flame burn,*
*Open the door, let Jesus return.*
*Take seeds of His Spirit, let the fruit grow,*
*Tell the people of Jesus, let His love show.'* [2]

Mr. Morris, a Welsh Headmaster, enthusiastically thunders out on the piano keys whilst missing some notes. Chesterfield School was a mixed bag of emotions, good memories along with battles between bent minds and racism. At playtime, I'd join my friends in games of marbles, finding joy in the simplicity of the pastime. The Victorian-era drains served as our makeshift boundaries, delineating the playing area. With colorful glass cat's eye marbles in hand, we took turns shooting them, aiming to be the first to get our marble into the dip in the drain and win our opponents pearl. As we played, the marbles, with their diverse shapes and colors, reminded us of galaxies and stars, igniting our imagination.

My Mother would drop me at school on a rota with my dad before going to work in factories, making electronic parts at 15 Ripaults Factory, Enfield and car components for Ford. My father, Vincenzo, worked at Poly-Lina before eventually making fluorescent lighting for General Electric.

Many an awkward nightshift, my Granddad and Nonna, would look after me in my first eighteen months to five years.

Brought up under Catholicism, my two brothers and I were taken to Church for communion, to learn sacraments at Sunday school with the Italian nuns. I found having to queue in line for communion a highly anxious event, which brought blushing hot sweats. The thought that my glowing red face might bring unwanted attention caused the Sunday routine to feel like a parade of shame. Sister Gandhi, one of the stern nuns who didn't like children, gave me the impression that she used to like striking me on behalf of anything my brothers did or indeed any other younger children's misbehavior, which made me the constant benefactor of a blessed slap or two round the head. Eventually, they sent sister Gandhi packing to a remote part of Africa. We sometimes went to the Catholic afternoon school next to Chesterfield School, in addition to the Ponders End Italian service. But to be honest, at that time I found Church rather monotonous and lackluster. Confession was an altogether embarrassing experience and I was never keen on saying Hail Mary at all, I felt insincere, or the feeling of condemnation if I did not repeat the prayer. Being Catholic was a part of my culture and Sicilian heritage. With the good also came the perception of shame and disconnect. We are down here and God is far up in the sky, watching, keeping score, ready to smite.

However, there was beauty in being taught at a young age by my mother to pray the Lord's prayer and to ask for God's protection over our family. As a child, I prayed for everyone and anything, even Rupert, my first teddy bear, who, after his first time in the washing machine, hung in the moonlight off the washing line with nothing but wooden pegs to hold him.

<u>When I was a child.</u>

*'When I was a child, I talked like a child, I thought like a child, I reasoned like a child.'* [3] and as a child, I enjoyed the stories and pictures I read in my colorful children's Bible and was profoundly touched watching Franco Zeffirelli's British-Italian epic film and television drama serial version of *Jesus of Nazareth*, with a young Robert Powell playing the serious but handsome blue-eyed Savior. (Even though Christ's eyes were brown). [4]

For some reason, I especially liked Michael York's passionate portrayal of John the Baptist crying out to make a way in the wilderness. I felt tears swell up inside when I saw people beating and spitting on the innocent Messiah who had helped so many people.

At eight years old, my mum bought me a colorful Bible for my communion, which was to be held in the Church of England. Even though we were Catholic, my brothers and I loved the pictures, particularly the one of a captured blind Samson calling on the Lord to help him *one more time* as he pressed on the colossal pillars to push them down.

After my two brothers were born, my mother began to have many mood swings. Occasionally, she would put on makeup, but I could still see her tears forming tracks in the mascara. She would constantly send me to the newsagents to buy her cigarettes and would smoke them as we watched the colorful Bollywood movies screened on BBC2, enjoying the cheerful moments of escape through the Asian songs being played. She was no longer lost in space but temporarily grounded as she smoked, drank coffee and smiled and we smiled too.

PROF. BEATRICE: "Some folks, when they take a sip of water, they're swallowing down their feelings. Others, without even knowin' it, hide behind a coffee cup."

JOE: "I wonder if cigarettes and alcohol have the same effect. After all, many people in pubs drink their sorrows not to dispel them, but to numb themselves. I don't hand tissues to my clients when they cry, but they are available if needed. Often, the clients I work with are content to let their tears mix with their mascara, blurring into one color that represents the merging of their lost identities and the emergence of their true selves from the sands of time, expressed through the canvas of a living, breathing body."

My father worked on rotary nightshifts and late evenings at a Poly-Lina factory that made all sorts of plastic material and I would often wait in the evening for him with my mum whilst Kojak (a New York detective series) played on our TV. My two younger brothers, *David* and *Mark* would be in bed.

PROF. BERNARD: "When we look at the world, we are operating through the subconscious mind. The programs in that subconscious mind primarily come from downloading other people's behaviors."

JOE: "Downloading... my mother, father, grandparents, siblings and my community in the first seven years of life?"

PROF. BEATRICE: "Yep, bein' intricate, with layers upon layers, we're like a big ol' sponge takin' in the ways of the world, pickin' up on the habits of folks we're 'round. Now, if our caregivers are savvy and know how to handle their feelings and mend their wounds in a good manner, well then, we're off to a mighty fine beginning."

Gingerbread Men.

Mum taught me how to make cakes, something I relished doing and enjoyed surprising her with. I used to take some of the pastry my mum used to bake for her Sicilian biscuits and gingerbread men. I loved the taste of the cinnamon, vanilla and almond cake dough and I would mold small dough men before leaving them to harden on the radiator.

I recall mum (perhaps as a kind of joke or due to learned behavior) pretending that she wanted to cut her finger off with a sharp knife, which led me to cry and beg her not to do that. She felt remorseful upon seeing my tears. I also remember another time when I was fully awake while my mum was making spaghetti in the kitchen, I saw the shadow of a dancing dog on the ceiling above in the corridor. I couldn't understand how the shadow was formed. These memories confused me.

I also remember my Granddad, my parents and some other visitors being encouraged by my Granddad to lift him as he sat on the chair using only their fingers whilst chanting something strange, though I remember my mum did not approve of the request.

JOE: "I had dreams in which hairy, fuzzy, gorilla-like creatures were trying to break through the front and back garden doors. As I approached, the creatures would attempt to force themselves in, causing me to press against the entryways in terror. I felt frozen and unable to run away, it was as if I were stuck in slow motion and at other times, it felt like some kind of cat was walking on my ribcage."

PROF. BERNARD: "In a typical sleep-paralysis episode, a person wakes up paralyzed, senses a presence in the room, feels fear or even terror and may hear buzzing and humming noises, or see strange lights. They may have the feeling of a visible or invisible entity sitting on their chest, shaking, strangling, or prodding them. Attempts to fight the paralysis are usually unsuccessful." [5]

JOE: "My younger brother David would also have nightmares of creatures stirring caldrons. Upon reflection now, could it be that we were processing the genetic imprints of terror and trauma inherited from my mother and my Nonno?"

PROF. BERNARD: "In the realm of epigenetics, environmental factors have the capacity to influence gene expression without altering DNA sequences, however, it's essential to acknowledge that while evidence supports intergenerational transmission of trauma-related symptoms, the underlying mechanisms of this process remain complex and are still under investigation. Meanwhile, the relationship between sleep paralysis and trauma is complex and likely involves multiple factors, such as genetic predisposition, sleep disruption and psychological stress." [6]

JOE: "I guess my brothers and I did not have the tools to process our emotions when we were growing up and this resulted in unresolved trauma in our household that led to generational family conflicts. One conflict even resulted in my middle brother having a difficult birth, where his umbilical cord became entangled around his neck. My mother attributed this to something her father had said to her during an argument: *'I hope your unborn child dies.'* "

These became vicarious memories that were not fully formed and coupled with the sleep paralysis episodes that I experienced from time to time, I found myself seeing myself in the world around me as if I were still in that environment of conflict and trauma. The feelings of fear, helplessness, and terror I experienced during those episodes seemed to reinforce the unresolved trauma from my past, making it difficult for me to process and move on. My mind's constructs remained stuck in time, endlessly plowing the ground of my consciousness, unable to move forward or cultivate new growth.

# The Ox

Enter Professor Virgil Maro, an Italian counselor in his 50s who cuts a striking figure of 'One Punch Man' [7] with his bald head gleaming in the light. His eyes, a deep wine brown with a golden glimmer, add to his captivating presence. He looks super cool! He chooses lighter clothing, intentionally contrasting with his contemplative nature. Draped around his neck is a long scarf, the color of orange sunlight, as if reflected onto a flowing river. It evokes the attire worn by monks or legendary Jedi from ancient tales. Despite its unassuming appearance, this scarf carries an air of mystery, as if it holds the key to unveiling deeper truths about the universe.

With a demeanor that exudes mindfulness and a touch of poetic elegance, Professor Virgil weaves words like a master craftsman. His linguistic prowess transports his students to the cobblestone streets of Florence or the sun-drenched hills of Tuscany, inviting them to immerse themselves in the beauty and romance of the Italian tongue. Each sentence he utters carries weight, transcending the mundane with profoundness. Drawing inspiration from his Buddhist beliefs, Professor Virgil gently encourages those around him to pause and immerse themselves in the present moment. He possesses an innate ability to tether people to the now, reminding us of the fleeting nature of existence. Using grounding techniques like prompting us to name five things we can see, four things we can touch, three things we can hear, two things we can smell and one thing we can taste, he leads us to confront our emotions with clarity and understanding. In his own distinctive way, he grounds us a little bit more.

Professor Virgil often offers a poignant reminder of life's impermanence. Infused with wry humor, he paints a vivid picture of a future where our physical forms return to the earth, nurturing creatures below. He declares in his Italian accent, 'Inna 70 yearsa time we will allla be worm food.' He also quotes Nietzsche's proclamation that "God is dead," a sentiment that may puzzle some, yet provokes contemplation on shifting belief paradigms and existence. [8]

Beyond his profound perspectives, Virgil isn't merely an academic, he's also a skilled psychologist and a published author. His afternoons are dedicated to counseling sessions, guiding individuals through the maze of their minds. Armed with his psychology knowledge and keen insights, he adeptly unravels the complexities within.

Professor Virgil, with his monk-like scarf and poetic wisdom, sits cross-legged in a pose of introspection and contemplation. His presence reminds us of the potency of mindfulness, the ephemeral nature of life and the interconnectedness of all. Amid a world often racing forward, he embodies a tranquil center, inviting others to embark on a journey of self-discovery, profound understanding and a spirit of humble service, much like the steadfast ox quietly toiling in the background, supporting the greater purpose.

Ghost in the Machine.

PROF. VIRGIL: "Ah Joe, caro Giuseppe! In the case of a child dreaming of escaping a slow-motion monster, the dream could symbolize feelings of fear, anxiety, or insecurity in their waking life. The slow motion might reflect being overwhelmed and unable to escape a tough situation, while the monster at the back door could represent a perceived threat to their privacy or safety. It's important to consider children's vivid imagination and susceptibility to media influence—so the dream could also manifest something from a movie or story.

Similarly, the concept of the Hungry Ghost in Buddhism, with its insatiable craving and suffering from uncontrolled desires, exemplifies the consequences of attachment and selfishness."

JOE: "The Hungry Ghost?"

PROF. VIRGIL: "Yes, the 餓鬼 (èguǐ). These beings are believed to exist in a realm known as the 'Preta realm' or 'realm of hungry ghosts.' Depicted with a pancia grossa and boccuccia piccola, it serves as a cautionary reminder to nurture mindfulness, moderation, and compassion to break free from the cycle of perpetual dissatisfaction." [9]

Michael S. Gazzaniga, a neuroscientist and professor of psychology at the University of California, Santa Barbara, is widely known for his pioneering work in the field of cognitive neuroscience. His research on split-brain patients has greatly contributed to our understanding of how the brain processes information and produces consciousness.

In his book The Consciousness Instinct: Unraveling the Mystery of How the Brain Makes the Mind, Gazzaniga states, "Regarding consciousness, we must broaden our perspective beyond the limited wavelengths that we habitually observe. It's analogous to a radio, where we, as the perceiver, possess the power to fine-tune our level of awareness and concentrate on the most salient details. This includes the diverse mental states that humans experience, from wakefulness to a hypnotic or even a sleeping state. It's reasonable to speculate that consciousness is ubiquitous, existing in all living beings, from mesmerized chickens to sharks experiencing tonic immobility." He invites us to consider a compelling question: "Do humans possess a physical 'off switch' that could be accessed by entities like extraterrestrials or ghosts, similar to how we provoke tonic immobility in animals?" [10]

Growing up, I wasn't filtering or consciously aware of those emotions. As a result, I implicitly relived them each time colors, sounds, smells, tastes, or feelings were triggered. Even the music of Bollywood would transport me back to moments of joy and even the smell of cigarettes would provide comfort.

However, when I subconsciously reacted to authoritarian figures, it felt as if those memories were happening for the first time. My subliminal mind couldn't be outrun. I knew I would have to face these memories in the future, but for now, I was a child stuck in the dark cosmos of time. I chose to ignore my problems and instead transformed them into convenient daydreams that provided me with comfort in alternative ways.

The state of our nervous system determines the state of the world as we perceive it. Hindsight is a good thing and if I possessed X-ray vision capable of seeing beyond flesh and bone, blood and water, what would remain visible is the intricate network of my nervous system. It essentially resembles a walking tree of interconnectivity. However, experiencing a series of traumatic events can profoundly shake the core of our authenticity, leading us to seek refuge in figurative 'fig leaves' such as addictions. I see the seasons of my life and as leaves fall, I find myself shrouded in different ways to shield against the harshness of reality.

As a child, I dreaded receiving my end-of-year reports from my teachers. When I entered infant school, I did not how to speak English and was granted some grace. However, as I progressed to junior school, years three, four and five came around and my mother would cry whenever she read the negative end-of-term reports. The disappointment etched on her face would manifest into anger at my failure to pay attention to education and how the teachers had written me off.

While I struggled in school, I heard punitive voices that would scaffold and feed my inner dialogue of failure. My mother would also remind me of her academic success and the amazing things she could have accomplished if given the opportunity. She was an intelligent girl who always topped her class received recognition for her achievements and was even recommended for higher education—a rarity for women during that time. However, societal constraints prevented her from pursuing her ambitions and her brilliance spilled over into other areas of her life, such as motherhood and creativity. She enjoyed being a mother, was a creative cook and continued with her poetry, sewing and storytelling. We had opportunities we could afford to waste, but her dad had denied her access to college or further education that would have nourished her career ambitions.

JOE: "Despite my academic struggles, I never lost hope that I would one day make my mother proud. While I may not have excelled academically like her, I discovered my passions and talents later in life. Reflecting on my childhood experiences, I now realize that my mother's unfulfilled potential was another root cause of her disappointment in my academic performance. It wasn't that she didn't love or support me, but rather that she possibly projected her unfulfilled dreams and ambitions onto me."

PROF. BERNARD: "Through rigorous introspection and therapy, we come to understand the necessity of disentangling our sense of self-worth from the fickle judgments of others. Joe, it became clear that the disappointment of others did not define your abilities or potential. This realization allows you to approach education and your personal ambitions with a renewed sense of purpose and confidence, rather than being mired in fear and a sense of inadequacy."

PROF. VIRGL: "Daydreaming and escapism are like old friends, embraced by young souls to navigate the labyrinth of life's challenges. They shed light on your emotional needs during those youthful days. the footprints of a youthful traveler etched upon the sands of time.

These ways of coping also play a role in shaping your thoughts about religion, spirituality and even those chats with friends about escaping future wars. Digging into these musings, you'll find questions about what's right and what's ethical, how beliefs guide you and how they impact the person you're growing into. It's like a journey of understanding yourself, where you start to connect the dots of who you are."

PROF. BERNARD: "Should there have been disruptions in your interactions with primary caregivers, therapy can assist in unraveling suppressed negativity. It's like when the idealized figure acts in hurtful ways, but we push those memories aside due to our inherent admiration for our mother. Imagine sitting on a warm patio, reflecting on these complexities—therapy provides a space to untangle these deep-seated feelings on such familiar ground."

These insights prompt me to delve deeper into the intricate tapestry of my emotions and personal journey.

PROF. BEATRICE: "I reckon one day, when you look back on it all, you'll see how therapy and them relationships in your later years done give you a real sense of security and emotional love. It's from that there foundation that confidence and independence done sprout up, as we've been aiming to mend them early hurts and ruptures in our life."


The Rupture.


One day, when I was six, my Dad borrowed my school bag for work and later, my mum found cigarettes in the pouch. Believing them to belong to me, she beat me black and blue—she beat the Jesus out of me—and accused me of doing something. She said I had to admit to it, or there would be more beatings from my father. Crying and convulsing, confused and terrified, I had no idea what she was referring to. So, I confessed to doing bad things at school, like not paying attention or having skirmishes or arguments with friends—any little thing I could recall. I apologized for it all.

It was only later, as I lay in bed with a lump on my head and welts on my face, tears stifled for fear of sharing, that she came to my room to apologize, offering me milk and biscuits. She had found out the cigarettes belonged to my father. She tried to comfort me, but I didn't trust her. Despite this, I still yearned for closeness, yet I remained on edge and slowly started to grow distant.

PROF. BERNARD: "On edge, it sounds as though you grew up in a state of hypervigilance, constantly on guard and ready to respond to perceived threats. You felt betrayed and violated. How might your six-year-old self express his feelings?"

JOE: "I felt hurt and scared. It was like when you trust someone and they do something bad to you and it makes you feel sad and unsafe."

PROF. BERNARD: "This heightened state was mentally and emotionally exhausting and it probably interfered with your daily functioning."

For years into adulthood, I would grind my teeth due to nerves, thus developing bruxism. My mother would place garlic on my belly button, saying it would help soothe me and rid me of the 'virmi', worms in our native language.

In my anger—which was inner sadness—and due to the unpredictability of my primary caregiver, in my self-soothing and my subconscious quest for comfort and meaning within the imprint of my world and upbringing, I became the bookworm kid at school. On book days, I would head to the library to check out picture books. I loved Asterix and Obelix, Tintin, Judge Dredd, Batman and dinosaurs. However, it was the supernatural that truly captured my attention. My mind thirsted for knowledge that nobody else seemed to possess. I wanted to know secret things, I really wanted that, I wanted to catch fallen angels, I don't know why, but things would only darken as I ventured down the wrong rabbit hole.

PROF. BEATRICE: "A real tough moment there, when your mom started pointin' fingers and hurtin' you, it left you all mixed up, distant and kinda not trustin' things. But from that, you started cravin' comfort and wantin' to figure things out, all the while facin' the ups and downs of growin' up and tacklin' some mighty deep feelings."

PROF. BERNARD: "Your path of seeking solace and understanding through reading, especially your fascination with hidden or mysterious knowledge, offers a window into how you coped with your surroundings. It's quite something how your mind is pushed to explore beyond your immediate world. Though, it's evident that these journeys brought about their share of challenges."

PROF. BEATRICE: "I truly appreciate you openin' up and trustin' us with your story. Your feelings are mighty important. Revisiting those memories and emotions sure takes a lot of courage. As we keep talkin', just know we're here to listen and support you in the way that feels best for you."

I caught a glimpse of a tear glistening in the windows of Beatrice's blue eyes as she looked at me.

April 4th, 2020.

PROF. BEATRICE: "What do you see Joe?"

JOE: "My five-year-old self... he's holding my mother's hand. I see her silhouette glowing in the sun's golden embrace... he's... I..."

Blue Skies, 1982.

It was a warm summer day in England in 1982. The sky was a rich, azure emerald and five of my close friends in year five, aged eight and nine, sat at a desk, looking at a full-color brochure for books that we could order. One of the books for sale was 'Mysteries and True Stories,' featuring a picture of a crashed spaceship on the cover. The review covered unexplained phenomena such as Bigfoot, the Loch Ness Monster, spontaneous human combustion, vampires and werewolves.

However, what particularly gripped my attention were the stories of UFO encounters. In hindsight, what deeply concerns me is encountering a story within a book that was entirely unsuitable for an 8-year-old, like me at the time. In this same book, there was an account involving Antônio Vilas-Boas, a 23-year-old Brazilian farmer who worked during the night to escape the intense daytime heat. On October 15th, 1957, he reported an extraordinarily unusual experience in his room. During this event, he described an encounter with another humanoid, but this one was a woman and she appeared entirely nude and alluring and they had an intimate union together.

This woman shared certain features with the other mysterious beings he had encountered, including a small, pointed chin and striking, cat-like blue eyes. Her head featured long, white hair, somewhat reminiscent of platinum blonde, but the truly perplexing aspect was the striking contrast with her bright red underarm and pubic hair. As an 8-year-old, this story left me feeling scared and profoundly perplexed. There was even an artist's depiction of this unclothed being, which only added to my confusion and discomfort.

Reflecting upon it now, I find it astonishing that such content could find its way into a book intended for children. Nevertheless, this occurrence represents just a fraction of what I've since learned about the books, including so-called academic science books, available today and the experiences and influences on young people in America, which can be exceptionally bewildering, especially for individuals of Generation Alpha and Generation Z.

### Fear is future-based.

This sparked a rich conversation among my friends and me, stirring my core emotions of hurt, fear and shame. I began to search for other ways to meet my needs, a way to forget the pain. A child who is constantly told off may not develop a sense of autonomy. The impact in later life might result in lethargy and constant doubt. [11,12,13]

There was Enzo, whom I called my best friend, his dad (also from Sicily) and his mum (from France). Enzo possessed a unique allure, a blend of handsomeness and confidence, tinged with a touch of arrogance. His presence radiated a magnetic charm that I often wished I could replicate. It was undoubtedly his Gallic side that stood out and I adored his mum's French accent. Then there was Asif, a young Muslim boy from India, full of wisdom and gentleness, who used to share his Monster Munch crisps with me at lunch. Colin, our Russian silent friend, had older brothers and sisters who bullied him and us at lunchtime. There was Mustafa, a boy of Turkish heritage, with whom we often fought with fists and then just as quickly made up and became friends again, promising never to break up or fight again. And then there was Fakeer (from Pakistan), who later changed his name to Sam.

Sam and I received the slipper a year earlier for our constant tagging game. We were sent to Miss Squires by our teacher for discipline because we were in the habit of playing 'You're it!' We were almost obsessive-compulsive in not wanting to be left as the 'it'. Miss Squires was notoriously strict and truly Victorian, the same teacher who had picked up and physically shaken Enzo in a fit of rage during the Christmas season when he accidentally knocked over the baby Jesus from the Nativity scene.

Fakeer and I were sent to the front of the class, bent on her knee, Fakeer first, receiving the slipper in front of an older class. Biting their lips, the older pupils tried hard not to laugh, whilst we faced them at an incline sideways balanced on Miss Squires' knee, receiving six strikes on our buttocks as she spoke with syncopated verse. *'You will not do this again!'*

I had known these friends since infant school and considered them the best in the world. A few years earlier in infant school, with permission from my teacher to go to the restroom, on my diverted journey I had walked into an empty class where upon looking at the teacher's desk, saw confiscated toys peering at me. I took the cap gun, the metal matchbox toy Jaguar car and the jet and stuffed them in my pocket. At break time in the playground, I told Mustafa, Sam and Asif that because I considered them friends I would each give them a present from my home.

PROF BEATRICE: "Well, it seems like you were tryin' to connect with your buddies by sharin' somethin' special from your stash. Grabbing them toys and handin' 'em out might've been your way of seekin' their attention and getting on their good side. Could be you just wanted to be seen as someone kind and popular, lookin' for acceptance and a spot in the group.

This move might also show a bit of a need for control or freedom and could've been a way to handle whatever was goin' on inside you back then."

JOE: "As fellow children of immigrants facing racism and imparted ignorance from the other children, they would pick on us and call us names. I could not understand why children were telling us to go back to our own country. I was born here, as were they."

Events in April to June 1982 were particularly confusing for me. We were on the receiving end of more discrimination from the English kids. England was at war with the Falklands, so I was called a dirty Diego, a derogatory remark to Argentinians and the name of their number ten midfielder, Diego Maradona, the best footballer in the world at that time, who at age twenty-one was aiding his country in the Spanish World cup.

I had no idea how children could marry the two countries of Argentina and Italy together and aim words at me that I'd never forgotten to this day: *'You greasy wop! You spag! Spag-hetti! F\*\*\* off and go back to your own country!'* They would yell at me in unison between spitting whenever they used me as piggy in the middle, tossing my knitted, woolly hat over my head.

One further memory of induced shame also came in 1982 when a male teacher from another class accused me of talking to Fakeer. While queuing for class in the playground, Mr. Hornsey, who sported a distinct unshaven, military-style mustache, approached me with a commanding tone and said, "Oops, did you not hear me?" before delivering a resounding slap across my face. My face flushed red with shame as I struggled to hold back tears. The students in my class were shocked by this unprovoked attack.

Enzo and Asif said the teacher did this because he was racist. When my mum picked me up at the end of school, I quickly told her what happened. She was furious, but no one at the school listened to her.

Puzzled and fearful, I considered myself a passive, peaceful child, who looked after my younger brothers from a young age, even occasionally when both parents were at work on overtime, dad returning from the night shift at 7 am and mum leaving home at 6 am.

I was upset as to why children treated us differently, my mum who had experienced racism whilst working at other factories, before later working at Ford Motors, had warned me that people are horrible and her words now resonated in me. I eventually grew up with a disdain and distrust of English folk, adults and people in authority. It was particularly satisfying for me and the two other Italian kids at school, when on the 11[th of] July 1982, one day after my birthday, Italy won the FIFA World Cup, beating West Germany by three goals to one.

Going to school the day after, on Monday and hearing Mr. Morris share an assembly on how he had rooted for Italy to win because of the way West Germany had cheated, fouled and played unfairly throughout the competition resonated with me. My foreign friends and I could rub it in the faces of the English kids, if they picked on us again, we could remind them that England had gone out in the early stages of the competition. It has taken a lifetime to deal with the remnants of distrust and prejudice toward cultures that have splintered me due to experiences with students and teachers in primary and secondary school.

Here we were on book day, and a conversation ensued that would send neurons flowing through my young mind for years to come. I imagined what it would feel like if there were no wars, no fighting, no hitting and if my mum could be happy and peaceful. My mind kindled and I felt transfixed, happy and comforted by my best friends as we discussed the idea of a second Noah's ark. I was also terrified at the thought of being left behind. It would be a spaceship sent from the heavens to rescue those who were good and there would only be enough room for those people who were worthy, for they would know our thoughts and deeds. The conversation left an imprint on my impressionable young mind that would continue to occupy my thoughts for years to come. I wanted my friends and family to be with me, yet at the same time, I did not know how my God would fit into the equation.

PROF. VIRGIL: "Depression is living in the past, anxiety is living in the future, and for a brief moment, you found peace."

JOE: "Yes! What was I trying to escape from?"

PROF. BERNARD: "As you look back now, it's like a piece of your nine-year-old self found some relief in sharing, almost like a break from logic, which can sometimes get in the way of dealing with emotions. It helped untangle a mess of suppressed feelings—those beatings, the racism you faced, the confusion of being slapped by your grandfather, and the heartache over losing his three-year-old son—all made worse by those racist teachers from the Victorian era."

JOE: "I just wanted my family to have a peaceful life. I remember that with tears in my eyes and my heart ablaze, as I looked at my Asian friends in assembly, I wished my family could have joined us in song, —

'Colors of day dawn into the mind,
The sun has come up, the night is behind,
Go down in the city, into the street,
And let's give the message to the people we meet.'" [14]

# Chapter Four

## Encounters of the Self-Concept

We all possess the innate capacity to heal from trauma, and experts suggest that individuals who are more self-aware tend to have better outcomes. The best external resource could be an adult who meets the child with respect in a place of safety. However, sometimes it is an animal, a tree, or a stuffed toy, but in my origin story, it would be the thought of entertaining angels unaware, angels of the flying silver disc varieties.

Jumping to the future, in 2015—2017, I found myself in university studying counseling. This time, in my third year, I am the only man in my class amid a motley crew of women who represent every form of diversity I am foreign to and who some expect others to walk on eggshells for. From feminists to the white privilege shaming mob, an over-sensitive, fundamentalist lesbian liberalist, a social worker, a Buddhist, an orthodox Jew, a black panther wannabe and me. I am (as I would also discover) a foreigner to myself. Luckily, the wise teachers from year two were there to ensure order and bring some balance to the frame.

Once a student's eyes are open, teachers, instructors and mentors appear everywhere. If you have ears to hear and eyes to see, then everything can teach us and then our most painful emotions can point to our greatest possibilities, to where our authentic nature is hidden.

People whom I would at first judge became my mirrors. The People who judged me were pushing me to my destiny, calling upon our mutual courage to respect our perceived truths. Compassion for myself would support my compassion for others. Over time, this cohort would help open me to the truth within, a truth that sets you free from anger masking sadness.

We held safe a space of healing for each other, through sharing, listening and entering one another's world. Healing occurs in a sacred place located within us all, for now, we see through a glass, darkly, but then face to face. Now I know in part, but then shall I know even as also I am known.

## Storytelling Self

PROF. BEATRICE: "For a solid relationship kin to happen, ya gotta take a good ol' journey down the road, crossin' a bridge that's waitin' ahead. For our healin', it's crucial to grasp that path. Our inner kid still needs our talkin' even if they ain't talkin' back yet. We don't gotta hide those feelings or say sorry for 'em, but if we don't claim 'em, we'll just end up tossin' 'em onto another soul in the bunch."

PROF. VIRGIL: "Can therapy facilitate regression to a therapeutic dependent relationship—una relazione terapeutica dipendente—necessary to allow the development of the previously undeveloped true self into a circle of love and strength?"

JOE: "How do I show therapeutic love to a client who feels lost at sea, without rescuing them or bringing a solution? This is my Epistemology: 'to seek knowledge.' I want to know."

PROF. VIRGIL: "What is your understanding of Person-centered theory?"

JOE: (As my pen glides, I often enjoy sketching) "It is a hypothesis —an idea, a blueprint based on supposition from pre-existing studies from varied therapeutic practices of counseling, collated to form an eventual modus operandi and to prove the idea behind it and to help the person realize who they are."

PROF. VIRGIL: "Impressive, a textbook response indeed! Person-centered theory, my friends, is like a master storyteller, weaving a tapestry of ideas to help us fathom the enigma of the self. It acts as a guidebook through the intricate labyrinth of our minds. It is not a panacea, however, from these very ideas springs forth the wondrous person-centered approach to counseling, a path illuminated by understanding and connection where clients can explore their emotions, thoughts and self-perceptions to promote personal growth and self-awareness."

During our triad group discussion about the formation of 'self-concept' and its underlying theories, I found myself deeply contemplating the origin of my self-perception.

JOE: "You know, as I reflected on my earliest childhood memories, I realized something quite profound. While I could vividly recall those moments, I hadn't really connected with the emotions tied to them. It's like those memories held all these feelings, but I had sort of filed them away as just part of my past."

Through therapeutic exploration, I gradually unraveled these memories, blending them with the submerged feelings they carried and allowing them to resurface in the canvas of my mind. So where did I acquire some of my thoughts from? I took a time-out to see it from a child's perspective and then my own as a child.

### Born to Relate.

PROF. VIRGIL: "Research by Donald Winnicott and Freud demonstrates that babies do not know they are separate from their mothers, they are interlinked in a mutual symbiosis. In essence, the baby is part of the mother and the mother is part of the baby."

JOE: "Virgil, that resonates with me! In essence, we are all connected and we all feel the need for healthy relationships. We are programmed to receive unconditional positive regard, wired for love and wired for communicating with one another in a way that expresses our true organismic self, our true selves. I want to express my true self and not be inhibited, suppressed, or denied from being who I am meant to be because of the 'self-concepts' and thoughts acquired in my early childhood or later years."

PROF. VIRGIL: " 'Welcome to Hotel California! You can check out any time you want, but you can never leave!'—But you can leave and in doing so, you will be able to cultivate the kind of relationship where the client feels accepted as an equal and is increasingly prepared to risk becoming vulnerable and open to exploring difficult and painful terrain, they must resist the temptation of erecting barriers to the development of intimacy."

PROF. BEATRICE: "Fairbairn, he had a notion that deep down, what we truly long for is to connect with others." —*Professor Beatrice paused and locked eyes with me.* "See, these emotions stirrin' in me right now, they ain't mine, they're yours." *– AE, Advanced Empathy, nudgin' her along.*

As a child, I recollect my father working hard and doing many years of factory night shifts to provide for his family. Being the eldest of three sons, with three and five-year age gaps, I wanted to do the right thing for my family. Honesty was an important factor for me as I cared for my younger brothers because this is what I believed my mum expected and there was nothing wrong with that. Is this where my origin of self-worth developed?

She would show us what love was by hugging my brothers and me, but there were occasions when she became moody and depressed. I was an empathetic sponge who felt her sadness. I believe this may have been her anger turned inward and suppressed, possibly manifesting as depression, some marital friction, or her own unresolved PTSD stemming from the coma and the loss of her mother, who tragically died in a road accident when my mum was sixteen.

Did I try to appease her by being extra helpful, taking the brotherly role, guarding my younger brothers and at other times avoiding her while being confused as to why she was temperamental?

Between the ages of six and twelve, I recall being bullied at school, but I also fought back on some occasions. I remember in infant school they used to give us a daily small bottle of milk. Once, I needed to use the restroom but did not want to miss the milk time and I ended up peeing myself, which made me feel embarrassed and annoyed at the teacher. Is this where shame crept in?

There were countless moments of joy—fun, quests, digging in the garden, and playing with frogs. Mum made cakes while Abba's music filled the air, and we danced to their biggest hit, "Dancing Queen." I don't know why I held on to the bad. We had such joy when we played the Demis Roussos vinyl "Forever and Ever," a mystical track. My brother and I would hold up the album cover, laughing as we thought he looked like a fat Jesus.

My earliest concept? Sudden thoughts of life and death, whether it was transference from my Mother because she yearned for her absent mother, or just myself lost in a moment of deep consciousness. I did not know, but I am mindful of the following early imprint. It dawned on me that one day, in time, my parents will grow old and they will die. I was gripped by a sense of loss and fear that time would pass. I loved my parents and I have never forgotten that thought, it wasn't morbid, it was alarm at realizing the inevitable. I did not want to lose the ones I love. Who does?

PROF. BEATRICE: "That awareness, that fear of losin' who we hold dear, sounds like it's been there with ya from way back, Joe. Wranglin' these feelings when we're young'uns, it's like stackin' up them bricks for a house. You lay 'em crooked, that whole darn thing might get shaky. Look like you twigged to the notion that the folks we care 'bout won't stick around forever and that sure etched itself in. No wonder these thoughts linger and splash some paint on how we tackle life's twists as we grow. And you know, if a person ain't able to handle themselves as a kid, they tend to wind up barrin' things off when they're all grown."

JOE: "That is something I was very good at, tuning out, not learning to self-regulate."

PROF. BEATRICE: "It's worth nothin', not the only way but surely one, ADHD comes about when a little one's brain goes into defense mode during tough times but can't do a thing 'bout it. It's like a survival trick that gets etched into the brain over the years of growin' up. Eventually, that very trick turns into a roadblock, 'cause that automatic 'tuning out' becomes the brain's default, kickin' in when emotions get rocky, or even when you're tryin' to pay attention. Messes up your knack for livin' in the here and now. Your mind's somewhere else."

PROF. VIRGIL: "As the Hoffman Institute espouses. *'Lack of self-regulation is evident in people who experience strong and distressing emotional states or impulses without being able to move through them and ground themselves. They act out the feelings, rather than experience and express them in healthy ways. This can reflect early life situations when nurturing adults could not be emotionally present enough to help the infant's immature brain to develop self-regulation.'"* [1]

My hand cannot keep up with writing this down with pen and ink, everything resonates as we share our thoughts and learnings at university. Along with shame and inconsistency and transferred uncertainty the constant ruptures and the attempts of my Mother's repairs, there was a mixed increase in the capacity for my self-regulation.

PROF. BEATRICE: "When you lack that sort of regulation, it clouds up your 'window of tolerance,' messin' with how you build connections. When you miss out on that responsive back-and-forth, you end up with a system that just can't keep itself in check."

Hence, reflecting upon my early years. I consider such reflection a disorganized attachment and a borderline personality, at best an insecure but organized attachment. I wanted connection, but I like avoidance. I was dismissive and preoccupied with thoughts of escape. So, it was not just my capacity with other people that was obscured but what was happening in my body too.

## The Therapeutic key

PROF. BEATRICE: "The mind, well, it's woven from what's goin' on inside your body, especially how it's connectin' to others. We're all a web of neurochemical stuff, from our gut to our heart, runnin' through our whole enteric nervous system, linkin' up the body, the mind and the brain."

PROF. VIRGIL: "As Ronald Fairbairn posited, we come into this world with our complete organismic valuing intact, destined to establish connections and to strive toward a state of wholeness, seeking to move away from the inner realm. Quote: *'The whole and intact ego (the self) is originally in full and unproblematic relationship with the other person... when the libidinal, or loving, connection is broken, blocked or compromised, the baby*

75

*takes inside the relationship which has now become ambivalent. She divides this jumbled mixture into its tolerable and intolerable parts.'* " [2]

My family's view of the world and their challenging history caused me to go into my moral defenses, especially after mum's transferred season of post-natal depression. I felt vulnerable, yet it felt dangerous to show my need for her, I no longer dared to be connected, we were disconnected. Hence, I can see now, that perhaps a part of me displaced my need for comfort onto other off-world desires, including science fiction (particularly my fascination with extra-terrestrials) because it gave some nourishment and nurture to my soul and some escapism to a better reality I longed for.

I distrusted humanity and repressed my anger, which resulted in years of mental fatigue without human contact or trust. I displaced my libidinal energy and became angry at the world and others, I did not have the knowledge, awareness, or tools to face the trauma of my childhood. I was not able to put it into words—the inherited persecutory energy from my parents hindered my core conditions and ruptured our bond and then a part of me followed. This broken bond, along with the racism I had experienced at school caused my mind to go underground in my subconscious until I eventually *zoned out*. Although my pain came from people, it should be people that healed me, if I allowed or dared to be vulnerable again. Yet this would take years.

PROF. BEATRICE: "Scottish Psychiatrist Ronald Fairbairn had this notion 'bout libido bein' like a search for objects, not just for pleasure, but to build bonds with things outside ourselves. In a perfect world, a kid's first bonds are with his folks." — *'Through diverse forms of contact between the child and his parents, a bond between them is formed. When the bond is formed, the child becomes strongly attached to his parents. This early relationship shapes the emotional life of the child in such a strong way that it determines the emotional experiences that the child will have later on in life because the early libidinal objects become the prototypes for all later experiences of connection with others.'* [3]

JOE: "So, is the therapeutic key therefore letting go of idealization? Can I dare to release, feel, forgive and allow the memory of the wound to facilitate self-repair? Why do I cling to the laws of fear—avoidance, fight or flight, hypervigilance, negative bias, rumination, limiting beliefs, social isolation—when, by the sounds of it, I should lean into the wound? I wonder if Moses felt this when he was asked to pick up the snake by the tail, to face his fear, his childhood trauma and become a leader?" [4]

## Exodus into New Worlds

Dad was one of the first in Albany Road to get a video recorder, the Ferguson video star3V29, 1982 model. I recall he had a copy of *The Ten Commandments* starring Charlton Heston. We invited all our godparents to have a three-hour, forty-minute screening at our house. My dad would also watch pirate copies of horror films on his own, *The Exorcist* (1973), *The Thing* (1982) and *An American Werewolf In London* (1981) along with other scary movies. I would sneak in and watch some scenes through the slightly ajar door. My young spirit is impressionable, I remember being terrified. I could not sleep on my back for years, convinced that some evil entity was under my bed, or something would burst out of my belly. I remember my parents were watching The Exorcist as I played outside with the neighbors' kids. The audio screams were heard in the streets as someone walked by and I was embarrassed to think that others thought someone in my house was screaming, so I told them it was what was on TV.

PROF. BERNARD: "According to the research, exposure to movie violence can produce intense fear in children that may last for days, months, or even years." [5/6]

The same year, 24[th of] October 1982, at nine years old, Star Wars premiered on LWT. (London Weekend Television) We recorded it and my two younger brothers and I watched it constantly. The themes of light overcoming dark were happy memories. Jedis waxed valiant against forces of darkness at a cost of suffering and sacrifice, a truly celebrated time of innocence when my younger brothers and I could play out the characters and have fun.

November 2015, NLM University Journal Recap.

JOE: "I've been out of school for three weeks since I broke my collarbone. It's funny, isn't it? Not a single call, message, or card from my work colleagues to check on me. Disappointing, really. Feels like I'm on a lonely walk, like some lone ranger. Defense mechanisms on overdrive, of course. But screw them, I can handle this alone. That's what I keep telling myself, using anger as my shield. Deep down, though, the disappointment stings. It chips away at my sense of worth in the workplace."

PATRICIA: "How are you finding the discussions on conditions of worth and empathy?"

JOE: "Enlightening, Patricia. Reflecting on how I restrain my own actualizing tendency. Feeling overwhelmed, honestly. The course material feels like a mountain and I'm not sure I'm equipped to climb it. Want to run home, eat, and sleep. Feeling incompetent when I can't grasp something, struggling to give myself unconditional positive regard. I impose conditions of worth on myself, thinking I should know it all. But it's a struggle to focus.

More self-confidence injected into me would help. Right now, it's all about how I see myself academically, stemming from childhood experiences, worrying about how teachers and peers perceive me, and feeling misunderstood in expressing myself clearly."

These factors made me want to employ the self-defense mechanism of running and hiding in my Nonna's wardrobe, where my brothers and I used to play, hoping that going into it would be like the cartoon film we watched, 'The Lion, the Witch and the Wardrobe.' We'd knock on the inner cupboard and hide ourselves in Nonna's fur coat, hoping to find an entry point that would lead to the hidden world of Narnia.

# Chapter Five

## School of Knocks

*'I remember that I was never able to get along at school. I was at the foot of the class.' — Thomas Edison* [1]

### 1983.

My last memory of Albany Road was in 1983 when we took a train to Milan to spend three weeks with my Auntie Maria, my mum's sister. Our cousin Giuseppina, a local DJ, would often mention us on the radio and dedicate the song *'I'm Walking on Sunshine'* to us.

Milan was a fresh experience for us, catching lizards in the sun, fishing with our Uncle and experiencing all the different flavors of gelato. We even went to the local youth group where hundreds of Italian children, also on half-term, deemed my brothers and me *too* English to be Italian. Too Italian for the English, now we were too English for the Italians. We really could not fit in anywhere!

Giuseppina, a creative and hip teenager, graced the airwaves with her DJ skills, captivating us with her hourly slots and heartfelt dedications. Her freedom, creativity and unwavering confidence mesmerized me as she pursued her dreams in media. I often found myself questioning the source of her confidence, wondering why I lacked such assurance. She felt like the older sister I had never known, unapologetically shaving her legs on the balcony while leisurely smoking, unconcerned about the gaze of a curious boy from across the street. Her audacity, however, earned her a reprimand from her disapproving mother.

One specific day stands out in my memory: an afternoon when the house was empty and Giuseppina took on the role of my babysitter. Trouble brewed when I couldn't resist the urge to expose her public leg-shaving escapade—an impulsive decision that would result in revenge. In the warm embrace of a Milanese sun, our confrontation reached its climax as Giuseppina cornered me, the embodiment of youthful rebellion. A resounding slap echoed through the air because of my actions. Instinctively, I retaliated, fingers entangled in her hair as our struggle intensified.

The unexpected return of our parents marked the end of our skirmish. Astonishingly, Giuseppina painted a remarkably different picture of our time together. With a straight face and a smile, she proclaimed me a model of good behavior, portraying our interaction as nothing short of harmonious camaraderie. I loved her even more!

The Soundtrack to my 1984-85.


*'Hello'- Lionel Richie.*
*'I Just Called to Say I Love You'- Stevie Wonder.*
*'99 Luftballons'- Nena.*
*'When Doves Cry'- Prince*


*'Take On Me'- A-Ha.*
*'There Must Be an Angel, Playing with My Heart' - Eurythmics.*
*'Frankie'- Sister Sledge*
*'19'- Paul Hardcastle*
*'I Want to Know What Love Is'- Foreigner*

In 1985, my parents moved to Connor Avenue, one road away from our old house and a ten-minute walk to my soon-to-be perdition, secondary school.

September 1985. On the first day of secondary school, I was late, huffing and puffing, as I entered the assembly of the new first-year students wearing my school uniform, white shirt, blazer, no tie, no shoes but spanking new white trainers. Among the new faces were some familiar ones who knew me from junior school who laughed as I entered the hall wheezing as the register and induction took take place.

Albany School, in Bell Lane, Enfield, was a real dump and my time there felt like some of the worst years of my life. The walk to school was one of navigating and looking out to avoid the glue sniffers, who resembled zombies with their vacant stares and unsteady gait, unaware of the grave risks they were subjecting themselves to through inhalant abuse.

In addition, I experienced bullying, engaging in two fights per year, facing rejection, more racism, underachieving and lacking additional educational support.

While there were pockets of enjoyable moments and my love for drama, overall, Albany School was characterized by a sense of grim animation. This school, much like many others today in disenfranchised areas, held a strong grip, marked by an atmosphere of heaviness and hopelessness that seemed to permeate, resulting in mechanized staff and students. Although many dedicated teachers begin with enthusiasm (seeking to effect change and make a meaningful impact by teaching and fulfilling their aspirations), unfortunately, the system can wear them down amidst the multitude of complex cases they must handle.

Occasionally, I would use my house key to tap the red school bell above the windows outside the classroom, mimicking the end of the lesson to skip class ten minutes early. This trick worked especially well when we had a substitute teacher and we would all rush to the playground, canteen, or home. Those were the days when we were permitted to leave school during lunch to eat.

Year four continued in a similar vein, I was thirteen taking a shower after Physical Education (or Phys-Ed as the Americans call it) when someone called my name and for no reason at all Michael Cargil punched me smack in the nose. Cargil had tried to break it, but he left me with a concussion and a bleeding nose.

Now the PE teacher, Mr. Sergeyev —for whatever twisted reason — decided to wait for the bell to ring to march me in my shorts and bloodied white vest to the medical room. Thus, I am paraded in front of hundreds of students who are making their way to the next lesson. Some laugh. Most stare. Others ask, *'What happened?'* I felt like a spectacle and laughingstock.

Mr. Sergeyev and some of the teachers or individuals in caring professions appeared to lack sensitivity and discretion in their actions. Thus, the impact of these interactions on my personal growth and development was significant, leading to a sense of mistrust, deepening feelings of shame and influencing my emotional well-being. I would bury these experiences, attempting to shield myself from their effects, only to later manifest the *'shame response'*—'a bodily-based affective response' [2]

PROF. BEATRICE: "...leadin' to a sort of separation between the autonomic nervous system in your body and the right brain, like they ain't talkin' right and it trickles down, creatin' a deep sense of shame in your gut."

JOE: "Some teachers require cognitive recalibration, in the form of being smacked with a wet fish across their face!"

Eventually, when a meeting was set for the bully (Cargill) to meet me, the same PE teacher who was also a Head of Year said that he had heard me swear before and that the student claimed I had called him 'A bastard,' which was absolute nonsense.

Mr. Sergeyev then proceeded to lie in front of my father, convincing him that I do curse. He claimed to have allegedly heard me use swear words before. My father then turned to me and asked if the accusation was true and if I had indeed done so, he stated that it was wrong. The meeting had been manipulated cleverly to portray me as the instigator. The bullying never stopped and the sense of injustice from the system's authority figures became more deeply ingrained. I also felt that my father had failed me as an advocate.

Trust was flushed down the gutter. Hate and anger buried themselves under my skin feeding off shame within and birthed a desire to escape this rotten planet or to avenge those who did me harm. This is the part where super villains are usually born but in 1986, I underwent a hernia operation, which revealed that I had been living with it for years. Apparently, I had torn a muscle while attempting to lift a large barrel of Italian oil in the garden when I was younger. This ordeal kept me out of school for a month. Surprisingly, upon my return, nobody asked where I had been.

<u>Ouija.</u>

Rejection used to be a friend of mine. Five so-called friends promised to pick me up one Saturday at 10 am and we would all go swimming to Pickett's Lock. Hours passed. I waited until 1 pm and then concluded that they were not coming. On the Monday back to school, Enzo, Colin, Marcus and Chris made no mention of attending swimming on Saturday. When I asked as to why they did not pick me up, they said they'd

Simply forgotten, the same so-called friends who did not defend me, but laughed when bullies put me in a giant metal bin and rolled me down the playground on my fifteenth birthday. As I tumbled inside the bin, the stench of stale litter assaulted my senses, mingling with the sickly sweet odor of discarded juice boxes. The rough texture of the bin's interior scraped against my skin, leaving painful abrasions as I endured the humiliating ordeal.

PROF. BERNARD: "Joe, it seems that during your teenage years, you were enveloped in a melancholic haze, burdened by the weight of depression, pessimism and a sense of diminished self-worth. It's as if your mind became fixated on the shadows, overshadowing moments of joy and contentment. This internal disconnection seeped into your relationships, coloring your perception of your first love, your primary caregiver and the world around you."

PROF. BEATRICE "Well now, it looks like when you felt the world givin' you the cold shoulder, you sorta gave it right back. Your hopeful outlook led you to push folks away, not knowin' it was stealin' your chance to truly connect and feel alive. But fret not, Recognizin' these here patterns is like findin' a trail in the tall grass – it's the start of somethin' big. It's a chance to dive deep into your story and find the road that leads to real change and healin'. You're on the brink of uncoverin' some powerful truths about yourself, and that's the first step toward findin' your way back home."

James Mayor and Perry Ward had also come from Chesterfield Junior School. James had been in my classes from my infant to senior school. Perry joined our senior class late.

Perry was a foul-mouthed, wimpy kid sporting glasses so thick he could probably read minds. However, he would impress his peers at my expense by constantly cussing me out. I knew I could beat him up, but he was under the protection of one of the toughest kids in the school, James Mayor.

Mayor was the infamous school bully who tormented all the kids in our class. He had a devilish glint in his eye that always sent shivers down our spines. One day, in elementary school, while we were playing in the schoolyard, he pushed me off a bench and my head hit the concrete with a sickening thud. A flash of lightning shot through my head and blood gushed from the back of my head, but I was too scared to cry. Mayor smirked and walked away as I lay there, dazed and confused.

The incident left a deep scar on the back of my head that never fully healed, an indicator that I should have had stitches. Although the nurses never called for an ambulance, I technically had been seriously injured. A year later, Mayor struck again, twisting my neck with a sadistic grin on his face. I felt a sharp pain shoot through my body and I knew I was in trouble. I couldn't move my neck without wincing in pain and my muscles and tendons were twisted for weeks. Despite the agony, I never went to the hospital for some reason and I still have scarring to this day that serves as a painful reminder of those experiences. In Beijing, in 2022, x-rays finally revealed an injury on my neck bones, caused by some impact. I had been carrying this burden for years.

PROF. BERNARD: "Being a victim of bullying can be a traumatic experience that can leave lasting emotional scars. As Gabor Maté explains, *'trauma is not what happens to us, but what we hold inside in the absence of an empathetic witness.'*" [3]

JOE: "Those experiences have undoubtedly shaped me, but I wasn't very good at defending myself, physically or emotionally, especially against those who were considered to have remarkable strength."

One hot summer after lunch in year five of high school, fifteen years of age, Mayor and Ward began sharing with everyone that they had fooled around with a Ouija board, a tool used for attempting to communicate with spirits or entities from the beyond through the movement of a planchette guided by participants' hands.

Mayor's mother was allegedly a medium and tarot reader. Though I was somewhat unfamiliar with these sub-genres of the Occult, my parents' beliefs led me to suspect their unwholesomeness. Ward enthusiastically recounted the events at his home, captivating most of the class gathered at the back of the classroom. As Ward spoke spiritedly, Mayor appeared frozen in time, seemingly affected and hypnotized by what he had witnessed. His mop of rich black hair occasionally nodded in moody acknowledgment.

Perry's voice carried a starry-eyed wonder as he recounted strange knocks on the door, deceased dogs barking, cat's eyes glowing in the dark and words that were formed by small glasses that moved on their own accord and telepathic voices and names of future people they were to marry.

As they told the story, many students were gripped with amazement, feeling a tangible, time-shifting presence settle among us—a peculiar shade that seemed to envelop our surroundings. Everyone who listened felt drawn into an open door of possibility and wonder.

Felicia Caruso, a shrewd Italian girl who sat at the front—her father Mario also being our ice cream van driver—wisely said, 'I do not want to know! I don't want to get involved in this madness. It's not good for you.'

Looking now to Ward and Mayor, many students began to request answers to who they would marry, how many kids they would have and whether they would get good grades. Some asked if they would become rich.

I also made a request—"Perry," I paused and looked at him excitedly in the eyes, "Would you ask them if UFOs are real? Would you ask them if aliens are real?" Ward and Mayor nodded, affirming they would. In that moment, unbeknownst to me, I had opened an unconscious door that fed into my quest for comfort and soothing.

*"And the soul that turneth after such as have familiar spirits and after wizards, to go a whoring after them, I will even set my face against that soul and will cut him off from among his people. Sanctify yourselves therefore and be ye holy: for I am the LORD your God."—Moses* [4]

PROF. BEATRICE: "Keepin' an open mind might allow the wrong things in and a weakened psyche can be more prone to negative vibes."

JOE: "The remainder of school proved negative, bleak, and unmemorable... I would carry the darkness with me, stemming from my inability to be heard or express myself, for years to come. Unfortunately, those who would later love me became the recipients of that rage—a rage that grew from the sadness, rejection, confusion, and suppression of emotion during my early school life, influenced by culture, esoteric knowledge, and wrong friendship groups. It was as if the pain I couldn't share reciprocated itself in my relationships, a cycle of hurt and reciprocity that persisted long after my school days were over."

Most teachers at Albany school wrote negative comments in my school reports, although I always received an A for Drama and a B for English Literature. It seemed that most would copy the one who wrote the first comment, even though they did not know me well. Math was never my strong subject at school (perhaps I had dyscalculia), but I made strong efforts in my concentration and my performance was above average. I deliberately sat next to Chris Turner, the top student. Therefore, it genuinely hurt to read

Mr. Quarterly's comment in my math report: *'Giuseppe spends most of his time in a world of his own.'*

PROF. BEATRICE: "Well now, it sounded like you might have been experiencing a touch of dissociation, which is a way our minds cope by sort of stepping away from reality when things get tough, or emotions run high. This behavior might have meant your inner self was trying to carve out a cozy mental nook where you could keep some distance from the tough stuff, giving you some breathing room from those troublesome feelings and experiences."

JOE: "Yep, pass me another Monty Python wet fish to smack the math teacher with, what an absolute bell end he was."

It stung, especially when other teachers who did not know me would write similar damning words in my A4 yellow report book, which my Mother would read with disappointment. Only Mr. Whitwer, my English teacher and Ms. Lewis, the drama teacher, saw the promise and creativity in me and encouraged my natural writing and acting abilities, which would play a part in my future.

<u>Year 5, June 1989.</u>

*'Right Here Waiting' – Richard Marx.*
*'This Time I Know It's For Real' – Donna Summer*
*'Leave Me Alone' – Michael Jackson*

At fifteen, I completed my final examination, *Economics.*

Time was called as pens and paper were placed down. Time to disband. Many students began to cry as the realization hit them that this was the last time they would see each other as friends at school. It had happened all too quickly and I slowly walked out of the gates none the wiser.

From June to the end of August 1989, my family and I spent a few weeks in Wood Green where my parents had invested and bought a property to renovate and eventually rent. I can't forget the huge cockroaches that splat under each shoe my brothers and I exterminated them with. Director Tim Burton's eccentric Batman had been released at the cinema.

In September of that same year, I returned to school as I had applied successfully for the sixth form of school. Upon my arrival, I quickly left as I felt underdressed to compete with the other students who had designer shoes and clothes. My low self-esteem and disbelief marched with me, never to return to the school of hard knocks.

JOE: "I left Albany School in September 1989 with good grades in drama and English, but burdened with depression, low self-esteem and suicidal thoughts.

I'd like to give a shout-out for the recognition of those others who attended Albany School and survived. Whether it be they who were constantly derided and called 'jungle bunnies,' 'malakas,' 'pakis,' 'pikie kids,' 'limeys,' 'dlobo,' 'spags,' or 'wops,' amid the challenges posed by the predominantly white, deluded students, nutty bitch-resting-face teachers, dilapidated buildings, or other obstacles, some of us persevered and made it through that shithole in the end."

PROF. BERNARD: "Joe, the racism you and your peers experienced at Albany School is deeply troubling. It's evident that such discrimination not only affects one's emotional well-being but also takes a toll on physical energy. Emotionally drained people often lack physical energy, as anyone who has experienced depression knows, and this is a prime cause of the bodily weariness that beleaguers many addicts."

The transition from the relatively safer environment of primary school to the harsher world of secondary school left deep psychological scars. Encounters with older, foul-mouthed bullies reinforced my negative self-concept. I had already experienced rejection from my primary school friend, Enzo and received bad reports from teachers, which triggered anxiety and fear of disappointing my Mother. I lived in constant fear, feeling isolated and rejected. This growing gap between my self-concept and true self had caused irritability and despair. I couldn't trust anyone, especially authority figures and believed the world to be a cruel place.

PROF. BEATRICE: "Folks who've been through real tough times can end up always watchful or stuck in that fight or flight mode."

JOE: "I guess I was scared that the world wasn't safe when my mind and body sensed danger in so many places. I used to think life wasn't worth living just because I didn't have a girlfriend."

PROF. BERNARD: "It's evident that this desire for connection is common among both young boys and girls, but it's essential to transcend this urge. Rushing or succumbing to the temptation of entering a relationship merely for the sake of it should be avoided. Instead, we should prioritize self-love and refrain from waiting for a prince to rescue his princess or vice versa. This principle applies universally, yet it's rarely taught."

PROF. BEATRICE: "You see, before that prince even arrives, he has a whole bunch of dragons to face right here inside—inner reckonings, you know. And that princess of the prairie won't find her prince until she learns to cherish the grassland of her heart without getting lost in narcissistic musings."

JOE: "Otherwise, we might wrongly blame the other person for relationship failures instead of acknowledging our shortcomings or unrealistic expectations. I'm guilty of that, sometimes venturing into dark places and creating unnecessary conflicts out of fear."

But in a world of instant messages and data, are we able to accurately read the messages of our internal compass as we suppress or battle our fears, who will help us get our feet back on the ground when we dare to say help?

# Chapter Six

## The Messenger

*'I saw a UFO... and it went down the river, turned right at the United Nations, then turned left and went down the river...'* — *John Lennon* [1/2]

Growing up, my brothers and I cultivated a mischievously witty sense of humor that bound us together. In addition to loving Bruce Lee films, during our younger years, we discovered a treasure trove of our mum's 7-inch vinyl records languishing in the playhouse in our garden. With our mother having no use for them, they became the perfect ammunition for our impromptu vinyl disc battles. We'd grab random titles, read them aloud and then launch them at each other with all the seriousness of knights in a vinyl-shattering joust.

I recall one instance when I'd call out to my brother, "Hey Dave!" and he'd respond with a quizzical "What?" right before a disc labeled "Here Comes the Sun" soared through the air. Another time, Mark would chime in with a shout of "All You Need Is Love," just as a vinyl missile hit the wall and exploded into sonic oblivion. Not to be outdone, Dave would retort with a playful "Love Me Do" as he skillfully dodged a circular disc "Help" whizzing towards him, which promptly embedded itself in the grass like a musical saucer.

Leaving the halls of Albany School alongside my middle brother, David, we found ourselves locked in a heated argument. Tempers flared and before I knew it, I hurled a makeshift projectile fashioned from accumulated rubber bands directly at him. As if in cinematic slow-motion, I watched in both horror and awe as the rubber bullet hurtled toward its target, fully aware of the impending calamity. Yet, with the agility of a seasoned ballerina, David deftly sidestepped the rubbery projectile, leaving me to marvel at his unexpected grace under vinyl and rubber band fire. Inevitably, the ball shattered the top pane of our garden door while our mother watched, a picture of calm amidst the chaos. I could feel her piercing gaze and I knew the wrath of Sicilian sanctions was upon me.

I pleaded with her, promising to find a job and make things right. At that moment, I was more motivated than ever to make amends for the damage I had caused.

With a glance at the job columns of the local paper, I saw an opportunity to redeem myself. The Enfield Town sorting offices were seeking postal cadets and I jumped at the chance. Donning the blue uniform, I made my Mother proud as I worked six days a week.

At sixteen years of age, the 5 am alarm call was an awful sound. You knew you were in Enfield when the birds woke up coughing, surrounded by chain-smoking postmen, most of whom were ex-military. Their distinct North London, Enfield accent, — an amalgamation of Cockney marked by the occasional glottal stop — flavored their conversations with a blend of urban flair and local inflections. And when they mentioned "waher" (water) and "buh-er," (butter) the distinct pronunciation gave away their Enfield roots. Amid corruption and surveillance from the postmaster generals, many postmen contemplated joining the Gulf War just to escape their sense of non-existence. But these messengers of life and joy delivered letters throughout Enfield.

The Enfield sorting office was a hive of activity, with packages being sorted and delivered left and right. But amidst the chaos, a group of postmen hid away in a corner, snorting lines of snow dust. Their eyes were wide, their movements jittery, as they frantically worked to keep up with the mounting piles of mail. The other half of the staff watched in disbelief as the snow-dust-fueled postmen zipped around like a pack of hyperactive greyhounds, making deliveries at an alarming rate.

Throughout the year, summer was a pleasant experience, delivering mail with my headphones on and listening to a selection of my audio tapes from Snap's *I've Got the Power* to George Michael's *Listen Without Prejudice* album. *Cowboys and Angels,* a stunning composition. The Pet Shop Boys' *It's a Sin* and then I discovered and became entranced with the first love of my life, Mariah Carey and her song *Vision of Love.*

In 1989, the Enfield sorting office sent a handful of us teenage postal cadets to King's Cross, Camden (believed to be the location of the legendary battle between Queen Boudicca and Roman invaders) for further training for one week. Upon arriving, we met several teenagers from various regions of London who were to be schooled in sorting skills. One teenager with Scottish roots was not popular with the other teens and on the last day of training one cadet from Enfield and two others from East London gave him a goodbye beating on the floor.

I wasn't part of the Scottish salutation gang. However, the prick named me as one of the teens who had booted him, which left me unable to defend myself as I could not bring myself to snitch and name the other local teens who had been involved.

I left the job in early 1990 after I was robbed at knifepoint in Enfield one road away from my Granddad's former home whilst carrying the postbag. A teenager with an Irish accent and dark green trainers held a knife to me and politely asked me for the mail in my hand and then the pouch.

Half asleep, in shock or indifferent, I gave him what he wanted before the realization of what had happened eventually settled in. To be honest, I couldn't care less. I was cold, tired and depressed. The guy did me a favor. This was before the advent of mobile phones and the Internet. The other postal workers mocked me teasing that I had been mugged by a Leprechaun.

After a short spell of stacking bananas in a supermarket and working alongside a twenty-year-old bully dating a fifty-year-old woman who stole cigarettes from the kiosk I went to the career office in Enfield and applied for a job that attracted my eye: 'Messenger wanted in the City of London.'

## The Cockney Heartland.

In May of 1990, I peeled away from Banana Ville, feeling ripe for a change. It was just the right time to plant myself in a new opportunity and sure enough, I applied and was offered the position as a postal messenger for Lloyd's Broker 'Cameron Guardian Assurance' based in Commercial Street, London EC2. I landed the job because the post manager who interviewed me, Lars Janssen, had also worked as a postman in his youth, so my previous experience proved to be valuable.

The train from Turkey Street to Liverpool Street took thirty-five minutes (give or take) if it was not delayed and then navigating the squeeze to avoid becoming a sardine on the next one.

In May 1990, at age seventeen, there I was traveling on a train. I am innocuous, slim, with jet-black hair. Good-looking yet lacking confidence. I found myself amidst a carriage full of suited, pretty people. Sitting across from me was the most beautiful blonde woman I had ever seen. It was an experience—a feeling of freedom, as if I were embarking on a voyage.

PROF. BERNARD: "Just as one embarks on a journey, Erikson (1963) postulated that life's voyage involves passing through psychosocial developmental stages. The fifth stage, he posited, exists 'between the morality instilled in childhood and the ethics to be cultivated in adulthood.' Young adults must acquaint themselves with the roles they may embrace as they mature, including those related to their evolving body image and sexuality. [3]

Success in this developmental stage hinges on the conviction that we remain faithful, staying on track to our true selves—a concept encapsulated by fidelity. According to Erikson, we come to terms with our changing bodies and commence the process of shaping our identities through ongoing exploration. With the appropriate guidance and positive reinforcement, we progress towards greater independence and a heightened sense of self-control (Marcia, 2010)." [4]

The sardine tin vessel landed at Liverpool Street and as I stepped out onto the bustling platform, I couldn't help but think about the unique rhythm of life in this city – where even the language, like the Cockney rhyming slang echoing from the East End streets, adds a touch of mystery and charm to everyday interactions. There I stepped off the 'hell and rain' in my 'whistle and flute,' to go to 'Captain Kirk' to make some 'bees and honey,' en route to Commercial Street.

Commercial Street. Let me tell you, that street isn't just any street. It's woven with history like an old patchwork quilt. The buildings around here are straight outta Victorian times, standing shoulder to shoulder with street art that holds more stories than your nan's knitting circle. It's where the past mingles with today's creative buzz, where the old-school industry mixes with the here and now—and as I set foot on those busy cobblestones, it's like the street was whispering, "Come and explore, mate."

It was in the deck or rather basement, with minimal sunlight passing through glass bricks molded into the pavement above where footsteps and Yuppies would wander on by, that I felt a sort of redemption for letting my parents down for quitting the postman job. Here, in this melancholy basement of mission control, where the sun only appeared fully at sunset, I set about to work for an insurance company in a five-floor building that rented two other additional buildings along the street for its indemnity staff across the busy street.

Working alongside two older messengers and a teenage printing assistant, I became the fourth member of a motley crew of cellar misfits and a microorganism for further imagination, yet it was here that I felt accepted.

Brick Lane was only a stone's throw away. The streets of the East End were saturated in legends of gangster stories. Lars told me of the areas where the infamous Krays and like-minded folk had frequented, including a small pub called *The Vic,* of which he was a regular.

As a postal messenger in the basement, we would open the letters, red stamp the checks and sort them into their groups, we would know the secrets of the company, the ins and outs, the claims, complaints and profits.

Bottom of the barrel, having access to highly classified material as well as hearing the stories from Stuart the cleaner about which man and woman from different departments had been sleeping in the medical bed after work on Friday and who else was sleeping with whom. Office affairs, gossip and secret alcohol cabinets in the insurance buildings were all but a by-product of the job. Office Politics.

That is just the way that part of merchant London rolled, always has and always will. I slogged from building to building to deliver the mail, collect the checks from department to department and meet and talk to staff from the aviation department to home, car and pet insurance, account departments and indemnity claims. The basement's electric stamp machine hummed and franked the letters throughout the day as we fed them in preparation for 1 pm and 5 pm deliveries to the post office.

In the middle of the street, nestled between Aviation and Pet insurance, there was a gay shop of sorts called *Expectations*, a peculiar, rainbow place. As an innocuous seventeen-year-old, I would see many interesting, leather-clad, handlebar mustache, bike chain-carrying characters walking along the street to enter Expectations. I would steer away from curiosity unlike the other postal messenger, Toby, who had an itinerant avaricious mind and would walk in enquiring of what products were on sale—or so he said.

Lars Janssen, postmaster and my boss, was a wise cockney who boasted that he was born and bred in the East end of London. To be considered an East Ender you had to be born within the sounds of the 'Bow-bells.' Janssen constantly reminisced about the history of the Boar War and his own World War Two evacuations, barrage balloons and the way it used to be and the way it should be.

"If it says *'Bisto'* [5] on the back of a bus, it doesn't mean they sell gravy!" Was one of his favorite sayings. Aside from his fondness for debunking misleading advertising slogans, he had another favorite saying that never failed to bring a smile to those around him. With a playful twinkle in his eye, he would often gesture towards his head and feet, illustrating his belief that life could be neatly divided between intellectual pursuits and physical pleasures. "Up here for thinking, down there for dancing," he'd say, his voice tinged with amusement as he emphasized the division between mind and body with a knowing nod. It was just one of the many quirks that made him the unforgettable character he was.

Lars, a gentleman of third-fourth generation Dutch lineage, adorned with concentrated glasses reminiscent of Velma from the Scooby-Doo cartoons, showcased a mop of fading ginger hair that hinted at his impending retirement plans.

Occasionally, Lars would educate me that Italy's tank design had five gears, one for going forward and the other four for going into reverse and switching sides. We would laugh together as I told him my Grandfather probably shot his mates.

The other messenger, Toby Logan, a frequent visitor to the Expectations shop, was a soon-to-be-married, twenty-year-old fellow hailing from Woking, Surrey. Sporting an extra few pounds, he exuded an air of slight paranoia, often seeking solace in comfort food, to change a common idiom, if we were *one sandwich short of a picnic* it was because Toby had probably eaten them. With an endearing touch of self-delusion, he went by the name Diamond Logan, convinced he was a sensational disco dancer straight out of the seventies. On the eve of the Christmas party, he would grace the floor with his John Travolta-inspired dance moves, inviting a mix of awe and amusement as he basked in the illusion of his magnificence.

Toby continually teased and baited Lars with political discussions and the increased budget for his forthcoming extravagant wedding, which had so far amounted to £20,000 ($25,000). His marriage was to include a horse and carriage, an extravagant wedding dress with a two-meter train to trail along the aisle, white diamond-laced tiaras, white and pink diamond-crusted suits and a wedding invite in the hundreds—all of which would later add to Toby's ever-increasing woes of debts and loans. Along with his debts and anger issues, I would watch and learn as he phoned banks requesting deferrals for fines and overdrafts, writing then creasing checks before posting them to buy himself extra days in delaying the magnetic check reading system. In addition, Toby would call the massage numbers advertised in *Loot,* a classified advertising paper, engaging in conversations with women about prices and services to relieve his stress. His voice would turn smooth as he attempted to woo his conversation partner, using these interactions to release his inner frustrations.

Finally, in the same basement, Fergus Finlay, also from the East End, was the company's internal printing man. A skinny, spindly teenager who grew up rough, talked tough and liked to say 'He who dares wins' a lot. Fergus was a proud teenager and very distrustful of people, often raising an eyebrow skeptically even in the most benign conversations. He would deliberately stand tall like a fighting cock, his posture exuding a mix of defiance and bravado. He once amused us when a woman phoned him to say that she was his long-lost sister. His dad, it seems, was exceedingly promiscuous, leaving a trail of offspring in his wake. Fergus had discovered over time that he had up to sixteen brothers and sisters, a family tree as sprawling and intricate as the cityscape he hailed from.

This rejection from his father played on him and resulted in a peculiar desire to study human psychology and hypnotism, which Fergus put to practice on whoever came down to the basement to collect stamps or order up printing of new letterheads. Fergus was the sort of chap who found it hard to display any emotions. He played the tough man and forever tried to uphold the tiresome image.

Lars was like a surrogate father to him and they both relished sharing stories of the East End.

Fergus' usual entrance routine in the reception area involved a sprint and a leap up the steps, then kicking open the front reception door with a flourish reminiscent of Thor, Son of Odin. However, one summer morning at 7 am, Fergus propelled himself so forcefully that he came soaring through the reception windows, cutting his wrists at the tendon. Blood gushed everywhere. His girlfriend (our receptionist) screamed hysterically, to which Fergus simply replied emotionlessly, "Oh shoot! Look at that," as he gazed at his exposed white veins, resembling puppet strings.

In my own dissociated state of mind, walking down to the basement, Lars and Toby enquired as to the noise upstairs, to which I replied, 'Fergus has had a small accident.' They ran upstairs to see the understatement, claret everywhere, Sandy the receptionist in shock and Fergus sitting holding his wrist with an ambulance on call.

The post room (mailroom) with its diverse characters, served as a vital artery in communication within the other departments. The mailroom knew just as much as the company directors at the top of the building and all about the secrets of commerce and Lloyd's negotiations, as well as the mechanics of its claims and insurance. There were of course moments of temptation that I fell into and things of a lascivious nature that I was introduced to. Some would say it went with the job, but the truth was it went with the territory.

We had our own soundtrack down here. A now-defunct Melody FM station played vinyl tracks from the thirties and forties and from delightful movie hour soundtracks.

Things used to heat up daily in the basement and like an amplified real-life House of Commons. Lars would throw stationery equipment, pens, rubbers, rulers and occasionally chairs at Toby as they debated over the politics of Conservative and Labor.

Toby also had an insatiable desire to be an audience member on almost every TV show broadcast and was constantly phoning TV studios for audience tickets.

Above us, the office directors on the fifth floor would each have their own globe decanter that opened to reveal a selection of fine spirits that were offered to clientele. We also had a secret stash of spirits in our filing cabinet with a lock that could only be released with a letter opener being inserted in such a way as to pry it open.

At age seventeen, I would have an occasional cigarette in one hand, whilst opening the letters and when Lars was away, we changed the radio station for contemporary music, for when 'the cat is away, the mouse is King of the house.'

1992-1993

*'Creep' - Radiohead*

*'Jump Around' - House of Pain*

*'Shape of My Heart'- Sting.*

*'Boom! Shake the Room'-DJ Jazzy Jeff & The Fresh Prince*

*'The River Of Dreams'- Billy Joel*

Toby's debt trap had left him with an unhealthy disposition. He was sexually frustrated, buried in unpaid bills up to his eyeballs and living from paycheck to paycheck. Consequently, he developed a penchant for provoking conflicts as a means of self-regulation. This involved displacing his frustrations onto those within his reach. Anyone unfortunate enough to be on the receiving end of his foul moods, triggered by relationship or financial woes, would face a Russian roulette of criticism, mockery, or bad manners—any minor excuse sufficed to make it a personal attack.

After Toby had vented his frustration on me (or if I had been lucky, it would be some other unsuspecting soul who came to the basement asking for stationery, stamps, or a tin of coffee from the stationery cupboard), he would flip a personality switch and enter a cognitive state of sorrow. Logan's split personality was distressing to be around, his volatile emotions would surface on most mornings after a phone call to his new bride, with whom he argued the night before, or after a call with the bank regarding his overdraft reaching its limit.

One time, when I stood up to him, he threatened to go to the fifth floor and accuse me of some injustice. However, I grabbed him in a headlock and told him to calm down, genuinely alarmed that I might lose my job. After a minute of pinning this twenty-nine-year-old down, he simmered down and then shifted from rage to laughter, saying that he wouldn't have gone up to the fifth floor. As a 17 year old, this only added to my sense of injustice that I would eventually carry into my first relationship.

Innocence.

.

PROF. BEATRICE: "Back in our young years, we hardly ever ponder the days to come. That innocence gives us the open road to savor the moment like few grown folks can. The instant we start fussing' about what's down the line, that's when we wave goodbye to the easy-goin' days of our childhood."

JOE: "I met Eleanor at work, about two years after I started. We were both nineteen at the time, and she became my first girlfriend. Her family home was always bustling. With her mum, dad, an uncle, two brothers, twin sisters, and three dogs all sharing a four-bedroom house in Hackney, it was lively, to say the least. Eleanor's mum was on a special housing waiting list, which eventually landed them a council flat in London Fields when we were both twenty-one.

Initially, my parents weren't thrilled about my choices, but they ended up being incredibly supportive. My dad even took on the task of painting and wallpapering our new place, while my mum made sure we had all the essentials, like cutlery and plates. I busied myself too, building a sliding mirror door wardrobe from my own imagination, to make the most of the space. Eventually, my parents helped me invest in a house in 1995, the same year our son, Lucas, was born.

Looking back now, I can see just how immature I was back then."

PROF. BERNARD: "Indeed, people often speak of our innocent birth, yet the reality diverges. We inherit an array of attributes beyond our control—identity and history woven into us like an indelible birthmark. We arrive with our gaze cast backward, yet as my dear Mother used to say, *'Di road ahead a call fi we fi move to di horizon.'* The journey ahead is to craft our innocence, a concept I've come to realize through my client work. Through growth and maturation, we shall reclaim the purity of youth."

Innocence had no enemy but time and still with a measure of unworldliness. I enjoyed my job. It was fun being in an environment with city folk. It was different from working alone as a postman.

I was suited and booted, sporting fine ties and shiny shoes and the girls in the bank paid me attention. I smoked John Player Specials and sipped on my glass of expensive whisky, smuggled into the hidden cabinets of the basement by Fergus.

One lunchtime in March 1995, I made my way to Bethnal Green where Ronnie Kray's coffin procession was going through. There was such a large crowd. Having heard so many stories from the different black cab drivers that drove me around London about the gangsters of the East End, I wanted to catch a glimpse of the once King of the East End's brother, Reggie, having heard stories from Fergus and Janssen, but I never had a desire to be a gangster or enter the world of violence and deceit.

Now, along with opening and distributing mail, the best part was a daily trip to the heart of London via black cabs every day, back and forth, throughout the city. Delivering and collecting insurance documents, large sums of money, making transactions from The Bank of England and the Royal Bank of Scotland. We would drive up Shoreditch High Street, past the boarded-up and burnt-out warehouses, toward Old Street. Apart from the occasional bus, the traffic was reasonable in those days and the odd blade of grass could be spotted growing out of the road. It is incredible what a difference a hundred yards can make. Then we would park near Leadenhall Market, which dated back to 1321, situated in what was the center of Roman London, originally a meat, poultry and game market. I would finish my cigarette and stub it outside Lloyd's building in Lime Street, located on the former site of East India House in London's main financial district, the City of London.

Presenting my blue ID to the red long-coated sentinels stationed like regal guards at the bank's entrance, I stepped into Lloyd's. The escalators seemed to ascend endlessly, leading me through floor after floor. Looking down, the grand clock at the heart of the building caught my eye, featuring a poignant reminder of Lloyd's most renowned maritime loss: the HMS Lutine ship's great bell. This bell, which tolls twice upon significant losses for the Lloyd's Names underwriting a risk, traces its origin to the frigate HMS Lutine, insured by Lloyd's and lost to the sea in 1799. Suspended within the cavernous atrium of the colossal underwriting room, it stood as a solemn testament to the risks of the trade.

# Chapter Seven

## Lime Street Hustle

Lloyd's Building 1 Lime Street, The City London, EC3M 7DQ.

I enjoyed ascending the never-ending spiral escalators, observing the view of the majestic Lloyd's clock and watching the frantic commotions of transactions in the professional financial atmosphere. The air thrummed with the pulse of commerce, punctuated by the clicking of heels on marble floors and the cacophony of business discussions. The grandeur of the soaring atrium greeted me, adorned with gleaming brass fixtures and the rhythmic tick-tock of Lloyd's timepiece.

I would meet people who insured space shuttles, the Queen's Jewels and even Bruce Springsteen's voice. Before the introduction of the Euro, billions of pounds and dollars were administrated through ink on paper delivered by people in pinstripe suits, sunbed tans, Botox lips and immaculate countenances. You could see it in their demeanor. They had put their security in their finance and wealth. You could hear it in their voices, you could feel it in the atmosphere.

With so much spare time on my hands in between journeys, I used to daydream out of the window of the black cab at all the suits and rich, gray matter of the busy, fast and ice-cold insurance world. So many hardened faces. Some were chained to money and power. So many pretty women were too and you need money for city women I was told. Working in the basement was somewhat fun, but I still lacked the belief to pursue ambition. I knew there must be more, but I felt constantly relegated to hopelessness and no promotion.

Now Eleanor and I had a relationship together that was built on the foundation of My Sandcastles. I was not a good man to live with. I was insecure, jealous and angry. She was my first rushed love, but it was a form of limerence. [1]

PROF. BEATRICE: "It's like you're wondering if this relationship was like a fantasy, where you needed it to feel good 'bout yourself. Did you have this idea of being saved from way back when? Growing up around tough stuff, did your inner child start dreaming up tales of a 'someday my Princess will come,' maybe turnin' it into a sort of self-centered longing?"

JOE: "Did my longing to be seen, to be loved, to be heard and understood turn my teen relationship into a one-person relationship, since I was the only one seeing it the way it wasn't?"

PROF. BEATRICE: "You're thinkin' it was all 'bout what you needed?"

JOE: "I was too young and inexperienced to see her for who she was."

PROF. BEATRICE: "Seems like that relationship could've fit your fantasy, huh?"

JOE: "Not that I was looking to right the wrong highlights of my past that happened."

PROF. BEATRICE: "But reckon, lookin' at it from a neurological or neurobiological angle, maybe it turned into a habit, like an attractor state in the brain."

JOE: "I'd never had a girlfriend and I was grateful for the attention."

PROF. BERNARD: "Indeed, Joe, the teenage years are a tumultuous time of growth and self-discovery. Peer pressure can indeed play a significant role, often leading young men to seek validation and acceptance through romantic pursuits. It's a natural inclination to crave connection and intimacy during this phase."

JOE: "Yes, despite that, I hadn't managed to let go of my unrealistic relationship expectations.

PROF. BERNARD: "It's crucial not to rush or fall into the trap of pursuing just any girl for the sake of it."

JOE: "Yeah, I get it now. Looking back, I can see I was really struggling with my own..."

PROF: BERNARD: "... Shortcomings and insecurities?"

JOE: "Damn, yeah. I was dealing with my own mess. I was a scumbag... a narcissist, always putting my own needs first, seeking validation and attention just to hold onto whatever shred of self-image I had left."

PROF. BERNARD: "It takes a great deal of self-awareness to recognize our flaws and challenges. But remember, Joe, acknowledging our past mistakes is the first step toward growth and change. It's never easy to confront our imperfections, but it's a necessary part of our journey towards becoming better versions of ourselves.

You're onto something crucial, Joe. Adolescence is a period of heightened emotions and evolving identities. It's understandable to seek companionship, especially when it offers a sense of belonging. However, as you've come to realize, genuine connections require a deeper understanding of oneself and a solid foundation of self-love. Rushing into relationships without a clear sense of who you are can lead to misunderstandings and unmet expectations. Remember, the path to meaningful relationships starts with cultivating a healthy relationship with yourself."

PROF. BEATRICE: "It sounds as though you didn't even have a start loving' yourself or knowin' who you truly were. That inner Prince might've thought he found his Princess, but that *inner* wounded child never managed to slay that fire-spewing dragon."

*'Like a bird that strays from its nest is a man who strays from his home.'* [2]

December 1993, did I fly too early? Now in London Fields, Hackney, relieved to leave home despite disliking the surroundings and crime. From my third-floor flat window, I saw a gang punch a six-year-old while attempting to steal his bike. In the grip of fear, a fleeting notion arose to acquire a Wembley Nemesis air pistol. The plan: a nighttime escapade aiming at the soft glow of London Fields' train lights. A curious belief that casting shadows could confront fear and deter thieves. Thankfully, the impulse remained just that—an impulse.

Lucas, our son, was born in August 1995. My parents helped us to invest in a house in Enfield and we moved in December 1995. Looking back, I realize how incredibly blind and ungrateful my younger self was in many ways, as my parents would alternate in looking after Lucas, whilst my own dad did nightshift work as Eleanor and I traveled to London.

A few months after our son's birth, my company merged to form a new company and moved to plusher premises in Talisman Tower, Lincoln Plaza, London E14.

After Fergus's hoped-for redundancy and claims payment came through due to his mishap of jumping through an old window, he departed for Scotland to be with his girlfriend.

Lars, Toby and I were confined to a smaller, open post room, no longer hidden in the basement's shadows but fully exposed to all other employees. Rumors of cutbacks and redundancies, however, continued to circulate. I felt that I didn't have much time left. I predicted the 'last one in, first one out' law of employment survival would apply. And since I was the last one in, I was likely to be the first one out.

With the desire to make a memorable exit, I now see that I had the drive and untapped talent, yet I lacked the knowledge of how to harness the gift within, the imagination, the discovery. Personal growth, self-discovery and the development of coping strategies or skills to overcome obstacles and unlock my full potential were sorely lacking.

Instead I joined the suits and plunged into the same flood of dissipation of office affairs and the like. Nevertheless, I don't think anyone could have ever envisaged the future ramifications of my extraordinary brand of policy that would leave many all shook up.


## The Policy.


On January 8th, 1935. Vernon Presley went out to have a cigarette at 2 am during the delivery of his child and when he looked up at the sky above their little shack, he saw the strangest blue pulsating light. *"He knew right then and there that something special was happening."* [3]

On a warm, sunny day in mid-May 1996, I stood on the 33rd floor of the Talisman Tower, taking in the view of One Canada Square, the towering centerpiece of London's Canary Wharf financial district. With its distinctive pyramid-shaped roof adorned in stainless steel and glass, the building stood as one of the United Kingdom's tallest structures. The flashing beacons atop the tower added to its striking appearance, catching the eye of onlookers below.

While reading a newspaper, I came across a short article on the craziest gambling bets ever placed. The two things I loved as a child were Elvis and UFOs.

"Oi, Lars, check this out, right? There's this British bloke who's gone and put a bet on, reckoning' that Elvis ain't dead and he crashed his UFO right onto the Loch Ness Monster up in Scotland. And get this, the odds were sky-high!"

Janssen and Logan laughed. Never a gambling man myself, I still read the article aloud. Suddenly, a seed of thought germinated within and like Jack's magic beans, quickly sprouted into a stem that would eventually reach to the sky to become a beanstalk to further populate my field of crop circles.

"If people are daft enough to chuck a few quid on somethin' daft, they'd probably do it for a giggle, just to say they 'ave. Cheers, Elvis!"

With my eclectic outlook, I envisioned creating a certificate or policy designed to protect against the humorous scenario of 'Being abducted by aliens.' This novelty item could be displayed on the wall and in a hypothetical sense, even serve as a form of insurance. The idea struck me as prodigious, especially if we could target this policy toward fans of 'X-Files' and 'Star Trek.' Drawing from my knowledge gained during my school days when I avidly read about and aspired to become a ufologist, [4] it felt like a natural fit.

After meticulously drafting and designing the certificate, my mind a whirlwind of ideas, I was determined to transform it into reality by seeking backing from an insurance firm. Fueled by Fergus's old motto, *'He who dares wins,'* and Toby's envious jests, I summoned my courage. With their echoes in my ears, I ascended the stairs to meet the top man himself, Mr. D.L. Sully. A prominent figure among Cameron Guardian Assurance's company directors, he stood by the towering building's window, sporting an Erol Flynn-esque mustache. An aura of authority surrounded him as his gaze swept over the sprawling London panorama below, surveying the cityscape with the poise of a true dominion.

Mr. Sully listened with interest and surprise as I enthusiastically shared the idea with him and tried to tempt him with the promise of free publicity for the firm. Sully smiled. I think that was the first time I had seen him smile. Sully agreed that there was something in it but suggested other ideas and possibly even starting some sort of club rather than a policy, although, he encouraged me that I could probably find someone who would cover the policy. Turned down, but undeterred, I sought out other alternatives and after many phone calls and laughs, I still had found no backer.

## The United Nations

Returning to the drawing board, I then proceeded to write to all the top bookmakers enquiring about the odds for a specific nature for the pay-out considering potential extra-terrestrial evidence.

Eventually, '**Ladbrokes Bookmakers**' wrote back and offered odds of 250-1 if '*The United Nations* [5/6] *– or the British Prime Minister (John Major), confirmed the existence of aliens on Earth.*'

With this in mind and with a little money saved for the future, I thought of a name for my company and logo, thus IBP (*I Believe Promotions*) was birthed.

Postulating that if one placed a bet of £160.00 ($200) on Ladbrokes' odds it would technically cover the certificate and me for around £40,000 ($50,000) on any potential highly unlikely claimant. However, though the certificate never mentioned or used the word *insurance*, upon reflection and future understanding I was of course in error. Despite putting a lot of thought into this certificate and its wording and creativity. However, it could be argued that there may be some issues with my *early assumptions regarding the backing of a bookmaker* to cover potential claims! I worded it as follows:

*'Congratulations! You have become the bearer of the first-of-a-kind certificate against the abduction of yourself or someone you have nominated by Extra-terrestrial entities.*

*Name____, picture serial no ____ and certified print number____.*
*In the event of a claim (subject to substantial proof verified by the United Nations and an unnamed licensed bookmaker). IBP guarantees to pay the abductee a maximum of up to £40,000. \*($50,000)*
*Please note, that claims become void if a third party (media) is notified and shown substantial evidence before IBP.*
*Regressive hypnosis is not proof of claim.'*


## Gray Mind Matter.


In my mind, technically, reasoning that I had the backing of a bookmaker, if anyone pulled a stunt to claim then I would have evidence and sell the rights to such a spectacular story. Searching and contacting a local logo designer in Enfield, I told him what I required, a picture of a world with the words, 'I believe' emblazoned across the globe. When complete, I ordered a customized black ink stamp to be made to professionally mark the certificates to be sold.

Ordering the printing of the certificate to commence along with four works of art specially commissioned by a professional oil artist, who was commissioned to paint me four works of art, but mid-way through the project he said it was too much graft and being under a deadline, I had no choice but to negotiate it to two pieces.

Instructing the artist *in my vision*, firstly a picture of a spaceship shining down intense light upon a Kurt Cobain lookalike (the lead singer and founder of 90's super grunge band Nirvana) who was being lifted in its tractor beam. I asked for a distinctive surreal look. The second picture was of a normal man metamorphosing from man-to-hybrid-to-Zeta Reticulan, known as a gray —the lizard-type creature.

PROF. BERNARD: "It appears that you were exploring a form of transhumanism that carries a certain prophetic quality, intertwined with the concept of non-binary identification, Otherkin or Therianthropes."

JOE: "They have names for that now? I've come to understand that it's a vision of a future influenced by the concept of advanced transpermia, [7] tarnishing the image of humanity to accept these emancipated wandering stars. I find it ironic that they are called grays as if representing the graying of our humanity and how our limbic system gray matter (referring to the gray matter or neural tissue within the limbic system of the brain, associated with emotions, memory and motivation) might play a role in processing these functions— Interestingly, a UFO belief system actually shrinks gray matter! Whereas human love increases it." [8/9]

Within a couple of months, the portraits were complete. I had left a lot of the creativity in the hands of the artist and when he had completed the pictures, we both thought that the painting of the man in the light looked like Jesus ascending. In the future, I'd eventually go so far during some future media concoctions to promote the artwork as the second coming of Jesus. I had spent almost one thousand pounds on getting the artwork photographed and printed by a local printer. Titling the two pictures, 'Metamorphosis' and the other 'Night Abduction.' Marketing and placing full-page adverts in specialist mystery and paranormal magazines such as 'Fortean Times' and 'UFO Magazine' –

*IBP – Paranormal Protection*

*'The Abduction Xperience'*

*IBP is proud to present an exclusive never before offered item.*

*A certificate against alien abduction.*

*Pick from two limited edition color prints, only 300 of each available throughout the world, signed by the artist, each with serial and certificate numbers.*

*IBP will do what no insurance or underwriter will do.*

*Your own renewable authentic black and gold officially stamped certificate which guarantees to pay out should you be abducted by Extra-terrestrials, subject to proof and evidence.*

*Ideal gift and collector's item.*

Along with a small ad in the American National Enquirer, my lack of knowledge about advertising led to miscalculations regarding sales and exposure. It would have been foolish to expect to recoup the investment from such a large ad space. Dividing the budget over twelve months for smaller ads would have been a wiser approach.

Despite initially overcoming the financial obstacles and committing myself to the project, I proceeded to call The Enfield Independent (a local newspaper) one Thursday afternoon to gauge their interest in what was touted as a world-first story. Speaking to a journalist, I explained the project and clarified the technical jargon I had learned from skimming through a few documents, thinking little of it at the time.

Wednesday, 31$^{st of}$ July 1996.

That evening, my girlfriend and I arrived home to Enfield to see the local paper on the floor with a **front-page headline boldly declaring**:

116

## UFO Policies go on sale.

An insurance first for Enfield. Enfield Independent *(Front page 31$^{st}$ of July 1996).*

*For those who are preoccupied with the possibility of Extraterrestrial interactions, an Enfield man has come up with the perfect solution—insurance.*

*Joe Tagliarini of Ingvar Rd, Enfield Wash, claims to be the first man in the world to offer a policy against just this eventuality.*

*For an annual premium of £17.99 ($22) or a special discount of £9.99 ($12) for residents of Enfield, you can be assured that your family, mortgage repayments and any subsequent medical and legal bills will be taken care of in the event of your untimely disappearance, temporary or permanent.*

*The obvious catch is establishing firm proof and as we all know, getting money back from an insurance company is as hard as getting green blood out of a moon rock. However, Joe has the perfect solution: Confirmation by the United Nations, a game-changer indeed.*

*'To prove that aliens have landed', Joe said, 'The required proof is for the United Nations or the Prime Minister to officially accept it.'"*

*Lionel Beer, founder of the British UFO Research Association, said: 'There is a lot of argument about whether this is something real or whether it is something that goes on in people's heads.'*

## Radio Interview collage.

GLR: "How does a person prove that they have been abducted by Outer space creatures?"

JOE: "The Roper Organization did this survey back in '91 and guess what, 2% of Americans thought they'd been whisked away by little green men. That's like a whopping 4 million folks, considering the population then. Now, if we ever fancy checkin' out if E.T.'s droppin' by, we could throw that space wanderer's cell phone under the microscope, get the UN or some smart lab types to give it a good once-over. And the Orson Welles Martian stories? A whole lotta folks been yammering 'bout these 'Grays,' that's what they call 'em, these beings they all reckon look pretty much the same." [10]

TALK RADIO: "Have you been abducted?"

JOE: "Nah, mate, ain't nobody scooped me up, no way."

BBC RADIO 1: "I would like to speak to somebody who's been abducted, how do you prove it?"

JOE: "Being the top dog in Paranormal Insurance Investigation (PII) if the proof's solid and I'm convinced, I'll shell out. I'm after some real, out-of-this-world stuff – like actual proper ET materials found on the claimant or their gear. Plus, gotta have more than one set of eyes on the scene to back up the story. And don't skimp on the deets, mate – I want the whole enchilada on the abduction, from the surroundings to the funky tech they used."

KISS FM: "What sort of tangible evidence are we talking about here?"

JOE: "If we're talking hard facts, I'm after the real McCoy – think chunks of exotic metal, radar logs and folks who can vouch for the story. And let's not forget the time warp some abductees go through. So, having gear to track electromagnetic stuff and other weirdness is a smart move. Oh and get a camera or mic to catch any odd sights or sounds – it's like our paranormal toolkit for a solid investigation... Come to think of it, why don't the claimant bag himself the ET?"

CAPITAL RADIO: "So, if you've had an otherworldly experience, you better have a decent camera on standby?"

JOE: "Yeah, that's the one – not one of them potato cameras that spit out blurry pics. Gotta go for a proper cam, maybe even a throwaway one."

FRANÇAISE 51: "How much is zee premium, Joe?"

JOE: "The premium's fifty-one quid, innit? But if you're reppin' Enfield like me, 'cause I'm Enfield's top lad, it's just a tenner... they're getting a proper forty grand... and it's like a two-in-one deal, coverin' you while you're out huntin' them beings from the stars, ya know."

LIBERTY RADIO: *(in hysterics)* "Thank you, Joe, Enfield's favorite and eccentric son. Please keep us posted and keep your eyes and ears open. Wow, whatever will they think of next?"

# Chapter Eight

## The Maverick Mason

On August 15th, 1977, the Big Ear Radio Telescope in Delaware, part of Ohio State University, received the most powerful narrowband radio signal it would ever detect during decades of observations. The signal lasted for just seventy-two seconds. (Interestingly, 72 is represented by the symbol Hf on the periodic table, indicating the element hafnium—a lustrous, silvery-gray, tetravalent transition metal). When an astronomer spotted the signal on a computer printout days later, he was so impressed that he quickly scrawled 'Wow!' in red pen across the page. The signal appeared to come from the direction of the constellation Sagittarius and bore the expected hallmarks of what SETI (Search for Extraterrestrial Intelligence) astronomers expected to see from an extraterrestrial civilization. However, despite many attempts to follow up on the find, the so-called Wow! signal has never reappeared.

Two weeks after the Enfield front page (August 1996) the same Enfield journalist contacted me to say that some ladies from Waltham Abbey wanted to meet me in response to the newspaper article, so he gave me their number and I met them outside at a Waltham Cross bus station.

I followed them in my red Fiat Uno to their house, which was a stone's throw away from Waltham Abbey Church. The Church where King Harold of *the Battle of Hastings* is buried. A unique church in the fact that if you look up at the ceiling you will see the star signs of the Zodiac—something that many still find surprising today but here is the reason for such vision, they signify the passage over time. The twelve signs are visible in the stars over the twelve months. In their confidence, the Victorian Christians put them there, for they knew their pagan origin, of course, but also that the church had appropriated them, giving each one a Christian meaning. For example, Aquarius, the water carrier—think of baptism, Gemini, the twins—think of the duality of Jesus, human and divine, sharing humanity and offering us hope of Heaven and so forth. The Victorians had the confidence to look bravely at things Christians today consider secular and temporal and interpreted them in terms of Heaven and eternity.

<u>Jigsaw Piece.</u>

I arrived at the house and entered their living room, where five ladies and a man had gathered to sincerely share their experiences and beliefs about a coming disclosure and that truth of the 'aLIEns' and UFOs was at an all-time high: a belief that the Government was not covering it up as much to prepare the world for its reality.

Sylvia, having grown up and lived in Swindon, spoke with an accent as she began to vividly recount her story of what she and many others had encountered in Swindon in the 1970s.

"One evening, in our street near a park, a strange whistling sound made all the residents come out to see a huge, metallic silver craft silently land on the park. No one was frightened. There was an extraordinary sense of peace and calm as we all watched it just sit there while it emitted a peaceful hum. Then a dog ran toward it barking and it shot off into the sky at an incredible speed."

I listened in absolute amazement. '*Wow!*' my inner child was delighted to see the books and discussions of my past come to life in the shape of meeting real-time witnesses.

Sylvia continued, "The whole town had seen the huge silver disc land and the next day army helicopters came with pomp and noise as if to override the former night in people's minds." Sylvia's story connected with my childhood memories and I was a convert, hungry for truth, having found a jigsaw piece in my quest. Real-life persons with real-life encounters in a room of other mature believers who also shared their stories.

A few months later, I was invited to Glastonbury with Sylvia and the same people, I took Eleanor and Lucas (who was two at the time) and we stayed for two nights in a bed and breakfast. Glastonbury had me truly refreshed with its views, greenery, mountains, history and mystery. The B&B where we stayed had many VHS videos of UFOs and I sat and binge-watched them all for that first evening. In the morning, we were invited next door to meet a woman who I believed was a druid. With her long white hair cascading down her back and wearing flowing white clothes adorned with dream-catching ornaments, she greeted us. She led her followers to form a circle, inviting us to join in, holding hands as she chanted, invoking Mother Earth and calling for peace worldwide.

After the meeting had finished, she approached and spoke to two separate women, they then cried and hugged her for what she had said. She then approached me and looked into my eyes, paused and said, 'Come and speak to me soon. You need to talk to me about your journey.'

She seemed concerned and empathic and I felt warm. I sensed I would have loved to have talked to her, but time was limited. Glastonbury had been an experience that opened another door and my mind felt evidence was gathering swiftly.

As we left Glastonbury, the memories of that mystical encounter lingered, weaving into the fabric of my thoughts. The warmth of the druid's words, the sincerity in her eyes — it all left me feeling a sense of connection to something greater. Back home, I found myself drawn to the media, seeking out stories and documentaries that explored similar themes of spirituality and connection with the Earth. Each piece of media I consumed seemed to reaffirm the profound experiences I had in Glastonbury, further fueling my curiosity and conviction.

<u>me·di·a</u>

[mee-dee-uh] noun

1. a plural of medium.

2. (usually used with a plural verb) The means of communication, such as radio and television, newspapers and magazines that reach or influence people widely: The media are covering the speech tonight.

2nd of August 1996, back in Docklands, my first TV appearance beckoned. My boss, Sully, permitted me. ITN (Independent Television News) and Vinnie Rogers came to interview me at work for part of the 6 O'clock news segment.

Rogers linked the story to the release of the film *Independence Day* where aliens invade the world on the 4th of July.

VINNIE: "If you can believe all the stories, particularly the ones that are coming out of America at the minute, a poll that was conducted over there a year or two ago suggested that up to 3.5 million Americans believe they have been abducted by UFOs. Meet Joe, he works as a messenger for an insurance firm in Docklands, but he's hoping to put his bosses to shame by cleaning up with his idea for a policy, he's offering insurance against kidnapping by little green men."

JOE: *(In my strong cockney, East End accent)* "Listen 'ere, mate. In the unlikely event that you get taken for a ride by some little green men and ya manage to bring me back somethin' substantial as proof - like the steering wheel of a spaceship or E.T.'s mobile phone - then I'll pay ya up proper."

VINNIE: "If you buy Joe's policy for £17.99 ($22) and you're abducted by Interplanetary visitors in the coming year, he is legally obliged *(No-I-am-not)* to pay you forty-thousand pounds ($50,000). But the cash will be no use to you on Mars, will it?"

JOE: "Most of 'em come back, right? About 98% of 'em. But as for that other 2%, well, I ain't makin' no promises there."

Mr. Sully later called me and said that he had shown his son my news articles, explaining the power of imagination and its business skill as an example of inspiration.

My fellow workers who had mocked me did not know what to think about the post boy who had created his policy and gleaned so much publicity and initiative that even the motor insurance manager at the firm had said that his team of three boy racers thought of something like that, he would have been grateful for the exposure. It sure seems that someone took notice.

The *Daily Mail* soon picked up on the story along with world media interest, appearing in all major tabloids, little by little gaining snippets of stories from journalists and the public alike regards to the phenomena.

Meanwhile, P. Boniface, a reporter from an insurance magazine had been phoned by Toby in his attempt to discredit me and having seen the headline from the Enfield Independent, briefly spoke to me about my certificate and then ran a headline stating that the Department of Trade and Industry were investigating me. As far as I was aware, that was not the case, so I felt annoyed. Logan in his usual split personality took the opportunity to continue to mock and threaten me with impending jail time, wishing me misfortune and arrest.

Meanwhile, Lars Janssen explained I'd done nothing wrong, but Boniface's news article would soon work out for my good, as a week later, the same reporter contacted me and told me that a certain Johnny Cradock wanted to meet me to discuss my policy.

### The City of Woe.

*"Through me you pass into the city of woe.*
*Through me you pass into eternal pain.*
*Through me among the people lost for aye." —Dante, Canto III*

Semi-surprised at the simplicity of submitting a story to the media throughout the somewhat comedy of errors, I was asked by a journalist to contact a broker who wanted to meet me. Johnny Cradock (labeled by the media as the insurance maverick) was notorious as such because he was the only person on the planet insuring people against Bovine Spongiform Encephalopathy (BSE) aka Mad Cow Disease and virgin births (apparently).

### From Potteries to Policies.

*"The man is in the wrong industry" –*
*Max Williams, Chief Executive, British Investment and Insurance Brokers'*
*Association.*

I first met Johnny Cradock in his office on Lime Street, which overlooked the Lloyd's building. Smiling with a mischievous Cheshire cat grin that even Alice in Wonderland could not have avoided, "I've just met Lloyd's chairman Sir David... He told me that I was the Einstein of the insurance industry!"

"That was nice of him," I reply.

"Yes," Cradock continues, "But I think he meant Frank rather than Albert." Cradock asked me if I would like to join him in having a bit of fun with the media.

Cradock, a product of the Potteries, a region known for its historical significance in the ceramics industry. Nestled in the heart of England, the Potteries earned its name due to its prolific production of pottery and ceramics, shaping the landscape with its rich artistic heritage. Born within the embrace of this creative crucible, Cradock carries the essence of his birthplace – the ability to mold and shape, to bring forth artistic creations from the very clay of his imagination.

Standing at an impressive 6 feet and 4 inches tall, Cradock's portly frame and rugby player-like appearance are complemented by round spectacles that frame his gray-blue eyes. He wore the mask of earnestness, though he claimed he often struggled to pick up on social cues and make true eye contact. Ironically, he believed that the nuances of sarcasm eluded him, endowing him with an endearing sincerity. His blonde mousy hair frames his face, adding a touch of youthful charm to his overall presence. His unwavering dedication to drawing and artistic expression colors his world with passion.

On the day in question, Cradock adorns a crisp white cricket suit, the ensemble harmonizing with his matching stripy tie. At thirty-five, he bears the marks of experience, having earned a law degree from the University of

Newcastle. His triumph over dyslexia to secure the esteemed Robert Maxwell Prize for exam performance is a testament to his perseverance and intellect.

Cradock's refined speech, flavored with the symphony of BBC English, carries an air of prim professionalism. Beneath this veneer, a delicate tapestry of dry wit and playful mockery is interwoven, often directed at journalists and the sprawling media landscape. At just twenty-three, I stand under the tutelage of a mentor who seamlessly embodies authority and clever subtlety. This intriguing fusion ignites my curiosity and commands respect, setting the stage for a remarkable journey of growth and learning.

Cradock specialized in business and insurance law but when he qualified, he gave up law and searched for ways to make some immediate money. The hypnotic maverick states he'd found work at Lloyd's of London by writing a begging letter that was along the lines of, *'My dad thinks I am useless, please help me to prove him wrong by giving me a job. I was given the role of tea boy or oily rag as it was known then.'*

He worked his way up and became a senior underwriter. Cradock took on many high-profile cases such as life cover for Ayrton Senna and covering the Rolling Stones, Michael Jackson and Elton John for cancellation or non-appearance insurance, on which he says he is now considered a world authority.

On other occasions, he would wear pin-striped suits, matching his bubbly, charismatic personality and along with his immense understanding of law and insurance, he had a boundless vernacular and amazing academic use of vocabulary, either that, or he knew how to baffle people by overusing big words.

From the nurturing embrace of the Potteries and the fertile clay of Cradock's imagination, a novel and powerful insurance Frankenstein is forged – a reflection of our shared journey through the captivating landscape of the insurance industry.

We teamed up and began to weave our web of charismatic prowess. I joined this mad tea party, which eventually led me to an unknown destination: the Garden of Storytime. It was a tea party quite like the one hosted by the Mad Hatter, where we engaged in bizarre, nonsensical conversations and portrayed characters acting out those behaviors, reflecting the whimsical and surreal nature of Wonderland. Absurdity and a lack of adherence to conventional social norms added to the overall dreamlike quality of the illusion and delusion.

Journalist, Bill Sebastian was following Cradock's antics with great relish. He had first met Cradock fittingly in *The Globe pub* at London Bridge the same Summer of 1996 while writing for a weekly trade title, *Capital Financial Courier*. Sebastian saw then the force of energy, which drove him, writing his lumbering and clumsy form, untidily crushing a stool as he wiped the overspill of Guinness down the side of the glass. He then wiped his finger on the edge of a beermat then licked it before looking at Bill through his half-inch thick glasses for a moment, asking: "Do you want a really big story?" Of course, he did.

Sebastian may have only been working for a second-rate free trade paper, but he was nonetheless a journalist and had been for six years. Cradock, having launched into describing the scale of upset Bill could cause through the research he was to do, planned to smuggle Bill into the Lloyd's of London Library, posing as an underwriter doing some confidential research for his insurance firm, N.O.B.L.E – This stood for 'Nigel Owen Brian Llyod's Enterprise.' The names were irrelevant. He picked them randomly from the phone book. A feeble set of names, he admits, but better than the first lot, Theresa Isabel Tanya. Cradock was a Lloyd's Name, he told

Bill and added that *'as a Freemason,'* he had not fallen prey to the fraud which had left so many other Lloyd's investors bankrupt. *'I was only on the syndicates, which made money,'* he explained, smiling unrepentantly.

Cradock and I began to spin a folly of entertaining deception. It seemed like a great joke at the time. Cradock wanted publicity for NOBLE, but his intent was twofold at first but then became threefold.

Firstly, he was to get back at the insurance regulator for ignoring his pleas for them to act against banks ripping off consumers with worthless but costly PPI (Payment Protection Insurance). The PPI scandal eventually culminated in £50 Billion (Sixty-one billion, seven hundred twenty million, five hundred thousand dollars as of 22nd April 2024) in compensation from the banks. Cradock was livid that banks were selling these insurances that were costly and riddled with exclusions that made them not worth the paper written on. He complained to the Government Regulator to take action against the banks, but the regulator wrote back saying they could see no evidence of PPI mis-selling. It would be another fifteen to twenty years before the banks were proven to have ripped off the public to the tune of £50 Billion. And they had to pay it all back. Hence, the influx of *'Have you been sold PPI cover?'* commercials.

Secondly, this venture into promoting unique policies would generate a lot of publicity for Cradock's own company, thus enabling him to sell a worthy version of PPI, which he would later handsomely do in the future.

Thirdly, the reason for hoaxing, as I can testify, was very easy and enormous fun.

Cradock took out a huge white book, opened it and showed me all the newspaper clippings and articles that he had collected on behalf of his company from his eccentric policies and outrageous quotes. He too had started this journey in early 1996.

Cradock wanted to partner with me and said that any policies or inquiries generated to purchase UFO certificates would be subsequently handed over to me to sell my resources. It sounded like a win-win deal to me.

Cradock, in addition to being rather mischievous concerning business, seemed like the sort of person not to be trifled with. His demeanor carried a hint of the wolf, keenly aware of his surroundings and quick to protect his interests. *"Watch this!"* he said, as he dialed a number.

A voice answered and he spoke in a professional tone about the Extraplanetary Policy and impregnation before passing me the phone saying match that and I did. With my knowledge of ufology, I fended off questions of claims and procedures, even though I hadn't a clue about real insurance or the person I was talking to. After the interview, Cradock looked impressed and said, "Do you know who that was?"

"No," I replied.

"That was one of the most powerful journalists in Britain. That story will go national and worldwide."

Reuters syndicated the story globally. The story became stories that would extend and go throughout the world for fourteen months and I could've continued. (June, '96—Aug, '97).

After I met with Cradock, I contacted Boniface to put him straight, he then wrote a headline stating:

*'Insurers hitch a ride on the alien bandwagon' - London Underwriting Digest 29/8/96.*

*The Enfield-based entrepreneur who made headlines by selling insurance certificates for alien abductions without proper licensing. Despite his unorthodox approach, he has found support from a multinational insurance company, which has underwritten the scheme and become his exclusive agent. In exchange for an annual fee of £100, ETSAFE– policyholders receive £1 million in cash payment if abducted by Spaceborne beings, The Enfield man has so far sold fifty-one certificates and received inquiries from the US. He plans to expand his business with an advertising campaign starting next month, beginning with The National Enquirer. Nevertheless, some responses to Tagliarini's offer have been troubling, with a few fanatics claiming that 'other-dimensional beings' will soon arrive to collect Earthlings in a modern day Noah's ark. Despite these concerns, the insurance policy has piqued the curiosity of many customers, even as some experts express skepticism about its viability.*

More radio and TV interviews ensued and I would tweak things and character vernacular just to make it more interesting.

JOE: "The presented evidence will undergo assessment either by a credible scientific laboratory or the United Nations. Recent findings from a survey revealed that a significant number of individuals, including 3.8 million Americans and three thousand Britons, assert that they have been abducted by extra-terrestrial beings. Such reports are commonly reported among the general population, suggesting the prevalence of this phenomenon." [1,2,3]

As I came up with more outlandish ideas for paranormal insurance policies, Cradock and I found ourselves selling them to the media faster than a werewolf can devour a juicy steak. I even made an appearance on The Y Files, where I pitched our complete package of protection policies to an audience of true believers. While on set, I had the misfortune of meeting a couple of wannabe vampires who were about as real as the special effects in a B-movie. But hey, at least they had a good dentist!

## THE Y FILES: File 11:11

INTRO: "From the unusual to the outlandish, would you consider insuring against being abducted by a vampire? If it's strange or paranormal, welcome Joe Dante, the world's first paranormal insurer from the East End of London to The Y Files."

JOE: "Check it out, mate. I read in the papers that some bloke put a bet on Elvis being alive, flying a UFO and riding Nessie, can you Adam and Eve it? Proper genius, if you ask me. Got me thinking, why not have a policy for when the little green men come and take you away, eh? So, I made one. You know how it is, people insure their cars and their gaffs, so why not insure against the unknown, yeah?"

"At the moment, we've flogged 1,947 policies, give or take *(I just picked a number out of thin air, to be honest - changed it later on)*. And get this, all our paranormal policies are the real McCoy, yeah? We're the first ones to do it in the whole world, mate. So, if you ever get lifted by Ufonauts, you know who to holler at, innit?"

INTERVIEWER: "What proof do you need if someone claims they've been bitten by a Vampire?"

JOE: "Now, if you wanna prove you're a vampire, your fangs better elongate, yeah? And don't come at me with that "I don't like garlic" malarkey, 'cos that ain't gonna cut it. You gotta have superhuman strength too, see? Some of my clients even wanted me to go all the way to Transylvania! We do insure travelers there now, so no worries, yeah.

Now, if you reckon you've been bitten by a werewolf, we'll stick you in a cage during the full moon, with your written consent, mind and silver bullets at the ready. And if you get spirited away by a Stargazer, no need to fret, 'cos 98% of them captives come back in one piece. We're expecting a claim any day now and as your paranormal insurance investigator, I'll investigate it myself and take a butcher's cut at all the evidence. I'll give it the proper once-over with all the analysis gear we've got, see?"

PROF. VIRGIL: "Mal di Luna?"

JOE: "Yes, media luna-tics indeed."

PROF. VIRGIL: "Ah, the monkey mind, swinging from one thought branch to another like a lunatic in the moonlight. Quite the challenge to wrangle, but mastering it leads to inner tranquility."

JOE: "But the media ensures that it trolls people..."

PROF. VIRGIL: "Indeed, the media's relentless barrage often fuels the monkey mind, transforming it into a masterful troll tra verità e illusione."

The media would go on to quote Cradock in print: *'You can never underestimate the stupidity of the British public.'*

Ironically, it was not just the British public who were underestimated, the rest of the world was about to follow suit. This occurred before the arrival of YouTube, yet the content still went viral on the fledgling Internet. Both viral content and ghost stories can capture people's attention and imagination, spreading rapidly and becoming embedded in the collective consciousness.

# Chapter Nine

## Ghosts and Redundancy

*London Weekend Television—September 1996.*

Cradock was contacted by LWT (London Weekend Television) expressing interest in the poltergeist insurance policy, for the program *After 5* (the sister show of *London Tonight)* and they wanted to interview a policyholder. Cradock duly called me.

PRESENTER YASMIN: "Is your house fully insured? If you are smart, you will have fire, theft and contents cover. But have you ever considered the need to protect yourself against the paranormal? Well, as Yasmin Pasha has discovered, hundreds of people have opted to do just that, with the very latest type of insurance policy."

(Ghostbusters intro music dubbed over voice).

YASMIN: "Remember the film Poltergeist, where an unseen phantom wreaked havoc in a family home, tossing furniture around and sucking small children into television sets? Well, of course, it was only a film, but have you ever wondered what you'd do if a Poltergeist or a ghostly presence invaded *your* home?"

CRADOCK: "We can provide up to a million pounds against attack by Poltergeists or impregnation by Poltergeists… but the attack is the major concern."

YASMIN: "For a premium of roughly one hundred pounds per year, Cradock's insurance company will provide cover for anyone unlucky enough to be plagued by a Poltergeist."

CRADOCK: "We've had considerably more than a thousand inquiries, all of which have been unsolicited. We have sold over six hundred and sixty six policies."

YASMIN: "So what kind of person would buy something that protects you from destructive unseen forces?"

(PROF. BEATRICE: "Here comes that young actor, Joe, don't ya know?"

JOE: "Yup, here *we* ghost again.")

Scary music played again with a film of me walking along a street with my hair messed up and on edge as if I had seen a presence. The cameraman hid in the bushes of his front garden and chased me indoors. Oh, the joys of light entertainment.

JOE: "When I was four years old, I saw what I believed to be the impression of a small child wearing Victorian clothes—a ghost, a poltergeist, or whatever you want to call it. It was quite frightening at the time."

YASMIN: "Motorcycle courier Joe forked out the premium for Poltergeist protection without a second thought."

JOE: "Why not take out insurance against it? As a professional ghost hunter, I might get possessed or have things thrown at me that have been levitated. I might even step in some ectoplasm, so why not?"

YASMIN: "But girlfriend, Eleanor and little boy, Lucas don't seem to be that impressed."

ELEANOR: "I think he's a *nutter*." *(Lucas, thirteen months old, nods in agreement and gnaws an apple.)*

YASMIN: "Surely not? But Cradock's certainly onto a good thing, he spotted this gap in the market after offering insurance against alien abduction and impregnation."

CRADOCK: "Quite simply, I've introduced the policy as a response to the genuine concerns of my clients. There are a considerable number of people who are deeply concerned that there are non-terrestrial beings and also the threat of abduction or interference by extraterrestrial beings or *ghosts*, perhaps."

YASMIN: "So how does somebody prove their claim to your satisfaction?"

CRADOCK: "It's not to our satisfaction, it's to the satisfaction of a panel of independent experts. We will take any evidence. We close no doors."

YASMIN: "The burden of proof is definitely on the client, however, that doesn't seem to bother Joe."

JOE: "It shouldn't be a problem. Levitation, I believe, should be the strongest proof point if the claims investigator comes to see it. Additionally, we can document any electromagnetic disturbances or anomalous readings during the levitation event. And if there are multiple witnesses, their testimonies would further support the credibility of the phenomenon. With these combined pieces of evidence, I guess then we'll have a solid case to present."

YASMIN: "Joe is off to America next month—on an aLIEn hunt and naturally, he's insured."

JOE: "Things will be covered at home if things go wrong or if I'm kidnapped by little green men or splattered with jelly!"

YASMIN: "Ha-ha, I mean, you know, obviously you have a sense of humor about this, but you do take it all quite seriously, don't you?"

JOE: "Oh yeah *(I flicked back my head to hide my smirk)* I do take it seriously. There is something out there."

YASMIN: "At the moment Joe's family is probably the most destructive thing in his life."

*(Lucas pulls a blanket off his head and throws Lego parts all over the floor, in accordance with my directorial idea).*

LUCAS: "Daddy!"

YASMIN: (continued) "But like hundreds of other policyholders, when things go bump in the night at least he'll have peace of mind. Well, in theory anyway." Yasmin quipped, her voice laced with a hint of skepticism.

*(Ends with scary music and camera shot zooming upstairs).*


September 1996, London News Network.


Dear Joe,

Thanks very much for agreeing to be interviewed for *After Five*. Your interview was excellent—very natural and relaxed. The cameraman and I enjoyed meeting you. We received a very good response to the report and I gather Cradock is now drafting a new insurance policy protecting against Vampire attacks. He's an enterprising man, isn't he? I hope your trip to America goes well. Please keep us posted *if you decide to make a claim on your policy* and keep us up to date with your UFO hunt. Once again, thanks for your time and trouble. Best Regards, Yasmin Pashsa. REPORTER. YP/ls.

## Leaving behind glass pyramids

September 1996, as expected, I was made redundant from my messenger city job after five years of service. Toby, the mocker, said it was because of my involvement with the jolly maverick. Lars said it was genuine redundancy. Regardless, I knew it was on the cards ahead of time. Three postal workers in one tiny room for all the staff to see where one couldn't swing a cat in there if one tried, was a far cry from the basement of Commercial Street. Facing No.1 Canada Square with its pyramid roof with flashing aircraft warning lights, I was not needed, thus, I was given my redundancy check and said my goodbyes to the glass pyramids in the sky, leaving Cameron Guardian Assurance with the specter of the legend of Carpenter.

I wouldn't see Lloyd's again until my *'ewe-nique'* Sheep Cloning Policy was created, which would involve an actual inflatable sheep. Cradock had acquired it from a shop in Soho.

Meanwhile, I did several quick part-time jobs, from early September 1996, working for the British gas mail room, franking letters in the day before then working full-time nightshifts (Oct. 96) for 'General Electric USA' (a fluorescent light company). No one there knew my past, but that would soon change.

## Libido Risk

Months later, the suggestion for libido risk came up in a pub discussion with Cradock, whilst we were simultaneously proceeding with the Poltergeist insurance.

It was at that time that I decided to create another character that would briefly appear as a pole dancer. Frank da Rimini was a British gas mail worker by day, but a part-time stripper by night. Taking advantage of my surroundings, I, Frank the dancing stripper, allegedly made a mailing error at the British Gas sorting office. Of course, I had nothing to do with any mail error, but at that time there was some news story of how British Gas had been responsible for an error that led to hundreds of thousands of customer letters being sent late or lost altogether. I had no idea where the base was or the error. I just took an opportune moment to blend my latest character with the time and space of my work surroundings for him to take the blame. At that time, I had been working in one of the British Gas HQ mailrooms sending out late bills, but of course, I had nothing to do with the real situation. Meanwhile, the Paranormal insurance interviews continued.

## TV Collage

CHARON'S CROSSING TV: "Now, most of us at one time in our life are forced to consider taking out insurance—the normal run-of-the-mill kind of thing, your house, your car, life insurance. But that is far too ordinary for the gentleman sitting beside me. Welcome to Charon's Crossing TV, *Joseph Carpenter.*"

CARPENTER: "Hello."

MINOS WATCH: "Joe, could you explain to our audience what type of insurance it is that you have taken out?"

CARPENTER: "I've taken out 'Paranormal Insurance', amongst other policies, which include and cover Cosmic pilgrim capture."

GERYON STREAM: "So, you've insured yourself against being beamed up or taken away by cosmic beings in Extraterrestrial spacecraft?"

CARPENTER: "Yes, that's correct. I mean, I haven't intentionally insured myself against otherworldly abduction, though it's worded as such. I took the policy out because in my eyes it's about making contact. And if I do, cha-ching! It's like a bonus reward for hanging out with extraterrestrial homies! If I manage to snap some proof of it, I'll be laughing all the way to the bank!"

NESSUS DC PRESS: "What prompted your choice to embark on this extraordinary undertaking? Your steadfast conviction in UFOs is palpable. Here in the United States, we encounter a wide spectrum of individuals who assert having encountered extraterrestrial phenomena, frequently sharing accounts of remarkable escapades. However, a substantial number of these recollections lack substantial evidence to back their claims."

CARPENTER: "Ever since I was a kid, I've been captivated by the supernatural. You could say I'm a full-fledged 'Paranormal Investigator,' always on the lookout for things that go bump in the night. While I do dabble in Poltergeists, the history of Vampires and Werewolves, my true passion lies in chasing UFOs. They're my top priority, my main pursuit and the apple of my eye."

STATIUS VISION: "Joe, have you been to see a Priest yet?"

CARPENTER: "Err … no, but I think they believe in them too. I think a Priest might consider them our space brother. Maybe *Jesus* was one."

ACHERON MEDIA: "How much did it cost you to insure yourself against a Ufonaut encounter or to get rewarded for it if anything happens to you?"

CARPENTER: "The premium cost me one hundred pounds and that covers me for a year. If E.T. turns up, then the pay-out is one hundred thousand pounds."

MINOSU ミノス・コネクト KONEKUTO: "One hundred thousand pound? With 3.9 million Americans, they say, claiming they have been taken up by エイリアン (Eirian). If we look at statistics, it appears to be a worthwhile investment, doesn't it? Interesting, so you're seeking your very own Utsuro-bune or Mitsuo Matsumoto moment, right? Venturing into the skies, pursuing UFOs, much like those intriguing tales?"

CARPENTER: "Yes, I suppose … although I've never come across those stories. I'm on a quest for connection with cosmic travelers, aiming to capture concrete evidence. This serves as my sole incentive and it happens to be the only opportunity available that qualifies as a legitimate interstellar pursuit amidst the realm of supernatural and paranormal phenomena. I'm eagerly anticipating a sky search near Nevada and if there exists a possibility of acquiring paranormal insurance tailored to my profession, why not seize it?"

CERBERUS NEWSNETZ ÜBERTRAGUNG: "What kind of proof will the insurance company need? Like in a car accident, photos of what happened along with your insurance details usually work. But how can you show evidence of a 'Nahbegegnung' (nah-beh-geg-noong) here? Most times, it's just people saying things that might not be accurate because of their thoughts."

CARPENTER: "Well I guess then they won't be accepting hypnosis regression as evidence, however, E.T.'s mobile phone I suppose, if I can steal that, or saucer debris or an unknown element, then surely that will suffice."

POSTE DE SAINT PIERRE: "They will undoubtedly seek concrete evidence, going beyond mere photographs or mere testimonies, won't they?"

CARPENTER: "If I can get camcorder footage, perhaps even capture the alien myself, that may be sufficient, but what if it has its own insurance?"

CRÓNICAS DE CATÓN: "*What put this in your mind* to do this? Is it because of the kind of work you do?"

CARPENTER: "You know what? I've been investigating the possibility of visitors from beyond for years and let me tell you, it's no joke. There are a lot of stigmas attached to this type of research, which makes it tough to get the resources we need to make real progress. So, when I heard about this insurance, I jumped at the chance to show my support for the cause.

It's not just about the money—although let's face it, that's a bonus—but it's also about taking this investigation seriously."

STYX NETWORK: "And so, by insuring yourself against the possibility of a cosmic kidnapping or transportation, you are sending a message that this is a real and important field of study that needs to be explored?"

CARPENTER: "Yeah, you could say I put my money where my mouth is. But more than that, I'm excited to be part of a movement that's bringing credibility to this often-misunderstood area of research, I want to be the one that crosses the bridge into the unknown and comes back with the golden egg."

NIMRODEU 님로드 티비 TV: "In addition to '외계인 보험' (Weigyein boheom), do you have insurance that covers unusual risks, such as those related to vampires or incidents linked to cults?"

CARPENTER: "Yes, I'm also covered against a conversion to Vampirism, a conversion from man to wolf and a possession by Poltergeists, it's a pretty fully comprehensive policy."

NIMRODEU 님로드 티비 TV: "Ah! Baempaiuh, Weeooulpeu geuligo Polteogaiseuteu!"

TIRESIAS NEWS: "Seriously, do you think the insurance company is going to believe that you were turned into a blood-sucking creature of the night? Unless you have some real proof like a bat wing sprouting from your back or a sudden craving for garlic, I don't think they'll be cutting you a check anytime soon. But hey, stranger things have happened in this world, right? Remember Vlad III, also known as Vlad the Impaler? He had a reputation that makes being a vampire seem like a walk in the park."

CARPENTER: "That's right, though they'll probably place me in a cage and have silver bullets on standby."

ULYSSES GTV: "Ha-ha-ha, so, do you believe in all these 'τρελά πράγματα' (tre-lá prá-gma-ta) or is it just wishful thinking, my friend? Are you secretly hoping they're real, or do you think they actually exist out there?"

CARPENTER: "The actual Poltergeists, UFOS and aLIEns I believe in more than the Chupacabra and Skinwalker side of things, but we do live in a strange world, so I wouldn't rule it out."

DELLA GHERARDESCA UNO: "So, the insurance company, they give-a you un certificato ufficiale o documento, you know, somethin' that assures they gonna protect-a you if an ET or perhaps Nosferatu decides to make an appearance right there in your own living room? I'm-a just-a thinkin', if I were the insurance company, I'd prefer some tangible proof of that commitment before I go ahead and hand over any of my financial assets!"

CARPENTER: "Pretty much! È una vera politica and in this day and age, garlic, crucifixes or holy water might not do the job, but that's why I have the full PI."

THE PIER PERSPECTIVE: "Paranormal Insurance, Nightwalkers, Shapeshifters, Close Encounters of the 4$^{th}$ Kind and Poltergeists…"

SORDELLO NEWS 24: "… People who file their teeth and hang out in hidden brotherhoods?"

MCB MINOS, CERBÈRE, GÉRYON TV: "My friends, let me tell you, I am not a skeptic, but I 'ad zis vision of a big, 'airy 'and comin' down on my shoulder!"

TV and radio reporters from Europe and beyond were eager to interview Carpenter, the policyholder, believing they had a compelling story. In truth, nothing could have prepared them (or me) for what would unfold later.

## CNN.

For the next month or so, Cradock, Sebastian and I found ourselves visiting TV studios or fielding calls from radio stations worldwide. Then, Cradock phoned me with news that CNN from America was also interested in filming him. At this point, I decided to subtly adjust my script.

CNN: "Is it safe to say that you hold this matter in deep regard?"

CARPENTER: "You betcha, I've got PI because I'm a seasoned investigator. And let me tell you, I've gathered some solid evidence that'll make those insurance folks sweat. I can't say too much right now, but I've secured a legit tape locked up in a bank vault that'll have them shaking in their boots. Evidence that'll blow the insurance company's socks off. If they thought this was some kinda gimmick, they're in for a rude awakening. Something happened and I've secured the proof to back it up. But you know what they say, good things come to those who wait."

To my surprise, CNN did not probe. I was calm and confident and did not care if they broadcasted the interview or not. Some journalists warned me to keep the tape safe. Others advised me to make several copies of it and not to trust the insurance company. "If he doesn't pay me, I'll go round and kick his head in!" I replied in an East End gangster voice.

I phoned Cradock and told him what I had said and we were surprised to see the interview aired on CNN news. The unbelievable stakes had just been raised and the wand had been passed to Cradock.

# Chapter Ten

## <u>Dis-clothe-sure</u>

With the stakes hitting close encounters levels, the wand of responsibility found its new bearer in Cradock. As we delved into the precarious realm of folly, I had mentioned libido risk to Cradock in a pub early in 1996 and suggested he send one to Bill Clinton. Months later he had come up with wording and phallic policy ideas. For the record, I had nothing to do with the Virgin or Immaculate Conception Insurance. I jokingly said to Cradock, "Who are you gonna get to hand over the check? *Richard Branson?*" Cradock paused and his eyes lit up through his professor spectacles and a 200-watt, anti-Christ bulb appeared above his head. A couple of days later, he promptly wrote to Virgin's Press Office and received a response back saying something like, *'Thank you for your inquiry, but Mr. Branson has a busy schedule this year.'*

A British film called *The Full Monty* (about a group of unemployed misfits from up North becoming strippers) was a roaring success at the box office. We decided to capitalize on stripper hysteria by phoning *The Sport* who snapped up the story straight away. A week later, Cradock phoned me to explain that Channel 5 TV was also interested in the story and would like to interview a policyholder.

I dialed the journalist's number and a receptionist with a French accent answered. "Can I speak to Stephanie please?"

"She is not here at the moment, may I leave a message for you?"

"Hi, Mr. Cradock from NOBLE gave me this number concerning libido insurance."

"Ah yes, I work for Channel 5's program, *Serious Hot Money* and we are very much hoping she can interview someone who has bought a policy for our '*Risky business*' segment. What is your name?"

Tues 21$^{st of}$ October 1996. 11:45am

At precisely 11:30 am, Cradock arrived at my house, punctual as always. However, the Channel 5 crew, scheduled for 12:40 pm, were running late. Cradock, who had a prior commitment, politely requested to be interviewed first and we accommodated his request.

During the interview, as the cameras rolled, the inquisitive reporters posed a question that often piques curiosity: "What is the most unusual item you've ever insured?" The question hung in the air, creating an intriguing pause. Cradock leaned forward, a twinkle in his eye as if he had been waiting for this moment to regale us with a remarkable story.

I couldn't help but think, 'This should be interesting.'

After a moment of contemplation, Cradock broke into a calm, confident reply, his words landing with unexpected gravity: "An African Chief's genitals."

The producer and interviewer laughed.

"No, seriously, there would have been a major impact on the tribe had he not been able to reproduce," Cradock added.

The straight man went on to talk professionally and seriously about all sorts of insurance, including reporters he insures who like to insure their faces, whether they are good-looking or plain ugly. They finished interviewing Cradock and thanked him for being such a professional.

The camera started rolling while my penciled-on goatee was still drying and improvisation ensued.

"What's your name and what do you do?"

"Ah, bonjour! I am François de Rimini and I dabble as a part-time stripper, you see."

"Tell us Frank, what part of your body have you insured?"

"I 'ave insured a particular part of my body, mainly ma libido."

"How much did the policy cost and how much are you covered for or how is insurance assessed?"

"Zee premium, it costs me £25 per year and zee coverage is £10,000 per unit, you know? I'm insured for £100,000."

PROF. VIRGIL: "Listen closely, for in the Third Stage of Freud's psychosexual development theory, known as the phallic stage, he delves into the depths of the human psyche. Here, he unveils the concept of libido—an unconscious, insatiable energy pulsating within us, consumed by unstructured and formless lust.

Now, let us journey into the vivid realm of Dante's Inferno. Picture the Second Circle, where the souls of the lustful writhe in torment. They are ensnared by their physical appetites, swept up in a tempestuous wind that rages relentlessly. It is a realm where desire reigns supreme, and the consequences of indulgence are etched into every tortured soul."

JOE: "Seems we've all been swept up in a tempest of desires, Freud and Dante included."

Channel 5: "Where did you hear about it and why did you decide to buy it?"

"I 'eard about it on from a friend and immediately thought zat someone in my profession should insure 'is work tools."

"Where do you perform?" she asked.

"I normally do my shows in London, but I've ventured up to the North, Manchester and Yorkshire."

"Like in the film, *Full Monty* that's based up North?" she asked.

"I 'aven't seen it, but my best mates wind me up about it 'cause they know wot I do, but I don't fancy performin' locally, mainly 'cause I don't want anyone to know. Besides, I'm just an amateur. I do wot I do just for a laugh and a bit of extra dosh."

"And women?" she probed.

"I already 'ave a girlfriend, you see. And I do not believe in 'quand le chat n'est pas là les souris dansent' – when the cat is not there, the mice dance. If I were to get into any bit of a bother, I might 'ave to put in a claim, you know."

"How much do you earn a night?"

"Ah, you see, eet can go from £50 to £250, depending on who you are and where you perform, but 'ow you say, ze competition, eet's fierce, especially for us amateurs."

"Is it mainly hen-nights?"

"No, it varies. 'En-nights, birthdays, that sort of thing. I even did an old-age pensioner's night once. I thought that would be tamer, but they're just as wild as the younger generation. I couldn't believe the energy they 'ad. Zimmer frames were swept aside."

"Is that you in your performing uniform?" She pointed at a picture of my brother in army uniform.

"Yes, but zat was a couple of years ago when I was at my peak, it's 'arder now to stay in shape. I 'aven't worked or done a routine in two months."

"So, what do women get up to? Are they well-behaved?"

"Non! L'habit ne fait pas le moine. —The habit doesn't make the monk. Zey 'ave no inhibitions. When ze women get togezzer, zey just don't care and some do get carried away, tendeeng to grab ze parts zat ozzers wouldn't dare touch. Zat's why I decided to insure myself. If I were to inadvertently injure my tackle or if a jealous female deed, zen I suppose I'd be safe in ze knowledge zat I could claim against ze loss of earnings."

JOE: "We did a few more re-takes and shots of me coming out of my house posing with my sunglasses, flicking back my hair and licking my eyebrows with a wet finger. The interview finished and the TV crew left. I notched another TV stitch-up in my journal under the title 'The Art of Self-Preservation: Insuring What Matters Most.'"

PROF. VIRGIL: "Indeed you did!"

JOE: "It was fun, I can't deny that."


Sunday, 10/26/96, 7:30 PM, Channel 5.


On the 26th of October 1996, my parents (who lived a couple of streets away) retold the story. My Mother was busy ironing, while dad took charge of making tea. The broadcast of the 'Risky Business' news segment played on the television.


NEWSREADER: "The need for insurance isn't limited to the rich, famous, or silicone enhanced. Even if your face isn't a fortune, another part (emphasized with a wide-eyed expression) of your body might just be!"

MUM: "I guess he's talking about insuring unique possessions." Mum continues ironing.

CRADOCK: *(on TV)* "Our clients encompass a diverse range, insuring various facets of their bodies—quite literally, every part you can imagine. This includes TV presenters who wish to safeguard their looks."

MUM: "He looks familiar. Isn't that one of Joe's pals?"

As I swing the front door open in slow motion, *'I'm Too Sexy'* by Right Said Fred plays, setting the mood. My sunglasses casually rest atop my head and I hold my keys with an air of nonchalance, elegantly flipping my hair with the other hand. The camera's lens gracefully traces from my feet to my waist, capturing every moment of this stylish entrance.

Mum and dad glance at the TV and then do a double take in unison. Right before their eyes, their son gracefully strolls across the lawn in slow motion, his goatee penciled on while the camera zooms in on his midsection.

DAD: "Lu, Lu, look!"

MUM: "Hold on, what's he up to? Is this some kind of home video? Oh my, what's he doing sauntering out the front door in leather sandals? There's a hole in his sock!"

JOE: *(on TV)* "Bonjour, mes amis. I am François de Rimini and I am what you may call a burlesque dancer. My shows mostly take place in local clubs here in London ..."

MUM: "Is this happening live right now?"

JOE: *(on TV)* "Zere is alwayz ze risk of an overenthusiastic mademoiselle getting carried away and getting 'andsy where she shouldn't, so I took ze logical step and got myself insured."

Queue the music again *'And I do my little turn on the catwalk'* as I strut in slow motion, my Elvis-esque hair meticulously combed, sunglasses adding to the nonchalant factor—almost picture-perfect, except for my choice of sandals and that hole in my sock.

JOE: (*on TV*) "Ze premium, it cost me just £25, but I 'ave ze potential to make anywhere from £25,000 to £100,000 in case of an injury."

NEWSREADER: "Okay, so you're not Caprice or Damon Hill and you don't need to insure a particular body part, but you still need insurance. How do you work out what type you need and how much you're worth?"

DAD: "What.. ma chi cavolo fa?"

MUM: "First he's selling assicurazione per gli alieni, now he's insured his kazoo, what the hell next, 'basta, enough'?"

DAD: "He doesn't give up! 'Uffa che palle,' I thought he'd finished all this crap,—'Lasciate ogni speranza, voi ch'entrate.'"

MUM: "I don't know how he has the audacity to do it."


PROF. VIRGIL: "In the process of developing a distinct psychosexual identity, boys experience castration anxiety, a concept from Sigmund Freud's early psychoanalytic theories. While Freud considered castration anxiety to be a common human experience, there have been limited empirical studies on this topic." [2]

JOE: "Castration anxiety?"

PROF. VIRGIL: "Castration anxiety, mio amico, is like a passionate opera playing in the minds of young ragazzi, where they fear their 'crown jewels' may be lost due to their own desires or deeds."

JOE: "Got it, grazie, good job I was acting!"


*The Washington Capital*

'City of London underwriting agency NOBLE has halved the premium on its Libido-all risks policy to £50 for £100,000 of coverage after Viagra's launch, predicting impotence will soon be a thing of the past.

Spokesperson Johnny Cradock said, "Demand for the policy has skyrocketed."

NOBLE has also sent US President Bill Clinton a complimentary $1,000,000 NOBSAFE policy as a birthday gift. Cradock added, "Mr. Clinton's affair with Monica Lewinsky exposes him to a serious risk of '......,' so we've sent him a policy to soften the..."

<u>Tenebris ad lucem.</u>

" THANK YOU SO MUCH, THIS A VERY GENEROUS OFFER, AND I AM CERTAIN MR. CLINTON WILL BE THRILLED "

In October 96, I returned to 'General Electric, USA,' a fluorescent light company where my father had connections and his line manager, Carol, offered me a job as a quality controller. Working the night shift, no one there was aware of my previous involvement in insurance, but that was about to change.

It was at that time, that a combination of my alter ego dancers, was still doing the rounds on some TV stations and a few months later, *Frank de Rimini* would also appear in *The Sport* on page seven. On the day of the shoot, a photographer came round and I had told Eleanor, my girlfriend, half the story. She was not impressed. I had chosen to look the part of an exotic entertainer. I wore my white shirt and jeans, sketched on another goatee beard using my girlfriend's eyeliner and slicked back my pompadour. The photographer said he wanted me to look like an Adonis, wrapped with just white bed sheets, hugging my body and a strategically placed football covering my modesty.

I promised my girlfriend that I wouldn't take my clothes off but I had a performance to give and so I sported my British Boxer shorts. With bed sheets around my body, I stood with one leg on a box guided by the photographer who assured me that in doing so it would show a definition or sculpture of the body. As he spoke, I tucked in my stomach and thought, 'Does he think I make a living being a stripper with a body like this?'

Weeks later, someone on the night shift was flipping through an old copy of The Sport and made photocopies of the story, then proceeded to tape black and white copies of my less-than-ideal photo shoot to all the factory columns at General Electric. This prompted me to quickly deny and remove them before my dad could stumble upon them.


## WHISPERS OF THE SECOND CIRCLE
Pg. 3. October 1996


### 'Low Libido Got You Down? Insurance to the Rescue!'

*Burlesque dancer Frank de Rimini wouldn't feel deflated if he couldn't get aroused, because he'd bag £100,000 ($127,000) instead. That's the pay-out he'd get under an amazing deal he's struck with a firm of specialist insurers. For a premium of just ($33) £24.38-a-year, the 23-year-old wannabe part-time stripper stands to land the bucks if he injures himself. And last night he admitted: "I am, how you say, almost looking forward to the performance anxiety. They could perhaps send Pam Anderson to, you know, assess me."*

*British gas clerk Frank, from Enfield, took out the policy when he decided to launch himself as a burlesque dancer. He said: "If a mademoiselle loses her control and grasps me, I may declare the loss of, well, paychecks."*

*Chief Johnny Cradock, of insurers 'Nigel Owen Brian Llyod's Enterprise', said: "We are talking about a permanent loss of libido. You couldn't just go down the pub, sink fourteen pints then claim £100,000. So far, around 1358 clients [3] have taken out the policy, including an African Chief insuring his genitals against infertility."*

Sky-None News picked up on the story and sent a car for me to be interviewed at their H.Q. I did my Elvis hairstyle and wore a leather waistcoat. I remembered walking into the busy newsroom packed with journalists and a few looked at me as if to imply, 'So, you're the stripper then?' I was nervous but *he who dares wins.*

Megaera Siren of Sky-None asked me off camera what I, Frank, did on stage as a dancer. The only dance I ever mastered was the moonwalk, learned from watching 'Breakin' the movie. So, I slowly shifted my weight onto my right foot, sliding my left foot backward as if defying gravity. With each step, I mimicked the smooth glide of Shabba-doo and Boogaloo Shrimp, creating the illusion of walking forward while moving backward. I stopped, and then looked into her blue eyes intensely, trying to catch my own reflection. As I improvised, I licked my finger and brushed it across my eyebrow. 'Well,' I said, 'I kind of shake my hips, move my torso and pelvis this way and that, and thrust one or both arms in the air as I glide around the stage.

I divulged to the pretty presenter that in addition to being a dancer, Frank was also responsible for the well-documented British Gas fiasco where one hundred thousand red bill letters were sent late and customers had engineers turning at the door threatening to disconnect their gas supply.

After the interview, Megaera asked me whether I would mind if she told anyone else about the incident. I said, *"No, tell who you want."* Before I went home, I suggested that one day we should go out for a drink. She agreed.

The next evening, I had a knock at the door and a journalist and photographer claiming to be from The Sunday Express was asking to speak to Frank da Rimini.

"Frank?"

"Err, yes?"

"My name's John... from the Sunday Express. We would like to talk to you about British Gas and your part-time job, can we come in?"

"Err, yes."

His face seemed familiar and I mentioned this to him. He casually acknowledged that he had made a few TV appearances in the past. Curious, he inquired about my work as a dancer, which clubs I frequented and the infamous British Gas incident.

Then came the unexpected proposition. He wanted to photograph me during one of my routines at a burlesque club and include a mention of the British Gas story. The mere thought of baring it all in front of an audience was a step too far for me, so I politely declined.

Undeterred, he persisted, asking where I typically performed. Caught off guard, I glanced at a local newspaper that had been left on the table and spotted an ad for 'Peak Glaziers,' a local double-glazing window company. I replied, 'The Peak venue in Yorkshire was my last performance but I haven't been fit for a while hence the increase in weight.'

They eventually left but had I been given prior notice and prepared something I'm sure Frank 'amorous' da Rimini would have been immortalized, but I had to go to nightshift.

Making lights in the night as a quality controller was a far cry from roaming London City via black cabs, listening to gangster stories and visiting the pubs with which they were associated when I finished the run early. Nightshift was supposed to be something to bide my time and ever since my brother ducked the elastic ball, I had never been unemployed and was always active. I would embarrass my dad, who'd managed to get me the job there, a 'shame and embarrassment' to him as I continued in my escapade of making a fool of myself all in the name of promoting weird insurance.

Along with Cradock's knowledge of law and insurance and our notorious track record of crafty stunts, throughout the months we continued to fool the whole world, making numerous disguised appearances on the same television stations such as CNN, NBC and other foreign Networks as we closed the net. Occasionally, I would be handsomely paid for interviews.

We each collected the clippings from the papers to continue to form our giant scrapbook along with the video TV appearances as a sort of head-hunting memento.

Cradock didn't do it for the money. He didn't need any. He liked to have fun jesting with publicity. At first, I too enjoyed the jokes and made sure I received payment from the foreign TV for interviews. A part of me acting and subconsciously seeking answers in my childhood request for UFOs, it depends on which way one looks at it. By now, I was proficient in storytelling along with Cradock. To be a good liar you need a good memory and I would need to exercise it as later I would reintroduce the world to Carpenter. Somewhere along the timeline of events, a threefold process would begin to organically unfold. I was the creator of the policy. Then I became Carpenter, who took out a policy to give the media the chance to interview someone who had taken out the policy. Little did they know that the creator of the policy was the same guy playing the insured and for the third act there would be the Gospel according to Carpenter.

# Chapter Eleven
## The Carpenter

*"Dove si legge tutto ciò, l'Evangelio più ardesse."*
*"Where everything is comprehended, the Gospel would have been more*
*ardently." — Dante; Purgatorio, Canto XXXIII*

On November 16th, 1974, The Arecibo message — an interstellar radio message carrying basic information about humanity and Earth — was sent out to the galaxy. It was a funky attempt to communicate with extraterrestrial life, with the hope that they'd be able to dig the message's meaning. The Arecibo message was beamed out into the universe via frequency-modulated radio waves, aimed at the location of M13, a global star cluster around 25,000 light-years away from Earth. M13 was a big, bad collection of stars that was visible in the sky at the time of the broadcast.

Fast forward 22 years to November 24th, 1996, Cradock and I had driven off the M1 motorway and were relaxing in the green room of a Northampton TV studio when it hit us, that message might finally be getting an answer. We were invited to a live TV debate on the paranormal in Northampton, our main goal was to hit the hospitality room. We chugged down beer like it was going out of style and took our seats in the front row. Just as we were getting comfortable, in walks Dave Davies, Kinks' B-side songwriter of 'You Really Got Me', looking like he stepped out of a time machine from 1964 with his purple velvet coat. He strolled around the room, waiting for someone to notice him before plopping down next to Cradock,

Sebastian and me. I turned to him with my best cockney accent and asked, "Alright mate, what brings you to this spooky shindig?"

"Just Aliens, man," he replied softly, looking a little embarrassed. Shortly after, five groovy chicks with autograph books came into the hospitality room and fluted their way over to the former Kinks man, who hugged them and signed their books with a flourish.

While hanging out in the green room, I met a bleach-blonde woman who had the appearance, vibe and sensuality of a serpent. She shared with me her trippy experiences of alien abduction by the grays and how they allegedly frequently visited her. She said that she had turned down offers of help from researchers to catch her tormentors. I turned to Cradock and we, both feeling pretty fly with all the spirit available, decided to liven up the stakes by suggesting we begin to test the public's reaction.

Cradock approached the producer, who had initially invited us to talk purely about paranormal insurance, took him to a quiet corner and said he had an exclusive for him, explaining what the good news was. "Bloody hell!" cussed the producer. "Great! I'll go and tell Nicki and we'll arrange something for more air talk."

Nicki Campbell introduced himself and laid out the TV show's format. Everything was grooving along smoothly and I drank a bit more to give myself some Dutch courage, "What the hell are we getting ourselves into man?" I asked my confidant.

"Making history, dude," Cradock replied with a sly grin.

Beyond the Insured.

"OKAY!" shouted the producer. It was time to go into the theatre.

Cradock and I made our way to the theatre and sat down. A comedian warmed up the audience and Cradock and I looked at each other telepathically: *Where did they get him from?*

The cameras went red for live broadcast and the credits rolled. As the camera panned the audience and passed us, I slicked back my hair, winked and nodded to the lens. It was caught on film and looking back at the replay, it is hilarious. The host interviewed all the other guests regarding the phenomenon and Cradock and I looked at each other again and heckled: "What a load a bull!"

As two guests engaged in a heated discussion about temperature inversion, phenomena created by advanced or unexplained technology, and the existence of extraterrestrial beings, the host suddenly moved over to us.

"... temperature inversion sends me over here," Campbell continues. "I want you to meet this guy over here. Now, this is a very interesting case. Now, you're an insurance man, aren't you? Mr. ... err ..."

"Cradock, Johnny Cradock from N.O.B.L.E." he replied.

"Now, you insure people against UFOs and having alien abductions?"

"Very much so. We set out with a simple objective in August..."

"There's a sucker born every minute, isn't there?" Campbell interrupted.

"Well, our objective was quite simple, to part the feeble-minded from their cash."

The audience laughed and Cradock paused quite seriously, causing the crowd to quiet down immediately. "Let him carry on," Campbell pleaded.

"Yeah, that was our simple objective. We've banked many hundreds of thousands of pounds from people who believe that there are off-planet life forms."

"Not only Alien life forms–but this is also taking it a step further when someone comes into your bedroom and grabs you and takes you into a spacecraft and attaches things to you," Campbell prompted.

"Very much so. Our objective was quite simple: to make money. However ..."

"However?"

"We have a claim ... we have been notified of a claim. I underwrite on behalf of four insurers, the capital worth of which exceeds one hundred billion dollars. We have a claim and there is an 80% likelihood that we will be paying that claim," said Cradock .

"And there's the claimant. Carpenter Joseph, what happened to you, very quickly?" asked Campbell, turning to me.
(Whilst being three sheets to the wind, experiencing a temporary shutdown of my prefrontal cortex and as I tried to access my inner voice, I ended up sounding like a young Michael Caine).

"So, there I was, mate, a Ufologist on a mission to uncover the truth about them mysterious flying objects. Two months back, I and my three chums decided to hit the skies and see what we could rustle up. And let me tell ya, what we found was nothing short of bloody mind-boggling. To cut a long *shory stort* (sic) err short (snigger) err ... we managed to snag some top-notch footage of a damn triangular object, as clear as day. But that ain't the half of it, mate. I proper got beamed up by the thing and we managed to get some bloody brilliant snaps and vids of it all."

"They took you?"

"Yes, I was... I passed out and I awoke in a craft with a dome shape, rather like a hundred-mile open greenhouse, rather surreal," I said.

"How would you know you weren't in a greenhouse?" asked Campbell.

"Listen up, mate. You might think I'm off my rocker, but I swear to ya, I could well have been in some kinda temperature inversion or something like that. But here's the thing, the camera doesn't bloody lie, does it? So, whether you believe me or not, the fact remains that what we captured on film was the real deal."

Cradock intervened and said: "The important thing is that we do not want to pay claims, we have assessed the validity of his claim."

"You've got this on camcorder?" asked the host.

"Yes, we've obtained what one might describe as extraordinary camcorder footage," remarked Cradock.

Professor Heinz Wolf shouted out: "It makes good publicity to pay the claim to get other people to buy your insurance!"

"That is a very skeptical view sir!" retorted Cradock.

"What did the Aliens look like?" asked Nicki.

"I managed to catch more than just a brief glimpse, mate," I said, "In fact, I had a long, hard stare at one of them typical aliens. You know the ones I'm talking about."

"Typical Alien?" Nicki inquired, evoking laughter from the audience.

"Yup."

"Your Typical Alien! Run of the mill alien!" Nicki teased. The audience's laughter persisted as the host transitioned to the next guest. It was a moment of historic comedy.

Cradock and I looked at each other and shook hands. Press releases and interviews would continue, as the story grew tentacles and became more refined.

PROF. BERNARD: "As my granpè used to say, 'in the world of tales, falsehood often takes a swifty ride, while the truth, caught off-guard, be struggling to even pull up its britches.'"

CE4

*In the UFO community, CE4 is an event in which a human is abducted by a UFO or its occupants – but should refer to "cases when witnesses experienced a transformation of their sense of reality." — Jacques Vallee.* [1]

CARPENTER: "I was out on a sky search and surveillance with three friends, at a UFO hot spot in Swindon Wiltshire, alongside me were three fellow investigators, we were armed to the teeth with lots of high-tech gadgets: infra-red cameras and sensitive microphones. As we were waiting in a field, suddenly, we saw a triangular craft overhead. While observing and filming the sighting of the craft, which was near a military base in Swindon, Wiltshire. I approached the craft, my colleagues carried on filming me and then a massive beam of light surrounded me and began to lift me before fully rising in the air. I passed out. But my friends captured it on tape, I was taken on board the star-shaped triangular spacecraft, which approached from the east. The event was witnessed by my three close friends and captured on camcorder along with DNA evidence of a transparent webbed claw I obtained from this Gray."

[Author's Note: 26 years later, on July 26th, 2023, the following story carries a distinct whiff of genetically modified cow dung. A Congressional Hearing on UFOs took place in the Rayburn House Office Building in Washington, D.C. This marked the first congressional hearing on UAPs since 1968.

Former U.S. intelligence officer David Grusch testified under oath before a congressional subcommittee, asserting that the government is concealing evidence of 'non-human' biological entities and extraterrestrial spacecraft. According to Grusch, these entities are distinct from any known human or animal species and are currently under scrutiny by the U.S. government. He refrained from disclosing the nature or origin of these entities. Grusch also acknowledged that while he hadn't personally encountered an alien body, he had heard from other sources about non-human pilots operating certain UFOs.] [2]

"After being captured by the beam of light, I came to. The inside of the ship was incredible—like being in a massive domed greenhouse. It was strange because although it was daylight, I could see the stars above the dome and there were miles of vegetation everywhere." *(This greenhouse part of the story had come from one of my interviews with someone who claimed he had been on such a craft and he wanted to take out my certificate a year earlier.)*

"I had a matchbox camera wired to my jacket, still filming as the alien creature approached. Its skin resembled polished silver, its fingers were eerily elongated, its head triangular and its eyes large, black and almond-shaped. It communicated with me telepathically, saying, 'Don't be afraid. We mean you no harm.' However, I panicked and punched it in the face before passing out again. Although I was on the craft for about 2 hours and 2 mins, only 42 minutes of earth time had passed and been recorded."

The evidence has been submitted to Insurance magnate *Johnny Cradock* and his brokers. It has been analyzed by scientists at Cambridge College and the insurers are to pay out Carpenter £1million. ($1,250,535.00) Cradock is in negotiation to sell the evidence to NASA or the highest bidder. The evidence collected must be seen to be believed. The event took place whilst in the town of *Swindon* on *October 8th, 1996.*"—*A random date chosen out of thin air and Swindon being the place where Sylvia had given me the 'Wow!' moment.*

It has been said that art imitates reality, like the objects of everyday scenarios or the images of nature. The results may not be the same as the real world because painters, writers, or creators often involve their life experiences and expectations in their works. I find it remarkable to note that the first number 1 single of 1996 was *Jesus to a Child,* George Michael's first solo number 1 for him in 10 years. This was followed by Babylon Zoo's only hit *Spaceman* hitting the top spot of top of the pops. Meanwhile, a global system called *the Internet* is also starting to take off.

Needless to say, Carpenter's story, the world's first Extraterrestrial abduction insurance payee and holder of non-human biological evidence, went into warp drive within the media. The story garnered attention through December and even made its appearance on TV news on Christmas Day. It continued to grace the front pages in Europe and even managed to secure a front-page spot in America. News giants SKY, CNN and NBC also featured the story, along with numerous foreign outlets expressing interest. Perhaps the most startling aspect of this stunt is the extensive reach it achieved and how readily people embraced it. The concept of freedom of information pairs best with a responsible outlook, rather than blind faith.

I posed with a fake £1-million check that Cradock made written out to Joseph Carpenter. A photoshoot of Cradock handing over the large million-pound check took place at my house. A young photographer came around and I suggested the idea of putting the Kurt Cobain-looking Jesus picture in the background. The photographer took two shots of Cradock and I shaking hands and him handing over the check. I then said to Cradock to lend me his spectacles as I put the check under my nose to copy the famous 'What no' man (a distinctive accompanying doodle character that became associated with GIs in the 1940s: in short, a bald man who was sometimes depicted as having a few hairs with a prominent nose peeking over a wall with his fingers clutching the wall saying, 'Kilroy was here' or 'What no' etc.). I said to Cradock under my breath, "What? No *real* check?"

The Kilroy check photo held under my nose went global, also appearing on the front pages of French, German, Italian, Spanish, Swedish and other European newspapers.

The photographer, Joseph Alvarez, who would later become a temporary friend, enthusiastically played along with our little charade. He leaned in and asked with a mischievous grin, "So, what's it like being a millionaire?"

I couldn't help but chuckle, 'Honestly, Mr. Alvarez, it hasn't quite sunk in yet. But Cradock and I are headed to *The Green Man* (British pub) clutching my oversized check.' As we strolled into the pub, I couldn't resist the urge to proudly announce, 'Guess what, everyone? I've won the lottery!' After all, who in their right mind would believe that I had just been paid a million bucks for an encountering frog type visitors from another dimension?

Across the Pond.


*Gillian Anderson on The Tonight Show with Jay Leno*
*Monday, December 16<sup>th</sup>, 1996.*

ANDERSON: "I was told that I'm going to be in London next week presenting somebody with a two-million-dollar insurance claim check, cause he's receiving two million dollars of Alien abduction insurance. They have that now."

LENO: "They have abduction insurance and they have alien pregnancy insurance now."


The respectable **New York Journal of Commerce** runs a New Year's Eve front-page story:


*'Been abducted by Aliens? No problem: File a claim!*
*Christmas Day turned into Independence Day for one British man who got*
*$1.6m after claiming an extra-terrestrial experience.*
*The evidence including the claw has already been sold to an unnamed US*
*media agency for more than the cost of the pay-out.'*


3<sup>rd of</sup> January 1997.


Diary entry by Bill Sebastian: Back to work after a media frenzy of a festive season, interviewed by former Radio One DJ Simon Bates the week before Christmas on Melody Radio. There have been hundreds of radio and TV requests to report this legitimate but amusing and unlikely news fodder. Bates begins by saying he had seen a story yesterday that he says he initially did not believe about selling someone an insurance policy against Galactic abductors. Cradock proclaims that he had been given enough evidence to satisfy him that the claimant had been abducted by otherworldly entities just outside Swindon and should therefore be compensated by the insurer for £1m.

So, today he calls Carpenter the alleged claimant, who tells Bates he's going to get his check for £1m the following day in a West End hotel presented by actress Gillian Anderson (who plays the character Dana Scully from the X files) sometime in the morning or afternoon.

Bates asks where Carpenter was abducted,

"Near a military base not far from Swindon." Carpenter goes on to explain he was out with a group of friends "... armed to the teeth with all manner of high-tech equipment – camcorders, infrared binoculars, Geiger counters, laser beams mounted on camcorders and a Boots disposable camera and we basically did a sky search."

On that night, Carpenter continues, "We managed to film a well-defined UFO, a triangular craft doing speeds that no conventional aircraft can do. It just stopped in mid-air. As my colleagues filmed it, I approached the craft so that later we could analyze the film by judging its height, distance and so forth. Anyway, as I looked directly above, an intense beam of light was rather like that of a police helicopter light because I've been chased by those a few times in my line of work. I was suddenly lifted off the ground and I passed out at this moment, but all this was captured on camcorder. That is the first part of the evidence. The second part ..."

BATES: "So, you managed to capture the whole 'being lifted' business on your camcorder?"

CARPENTER: "Absolutely, my three friends recorded the entire thing."

BATES: "Ah, I see. And at which base in Swindon did this remarkable event take place?" *(Joe didn't even know there was an airbase in Swindon, apparently, they have two, thus responding)*,

CARPENTER: "I can't tell you, I want to keep it secret...I was transported onto a huge triangular spaceship where I passed out, but not before gathering the necessary evidence."

BATES: "Joe Carpenter, who had an extraterrestrial encounter on October 8th just outside Swindon, listen, you can be as cynical as you like, but a million pounds is crossing his silver palm tomorrow in a West End Hotel, morning or afternoon. He was abducted by Space Aliens (starts to lose composure and laugh) just outside Swindon, where he punched the lights out of one of them, brought back some DNA (sniggered) and took photographs (regaining professional composure) with his Boots disposable camera. (Three-second pause as he laughs) You heard it first here on *Melody*. (Desperately trying not to laugh but failing) ... Back in a sec!"


4th of January 1997, 3pm.


A TV crew from Channel 9 Australia suddenly turns up at Cradock's office. Journalist Michelle waltzes in, her lips so plumped with botox they could double as inflatable pool floats, her blonde hair seemingly styled by a team of overenthusiastic squirrels. "It's in a bank vault, but I can tell you what I saw," he responds. They managed to phone me, Michelle brazenly asked what I had seen and where I had been, as if I owed her an explanation. Journalism and media, often driven by ego and manipulation, assert an entitlement to demand information and shape narratives according to their whims.

CARPENTER: "Literally hundreds of blonde Sheilas, Pamela Anderson lookalikes. It was just like being in Heaven,"

MICHELLE: "Sorry, what did you say?"

CARPENTER: "They said, *'Take me, Joe. I'm yours.'*"


Another unsolicited German TV station, who had interviewed Carpenter a year earlier but was late and overstayed their twenty minutes by two hours also demanded an interview with their top reporter Yahim on the case who insisted on seeing footage of what was seen on-board the spacecraft.

JOE: "I saw these two lights moving ahead of me from left to right. And then I saw Elvis."

YAHIM: "What is Elvis?"

JOE: "You know, *'thank you, thank you very much, ah hah,'*" I said in my best Elvis accent.

YAHIM: "Are you taking the peas (piss)?"

JOE: "Look, I can't speak right now. I'm currently in a hotel in a remote part of Scotland—Bonnybridge, to be exact. I can meet you there if you'd like. I found the hotel name in that area using the Yellow Pages. I told him he could come to meet me there."

I never heard from Yahim again.


The TV Breakfast that could have been.


October 30th, 1938—*War of the Worlds* was broadcast on CBS Radio, including KNX (1070 AM) in Los Angeles. In his radio adaption of H. G. Wells' book for his program "Mercury Theater on the Air," Orson Welles scared the nation into believing that Earth was being taken over by

Martians. Panic ensued, as listeners believed the program was broadcasting real news bulletins. Or at least that is what we have all been led to believe. [3]

Early January 1997, I was invited onto Channel 4's *The Big Breakfast* (which had millions of breakfast viewers) but turned it down because I knew that if the presenter tried to make a joke of things I might not fare so well on live television. I also joked with the researcher that I would show the public what Zig and Zag (the alien puppets) would look like in the nude, i.e., a giant pair of hands. She laughed and said, "No, you would upset the millions of kids watching."

TAKE ME JOE, I'M YOURS

*The Big Breakfast* had phoned me on the same day that I had been bombarded with other telephone interviews, she was one of the last to phone and because I was tired from nights, I let my guard down and told her the truth policies and stunts, even about my libido insurance appearance on EBN News with a cucumber stuffed in my jeans.

She still wanted me to appear on the show as the world's biggest hoaxer, but I declined. When I was more awake, I tried to rearrange and convince the producer to join us in creating a mock reconstruction of evidence footage to show the viewers and join our journey, but we missed the slot. I can only imagine what that would have done to the world had Channel 4 joined our Orson Welles production.

# Chapter Twelve

## The Canadian and the War Correspondent

6<sup>th of</sup> January 1997.

Shortly after Cradock received a long email and three faxes from the following.

Michael Deloir, Concordia University, Montreal, Canada.

6/1/97:

*In response to our sixth phone conversation, I'm sending you the info. Hope everything is to your satisfaction. Hoping to hear from you.*

*To whom it may concern, I, the undersigned Christian R. Page National Director of SOS OVNI, Quebec, confirm that Mr. Michael Deloir is a serious UFO investigator affiliated with a group of researchers from the Montreal Concordia University. This group, directed by the well-known Canadian Psychiatrist Dr. Jean Roch Laurence, specializes in UFO abduction phenomena. Hoping that this information will be useful, please accept Dear Madam/Sir the expression of my high consideration. Sincerely, Christian R. Page, National Director.*

8/1/97:

To: Johnny Cradock. Ref: Michael Deloir.

*Dear Sir,*

*Mr. Michael Deloir has been actively involved in the investigation of reports of alien kidnappings that my laboratory has been conducting for the last three years. Mr. Deloir has been and is still working as a field investigator on numerous cases in Quebec and is attached to my team as a research assistant. Do not hesitate to contact me if you need more information. Sincerely, John Roch Laurence Ph.D Associate Professor of Psychology Department.*

So, Cradock gave Michael Deloir my number. Deloir would call me three times over the week and explain who he was. He mentioned that he was flying over to Paris on Friday, January 24th of that year and would be popping over to London, staying in a hotel, with the hope of meeting me.

"There's no need to do that, I wouldn't want you to go out of your way," I said.

Deloir insisted: "I want to, I'm an investigator. I have to check this out."

I didn't want to meet or deceive this guy or waste his trip from Canada. Since he wasn't a journalist, I decided to be straightforward.

"It's a hoax. I made it up. I created the policy and we decided to take things a step further."

Deloir didn't believe me.

"Why would an insurance company put their reputation on the line?"

I felt like saying, "You don't know Cradock." Instead, I continued and in the conversation of our delusion, heard myself make some sense, "As a child, I believed and when I started my IBP certificate, I wanted to share the thrill. But then, when I'd been given the power of the media, I didn't exactly plan to give the E.T. and Alien policy the PR it received. I didn't plan to give it propaganda in a way nobody else has done before, but along the way, I met and interviewed some credible people with stories that resonated with me. I could never have done this any other way. I wasn't expecting this."

I felt bad for Deloir because he was not a journalist, but another piece of the puzzle had come to me. I was talking to a serious investigator and believer in the field. So, I decided before I continued with the full story, I wanted to know and to ask him what he has found, seeing as he claims he's been investigating it for fifteen years. He wouldn't tell me, though I kept insisting. I said I wouldn't tell him anything then. Eventually, he said he had found what appears to be an implant, which suggests it comes from an alleged abductee. That was interesting to know as he claimed he hadn't released his data yet. I asked him, "Do you work for the Government? Are you checking me out?"

"Why are you asking me if I work for the CIA?"

"I asked you if you work for the Government, why did you say CIA?"

"It's the *same* thing," he replied.

Deloir continued and told me there is a person he knows who has two million dollars in a bank put aside and would pay someone who could show him conclusive evidence of ETs and UFOs.

"I told you, it's a hoax."

"What do you mean?" he asks, "Have you made some sort of video and DNA to make it appear as if it's genuine?"

"No! I created the policy and took it a stage further."

Deloir, utterly confused, still didn't believe me, not wanting to take no for an answer. He thinks I'm involved in some co-government conspiracy to withhold the truth, the truth being in his mind that I have some kind of evidence or motive.

"I still must investigate. Why would an insurance company pay you for a hoax?" he asks.

"They haven't paid me," I reply.

"But it's all over the papers, all over the world, all over the Internet. I've spoken to Mr. Cradock. You've received $1.8m. Please show me the evidence and if it is genuine, our client will pay you. Mr. Cradock categorically states he has seen the evidence, believes it is genuine and is currently in a bidding war with NASA and tech companies in America, to acquire the DNA."

"Look, Mr. Deloir, I have told you the truth. The whole story was a prank, not even elaborate, if you don't believe me ask Cradock, tell him I told you."

"Why would the insurance company risk their reputation over this?" He asked again.

Deloir eventually stopped questioning and decided to wait until morning to phone Cradock.

Once again, Cradock stuck to the story we had brilliantly executed. Deloir was now awfully perplexed. He even asked Cradock whether he would hire him to investigate whether the insurance company had been conned, as managers of insurance companies don't lie. The mind game had Deloir's prefrontal cortex in a spin.

Deloir phoned me for the third time and asked whether I was still sticking to my story.

I continued, slightly annoyed at his persistence, "Listen! I could've sent you back to England on a wild goose chase if I wanted to, but I opted to tell you the truth. You should know that ufologists throughout the world are full of misinformation, as I found out myself. This one is dedicated to them. They all talk the talk, claiming they have this footage, this evidence, this implant, but they never show anything other than footage shot with a potato camera! If you're upset, I could argue with you that I generated a catch-twenty-two situation. As I told you before, more minds may be open throughout the world now that they've been tested. But I kind of feel bad. I've met some interesting people along the way and how else was I going to find out what is true and false? I didn't exactly plan it this way."

I asked him one question about a rumor circulating in the UFO community regarding forthcoming disclosures. He didn't want to comment, but after I repeated the question several times, he and I stopped taping our conversation and in a serious tone, replied: 'Live the life you have to live, we haven't got long.'

What he meant by that I do not know, but it made me shudder and reflect on end-time scenarios.

"Do you realize what you've done?" Deloir continued in his patronizing professor-rebuking child mode. "You've done the Government's work for them. They should be paying you for this. The cover your story has been given, you have no idea, the number of people who believe you. This is worse than the Roswell footage, [1] disinformation of this kind is extremely dangerous. You have damaged the subject. Now, if I were to release my data, people would say it is fake. You, as an investigator, should know that."

Deloir went on to say that he would try and undo the damage I had done by speaking to a friend in the media before he put the phone down. Three days later, Cradock received a fax from Canada. We had made the front page of Canada's National Paper, stating that the Alien insurance story was exposed as a hoax thanks to Mr. Deloir. I don't know why they thanked him and gave him the credit for exposing us. I told him the truth to not waste his time. Looking back, I should have treated him like a journalist and taken him on a wild goose chase or perhaps sent him to Scotland like Yahim, the German reporter.

Several radio interviews were requested and Cradock was happy to oblige.

MELODY RADIO: "So, Mr. Cradock, what do you have to say about this accusation?"

Before the DJ could even finish patting himself on the back, Cradock responded in his professional voice, "Do you honestly believe, as do you or anyone else listening, that Joseph 'The' Carpenter was taken by a star-shaped UFO, which approached from the east and was witnessed by three friends?" Cradock assured me that all the DJ could do was acknowledge the joke and laugh along with millions of others, except for one. But we would continue to keep the story alive, sending mixed messages eagerly devoured by media enthusiasts, prolonging the fun as I continued to engage with journalists.

*"Mr. Carpenter denies he is a friend of Mr. Cradock and rejects claims the whole affair is a hoax. Well, they would say that... but once the footage is released..." he said. "The footage is a recording made of the UFO by Mr. Carpenter using his camcorder, being held by the policy underwriters. Which are... ?"*

*"A consortium of European underwriters," replied Mr. Carpenter.*

*"And Mr. Cradock?"*

*"I don't know what he is. I've only known the guy for two weeks," said Mr. Carpenter. "But if the check bounces, I'll go around and kick his head in!"*

## USA Today.

*"At first, I thought it was the searchlight from a police helicopter. But then it started lifting me off the ground and I realized it was an anti-gravitational beam. It took me up about 50 feet. I was so scared the world passed through my bottom and I passed out."*

## The Swindon Times

*"There was a claw or fingernail or some plasma, it's not*

*of this earth, I doubt if Steven*
*Spielberg can pull that one out of*
*the hat... I just want to get my*
*money, then maybe make Gillian*

*Anderson an indecent proposal*
*and then go away probably*
*somewhere hot."*

## The War Correspondent.

February 1997.

As I began an interview with Tim Leach, a former head of the Foreign Correspondents' Association for ITN and BBC, as well as a seasoned Zimbabwe reporter, a particular story etched itself into my consciousness, resonating with the inner child within me. Tim had come to interview me and he began to earnestly share that in all his years as a war correspondent, where he had witnessed some of the worst human atrocities in recent decades, nothing had frightened him more than the interviews he had conducted with children in Africa. After years of being exposed to human horror and suffering from post-traumatic stress and the possible fallout of those experiences, he had held no beliefs in anything until three years prior, in 1994, when he interviewed a cluster of over one hundred school children (aged between six and thirteen) in Zimbabwe, Ruwa.

On September 16th, 1994, more than a hundred children at Ariel School claimed to have witnessed a silver craft landing and had telepathic interactions with humanoid figures—commonly referred to as 'the Grays.' Tim and his colleague were thoroughly convinced that the accounts shared by these children were genuine. These entities engaged with the children for approximately 15 minutes before departing in their silver saucer. They left behind telepathic messages conveying warnings of impending environmental disasters and a crisis stemming from mankind's misuse of technology, all imprinted upon the young minds that still traumatize them to this day.

Tim's narrative resonated deeply with me, tapping into the childhood hope of finding salvation from a troubled Earth through the intervention of alien saviors—a notion deeply rooted in my subconscious, representing escape and radical change. At that time, the internet was still in its infancy and YouTube had yet to exist. Tim became the fifth person to share a detailed investigative story, but this chilling account involved the Fifth Kind, encompassing direct communication between children and aliens.

The first had been Sylvia from Swindon, followed by the bleach-blonde lizard woman in the TV studio's green room, then Deloir the Canadian and Alvarez with his accounts from Brazil of an alleged UFO crash and alien capture in Varginha. Alvarez also shared the phenomenon of constant midday skylights captured by unflinching journalists and media outlets in Mexico that had accepted the extraordinary as mundane. Tim Leach, BBC's War Correspondent, added another layer to my childhood apocalyptic yearning for solace and affection and it shook me.

At each step of the way, it seemed that my request to James Mayor and Perry Ward through their Ouija board was coming to pass. It all began with our Ouija board sessions, where I reached out to James Mayor and Perry Ward for guidance. Now, I found myself back where I started, sitting with a piece of truth that had emerged from Tim's interview with the children at Ariel School in Ruwa, Zimbabwe. It was like assembling a jigsaw puzzle, with each interview providing a crucial piece of information for my quest as I navigated the valleys and wrestled with the angels of my imagination— much like Jacob of old, who emerged from such struggles a changed man. [2]

PROF. VIRGIL: "Ah, our dear Dante embarks on a voyage up the purifying slopes of Purgatory, where departed souls hope to find solace.

Picture this mountain as a multi-tiered haven, with each level reflecting one of the notorious seven deadly sins. Guided by his newfound companion, the wordsmith Statius, Dante ascends this celestial ladder, the 'scala,' unwinding before them, guiding their ascent toward the pinnacle, one enlightening step at a time."

JOE: "I can only imagine the symbolism and depth behind his journey."

Meanwhile, amidst this allegorical journey, news articles in Germany, France and Italy hail Joseph Carpenter as a billionaire, attributing his newfound wealth to a 2.5 billion lira award from NOBLE, ostensibly in recognition of his proof of an otherworldly encounter. This news ignites both skepticism and curiosity regarding the possibility of extraterrestrial encounters. While the world remains preoccupied with the implications of such events, Dante's ascent up the scala of Purgatory serves as a poignant reminder of the spiritual journey toward redemption and the purification of one's sins. Soon, as if beckoning us to join Dante in his ascent, the steps to Rome beckon.

# Chapter Thirteen
## All Roads Lead to Rome

*"Y'see, when that lawless fella shows up, it's gonna be like a devil's sideshow, full of fake magic tricks, signs and spooky stuff. And those folks who ain't seein' the truth, well, they'll be headin' down a bad path. They're skippin' on love for the truth and that's where they get lost. Then, the big guy upstairs sends 'em a major illusion, makin' 'em believe the big ol' fib."– Prof. Beatrice [1]*

Despite spilling the beans, Carpenter's story still had Element 115 propulsion and apparently, no one in Italy had read the disclosures from Canada that had also been printed in *The Times* Newspaper U.K. So, we would continue to manipulate the media airwaves to achieve our momentum.

The breakthrough in aerodynamic lift came three months later in March when Carpenter and Cradock were invited to Rome, Italy, to make an appearance on 'The Maurizio Costanzo Show,' the Italian equivalent of Oprah.

*Cradock Receives another FAX: 4 FEB.1997 19:04*

*To Mr. Johnny Cradock, we are writing from the Maurizio show studios. Our show is the most famous talk show in Italy, which has been on the air for over fifteen years hosting guests from all over the world. We would be honored to have you and your client Mr. Joseph Carpenter on our program. We are paying for your trip and your hotel in Rome. Hoping that you will accept our invitation, I'm sending you our fax number, yours, sincerely 'Adamo Lorenzetti.'*

Italian TV had not done their homework, or the mixed messages had them probing. Either way, I could not care. We were going to Rome, baby!

7<sup>th of</sup> March 1997

*'Wannabe'– Spice Girls*
*Number 1 Song in the UK.*

I had just finished a night on the graveyard shift and arrived home at 7am. Cradock met me there and we were promptly whisked off and driven to Heathrow for a business class Alitalia flight to Rome to appear in the Maurizio Constanzo Show.

Four hours later, we arrived in Rome. We were collected and driven, briefly seeing the romantic Mediterranean views before being booked into the beautiful Ritz Hotel. When Cradock and I arrived, we needed a drink and approached the desk to introduce ourselves and book in. The receptionist handed us a key card to our rooms and mentioned that when we ordered food and drink, we should mention "Maurizio," and all our costs would be covered.

As soon as I entered my room, I was impressed. Deluxe bed, a splendid balcony view to observe the elegantly dressed Romans and a fridge laden with booze. After settling in, we went into the hotel's restaurant and ordered Italian food.

"What drink would you like, Sirs?" asked the waiter.

"I fancy a coke," I said.

"Sod the coke, can we have your wine list please?" replied Cradock.

"What do you recommend?" Cradock asked the waiter, "What's the most expensive?"     The waiter held up his hands and pulled an Italian face, suggesting, '*No, it's up to you, leave me out of this!*'

"No, come on please, I insist I want a bottle of your finest," Cradock pressed. The waiter did as he was asked and came back with a bottle of Chianti reserve. "1987, a good year," said Cradock.

"Yes, a very good year," replied the waiter.

"Rome wasn't built in a day," I said to Cradock as we tucked into our venison. "It's going to be stitched up in a day. Thanks for the chianti, *absolutely lovely* it was."

Later that same afternoon, we were driven in a celebrity car to the famous Italian TV studios and after a short drive, we arrived and disembarked from the car in the midday Roman sun. We entered the theatre at the back and several hundred people were waiting to see who got out of the car. We donned our sunglasses like English movie stars, waving at the crowd. We then met and were briefed by the producer, before meeting my female interpreter. I then met Maurizio Costanzo, whose show it was— journalist, screenwriter and film director. Although, I did not know his profession and skill set at the time.

Before and after the show I met a soldier who had claimed that whilst on duty he and his fellow soldiers had seen silver metallic UFO discs on his tours within the military, he sincerely asked me if I could give him an answer as to what it was he saw, which had concerned him for years, but I could not give him any resolution, except that I believed him and perhaps he should write a letter to the United Nations. I felt a bit guilty, but I did not come to put people for or against me in the debate, I came to meet, seek, have fun and by unintentionally subconsciously making myself a scapegoat in pursuing a

184

childhood question. The world indeed needs discernment. It was not my time. My delusion carried me to find my answers.

We stood at the makeshift studio bar and sampled more of Italy's finest. We were in an extremely merry mood when suddenly a gorgeous blonde walked by to talk to the producer. "Oh my, blessed bosoms!" said Cradock as subtle as a brick.

"She must be the Marilyn Monroe of Italy," I said, as she walked past us again in seventies enchanting clothing.

The elegant young lady smiled and to our surprise addressed us mere mortals.

"Are you appearing on the show as well?" she asked in a perfect Italian American accent.

"Yes," we answered in unison, our jaws dropping.

Cradock introduced himself and kissed her hand dramatically before explaining the reasons and introduced me as his client who had been recently paid a million pounds after subsequently being abducted by the Grays and proving it.

"Ah, you are Mr. Carpenter!" she interjected. "Yes, I have heard of your story here in Italy and Los Angeles. What an amazing story. Is it true?" she asked, wide-eyed.

After being awake for almost thirty hours, flown for four hours on a plane and having drunk a vat of vino and eaten plenty of venison, I replied, "It's true, the footage, the creature, all of it, it's true."

I approached the researcher and asked him: "Can I have my photo taken with Maurizio? My mum is a great fan."

"Yes, I'll ask him, it shouldn't be a problem," he said. "You'll meet him in a minute as I have to discuss the show format with him and he usually likes to know some background about each guest beforehand," he added, somewhat cryptically. "He's got a fantastic memory. He used to be a Magistrate."

I walked into Maurizio's room where he had completed his make-up for the cameras. Maurizio was of advancing age, silver-haired, short, with a small pot belly, sporting a stout white mustache. A smaller version of actor Bob Hoskins. The translator introduced me. I said hello and shook his hand. "So, you're Italian, then?" Maurizio asked. I'd been forced to give my real name on my passport when the flight was booked. "Where are your parents from?" he asked again.

"Aqua Viva, a small village in Sicily," I replied.

"All the newspapers called you Carpenter. Why did you change your name?"

"It's a rough translation of Tagliarini and easier to pronounce and stops people from tracing me and asking for money," I replied.

"You are a clever man, you know what you are doing."

Craddock and I were then led to the green room, a chaotic yet oddly glamorous backstage haven. I was promptly seated and besieged by a very camp makeup artist wielding a large brush, who proceeded to vigorously dust my face with enough matte setting powder to rival a bakery's flour supply. Meanwhile, Craddock lounged nearby, barely touched by the brush, looking smug as he escaped with just a light dab.

Cradock was seated in the front row, while I occupied a leather plush sofa on stage with my lovely interpreter by my side, alongside other Italian actors and celebrities seated on another sofa. I had my lapel microphone on and with my pretty translator next to me, I was ready to go. A couple of minutes later, the opening music began and the credits rolled on a monitor on the floor as the enormous crimson curtains slowly parted.

The curtains slowly opened and to my amazement, I was seated in front of a live auditorium of thousands of well-dressed Romans clapping as the credits rolled.

"Oh my God. Is this the Albert Hall or what?"

My heart beat like a drum. With the effect of wine numbing me, I combed the well-dressed audience looking for a friendly face and there for a moment, I thought I saw it. There, in the front row was Cradock with his huge Cheshire cat grin. I shall never forget that moment for the rest of my life. In his quintessential pinstripe, white English cricket suit, he pointed at me, winking then screaming like a wild pop fan and did his very, very best to make me laugh, silently mouthing, "Look at this, this is bloody amazing!" I gasped at the magnitude of the auditorium. "Oh, my days! What on earth had I stepped into?"

I managed to keep a half-straight face, just! Fortunately, a beautiful woman interpreter was sitting next to Cradock watching him and looking at me as if she could read my mind. She smiled and I smiled back and felt relaxed.

Maurizio introduced the guests one by one. I was fourth in line and as he introduced me (in Italian) he said, "When we heard the story of an Englishman abducted by UFOs, we couldn't believe it and invited him on the show, then he arrived and revealed his true identity! Yes, it is true. Italians do get around. Joseph Carpenter is a name he created for himself. His parents are Sicilian. His real name is *Joe Tagliarini*."

It is funny how the phenomenon of being on stage acting seems to make you play the part confidently and disinhibited. I calmly scanned the audience's faces and some didn't know what to believe as soon as it was revealed I had Sicilian blood.

"We'd like to talk about your amazing experience with aliens," replied Maurizio via an interpreter.

I proceeded to describe my story and insisted I hadn't been drinking or smoking any funny stuff.

"The actual footage I provided to the insurance company is so good I'd have to be a close friend of Steven Spielberg to have faked it." I continued to scan the audience for their reaction. Some of them laughed and nodded their head. Some had a serious look on their face.

"What did the Alien look like?" asked Maurizio.

"It was five feet high with a triangular head and almond black eyes."

"Like Betty Boo?" interrupted Maurizio and the audience laughed while the interpreter translated it to 'Like a Walt Disney character?'

"Like Mickey Mouse on drugs?" I replied. The camera was blurred on my face but quickly focused sharply. *(Whoops, the wine speaking).*

The interpreter changed it to, 'Like a mouse on hallucinogens.'

"Like a giant mouse? You mean it had big ears and big eyes? Please continue," asked Maurizio.

"Not big ears, but yes, it had two large almond-like eyes, a slender, slim body, dolphin-like skin and two tiny slit nostrils," I replied.

"Like scales?"

"No just smooth-looking skin."

"BAMBI!" Interrupted the seventh guest, Cato of Utica, a professional actor/comedian.

'The estraneo looked like Bambi?' said my interpreter. I knew what he said and what he was up to, but I played it cool.

"It *was* Bambi!" he insisted.

"Hey, come on. This is an Extra Terrestrial he's describing, have you ever seen one?" asked Maurizio.

"No. I've never seen one and hope I don't, but first, he said it was a mouse on hallucinogens and now it sounds like Bambi. He's having a laugh, Maurizio," replied the actor.

"But we have his insurer here..."

Before Maurizio could finish the audience clapped and laughed.

"Let him finish..." said Maurizio as he waved his hands in the air, decreeing order.

"I'm not convinced, Constanzo," replied the actor, pulling a face and nodding in comedic disagreement suggesting, *You can't pull the wool over my eyes.*

"I don't really care," I explained. "They said the moon landing was a fake but at the end of the day I've earned my million pounds... so..."

The actor placed his finger under one eye and pulled down an eyelid, a well-known gesture in Italy known as *occhio*, 'eye' meaning stai attento, *pay attention, I'm watching you* and to suggest one's partial role in the Mafia. "Ah well... nice one. Respect to you. I understand your motives," the actor nodded in agreement.

The camera turned to the Cheshire Cat in the audience who in turn passionately clapped with the Roman audience. I continued describing the event, including the claim that I had hit the creature before being returned to Terra-firma.

"Once back on the ground, we analyzed the footage."

"Why did they pick you?" asked Maurizio.

"We had been given a tip-off by fellow military researchers that this would be the place to make contact with E.T.s."

Another guest interrupted, "Permit me, why did you insure yourself?"

"Good question," replied Maurizio. "Why did you take out this insurance?"

The camera turned to the audience members and in particular Cradock, who anxiously waited for the answer. 'Yeah, why did you insure yourself?'

"I'm a paranormal researcher and have been investigating the phenomena for several years and when I heard about the policy back in January, '96..."

"... He decided to insure himself!" Maurizio interjected.

"Yes, but I would like to insure myself for my car, my house and my belongings with my insurers, from where did this insurance company come up with this generosity?" asked the skeptic.

At this point, the spotlight turned to Cradock again.

"We have the manager of the insurance company here with us. Let's see what he has to say," said Maurizio. And with the first break, I'd had all morning, the cameras turned to focus sharply on Cradock –and the straight man of the double act went to work his magic.

Good evening, Mr. Cradock. Is this a stunt?" he asks. "After all you have been flown from England to a hotel, eaten well and appeared on national TV."

*(I wonder if he's seen our bar bill).*

Cradock in a deeply sincere tone responded.

"The evidence Joe has provided is extremely .. I say again extremely compelling,"—"As you may be aware, insurance companies do not pay out unless there is sufficient reason to so. The evidence in question has been sold to an American media conglomerate for more than £2 million.

The insurance company is a *con*sortium of European insurers, including Italian insurers." Cradock's voice was deep and serious, with every word etched in suspense, manipulating the dramatic tension as the heart of the story echoed across the Roman theatre.

Cato sat at attention, like a deer in headlights, eagerly awaiting each word's translation. His expression betrayed awe as he witnessed the grand performance unfold before him.

"We have a capital exceeding $1 Billion... Mr. Carpenter has provided us with compelling evidence to validate his claim... and based on that we have decided that we must pay him."

"Because of the footage?" asked Maurizio

"You are no doubt aware that insurance companies do not pay claims without very good evidence," replied Cradock.

"Either that or for very good publicity!" declared Cato for the third time, with the audience approving and clapping.

"The evidence is compelling and on the basis of the evidence that Mr. Carpenter has provided, we have sold that evidence for £1.8 million to an American corporation," replied Cradock with an earnest expression.

Suddenly, the audience fell completely silent.

"1.8 million pounds sterling?" asked Maurizio.

"1.8 million," repeated Cradock.

"The footage concerning Mr. Carpenter? Do you think there is any likelihood of us having this footage to see after it's been aired in the States maybe?" asked Maurizio.

"It has been sold to a multi-corporation company and will be aired in Europe in due course," he replied.

"The footage will be released this summer for all to see," I interrupted.

"Mr. Carpenter, there was also some other evidence you mentioned, a claw, was it? Is that true?"

"Yes. There was a claw.. a form of DNA left tangled in my coat. I presume it ended up there when I lashed out and hit the creature."

"What did it look like? What was the substance like?" asked Maurizio.

"It was like smooth cling film. That's one way I can describe it."

"Was it jelly-like?" asked Maurizio.

"Soft, dolphin-like, sleek and velvety."

"The insurers have that claw also?" asked Maurizio, pointing to Cradock.

"Yes, they sold all that evidence, including the claw, to the American company, so, obviously, if the Americans are happy – then no one's a loser."

"That's certain? Even the insurers are winners? Let's sum this up, they've done good business and the insurers have sold the evidence and documents and recouped their money twice over. Carpenter has made himself a million and a trip to Italy. Now, even I recognize a life touched by luck," concluded Maurizio.


PROF. BERNARD: "Our entertainment industry has a subtle and ongoing influence on society, often encouraging people to look up to either a paternal figure or superficial, empty-headed individuals."

PROF. VIRGIL: "Ah, the world, she wears her blindfold well, doesn't she? Yet here you stand, in this little oasis of clarity. Of course, out there, it's a never-ending parade of captivating distractions, meticulously crafted to coax those pleasure-loving synapses of ours into a rhythmic hypnotism. Whether it's caped crusaders rescuing kittens or the theatrics of reality TV, we can't help but succumb to the allure of grandiosity and those larger-than-life personalities."

JOE: "I should've been an actor in another life, my eyes are open now."

PROF. BEATRICE: "You see? This constant influx of entertainment can kinda numb us down, messin' with our emotional balance and clear thinkin'. It's like we get caught up in all the drama and forget 'bout the real world out there. And lemme tell ya, those folks creatin' the content we gobble up, they ain't exempt from their emotional battles and scars. Many famous faces deal with sky-high expectations, leading to anxiety, depression and such. Now, don't get me wrong, show business has got its upsides, bringin' joy and inspiration, but it's also important to keep an eye on how it might mess with our minds and the struggles faced by those bringin' it to us, ya know?"

Maurizio asked Carpenter his final question: "Are you still doing sky searches?"

"Yes, I am and I'm investing in larger and more sophisticated cameras," I replied.

The show itself continued for two hours, covering various topics, including libido, voodoo and a guest who explored the possibility of time travel, each getting their 15 minutes of fame.

I noticed Cradock fall asleep, suddenly the camera zoomed in and the presenter joked: "It's all too much for the audience to take, even Mr. Cradock has fallen asleep!" The beautiful woman (his translator) who sat next to him gave him a nudge and he sat up to attention. The cameras turned to Cradock, "The footage will be released this summer for all to see. Meanwhile, Joe and I have an audience at the Vatican with his Holiness the Pope at 10.30 tomorrow, to view the footage and DNA." The audience gasps and my face turns serious. *"Holy cow! He's mentioned the Pope. Dear Lord, please don't bring the pope into this."*

I had visions of the Pope eating his popcorn watching us while he waited for the revelation of ET, [2] only to discover that a Sicilian and Englishman were coming to visit him and suddenly spluttering it out in English and a thick Italian accent, *'Hey Luigi, is it true Joey and Johnny are coming to see me tomorrow? I cannot see it in my diary.'*

The show ended, the curtains drew closed and the spellbound audience clapped. Maurizio approached me and said again, "I think you're very clever. A smart boy, good luck."

We were driven back to The Ritz to have something to eat and drink. After all, we were never going to be there again.

"Two bottles of your finest Chianti please," requested Cradock, which was later followed by a glass of vintage port as we finished our venison.

Later that night, Cradock approached a Swedish woman. We'd been drinking gin and tonic in the evening. Cradock was a bit worse for wear so I looked after him or he could hit headlines for all the wrong reasons. Suddenly, he asked her, "Where's your husband?"

"Dead," she replied, puzzled.

"Congratulations!" replied Cradock.

I quickly replied, "It's alright, we're from Britain. Monty Python?"

Before we went back to our rooms, Cradock put in a request for an early wake-up call for 7am for a cab to pick us up at 8am to take us to the airport to give us enough time to sample Italian breakfast. At 8.15 I awoke and knocked on Cradock's door. We rushed downstairs, handed in our keys and said goodbye to the hotel staff, having missed our breakfast.

We jumped in the car to the airport. The Vatican would have to wait.

# Chapter Fourteen

## Strange But True

*"Nel mezzo del cammin di nostra vita, mi ritrovai per una selva oscura, ché*
*la diritta via era smarrita."* [1]
*"In the middle of the journey of our life, I found myself in a dark forest, for*
*the straight path had been lost."—Dante, Canto I*

On the 22nd of February 1997, Dolly (the world's first cloned sheep) was announced to the world to a frenzy of media attention. The Roslin team chose to announce at this time to coincide with the publication of the scientific paper, which describes the experiments that produced her. Dolly captured the public's imagination—no small feat for a sheep—and sparked a public debate about the possible benefits and dangers of cloning. In the week following the announcement, The Roslin Institute received 3,000 phone calls from around the world.

On the flight back from Rome, I shared my idea for the '*ewe-nique clone policy*' with Cradock. His eyes lit up and he began contemplating a suitable press release, complete with the possibility of Dolly Parton presenting a phantom check. We planned to get to work as soon as we returned from Rome, once the Chianti had worn off.

Cradock promptly called the press to introduce this innovative policy. He also asked if I could make an appearance at Lloyd's to pose as the policyholder for our new clone policy. I had already crafted a new character for the occasion. During our car ride to Lloyd's, I explained to Cradock that

I would adopt the identity of Gene Demetris Roussos, a wealthy Greek individual. Gene had purchased a clone policy for his future, intending to undergo cryogenic freezing before his demise. The plan was to revive him once medical science and technology advanced sufficiently. Gene's motivation for taking out this policy was to prevent a potential clone from claiming his inheritance and assets ahead of him.

However, Cradock suggested that this storyline might be a bit challenging for the British public to embrace. So, we tweaked it to involve the clone of a lottery winner entangled in a dispute over eligibility for the prize.

Upon arrival to Lime Street outside Lloyd's, Cradock said, "Check this out!" and from his bag pulled out two blow-up sheep. "I bought these yesterday from a specialist shop in Soho! This one is Dolly and this one is Curly." I was to pose with our mascots outside the steps of Lloyd's (or at least that was the first idea.)

I wasn't too keen on posing with the knowledge of where the love sheep had come from, so I suggested to Cradock we should try and get one of the Lloyds' guards to hold it. Once again, Cradock's face was a picture of a mischievously possessed schoolboy. "Yes, but how do we get him to pose with the inflatable sheep?"

"Simple," I said, "We tell him it's for comic relief raising money for an animal hospice in Wales for distressed sheep."

The photographer arrived at Lloyd's and we told him of the new photo shoot. He liked the idea and Cradock pounced upon a red-coated guard, who had just returned rosy-faced from a pub lunch.

"Good afternoon, Sir. My colleagues and I are raising money for animal welfare charities and we would like to invite you to help us with a publicity stunt, raising money for an animal hospice. I wonder if you'd be kind enough to hold these two sheep for me to take a photograph."

The smartly uniformed waiter was unquestioningly obliging and more than happy to do so. As we drove back, we couldn't stop laughing, pondering on whether the Lloyd's Chairman would go crazy when he read the papers to see one of the joyful Lloyd's guards posing with inflatable Soho sheep under headlines about cloning insurance. Dolly would be unavailable for comment.

The cloning story made it in several articles:

*NOBLE PIONEERS'*
*CLONE INSURANCE*
*COVER.*

*City of London*
*underwriting agency*
*NOBLE has today*
*announced the launch of*
*CLONESAFE, a clone*
*insurance.*

NOBLE

spokesperson Dickie Bingham said, "Following the announcement that cloning technology can create a replica of any living being, we have decided to launch a policy

BUY ONE, GET ONE FREE

that will cover policyholders against being compromised financially by a clone of themselves."

Spokespersons from both Universities of Edinburgh said, "With the emergence of cloning technology, it is completely understandable that people are concerned about the risk of discovering they have a clone."

" NOBLE TODAY CONFIRMED IT HAD WITHDRAWN ETSAFE "

CLONESAFE costs only £100 ($120) for every £100,000 ($122,000) of cover.

Throughout the year of puppeteering perplexity amid the media, we continued the fun and merriment. I occasionally took money for interviewers to talk as the character of Carpenter who had been paid a million for the evidence on behalf of Lloyd's of London. Yet, I was stuck trying to offload my thousands of unsold certificates and posters. Another bold German reporter asked me for camcorder footage. I said I'd lost it on the plane back from Rome. He still insisted he was coming round, so I said, "Listen, mate, are you telling me you believe that stuff about Carpenter?"

The media were informed that we had sold over 24,000 Alien insurance policies, including selling the insurance policy to the Heaven's Gate Cult. However, the reality was quite different – Cradock and I never actually sold any such policy. *Those policies simply did not exist on our end.* If anyone inquired about purchasing a certificate, he would redirect them to me, resulting in some intriguing phone conversations and investigations with peculiar individuals. I never sold a single policy, rather, it served to gather more investigative stories and testimonies.

## Fleecing the Flock: A Tale of Sheep and Trolls

In October 1997, I stepped away from the world of makeup and media hoaxes. Cradock extended an invitation for me to join him on his journey, focusing particularly on the abominable snowman and the Yeti insurance concept I had previously suggested. However, our paths eventually diverged.

By July 2024, Cradock shares my belief that the theme of UFOs and the majority of associated images is fabricated. He also alludes to two theories: Illuminati and Discordianism.[2] In simple terms, these theories suggest they are creators of confusion and delusion. It's almost like something out of a comic book villain's playbook, echoing what the DC character Joker, Batman's notorious antagonist, would famously say: *'Why so serious?'*[3]

Discordianism embraces paradox, randomness, and absurdity, often promoting skepticism and a playful approach to belief systems. It's characterized by its humor and rejection of dogma.

We both agree that propaganda used to persuade people to believe something. Nowadays, it's more about trolling lost sheep, making them question their beliefs and the very nature and fabric of truth itself, shaping society, controlling academia, and effectively taking over the airwaves on the basis that it generates more clicks. This caters to a nation of decadent, degenerate narcissists and non-entities with profound personality disorders, fueled by the media and the echo chambers of their minds. Nobody challenges them; they are incapable of critical thinking, with axiomatic beliefs ingrained within them, and incapable of any form of challenge.

Furthermore, Cradock believes that China will be the world's savior, bringing order as Western civilization crumbles.

Nevertheless, I am done with seeking Yetis, and I was never impressed with the Great Wall of China when I lived and walked it. Given what I see on this earth, which would be the better of two worlds amid trolls that lead the minds of people like lambs to slaughter.

## Skubalon.

*'It's why fake news outperforms real news, because studies show that lies spread faster than truth.' - Sacha Baron Cohen*

News, most of which I consider unworthy even as manure on my farm, is undeniably driven by agenda—an intriguing amalgamation of money, drama and its influence on cognitive processes, particularly the prefrontal cortex and hippocampus. You no longer need a Ouija board, all you have to do is switch on your TV or radio!

When delving into the data pertaining to the vast realm of media, it becomes evident that the term 'media,' which has its roots in the Latin word 'medium,' signifying the middle or intermediary, is now a polluted mainstream—a river of filth, serving as a conduit for the transmission of the unseen, defeated, fallen realm.

Amidst this labyrinth of media entities and emerging companies, I present the top 10 contenders, each with its corresponding market capitalization.

1. Comcast - $186.70 billion
2. Thomson Reuters - $58.53 billion
3. Naspers - $32.54 billion
4. Warner Bros. Discovery - $28.22 billion
5. Fox Corp. - $14.76 billion
6. News Corp. - $12.15 billion
7. Paramount Global - $8.96 billion
8. The New York Times Company - $7.24 billion
9. Nexstar Media Group - $4.70 billion
10. IACI - $4.64 billion

The collective market capitalization of these 10 companies stands at approximately $359.28 billion! [4]

In a world dominated by financial juggernauts, Cradock emerged as a contemporary crusader, driven by an insatiable thirst for justice. His mission he states, was clear: to untangle the intricate web spun by banks peddling worthless Payment Protection Insurance (PPI). This scandal would eventually rock the very pillars of the financial realm, resulting in a monumental restitution of £50 Billion ($65 Billion). Undeterred by regulatory indifference, Cradock embarked on an unwavering quest, unveiling undeniable proof of PPI mis-selling and advocating for the millions ensnared in this massive deception.

Yet, Cradock's ambition reached beyond mere retribution. Amid the ensuing chaos, a shrewd strategy unfolded—one that propelled his company into the international limelight. His ingenious move to endorse innovative policies not only exposed the rampant PPI misconduct but also paved the way for a future where Cradock championed an authentic and invaluable version of PPI. This audacious endeavor marked the dawn of a new era, forever revolutionizing the insurance landscape.

THE NATIONAL MEDIA ARE AWAKENING TO THE RACKET OF BANKS' PPI MIS-SELLING

Meanwhile, Carpenter's legend remained shrouded in mystery, whispers suggest he now resides on a distant island in Bermuda, symbolizing the darkness through which a candidate for initiation must pass. With that, the media's last known connection with him vanished, and the strings of Geppetto were cut. Like a sunken Lutine ship disappearing without a trace, I can confidently say with a smile that he is indeed dead. This story stands as the only artifact that, like a bell, rings the warning: 'Do not be deceived.'

# Land of Smiles.

*Soundtrack: 'Despacito' by Luis Fonsi and Daddy Yankee (feat. Justin Bieber)*

In July 2017, I found myself not in Bermuda, but astride a motorbike atop the lofty hills of Thailand. Here, I was busily checking off items from my bucket list, my gaze sweeping across the expanse of palm trees and the breathtaking vistas of paradise. This moment marked a pivotal juncture in my life – a period of detox and defragmentation aimed at reclaiming the years I had surrendered to white knight relationships and the semi-beta life I had lived.

Amidst the lush surroundings, I embarked on a quest for healing, intertwined with the lessons of fundamentalism that had taken root during a shift in the education system. A system that seemed intent on spotlighting my so-called white privilege. However, in certain corners of some British international schools in Asia, you'll find plenty of snakes in suits and ties and mosquitoes in pencil skirts.

However, it was here that the taste of coconut water became a revelation – a refreshment as fresh, delightful, exquisite and wonderful as the newfound clarity coursing through me.

The sight of blooming flowers summoned a troop of beautiful butterflies, evoking memories of my childhood days when I used to capture these delicate creatures. This stark contrast to the nightshifts that once held me captive in the heart of London served as a poignant reminder of the transformation that had unfolded.

At this moment, a whisper of encouragement reverberated through time and space, a message directed back to my former self, 'Joe, hang on in there. You're stronger than you know and brighter days await you.'

<u>1997+.</u>

PROF. BEATRICE: "What do you see Joe?"

Nightshift had evolved from a temporary solution into an ongoing routine, marked by uninspiring nights that buried my creative talents and left me feeling purposeless. During this period, I struck up a friendship with Joe Alvarez, a photographer and journalist. The same journalist and UFO researcher who snapped that picture of me holding the million-pound check. Surprisingly, he appreciated the humor behind it.

Alvarez was deeply immersed in various conspiracy theories involving the government and extraterrestrial beings. His unwavering belief in the existence of UFOs was evident as he shared countless stories of the people he'd interviewed during his journalism career. For a moment, I found myself drawn into his world of spiritism, unconventional explorations and prescriptions. Together, we explored places like Avalon in Glastonbury, a location steeped in beauty and history, rich with tales of King Arthur and Merlin. Additionally, I had the privilege of having a backstage journalist pass that granted me access to concerts, where I could watch bands like *The Prodigy* and *Placebo*.

PROF. BERNARD: "It appears you continued to wholeheartedly immerse yourself in the study of a subject that had captivated you from a young age. In your quest for answers, you assumed command of your very essence to unveil the truths underlying these phenomena. Your unwavering dedication led you to association with practitioners of the occult, which, in turn, resulted in the transformation of a fragment of your authentic character. Throughout this journey, your inner child and teenager assumed prominent roles."

JOE: "Although I take full responsibility for my actions, my conduct at home became a source of distress. I am not proud of how I treated Eleanor. My dark wounds began to surface, mixed with the constant barrage of journalists probing into things that had never been properly dealt with."

As the weight of my past actions bore down on me, the story of Carpenter remained in reams of fax rolls with reports in the following unedited titles:

**U.K.**

The Guardian

Sunday Express

Mail on Sunday

The Times

Independent

Mirror

Scotland on Sunday

Daily Record

Metro

North Wales

Daily Post

Scottish Herald

Manchester Evening News

London Evening Standard

The Financial Adviser

**International**

The Toronto Star

Manchester Evening News

Hobart Mercury

Associated Press International News

Tasmanian Country

Omaha World Herald

USA Today

Chicago Tribune

Seattle Post

Seattle Times

The Virginia Roanoke Times

Los Angeles Daily News

CNN Worldview

CNN Inside Business

CNN The World Today

Newark Star-Ledger (New Jersey)

Port St. Louis News (Florida)

Charlotte Observer (North Carolina)

Broadcast News (Baltimore)

Daily Record

Miami Herald

National Underwriter

Capital (Germany)

The Ottawa Citizen

The Pittsburgh Post

The Columbian (Vancouver)

Salt Lake City Desert News

San Diego Advertiser

New York Daily News

New Orleans Picayune Times

Sydney Daily Telegraph

Ottawa Citizen

San Diego Union Tribune

Washington Copley News Service

Chattanooga Times (Tennessee)

Detroit Free Press

Dubuque Telegraph Herald IA

The Oregonian

Dallas Morning News

That's just from the shorter of many fax rolls. Sebastian, Cradock and I observed that *it was the folk of North America who had the greatest hunger for news of all things alien.*

I ended the media acting on the 18[th of] June 1997 after a reconstruction and filming for the then popular ITV (Independent Television) paranormal show *Strange But True*, which garnered twelve million viewers in the UK alone. In my final TV show, with Michael Aspel, it claimed I came forward to surrender the truth of the story. In truth, I did it just to push the boat out a little more, to gain a genuine actor's payment and to end with a swan song.

I'd meet the actor who was to play me in the reconstruction. I'm told he resembles me, but when we were introduced, he didn't look anything like me. The only similarity was his dark hair.

The presenter asks: "What do you think, Joe?"

"He's my doppelganger," I fibbed. "People won't know the difference when they see this on the telly."

Filming dragged on for about five hours before the film crew left for Alexandra Palace (which sits atop a hill in the Alexandra Park area of the city, offering panoramic views of London) to film a reconstruction using triangular light special effects and inflatable dolphins as the Interdimensional entities. The idea was to cast a light on the dolphins to make them look extra-terrestrial creating shadows.

JOE: "Of course, I knew who I was, part wannabe paranormal insurance salesman and investigator, part actor, part lost youngster looking for purpose, though I couldn't believe at first that people had embodied the idea and believed Carpenter's story."

PROF. VIRGIL: "Ah, but here we stand, where the tangible remains a specter and the phantom becomes as real as your morning espresso. It's as if the absence of evidence decided to don a mask and dance a more captivating tango with our imaginations. A spectacle where the brushstrokes of words and the symphony of descriptions hold more sway than a battalion of alien souvenirs. You see my dear friends, the pen, or perhaps I should say the keyboard, truly is mightier than the unidentified flying saucer. Our words, our linguistic dalliances, not only craft our identities but also seem to whisper secrets to destiny herself."

JOE: "Yet drama with the additional language enhanced the perception of our deception. Language is intricate, contextual, and powerful—it taps into humanity's innate desire to connect with something greater than ourselves. But we are not called to be rescued but to discover who we are. It is our mind that needs redeeming from all the distractions, fear and fake news that swarm us like ferocious locusts."

Throughout my odyssey, I'd mingled with those who had seen UFOs, met aLIEns, claimed to be Vampires and journalists who spoke of unions with Incubus and Succubus spirits. I'd become disrespectful to many and myself. Nightshifts didn't help. I had destroyed my relationship with Eleanor and was unfaithful. I was now in debt due to the failed 'I Believe' poster and certificate business, yet the paradox was that many people thought the lie was true, that I was indeed a millionaire.

Despite publicly confessing, my personal life was filled with a galaxy of emotional ties and physical clutter accumulated over the years, as my parents and brothers had warned me that the joke, though initially funny, was bringing embarrassment to everyone.

In August 1997, *'Strange But True'* aired on UK TV, effectively closing the claim. This indicates that the insuring entity, self-insurer, facility, or provider had settled or otherwise resolved the issue, with or without an indemnity payment to the claimant. [5]

### Communion.

*'Rather, we have renounced secret and shameful ways, we do not use deception, nor do we distort the word of God. On the contrary, by setting forth the truth we commend ourselves to every man's conscience in the sight of God.' – St. Paul.* [6]

Enfield has made a unique imprint on the world stage, known for the Enfield hauntings and Poltergeist of 1977 that occurred just a mile away from Green Street where I lived. The area is also notable for being the childhood home of William Henry Pratt, later known as Boris Karloff, who played the iconic role of Frankenstein.

*Soundtrack "Angels." (1997, December 13, No.1). Robbie Williams*

On Wednesday, December 10th, 1997, Lucas's mother and I took our son to a Church of England near Green Street, Enfield, to be christened, succumbing to cultural pressure from my parents. During the ceremony, a Ghanaian priest asked us to renounce the works of Satan and dedicate Lucas to the Lord. As I prayed out loud, I remember feeling a genuine connection to the words I spoke.

The prayer was as follows –

MINISTER: '*Dost thou, in the name of this Child, renounce the devil and all his works, the vain pomp and glory of the world, with all covetous desires of the same and the carnal desires of the flesh, so that thou wilt not follow nor be led by them?*'

JOE: '*I renounce them all.*'

MINISTER: '*Dost thou believe in God, the Father Almighty, Maker of Heaven and Earth? And in Jesus Christ, His only begotten Son, our Lord? And that He was conceived by the Holy Ghost, born of the Virgin Mary, that He suffered under Pontius Pilate, was crucified, dead and buried, that He went down into hell and also did rise again the third day, that He ascended into Heaven and sitteth at the right hand of God, the Father Almighty and from thence shall come again at the end of the world, to judge the quick and the dead? And dost thou believe in the Holy Ghost, the holy Catholic Church, the Communion of Saints, the Remission of sins, the Resurrection of the flesh and everlasting life after death?*'

JOE: '*All this, I steadfastly believe.*'

MINISTER: '*Wilt thou be baptized in this faith?*'

JOE: '*That is my desire.*'

MINISTER: '*Wilt thou then obediently keep God's Holy will and commandments and walk in the same all the days of thy life?*'

JOE: '*I will.*'

MINISTER: '*O merciful God, grant that the old Adam in this Child may be so buried, that the new man may be raised up in him. Amen. Grant that all carnal affections may die in him and that all things belonging to the Spirit may live and grow in him. Amen. Grant that he may have power and strength, to have victory and to triumph against the devil, the world and the flesh. Amen. Grant*

209

*that whosoever is here dedicated to thee by our office and ministry may also be*
*endued with heavenly virtues and everlastingly rewarded, through thy mercy, O*
*blessed Lord God, who dost live and govern all things, world without end. Amen.*
*Heavenly Father, by the power of your Holy Spirit, You give your faithful people*
*new life in the water of baptism. Guide and strengthen us by the same Spirit, that*
*we who are born again may serve You in faith and love and grow into the full*
*stature of Your Son, Jesus Christ, who is alive and reigns with You in the unity*
*of The Holy Spirit, now and forever.'*

ALL: *'Amen.'* [7]

## A Cinematic Catalyst.

*"Il cammino verso il paradiso comincia nell'inferno."*
*"The path to paradise begins in hell." — Inferno, Canto III* [8]

A couple of weeks later, on Christmas Eve in 1997, Eleanor and I
watched the film premiere of Forest Gump on TV. We had seen it together
at the cinema before, but this time as I watched it, several scenes began to
speak to me. Tom Hanks' character, Forest, suffered tremendous loss in his
life - his friend died in war, his girlfriend left him and then he discovered a
son he never knew he had. Something stirred in my heart and I began to sob
uncontrollably. I couldn't understand why. I rarely cry, especially when
watching a film for the second time. But the emotions were too much to bear
and I tried to hide my tears from Eleanor. When she saw me crying, I reacted
poorly and pushed her away, telling her I didn't love her anymore. In a fit of
anger, I spoke words that burned any remaining bridge between us and
destroyed our relationship like wildfire.

# Chapter Fifteen

## Fire In The Sky

*'I saw Satan like lightening falling from heaven.'* — *Yeshua*

Friday, January 19th, 1998, 'forty days' exactly after Lucas's Christening, Eleanor returned home from work, packed her clothes in two black bags and left in a pre-prepared moment, saying she would be back for Lucas. I watched her from the window leave in a friend's car. I do not blame her at all.

Three days later, Monday 22nd of January, whilst I was at my parent's house, two police officers knocked on the door. "Are you Joseph?"

"Yes."

"Where is Lucas?"

"He is here with me."

"We have his mother waiting in the car. We need to take him. We have custody papers."

I changed Lucas's nappy and told him, "You are going to see Mummy now."

The policewoman was very gentle and could see I was in shock and disorientated. I walked Lucas to the front door and handed him to the lady who walked him to the black cab where his mum waited and then they drove off. At the same moment, the phone rang. I answered it and it was a wrong number, which was even more confusing. In the twinkling of an eye, my world would begin to shatter.

When my parents returned home, my dad asked, "Where is Lucas?" I explained what had happened and for the first time in my life, I saw my dad cry, "They have taken my Lucas away."

## The River Styx.

The River Styx, derived from the Greek word meaning 'detest,' holds great significance in Greek and Roman mythology, serving as the boundary between the realms of the living and the dead. Within 'The Divine Comedy,'[1] it resides in the fifth circle of Hell, under the watchful gaze of Charon, the demon ferryman who transports condemned souls to their eternal torment. Dante and Virgil navigate this river with the assistance of an angel's boat, symbolizing the transition between worlds. This journey mirrors my departure from one realm and my entry into an uncharted future.

I took a week off from work and during that week, I went to court to gain access to my son. I was granted the right to see and take care of him every two weeks while the courts decided on the future of our parental guardianship. In court I remember saying sorry for what I had become, the judge was presented with a copy of the News of the World article that depicted my insurance story, which I was now ashamed of. However, the judge glanced at the article, looked at me and then commented that I was a clever man. This unexpected compliment took me by surprise.

Returning to work the following week of the night shift and each morning that followed was the most painful, heart-breaking time of my entire life. A pain I had never experienced before and will never forget. I was alone, I felt abandoned, totally separated and empty. The silence was deafening, a thousand thoughts spun in my head, the past, present and future blurred in front of me as I looked at the toys in front of me, but Lucas was not there to play with them.

PROF. BEATRICE "What do you see Joe?"

JOE: "My two-year-old son is excited to see me as I come home from night shift. He is welcoming me home at the top of the stairs, saying 'Hello daddy' … but he isn't there anymore."

My girlfriend's perfume and lipstick were still on the dressing table. The perfume smelt good, but she wasn't there either. It was a ghost house. I spent weeks looking out of the window, expecting them to walk home at any moment, but they never did. In another room, there were paper cuttings, videos and unsold posters, all centered around my exploits. I stared at them with a mixture of disgust and hatred, feeling sick to the core of my being and wanting to vomit. I cried incessantly, praying for my family to return or hoping to wake up from what seemed like a terrible nightmare, yet this was my harsh reality.

I'd spent so much time and money—literally thousands of pounds— on diabolic inspirations. There were hundreds of hours, literally months' worth of documentary material. When would I ever watch this stuff? What was the point of collecting it? The painting of the man caught in the light beam hung in the center of the living room. It had become a token of a stronghold that consumed my house and life. I had neglected my family for this delusion, prioritizing it over meaningful connections and moments with those I love. As I stood in the shadow of my obsession, the weight of terror bore down upon me, twisting my realization into a nightmarish horror that sank deeper with every heartbeat.

PROF. BEATRICE "What do you see Joe?"

JOE: "My five-year-old self is holding my mother's hand. I see her silhouette glowing in the sun's golden embrace, radiating youth and beauty. This is... this is my first memory of her, we are at the park, the grass is so ... so green... The breeze is blowing the back of her jet-black hair and... (pause) she's... mum is turning slowly towards me..."

January 1998.

My broken-hearted mother came to my house and in the evening, we took all the posters, cuttings, news cuttings, the United Nations betting slip, the certificates, collection of sci-fi tapes and put them in a heap in the back garden. I doused the junk with petrol, lit a match and watched as the flames began to lick the two giant oil paintings. They stared at me as the fire crackled in the evening sky night, the pictures screamed with the linseed oils, wood and trapped air–a symbolic scream. We burnt everything to do with the trash I had amassed. My life flashed before me, everything I'd done from as far back as I can remember to the present. My Mother commanded evil to leave the house and never to return.

*'Many of those who believed now came and openly confessed their evil deeds. A number who had practiced sorcery brought their scrolls together and burned them publicly. When they calculated the value of the scrolls, the total came to fifty thousand drachmas.' — Luke the physician* [2]

<u>Addict to delusion.</u>

"Addiction is passion's dark simulacrum and to the naïve observer, its perfect mimic. It resembles passion in its urgency and the promise of fulfillment, but its gifts are illusory. It's a black hole. The more you offer it, the more it demands."— Gabor Maté. [3]

Returning to work a week later, one long lonely night, I cried alone in my office, with flashbacks of everything I'd done to Eleanor and Lucas screaming with night terrors because of the atmosphere of the home. What I held inside me not only trapped me, but my household and I never made the connection. I should have known better as a father. I'd become a glutton, a thief, a liar, an addict to delusion, a hitchhiker on an interstellar odyssey of delusion, a shipwrecked star sailor entangled in lifeless, *wandering stars*.
Feeling ashamed and disgusted and with my mind in pieces, I wretched out the realm of my defilement, calling out to the God of my childhood. I didn't know how, yet I cried and spoke to God for half an hour with all my heart in the quality control room where I tested fluorescent lights and then went for a cigarette to the designated smoker's room. (Soundtrack.—'The Sound of Silence', Simon and Garfunkel, 1964).

<u>The Visitor.</u>

In the hushed corridors of a Carmelite monastery in 17th century Paris, a young monk moves with quiet grace, the soft swish of his broom echoing through the stone halls. With each stroke, he sweeps away dust and debris, but his mind and spirit are elsewhere, immersed in prayerful communion with the divine. Nearby monks and visitors from around Europe pause in their own duties, captivated by the aura of reverence that surrounds the humble figure. In the simplicity of his task, they feel the presence of God, as if the very act of sweeping has become a holy offering. Brother Lawrence, whose presence transforms the mundane into the sacred, becomes a beacon of spiritual devotion for all who encounter him. This is a time when faith permeates every aspect of life and Brother Lawrence embodies its essence with every movement. [4]

In the year 1998, approximately three centuries after the events in the monastery, a gentle soul was seated in a smoky room, his presence a quiet echo of the past.

I went for a cigarette and the usual crowd of colorful characters were in the smoker's room, the night workers who did not know what to make of me. Vince's son, an eccentric TV star who was potentially a millionaire in disguise, one minute the insured naked poster boy, whose picture had been photocopied and placed upon the pillars of the factory like a blind Samson, the next minute paranormal insurance investigator and then a person who had a close encounter of the fourth kind. They knew nothing of the recent events at home.

What was a millionaire doing on the night shift? I was a Martian to them. There were eight people all puffing in the smoking room. A new part-time worker was in their midst. He was not smoking. He seemed out of place, a 33-year-old black man with a calm and bright smile. I had walked in mid-way through their conversation,

"Well, *technically* the Romans crucified him."

"It was the Jews and bloody good riddance, they should've cut his head off."

The night shift pack aimed their comments at the young black man who remained calm and with a look of love, continued to speak with gentleness.

"No, *you—me—we* killed him—with *our sin*."

Many who had finished their cylindrical dummies cussed and left the room one by one.

"*Bullshit!*" proclaimed Steven. He was the last smoker to leave the room. Steven, whom I later nicknamed Legion, asked me, "Who do *you* say *Jesus* is, Joe?"

Remaining silent, it was just me and the young black man with a smile that pierced the smoky room. As he went to leave, I reached out to him, seeing that he was authentic. I asked him for his help. I told him about the situation that had happened in my life, he placed his hand on my shoulder and said, "Father, I thank You for this man." I felt a warm peace surround me.

*'But when it pleased God, who separated me from my Mother's womb and called me by his grace.'* [5]

His name was Emmanuel *(God with us),* a pastor in training from Akim Oda in Ghana. Emmanuel Ampofo Danso had the most beautiful, flawless coffee-colored skin that reflected the sands of space, time, and starlight. His teeth were the whitest I had ever seen, and he spoke in beautiful King James English. Over time, his eloquent speech gradually transformed my cockney slang into a more refined vernacular.

Throughout the week, I stuck to Emmanuel like glue as throughout the night he told me about Christ, the men in the Bible who had made mistakes and yet God redeemed them and how God as a Father loved me. It was about the third night as he spoke and I suddenly felt what was a warmth that fell upon me. I could *sense* Jesus. I knew He was real.

*'While Peter was still speaking these words, the Holy Spirit came on all who heard the message.'* [6]

An envelope of peace and love fell upon me and suddenly I loved! I wanted to share what I was hearing with the people on the night shift. I don't know why, but I loved them, it was amazing. My hate left and as I listened, love came in its place.

> *'So light up the fire and let the flame burn,*
> *Open the door, let Jesus return.'* [7]

It was a tangible, peaceful presence, a molten lava kind of love that flowed from my head to stomach to toe. Solid, accepting and beautiful, like I had finally found a home, what I had been looking for since I was a child. I was like a yellow chick hatching out of an egg and chirping for Papa, for Mama, for the first time. Deep tears from the depth of my being, I was transported back to love.

> *'Take seeds of His Spirit, let the fruit grow,*
> *Tell the people of Jesus, let His love show.'* [8]

I looked at my fellow workers, most of whom I did not like, and I felt consumed by love for them. I wanted to hug them, to share with them the incredible news I had just heard. It was real, it was amazing, and I wanted them to feel it too.

# In The Realm of the Holy Ghost.

PROF. VIRGIL: "Ah, my dear scholars, in the scholarly musings of Worthington, E. and his esteemed companions (et al.), we encounter a quartet of avenues through which the delicate dance of spiritual experiences is perceived. We have the divine rendezvous (a rendezvous with God, if you will, *religious spirituality*), the human waltz (*humanistic spirituality*), the nature ballet (*nature spirituality*) and the cosmic tango (*cosmic spirituality*). In each of these thought realms, spirituality takes center stage, intertwined and twirling with these entities, forging connections and weaving integrations like the steps of a grand ballroom affair." [9]

JOE: "*Four*? Wow. Yes, I guess this is the only true CE4—Close Encounter of the fourth kind, without the need for exotic technology, this is the only 'reality transformation' that one needs, a pure untainted reality. This is home, this is the realm of the Holy Ghost. This is the domain of love, the encounter with the Spirit of truth, the Comforter, the true Intercessor and Counselor."

Emmanuel, as a temporary worker who had come in to help General Electric with a large florescent order, would speak of the love of God and how once he used to work in a bank in Ghana and courted many women and forced his girlfriends to have abortions. He said that one day he happened to hear of a man speak of the love and forgiveness of God and it was upon hearing the words and love of Christ that he had an encounter that later led to his quest to train as a Pastor.

I had such love for this man. I'd only known him a short time, but the words that he shared with such purity and sincerity, I could not imagine his former life being what he had once said he was. I even remember saying to him that he should not share his past concerning women and abortions. He simply smiled and gently said in response, "It is for the glory of God that I am what I am by the grace of God and many hundreds of people will come to know the forgiveness and love offered to all."

Testimonies included how the Holy Spirit would speak to him and show him things of the past and things to come and how real the presence of Christ was. I gleaned everything that he had to share. I recall picking Emmanuel up in my red Fiat Uno and he would share with me how the Holy Spirit had told him I was on my way and which road to meet me at. The way that he spoke of a personal relationship with God was fresh to me and it made sense within.

On one car journey, we stopped for petrol. My petrol car key broke awkwardly in the petrol cap and I could not remove the key from within the cap. This had never happened before and I told Emmanuel as he sat in the passenger seat. He simply smiled, rose and said, "Thank You, Father." He placed his fingers above the cap and the broken key magnetically moved out. Then he sat in the car as if no big deal.

One night shift, where Emmanuel worked with six-to-eight-foot empty florescent glass tubes that were packed in a metal crate, containing about eighty of these unfilled tubes, one crate fell near him, missing him by a few centimeters. He breathed a sigh of calm relief and said, "Thank You, Father."

These falling glass lamps could have easily maimed or killed, yet this gentleman was a walking epitome of chill.

My brother, David was on leave from his army post in Kosovo and had sustained an injury on his knee that could make him fail a forthcoming practical health course and put him out of service for his application to become a military policeman. I brought Emmanuel to meet him, he placed his hand on his knee and the pain left instantly and enabled David to be healed and eventually pass his course. David acknowledged that had it not been for the prayer he would have failed.

Emmanuel was only at General Electric for two weeks and upon leaving he gave me the radio frequency of a station called Premier Radio, something that I would be eternally grateful for. The sermons, the songs, the teachings and the testimonies, all helped feed my spirit and I had the opportunity as a quality controller to listen during each quality check. Premier radio helped me to grow tremendously during those nights. Sometimes I would stand on a high perch with the huge metal doors open, watching the sunrise as I listened to beautiful music that gave me hope.

In mid-August 1998, Emmanuel and I embarked on a visit to KICC (Kingsway International Christian Centre) Church, once nestled on Waterden Road in the vibrant London Borough of Newham. As we stepped into the warehouse-turned-sanctuary, the air hummed with anticipation. A visiting African preacher, his voice resonating with passion and conviction, urged the congregation to open their Bibles and turn to Genesis 1:1, *'In the beginning, God...'* The words hung in the air, heavy with significance.

The preacher closed the Bible and with a long pause and a smile, began to speak of the life-speaking Creator. I was so moved by the simplicity and bliss of the exposition from that one sentence that as we embarked on a journey through the timeless verses of creation, I began to speak in an unknown language as the Spirit gave me utterance. It was a wonderful moment. I felt lifted. I felt light. I felt *connected*.

I found myself returning to the night shift and using the soothing power of singing and speaking in a beautiful and enigmatic language of sounds, which helped me transcend the moments of mental exhaustion.

PROF. VIRGIL: "Now, isn't it intriguing that the way we use our language—speaking in tongues, singing, praying—can provide us with a backstage pass to our brains? [10] It's like a choreographed dance, where the frontal lobe takes a brief respite, allowing the parietal region to take center stage. This region, my curious companions, deals with how we perceive ourselves in the grand play of existence. Now, permit me to introduce you to something known as the 'Voo sound' [11] — a discovery and practice by Peter Levine (though, as they say, there's nothing new under the sun).[12]

Apparently, the sound of vowels can awaken the vagus nerve, which acts as the ultimate telephone line connecting the brain and the body. Oh and have I mentioned the hum? Yes, the delightful hum, our very own brain's elixir mixer. Our hum can even whisper soothing messages to the vagus nerve, helping it monitor our heartbeat, blood pressure and the adventures of our stomach. It stirs up endorphins, those natural mood-lifters, making us feel as if we're floating on a cloud of joy. You might even call it a bit of reversed engineered 'somnium,' ushering in relaxation and sweet slumber."

# Chapter Sixteen

## Somnium

*"The most necessary practice in the spiritual life is the practice of the presence of God, whereby the soul finds her joy and contentment in His companionship, talking humbly and lovingly to Him always and at all times, without rule or system... to talk to God anytime with simplicity of heart."*

—*Brother Lawrence of the Resurrection.* [1]

In February 1998, amid the process of healing from my fractured relationship, my Father assumed the responsibility of renting out the rooms within my three-bedroom house. One of these rooms found a tenant in the form of Branislav, known simply as Brian, hailing from the heart of Bratislava, Slovakia. Another room was occupied by an Englishman named Trevor.

Brian possessed an aura of youthful charm, his demeanor marked by a captivating blend of boyish innocence and emotional depth. His expressive brown eyes conveyed a multitude of sentiments, a window into a soul capable of grappling with the most intricate tapestries of emotions and inner conflicts. He bore an appearance that was both attractive and approachable, his presence radiating an air of vulnerability and sincerity that drew people in.

Physically, Brian's form was a testament to his athletic endeavors, a lean and toned build that hinted at his history of engaging in physical pursuits of rock climbing and skateboarding. However, beneath his external strength lay a wellspring of unspoken emotions and internal struggles. His voice, using English as a second language, was a soothing cadence of measured words and held an undertone of quiet contemplation, mirroring the depths of his journey. Each syllable seemed to reflect the delicate balance between his suppressed feelings and the impending liberation they yearned for.

Before venturing into the role of an au pair, Brian had extended his compassion and patience working as a nurse within the walls of a mental unit in Bratislava. There, he used clay as a means of therapeutic connection, a patient craftsman sculpting both art and hope. This previous chapter in his life echoed in the tapestry of his character, infusing him with a profound understanding of the human psyche.

Brian's path to the U.K. was paved by a desire to escape the shadows of his estranged father's passing, seeking solace and renewal within a foreign land. Initially embarking on the role of an au pair, he soon traded the challenges of wrangling restless children for the trade of Peter, a painter and decorator with a singular leg. Through shared experiences, Brian and I forged a camaraderie that has woven itself into our collective memories.

Even now, we share laughter over the recollections of our early escapades. I vividly remember the night when Brian, his post-communist roots betraying him, saw police helicopters alight in the night sky, their flashing beams piercing the darkness. In his conviction, he feared deportation, a consequence of his perceived deviation from the confines of his au pair visa. Amid my amusement, I advised him to take refuge in a cupboard, the echoes of my laughter reverberating through the night.

Trevor, on the other hand, was not what he appeared to be. He bore a face resembling Roger Ram Jet, with his blonde hair and scattered freckles. Yet, his countenance held a veil of deception, an expression that seemed to conceal a web of lies. He projected an image of a professional businessman, but his reality told a different story. Struggling with alcoholism, he engaged in the questionable habit of opening my mail, amassing a collection of unpaid-for VHS horror films from Blockbusters and failing to meet his rent obligations. So, upon my instruction, my dad gave him a one-month notice in March. During that time, I had a dream that a strange, scruffy-looking man had burst into my bedroom, peering over me, but I had remained calm.

It was mid-March, that Trevor and his scruffy-looking six-foot dad, came into my house, drunk and on the warpath. I was in my bed asleep at 5pm. Brian was downstairs in the living room when an angry, disheveled man walked into the living room to accost who he thought was me. Brian looked at the angry man in disbelief and awe, "You look exactly like my dad!" he cried, which defused the ruffian.

"No, no, not him," replied Trevor, who redirected the neutralized inebriate upstairs to my room, where he burst into my door blocking the frame with his huge disposition. Trevor hurriedly emptied the contents of his unpaid rented room. Meanwhile, Brian in the living room was waiting for the sound of punches to rain down on me, once he had figured their wicked intent.

I cannot recall what I said, but I remember my dream fitting the description. I spoke calmly and peacefully. Then they both left in a hurry. Trevor, having not paid his rent, left his VHS collection behind and whilst a blissful Brian was still mesmerized by the visitation of his lookalike Papa, waved goodbye to the scruffy drunk, holding and pointing to a photo of his father, "Look! My dad is in this picture!" Brain, still smiling, further defused them as they punched a dent in my red Fiat Uno.

Brian came from a peaceful village in Bratislava and when he told me his turn of events, he pulled out a photo of his dad and it was indeed a spitting image of the ruffian. We could not stop laughing at God's sense of humor and retelling the story often.

I didn't rent the other room again. One April on an Easter night shift, before Brian slept in his room, he had spoken to God for the first time before going to sleep, "Jesus Christ, God, if you are real, reveal yourself to me."

It was in the same morning that Brian recounted his story that during the night he had a powerful dream. "I saw an obelisk of light and a face shining down on me, amid a beautiful trumpet sound from the blue sky. I cannot describe it, it was similar but far more beautiful than when a Windows computer boots up. [2/3] It was a vision set in the future: I was married, I saw her face and we were doing Christ's work." – His dream was in 1998.

Later that year, Brian returned to Slovakia. While enjoying the film soundtrack of 'Prince of Egypt' that I had gifted him for the plane ride back, he became convinced that he should go to Israel. Upon returning to Bratislava, he joined a Church fellowship where he shared his adventures in Enfield. However, his journey took another turn as he once again bid farewell to his friends and family, flying out to Israel. Unfortunately, upon arrival, he was detained due to missing documentation and promptly deported back to Slovakia on the same day. We still laugh about it together to this day.

Brian eventually became an award-winning journalist and was sent to the USA for voice training in news delivery. He also received training as a cameraman. In 2008, he married a Christian artist and became a pastor and children's TV producer upon returning to Slovakia.

Brian returned to visit a few years later and we went on a trip to Ireland, visiting the Giant's Causeway in County Antrim and camping nearby with the missionaries he had met in Slovakia. We still laugh today about one time on a caravan site when Brian, wearing light green cotton trousers that were short above his socks, was approached by two young children. In thick

Northern Irish accents, which we still hear today and laugh about when we recount the question, they asked, *'Hey, Mister! Are there them paddle pushers you're wearing?'*

Brian later reminded me of my trip to Bratislava shortly after that Ireland visit. I was there to teach a group of fifty children a different Bible story each day for their Bible camp. During one break, I oversaw those same fifty children on a grass playground. I had to come up with a game, so I said, with my Slovakian translator interpreting, "Okay, you must chase and try to catch me." I ran, zigzagging left and right. I was out of breath when five children caught me. I said, "Okay, okay, you've caught me, that's enough." However, without my translator, all fifty piled on top of me and each other, one by one. Brian humorously reminded me, as he picked up the dominoes, "Josef, if we're going to make a game, we need some rules."

*July 1999.*

*'If You Had My Love' - Jennifer Lopez*

Smitten by my encounter and in a deep state of meditation, my mind was renewed over time. I would improve my inner environment, thoughts, beliefs and emotions, slowly shifting my life as I found help from within that had come from above before time began. I would walk past machinery and the machinery would suddenly come to a halt. People did not know what to make of me and said that my aura had done that. I would place thirty pence into the food vending machine and £1.00 coins and free cans of coke would come out. It would only happen to me, no one else and on several occasions. I did not pay too much attention, it just seemed natural, but I was very aware of the presence of God.

Over the passage of years, the Indian Hindu workers of the night shift bestowed upon me the title of *Guru*. The Nigerians and Ghanaians, recognizing something deeper, referred to me as the *Man of God*. Among the Greek community, I became known as *Jesus*, while the trio of Sicilians affectionately called me *Padre Pio*. A Moroccan voice branded me an *Infidel*, while the English humorously labeled me *Numb Nut*, a term steeped in U.K. Street slang for playful mockery. These monikers, lighthearted as they were, captured the essence of our interactions. As time unfurled, my companions would confide in me, sharing their beliefs and revealing their traumas, even their own encounters with phenomena.

In return, I shared the story of my encounter with love, forging connections through our shared humanity. Our camaraderie, nurtured through the night, embodied a unique form of affection. The paradox was that as the years went by, my fellow nightshift workers shared their beliefs in Aliens, Nostradamus and their own experiences.

One night, my hands were full as I carried several white-coated glass lamps in my hand to be tested, but the door to the bridge to the other side was shut, so I said, "Angel, open the door for me, please," and sure enough, the door opened right on cue, enabling me to not drop a lamp. One Friday, when I went to collect Lucas (now four years old) from Hackney (the eastern corner of the sprawling metropolis of London) for my weekend with him, we sat on a bus and in front of us were two unoccupied seats. I told him, 'Lucas, in front of us are two angels.' One minute later, the bus stopped and a woman boarded, taking a seat in the empty row while holding a birdcage with two canaries inside!

I and two other Ghanaians and a Nigerian would meet nightly during our breaks and lunches as we would read, study, argue, share stories and debate.

As a quality controller, I had a room all to myself where I had a whiteboard and I would write with my marker pen one of the first things that I memorized that I found inspiring. It was as if the words jumped out of the page:

*'The Spirit gives life, the flesh profits nothing. The words I have spoken to you are spirit and they are life.'* [4]

Apart from a handful of GCSEs (General Certificate of Secondary Education) I didn't qualify my name and I was stuck in a job that often felt like penitentiary. It was all well and fine that angels were in the room with me, but be that as it may, I had a sense of better things than remaining on the night shift inspecting lights as a quality controller and making pizzas by day at Pizza Hut four times a week.

I then began to circle, underline, speak and exegeses the sentence to an invisible group of imaginary students as I shared the verse. I began to cry as I imagined seeing a class of students, but I had no idea how I would get this dream to become a reality.

General Electric USA was the place that humbled me. I could see the sacrifices of how hard my father worked, both hands holding a huge gunning appliance that would propel paint into clear glass six-foot and twelve-foot tubes amid a cacophony of factory chemical smells. Thousands of fluorescent lamps were coated in a few hours. With my father's arm muscles bulging, I witnessed the heavy labor of sweat he endured to provide for his family. Whilst dad worked permanent nights, mum worked at Ford Motors on rotating shifts, so I would sometimes wait for her at a different bus stop. She too worked and labored hard for her family, saving for her children, thus enabling all three sons to place deposits on their future homes. She had been working since the age of sixteen, since arriving from Sicily, having to learn English. She then lost her Mother in a lorry accident the same year. Together, mum and dad saved all that they had to purchase their first home in Albany Road in the mid-1970s before later moving a nearby street. I never truly understood their sacrifice, commitment, trauma and discipline until I became a man.

PROF. VIRGIL: "We consider the potency of spiritual discipline in assuaging distress. Indeed, spirituality and religion are bedrocks of human understanding. Your acute self-awareness appears to have gracefully guided you through the subtle nuances of therapeutic encounters, all while embracing the collective wisdom blossoming from the dynamic interplay between Emmanuel and yourself—a symphony orchestrated by the Santo Spirito, if you will."

Journal entry: 1$^{st\,of}$ October 2016.

Who am I?

As I reflect on the origins and influences shaping my self-concepts, I ponder their ongoing formation, potential distortions, and the journey towards maturity for alignment with my true self. Who am I? Why do I perceive the world in this way? What is my purpose on Earth, and how can I authentically express myself? How can I cultivate meaningful change in my thought patterns, and what experiences shaped my self-concept? What falsehoods have I accepted about myself and others? Ultimately, it seems we are all interconnected, yearning for fulfilling relationships. Love, recognition, warmth, and connection are universal desires, almost ingrained within us to seek unconditional positive regard.

PROF. VIRGIL: "Discovering who we truly are often involves unraveling the layers of societal conditioning, alongside our upbringing,

230

cultural influences, and personal experiences, while embracing the authenticity that lies beneath."

From early 1998, I attended Emmanuel's Church for six months, taking Lucas at the weekends with me from the age of two and a half. New to this charismatic scene, I thought that I was the only white Pentecostal member, thus shielded from a lot of things working nights. I enjoyed the sermons. They seemed spot on and related to whatever situation I found myself in and being the only white guy in an all-African Church didn't bother me at all. All I felt was love.

Emmanuel and I parted company in late 1998. As wonderful as that early exposure to the Pentecostal scene had been, it began to feel cumbersome and stunted. I would later join an Elim Church in Edmonton in mid-1998 that I attended until 2005. I last heard from Emmanuel Danso in 2006. He had returned to Ghana, married and had a daughter. However, in 2007, I received an obscure letter from his wife in Ghana stating, "Emmanuel has kicked the bucket." He had sadly died in the *Robert Mugabe Camps* evangelizing. I do not know the exact details, but I am grateful for the spiritual discipline, foundations and impact he made on my life and my family in 1998.

JOE: "I felt a sense of transcendence or connection to something beyond myself to begin to better understand my intrinsic resources for flourishing. I would feel a connection while engaging in meditation over scriptures, while exploring my primary attachment figures, aiding me to feel a connection in the acceptance of my human experience during my therapy."

PROF. BEATRICE: "Carl Rogers pointed out that there's this kind of indescribable, spiritual aspect to his connections with folks, especially when things get deep in their sessions: '*At those moments it seems that my inner spirit has reached out and touched the inner spirit of the other. Our relationship transcends itself and becomes a part of something larger. Profound growth and healing and energy are present.'"* [5]

Rogers's description of his transcendental experiences in counseling exemplifies the potential for spirituality and significant encounters for others and myself regardless of the topics explicitly being discussed in therapy. Such encounters are spiritual not because of the content they address or the framework they put on clients' lives, but because they are *'a living encounter with the fullness of existence.'* [6]

JOE: "A living encounter with the fullness of existence! Wow that's' beautiful!"

My teenage insecure attachments and ambivalence sought nourishment that departed from an upbringing of Catholicism to New Age teachings and then later turned lopsided to the charismatic circus of Pentecostalism and its legalism, tithing and cursing, along with its literalism and 'dualism' of separation of body and spirit, *"A view incorporating the idea that there can be two kinds of reality, one natural, material, or physical and the other supernatural, immaterial, or metaphysical."* [7]

The reality is that the presence of God is always with us, sometimes, I lose awareness of His presence. There is no separation between God and me. We simply exist as one.

*'I and My Father are One.'* [8]

*'... so that they may be One as We are One.'* [9]

*'I will ask the Father and He will give you another Advocate to be with you forever—the Spirit of Truth. The world cannot receive Him, because it neither sees Him nor knows Him. But you do know Him, for He abides with you and will be in you. I will not leave you as orphans. I will come to you. In a little while the world will see Me no more, but you will see Me. Because I*

*live, you also will live. On that day you will know that I am in My Father and you are in Me and I am in you.'* [10]

## New Identity

However, as was in my case the trap with many denominations and even therapeutic theory, is that it can be taken too literally as a formula to treat problems and emotions, without releasing or exploring the inner world. Adolescence was as it is for all of us, a challenging, biological and social developmental process and I had no one to support or understand my individualized and idiosyncratic religious or new age context, which influenced my intrapsychic worlds. Furthermore, there are key psychological changes that occur during this period *"which involves the formation of a new identity."* [11]

Emmanuel's Pentecostal scene was great at first. I was grateful for the grounding I received, but I began to swiftly feel that I had outgrown it in addition I found that while I sought to unpack my new identity, the setting it instigated was legalistic and littered with work-based mindsets, in the sense that you must attend prayer meetings and the mandatory tithing to be a member of the Church felt very un-liberating. I attended Emmanuel's Church for about six months. After praying, I had a dream of where my next Church journey was to be.

I visited a handful of churches in Enfield and found them to be as dead as a dodo in terms of vibrancy, energy and passion and felt they lacked soul, but equally if not more so as legalistic, plastic and detached from the awareness and presence of Christ. I hated hearing about the workings and mindset of a Long-Distance Relationship, a deity-like answering machine that wavers in his presence due to our sins, flipping moods like a switch, bipolar-like, after our missteps. It's like some Santa Claus keeping tabs one day, then morphing into a thunderbolt-throwing Zeus the next.

Or the lament of the story of Job under an old covenant pre-Christ reality and belief that God inflicts and permits disease which went into direct violation of John 10:10,

*'The thief does not come except to steal and to kill and to destroy.*

*I have come that they may have life and that they may have it more*

*abundantly.'*

### Tramway.

I told God that I wanted out and I began to pray to find another Church. I was beginning to lose hope of finding some like-minded believers. One night, God gave me a dream of a Church and I picked up the Yellow Pages and began to look for churches within my area. 'Tramway Elim Fellowship' [12] was in the book and I rang. I was surprised to hear the voice of an English lady with a Liverpool accent whose name was Helen. I was surprised to hear of a Pentecostal with an accent other than that of a Ghanaian. I discovered I was not the only white, tongue-speaking mystic.

Upon attending the Church service on Sunday, it was per spec to the dream that I'd had the week before, from the entrance to the door and even the person who greeted me. I knew that I had found the place that I needed to be. A visiting Scottish speaker, Alex Tee, shared the testimonies of churches he had planted in Kenya and all the things that God was doing in his outreach missions. The Church was pastored by Terry Mortimer and associate Pastor in training, Vinney Davenport, whose wife Helen had answered the phone earlier during the week. That same evening, I brought my mother to visit for the evening service, where she heard the word and later went up for prayer. Alex Tee prayed for her and placed his hand on her forehead and she felt the Holy Spirit's heat enter her body. In that week, she began to write poems and songs in an unstoppable flow and over the next two years, both my two younger brothers and dad had their own experiences. Even Lucas's mother attended once and had an experience saying that *Christ had let her into his heart.*

Both Terry and Vinnie were remarkable expositors and often they would change their flow and direction, dispensing with their prepared notes. It was a real season of joy, we even had a visiting speaker, Pastor Miguel Angel Escobar, from Chile. During his sermons, including one attended by Helen, a peculiar phenomenon occurred, some people received gold fillings in their teeth.

I even took photos of Helen's new gold tooth. Naturally, some questioned why God would do this, replacing amalgam fillings with gold. Some offered explanations, such as 'If God can change water to wine, then He can change base metal into gold,' or the light-hearted suggestion that 'Gold is what the streets of Heaven are paved with and perhaps Angels from that dimension were sweeping the floor as the man from Chile spoke.'

After pondering on this and researching that amalgam is a mixture of metals, consisting of liquid (elemental) mercury and a powdered alloy composed of silver, tin and copper. Approximately half (50%) of dental amalgam is elemental mercury by weight. The chemical properties of elemental mercury allow it to react with and bind together the silver/copper/tin alloy particles to form an amalgam.

It appears to me that God has a way of removing poison or toxic mindsets and revealing the gold within us.

*'Instead of bronze I will bring gold and instead of iron I will bring silver and instead of wood, bronze and instead of stones, iron. And I will make peace your administrators and righteousness your overseers.'* [13]

Many young believers can follow these signs and wonders, get a puffed-up ego and lose their grounding and understanding in their God-given identity of righteousness. I no longer follow signs, signs follow me. 'And *these signs shall follow* them that believe. They went forth and preached everywhere, the Lord working with them and *confirming the word with signs following.'* [14]

I stayed at Tramway (Edmonton, North London) from the winter of 1998 to early 2005, immersing myself in teaching Sunday School. In 1999, I led mission teams in Albania, where Tirana, the capital, was amidst a tumultuous transition from communism to democracy. Despite the backdrop of political unrest and economic instability, characterized by colorful buildings and lively street markets, Albania's countryside offered rugged landscapes with rolling hills, picturesque valleys and traditional villages. Here, wild dogs roamed freely amidst the rustic tranquility, reflecting the untamed spirit of the region. During my time in Albania, I shared the good news, delivered food parcels and walked daily with cows, meeting humble farmers and embracing an organic lifestyle. It was then that I stumbled upon a dusty Bible, where someone had scribbled, 'I saw God smile at me through a child today.' That moment changed my perception of God, making Him even more present and I couldn't help but cry.

My journey continued with mission trips to Belfast, Slovakia and Lebanon, directing drama and adding a monthly preaching slot. In one of my first sermons, I passionately delivered a fiery message to the congregation, complete with hellfire imagery, but I'm grateful for the pastor who gently took me to one side and said, 'Joe be a shepherd, not a butcher.' Additionally,

I had the pleasure of writing scripts and an album that was performed to packed-out services.

These were truly beautiful times of the formation of understanding my new identity, not adding to it, or receiving upgrades or new levels, but *a journey of revealing what was already within.*

The first rap track I wrote and sang about Joseph's (Gen 37) life had a prophetic quality to it.

20 Silver Shekels.

I'm a boy from my father's hood,
My colors got me, mis, mis,
misunderstood
My own kin stitched me up,
Got me black and blue and cut.
I'm living in exchange for
scapegoat colors blood.
Now I'm up to my ankles and
knees in innocent mud.
Ain't bringing back no word for
me.
Into this place I go, not so boldly.
You see my brethren have sold
me,
I've been—Betrayed and stripped
of my destiny,
20 shekels —they— put a price
on me,

What they tell father is a mystery.
My spirit's jumping,
Got my blood pumping,
My future's stumping,
But I'm still jumping.

*CHORUS*
20 silver shekels put a price on
me,
But I know this ain't my destiny.
I'm coming out, out of slavery,
No victim mentality.

I came to my own, my own
received me not,
sold into slavery, rejected and
forgot,
But I'm gonna make it, I'm
holding on,

Though I don't understand
what's going on,
*'What's going on?'*
This ain't no Marvin Gaye,
But I know I'll find a way,
Into a foreign land now I go,
With only a dream and faith to
show,
Egypt's calling me,
Sun baking down on me
Sun-kissed, chains and handcuffs,
The fed master calling my bluff,
Holding me down with cords of
oppression,
But I stand firm in my
confession,
I'm a boy from the hood
misunderstood,
But I know God meant it for
good.

*Go to the chorus.*

So far away, the light of day.
This ain't the place I wanna stay.
Oh Lord, I feel so alone,
Daylight come and me wan' go
home.

Potiphar me serve, me don't
deserve.
Me gonna swerve this is absurd,
A thousand voices begging to be
heard,
My voice drowned out even
though I shout,
Temptation calling me,
Foreign gods surround me,
Lipstick, powder and paint,
If me look in the mirror, me
gonna faint,
Everything crisp with the hair
lacquer,
No way man it Chaka — Chaka!
If I eat all this food, it gonna get
me fatter.
Oh, Lord, get me out — out of
this gutter.

*Chorus + extension*

This ain't no conspiracy, I'm
coming out,
Out of slavery,
The Lord is here, here with me.
My savior has set me free.
The Lord's gonna come get me.

This ain't no conspiracy,                    My savior has set me free.

PROF. BERNARD: "Daylight come and me wan' go home' — It seems like writing music and drama have been and continue to be very therapeutic for you. They combine creativity and fellowship, both of which are beneficial for the mind and overall mental health. It sounds like they bring you joy and fill your mind with positivity."

PROF VIRGIL: "'*Dio ha scelto di far conoscere tra i Gentili le gloriose ricchezze di questo mistero, che è Cristo in voi, la speranza della gloria.*' – 'God has chosen to make known among the Gentiles the glorious riches of this mystery, which is Christ in you, the hope of glory.'" [15]

### Up to my ankles and knees

I met my first wife at Tramway, but that's a different chapter in my nine wilderness years. Unfortunately, not all stories have happy endings. I realized that I didn't love myself as much as I should have, allowing myself to be belittled. When the leadership at Tramway changed, it marked the beginning of what I'd call 'Ego-Wars.' I observed immaturity not only in the Church but also in its system, perpetuated by egotistical leaders behind the scenes who gossiped and sought power. A new Pastor arrived at Tramway and ultimately, it lost the vitality I once knew. I decided to leave, never to return to the mechanical institution that some churches have become.

Although I am eternally grateful that both my parents and my brothers came to 'experientially know' Christ around that time, there was a deeper significance to this spiritual awakening. Even my Granddad, once considered hard-hearted and misunderstood, whose strained relationship with my mother caused her to draw comparisons that stung, found solace in a transformative experience. I understood that my Granddad had been deeply affected by the trauma of war and the loss of his wife. However, it was my brother David, also a soldier, who led him to Jesus before Nonno passed away on Christmas Eve, 2004, just a day before his birthday. As a family, we continued to grow and evolve on our journey, guided by the Holy Spirit with each step of faith we took. This journey led us to a state of transcendence, where we fully realized our true selves through our understanding and relationship with Christ. Through this process, we deepened our understanding of ourselves and our place in the world, all while being guided by the Holy Spirit. In therapeutic terms, self-actualization is often defined as a state or process in which an individual reaches a state of transcendence and fully realizes their true self. By remaining open to the guidance of the Holy Spirit, we recognized that, like clay in the hands of the potter, we were taking steps of faith towards this process of self-actualization and the renewal of our minds.

"After saying this, he [Jesus] spit on the ground, made some mud with the saliva and put it on the man's eyes." [16]

# Chapter Seventeen

## Step of Faith

April 2017, NLM University.

PROF. BEATRICE: "The Actualizing Tendency, y'see, it's like the real cornerstone of Person-Centered Counseling. It's this drive that Carl Rogers thought every living thing possesses. The deal is, all organisms have this one big urge to grow, keep going, and make themselves even better." [1]

Rogers believed that all living organisms had one basic tendency and striving. No matter what the conditions, the organism would try to grow, develop and enhance the experience of the organism and at the very least, maintain it. This means that we are always trying to grow and develop to the best of our ability in whatever circumstances that we find ourselves in, considering our self-concept. Potentially damaged but ever-present, Rogers believed that 'The Actualizing Tendency' can, of course, be thwarted or warped, but it cannot be destroyed without destroying the organism. [2]

This is to say, that the actualizing tendency can be impacted and thwarted by the conditions around us, but it cannot ultimately be destroyed. This means that Rogers believes the Actualizing Tendency is ALWAYS present and in action as long as we are alive.

Within me, the 'Actualizing tendency' of wanting to find and be me, to be liked and affirmed and to do good was denied and I began to believe more lies, that English people and their system did not allow me to be my truest self because they and it didn't defend me.

In its earliest origins, the core self is forged in the attunement contact with the parent. Its healthy development needs the atmosphere of what Carl Rogers had called, "Unconditional Positive Regard." It requires that the adult world understands and accepts as valid the child's feelings, from which kernel the core self will grow.

*"A child taught to still the voice of her innermost feelings and thoughts assumes automatically that there is something shameful about them and therefore about her very self." – Gabor Maté* [3]

Over time, through the help of my cohort and counseling, I discovered core conditions that facilitated a transformation in the way I thought and felt about myself. Counselors, in theory, facilitate this through *Unconditional Positive Regard*, a process that can be likened to a therapeutic puzzle slowly revealing another part of me, pointing me toward my true organismic self — the essence of my identity, values and experiences shaping my thoughts, behaviors and emotions and embodying my authentic, integrated expression.

I understand that to comprehend others, I must first understand myself. I aspire to overcome any remnants of the giants I once wrestled with, loneliness, fear, rejection, distrust and lack of confidence. My goal is to remain in tune with myself and serve as a vessel of communication that fosters deep connections between people. One of my cohort members, Pat, aptly remarked, *'Change how you feel, for life is a stream of boundless adventure.'* Counseling, in many ways, is like holding up a mirror to oneself, offering insights into our emotions, thoughts and behaviors. It allows us to see ourselves more clearly as we renew our mind to the truth of who we are.

However, back in time, 2003 seven years at General Electric came and went. I wish I could say that I used the time wisely, it was a place of growth, endurance and character-building. It was the place where I resisted, cried and died. Habits were broken and new ones spoken. I wasn't consistent but love is consistent. I loved the presence of the Holy Spirit.

<u>Life is a stream of boundless adventure.</u>

As a quality controller, I would continue to write with my marker pen. I would imagine teaching classes, in another room there was a twelve-foot by twelve-foot round sphere used to test the luminosity and conductivity of the lights. It was coated in special pure snowy paint on the inside with a hollow echo chamber into which fluorescent lamps went to be tested. I would often walk up the three steps into this sphere-shaped landing module, imagining that I was speaking edifying words to many people, as my voice echoed in its chamber. At the same time, I would cry. There was a desire in my heart. Something ignited within. I colluded with negative feelings and some feelings can lie to us, I felt stuck in time, without a decent qualification, experience, or confidence, but then a still small voice of hope rose from within and asked, *'Who qualifies you?'*

*'You do!'* I cried.

*'Well, step out and watch what I will do for you.'*

One night, after many discussions and conversations with my Pastor at Tramway, I handed in my notice on Wednesday, the 22nd of October 2003, having stepped out in faith to work for a charity called N-Flame, which delivered PSHE lessons in North London schools.

Coincidentally, two other people on the night shift (unbeknownst to each other) had also handed in their notice the same week. One, also a quality controller from the compact department, resigned to work in a wine bar. Another worker, the one who said, 'They should have chopped Jesus's head off,' had secured employment to work at Greggs the bakery.

To me, this served as confirmation that I was on the right path to leave, especially considering my familiarity with the story of Joseph from Genesis. The prisoners who had kept company with Joseph in prison included a butler who poured wine into Pharaoh's cup and a baker who, unfortunately, lost his head after displeasing Pharaoh. What were the odds of such a parallel?

Seven was symbolic in ancient Near Eastern and Israelite culture and literature. It communicated a sense of 'fullness' or 'completeness' and I had spent seven years in the shadows of the night crafting lights, having shared my genuine encounter with every other worker over those seven years. Some mocked me but then loved me. Many were sad that I was leaving.

I kissed, hugged and blessed every single man and woman on the night of my goodbye. Steven aka *Legion*, who had inadvertently acted like sandpaper, who had cursed and mocked me for years when I had shown him love, was sad that I was going, but they had seen a life transformed from a mess to a message.

**ATTENTION OF**

Human Resources                                    Joe T

General Electric USA,

Lincoln Road                                       Clock Number THX*1138

Quality Control Dept                               Department Nightshift Linear

NCC-1701

ENFIELD

EN ***


Wednesday 22$^{nd}$ $^{of}$ October 2003


*Dear Sirs,*

*After seven wonderful life-changing years at General Electric Company*
*working as a Quality Control Nightshift, I am hereby giving a week and a day's*
*notice of resignation. I will finish my last night on Friday 31$^{st}$ $^{of}$ October at*
*2:45am. I will clock out for the final time and hand in my security entrance pass.*
*Please, can the correct documentation, final pay slip and any other data be given*
*to me as soon as possible? On Friday 31$^{st}$ $^{of}$ October 2003, I shall walk out and*
*kneel at the iron gates of GE and thank God that though I came to many as an*
*alien and an enigma, I received the light in a place where we make lights amid*
*hidden gems and characters. He indeed has a sense of humor. I am moving to*
*pastures new and will be the brightest light GE ever played a part in making.*
*Once again, thank you for employing me and playing a part in my destiny.*


*Yours Sincerely,*
*Joe Tagliarini*


## Lebanon.


Sponsored in part by Tramway and living by the tenanted rental of
my two rooms, I began to work for N-Flame, going into London school
lunch-time clubs and classes, delivering themes on euthanasia, the sanctity
of life and the Gospel. N-Flame would also allow me to go to Beirut in
Lebanon for ten days to deliver the same lessons and missions in an
international school.

In April 2003, in Lebanon, I encountered a twelve-year-old boy who had drawn pictures of buildings being blown up by suicide bombers and planes crashing into buildings. He boasted that he wanted to do the same in the future. To shock him into realizing the gravity of his words, I scrunched up his drawing, but he only laughed at me, and my actions seemed to fuel his fascination with violence. Reflecting on the incident, I can't help but wonder what growing up in a nation where occasional bombings from neighboring countries serve as a reminder to live by 'an eye for an eye, a tooth for a tooth' does to a child.

In August 2004, I entered into my first marriage and thereafter secured a job as a teaching assistant in North London, where I formerly ran lunchtime clubs with the Christian Charity Nflame. I worked at the same school for fourteen years, in what was then the fourth-largest secondary school in London.

Over time, I climbed the ranks from teaching assistant to learning mentor to qualified therapist. Each day, I worked with challenging students who struggled with low self-esteem, anger issues and challenging home lives, many of whom reminded me of myself. I worked with gangs, fatherless children, traumatized individuals, those with anger issues, students who claimed to have seen ghosts and the misunderstood on a one-on-one basis and in group settings. They felt like my family and I even developed unique self-esteem resources and sent them off to be printed when I set up a small business venture to support the teenagers I worked with. They loved the decks and together we learned key therapeutic words and created narratives of self-exploration, aiming to make them think outside of the box.

# The Scarecrows

*"'If I only had a brain.' Harold Arlen and E.Y. Harburg prophesying the man-made global warming movement."*
*– Joe Tagliarini*

During my collaboration with school psychologists, I was surprised to discover that a well-regarded and respected psychologist believed that the Earth was overpopulated and that a virus might be necessary to reduce the human population for the sake of sustainability. Encountering such a negative perspective, especially among educational psychologists, was concerning.

Unfortunately, certain education systems do not encourage future generations to foster a culture of critical thinking or provide practical solutions. They advocate going green to save the world from complete doom, yet we have a generation of young people who passionately champion environmental causes and identity politics, but can't even be bothered to make their bed in the morning and know very little about taking responsibility. They stand tall in their convictions but lack the substance to truly protect the fields of their own future.

Enter the Greta Grumble Apocalyptic Gang, those who glue themselves to the motorway, ignorantly ignoring their former Greenpeace co-founder, Dr. Patrick Moore. Moore states that if Net Zero is successful, half the population would die of starvation, "If we banned fossil fuels, agricultural production would collapse. People will begin to starve and half the population will die in a very short period of time." [4]

Meanwhile, governments and corporations, willfully ignored by mainstream media that is full of slothful morons and freemasons promoting confusion and delusion, exploit the green agenda by raising oil prices on diluted fuels. Furthermore, complete demonic organizations aim to usher in a new age where they have patented and manipulated seeds and crops. [5]

## The Perfect Cube.

When discussing the overcrowding ideology, let's put the issue into perspective. Consider that the state of Texas is the second-largest state in the United States, covering approximately 268,597 square miles (695,662 square kilometers.

The number of people that could fit into the state of Texas would depend on factors such as population density and space requirements. Assuming a population density similar to New York City, with approximately 27,000 people per square mile, the entire world's population could fit into the state of Texas with some room to spare. [6/7]

With a population of around 67 million in 2021, the land mass of buildings in the UK accounted for approximately 10.6% of the land area in 2011, which is equivalent to around 44,000 square kilometers or 17,000 square miles, thus each person in the UK could have approximately 655 square meters or 7,050 square feet of land and space. [8/9]

However, I'm not advocating for this, as I do value my personal space. These scenarios are hypothetical and would require significant planning and infrastructure to accommodate such large populations in one area.

A spiritual revelation, offering solutions and inspiration, along with creative thinking literally outside of the box, can be found in the book of Revelation, as explained by Randy Alcorn, the founder and director of Eternal Perspective Ministries, in his work 'Heaven.' The city's precise dimensions were meticulously measured by an angel and are reported to be 12,000 stadia, equivalent to 1,400 miles or 2,200 kilometers in length, width and height (Revelation 21:15-16). While these proportions may carry symbolic significance, it's worth noting that Scripture specifies that these dimensions are presented in 'human measurements' (Revelation 21:17). If the city indeed possesses these dimensions (and I have no reason to doubt it), what more convincing proof could God provide?

Imagine a city of this magnitude, placed at the heart of the United States, spanning from Canada to Mexico and from the Appalachian Mountains to the California border. The New Jerusalem offers an astonishing abundance of square footage.

Even more remarkable is the city's towering height of 1,400 miles. Some interpretations suggest that this represents the reach of the city's tallest spires and towers, surpassing the height of other structures. If this interpretation holds true, it resembles a *pyramid* more than a cube.

No concerns arise about Heaven becoming overcrowded. The ground level of the city alone covers nearly two million square miles—forty times the size of England and fifteen thousand times larger than London. It dwarfs France, Germany and India in size. And remember this only accounts for the ground level.

Considering the dimensions of a 1,400-mile cube and assuming that the city comprises multiple levels (although we cannot be certain), with each story being a generous twelve feet high, the city could potentially accommodate over 600,000 stories. If these stories were on different levels, it could accommodate billions of people within New Jerusalem, providing ample square miles per individual. [10]

Imagine if we had an academy that taught young minds that there are no limits. As beings created in the image of God, instead of promoting and perpetuating doom, gloom and apocalyptic narratives, they could be inspired to continue stewarding the planet, finding new ways of technology and solutions that do not cripple people.

## Academy.

One day, when the school appointed a new Headmistress, whose vision was to rearrange the landscape and make the school into an academy, she had the learning mentor's post deleted and I had to reapply and interview for the new position of counselor. However, I had favor with one of the senior leaders, Mr. Les Rocket, (real name!) who had promoted me each step of the years. I later found out that he knew of my past involvement in insurance and that I had become a Christian and he thought I was a genius.

I secured the position of Counselor in training in 2012 and was sent to NLM University in Tottenham to begin my four-year training. (I'd like to say that it's a Shakespearean village where Princess Di used to go to walk the Queen's corgis too, but alas it's a bit more gangster than that). For the next two years, I fought tooth and nail. I thought I knew it all. I was a part-fundamentalist who had seen my share of miracles and phenomena. What the world needs is dogma and repentance. What a prick in the goads I was.

Life will not be all blue skies and rainbows. The dog will bite. The bee will sting. The university years were one of growth and further discovery, but with every step of the way, marriage, ill-health and hostile wombs afflicted and blurred the passage of time.

Yes, my spiritual encounter with Christ was real and tangible. Yes, I had seen miracles and phenomena, but somewhere along the way I was burnt out and wounded.

November 2023.

*Soundtrack, "Flowers" by Miley Cyrus, the most streamed song of November 2023.*

I discovered a hill in Chiang Dao, Thailand and rode my hired motorbike to the summit. Unaware of the existence of rubber trees, known as 'Hevea brasiliensis' or 'ton yang' in the Thai language, I was pleasantly surprised by the breathtaking view that instilled a sense of freedom in me. I found myself surrounded by lush greens and soothing blues, sipping on coconut water and inhaling the exotic scents of spices and oils. I was in the Land of Smiles once more. As I gazed upon this paradise, the sun kissed my skin and I reminisced about my second visit when I marked the completion of my fourth tattoo, this time featuring delicate flowers, a long-awaited addition to my bucket list.

When I first embarked on my spiritual journey, I had a knack for memorizing Scripture. I endlessly quoted verses verbatim. Every sentence I uttered or wrote had to be backed up with a specific passage. There were moments of cognitive dissonance, where I couldn't express love to someone without citing a verse reference or telling them that God loves them but requires them to do XYZ first. I was swinging between two trees, 'The tree of life and the tree of the knowledge of good and evil.' Yet, something deep within me knew that this was not the heart of God the Father, nor the true face of Christ, or the essence of the Holy Spirit. Oh, what bondage!

"It is finished," said Jesus as He hung cursed from a tree. 'Christ hath redeemed us from the curse of the law, being made a curse for us, for it is written, *cursed is every one that hangeth on a tree.*' (Galatians 3:13). Jesus took upon Himself the curse of sin and the penalty of the law on behalf of believers, providing redemption and salvation. Did I receive the Spirit by believing what I heard, or by following hoops, rules, syntax and law? *11*

Jenelle from New Braunfels, Texas. "Well, Joe, you know, religion can sometimes get all tangled up in its rules and such, but when it comes down to it, God is all about love and wisdom. It's like we're sittin' under a cozy quilt and at first, we might see some rough patches and colors that don't quite match. But as we start to see things from a different angle, we realize there's a real beauty underneath it all. Love, my friend, that's the heart of it all. It's like God's love is this beautiful symphony, orchestrating everything just perfectly."

I eventually saw that for every literal concept I tightly gripped from Scripture, I would be challenged by another dogmatic voice with his or her literal scripture in hand, which seemed to contradict the scripture I was gripping. It wasn't the voice of God, it wasn't the voice of the devil—it was the voice of religious dogma.

I began to realize that many can turn the Bible into their version of the Tower of Babel, scattering all who read it into different camps of belief and denominations. This results in endless divisions where nobody can hear each other because we worship the denominational language we choose to speak.

Thankfully, the Holy Spirit started tutoring and stimulating me to loosen my grip on human language. I dislike it when people say that they are *addicted to Jesus*, I understand in one respect what they mean, but we are not called to be church junkies, especially after I realized I had developed a language and miracles addiction mixed with cognitive dissonance, which was dumbing down my spiritual growth and journey. I don't need to smuggle Jesus into anything; He already is, was and is to come.

As individuals with addictive behaviors, the theory suggests that our orbitofrontal cortex and its associated neurological systems have been deceived from childhood onwards into prioritizing false desires over genuine needs. This phenomenon is known as 'salience attribution'—the process by which specific stimuli selectively capture one's attention, with a heightened focus on various triggers, often linked to dopamine release and motivational drive. [11,12,13,14] Consequently,

behavioral addicts experience a sense of desperation and an urgent need to satisfy these desires immediately, as if they were truly indispensable. — The Holy Spirit intervened to initiate my healing process, guiding me to shift my focus from the literalism and language of men to the love and light of God, for it is, as Dante said, "L'amor che move il sole e l'altre stelle." [15] — It is love that moves the sun and other stars.

However, before that, there would be a chapter and battle with the counterfeit new ages, therapeutic boundaries and a journey of awakenings.

PROF. BEATRICE: "What do you see, Joe?"

To all those who are looking for home. It's okay to get lost along the way, for to be lost indicates you have a home to go to, what that looks and feels like is a journey of the mystery revealed.

To the Ecclesia, thank you for showing me the path.
For my parents whose love, sacrifice and humor live within me.

When you fall, get up, dust yourself off and apologize to the dirt for forgetting your position in this world! You are the author of your own autobiography, your story is epic! You've only begun to write the most breathtaking chapters!

— Pete Cabrera Jr

# Interlude

PROF. BEATRICE: *(Whispering)* "What do you see Joe?"

JOE: "My five-year-old self is holding my mother's hand... I see her silhouette glowing in the sun's golden embrace, radiating youth and beauty. This is—this is—my first memory of her. We are at the park, so green... The breeze is blowing the back of her jet-black hair and she's—she's—mum is turning slowly towards me..."

The recognition of trauma marks the genesis of resilience because it signifies a departure from denial and evasion of emotions. Resilience blossoms through nurturing this awareness, acknowledging and embracing the wounded facets of ourselves and tending to them. Amidst this expedition, diverse avenues and techniques pave the way to finding solace, yet it starts with acknowledgment and self-understanding. Self-compassion becomes the gentle hand that guides us through the labyrinth of our pain, offering understanding, kindness and forgiveness to ourselves as we navigate the depths of our experiences. It is in extending this compassion inward that we build the foundation upon which true healing and resilience can thrive.

*"I suppose that since most of our hurts come through relationships, so will our healing and I know that grace rarely makes sense for those looking in from the outside."* — *Paul Young.* [1]

We arrive in this world intimately connected to our instincts, our visceral compass guiding us through life's labyrinth. However, when the weight of trauma overwhelms and the solace of support eludes, a defense mechanism emerges—detachment from our emotions until our authentic selves fade into obscurity.

Employing free association—a method that unearths genuine thoughts, memories and emotions by articulating unfiltered musings—The Reluctant Counselor, Volume 2 embarks on a journey through time, knitting together past, present and future to unveil the intricate web of my cognitive processes. Revisiting this journal, I confront the discomfort of clarifying thoughts and delving into shadowy recesses, yet find solace and release in the process.

As we navigate this introspective voyage, it becomes evident that shepherding ourselves through the labyrinth of our minds is not merely a task but a profound act of self-compassion and understanding.

## Shepherd

You don't need to be a follower of organized religion, attend church services, or listen to sermons. It's okay if these pursuits aren't your preferred way to start your day, like a classic vanilla latte or a cozy gingerbread treat. I've been right where you are, feeling the urge to snap at the world of institutions.

Yet, we must steer clear of belittling those who find solace in these practices by labeling them as mere 'sheeple' or by speaking ill of pastors and ministers. While a few may tarnish the reputation, the majority in these roles have genuine intentions, seeking neither harm nor manipulation.

It's natural to carry disappointment from a negative church experience, but it's crucial not to let it consume you, monopolizing your thoughts. Keep in mind that most church attendees are driven by kindness and good intentions. Perhaps, much like my own journey, your grievances lie less with others and more with a former version of yourself. Disappointment is not a fruit of the Spirit. The Trinity always has a better plan. –"Hope does not disappoint us, because God has poured out His love into our hearts through the Holy Spirit, whom He has given us." – Romans 5:5 Berean Bible.

Your feelings are valid and it's understandable to have reservations. But consider the possibility that, just like your preferences, your perspective has evolved. Channel your emotions towards growth rather than resentment.

I grew tired of hearing people bash churches and Christianity in a shallow manner, although I will wholeheartedly state, that Christ did not come to make a religion *nor was he a Christian.* [2/3/4/5/6]

Connecting to God, emotional comfort, spiritual development, time for contemplation and reflection, the presence of the Holy Spirit, growing closer to Jesus and community are 7 key aspects that can significantly contribute to a meaningful church experience.

Constructive criticism is one thing, but constant mockery and negativity are not helpful or productive. I realize that leaving a certain type of church can be challenging, but let's shift our focus to finding positivity and saying 'amen' to things that we do agree with, rather than simply saying 'no.' After all, we are all under the same divine insurance policy.

To the Ecclesia, thank you for showing me the path.
For my parents whose love, sacrifice and humor live within me.

258

And in the words of St. Paul to Timothy '… because we trust in the living God, who is *the* Savior of all men, *especially of those who believe.*' [7]

## Divine and Heavenly Insurance Policy.

We have a divine and heavenly insurance policy, which is the word of God, we are backed by angelic forces that come to our aid when we invoke the name of Jesus. We have security in our Father's faithfulness. He has never been defeated in battle and can never be defeated.

In September of 2003, one month after waving goodbye to General Electric USA, I began working for a Christian charity called N-Flame, going into School lunch-time clubs and delivering life skills workshops for students. This later allowed me to go to Lebanon and briefly work in a Muslim school. Working with N-Flame was a faith venture. The Lord blessed me for it, having rented out the other two rooms in my house and receiving sponsorship from Tramway in Edmonton to do missions. It was there that I met my wife-to-be, at Tramway, one evening in mid-2003 whilst giving my testimony and we married in August 2004.

After gaining experience working for the charity, it became apparent that missions and sponsorship were not going to pay my bills in the long term. So, I juggled several jobs, in addition to working as a waiter, I also went to work as a checkout operator in a supermarket, whilst at the same time attending university to learn how to become a Primary School Teacher.

Math has never been my strong point, no patience, let alone to teach it to others. Shortly after, in December 2004, I was fortunate enough to apply and acquire the position as a Teaching Assistant at one of the schools where I'd worked in the lunchtime clubs, helping challenging students with low self-esteem, anger issues and home life challenges. As I began working closely with these students in my new role, I couldn't help but see reflections of my own struggles mirrored in theirs, tapping into my own inner child. For instance, there were students who struggled with expressing their emotions constructively, much like I did when I was their age. Others faced similar family issues that I had experienced growing up. Recognizing these parallels between my inner child's experiences and the challenges these students were grappling with allowed me to empathize with them on a deeper level. It also motivated me to find effective ways to support them in overcoming their obstacles and building confidence in themselves.

From there, over time, I was promoted from behavioral mentor to learning mentor and my gift to the youth was evident to all, before being sent to University to train as psychotherapist.

### Return to sender

My marriage in August 2004, however, would prove to be one I was ill-prepared for, with frequent infirmities exacerbated by my wife's childhood traumas, stemming from her parents' conflict. Born in Zambia (yet her parents are from the Caribbean), she lived in London until she was ten. The family then transitioned back to Zambia, specifically Lusaka, due to her father's work contracts that required travel.

Growing up in Lusaka, Míkáylà also faced bullying within both the U.K. and Zambian school systems — she found herself caught between cultures, with her accent being perceived as too British for the Zambian kids and too Caribbean for the British London school.

Growing up, she developed uterine fibroids, high blood pressure and similarly to me, a brain full of dogma and legalism, which had been instilled by charismatic churches in Zimbabwe and London.

During my white knight phase, when rescuing was second nature, I found myself deeply enamored with her, often prioritizing her needs over my own. Yet, beneath it all, I couldn't shake off the lingering grip of limerence, an intense longing that persisted like a stubborn splinter. Drawn to whom I believed was a deep student of the Word, she had once been a deliverance minister at Kensington Temple, but there were some red flags that I chose to ignore out of loneliness and in the name of religion.

I'd later pay the price of hoping to see things change, but eventually, after enduring nine years of a confusing situation, I hit another bump in the road.

Feeling adrift while constantly trying to meet my wife's mental, emotional and overall well-being, things wouldn't improve. No Church could heal her, it was a disappointing time for us both. She had tried years of fasting, abstinence, hours of prayers, breaking off so-called curses and generational bloodlines became a mantra of justification, but nothing ever changed.

Somewhere along my spiritual walk, things were going fine, my encounter with Christ was tangible and miracles thereafter were undeniable to the extent that all my family had come to experientially know Christ. David, my brother, whose leg healed, was the one who eventually led Granddad to know Christ.

It felt like the stagnant ecclesia was playing the devil in disguise that left me pear-shaped with its ideologies and dogma. I'd been taught and I thought that I must beg, fast, plead, tithe, make financial sacrifices, or have some kind of formula or use the Name of Jesus almost like a magic spell to get people healed.

Believing that perhaps we had unconfessed sins in our lives, perhaps some kind of generational jinx plagued us, or that not tithing was the cause of bad health. A combination of a remnant of African Church legalism and God being some kind of Mafia hitman to stop the demons, that we'd both been indoctrinated in. Yet, these dogmas, these jail house rocks were in direct violation of the knowledge of *'Whom the Son sets free, is free indeed.'* [8]

I yearned for my marriage to thrive, yet right from the outset, there were enigmatic challenges that lay beyond my grasp, leaving me in a state of desolation. Overwhelmed, perplexed, fueled by anger and tainted by jealousy due to the intricate web of circumstances, I bore the weight of resentment. How could she profess an absence of love? Míkáylà was consistently under the sway of potent medication to reduce the pain of her list of infirmities, inducing words and actions that undoubtedly sprung from the drug's physiological and cognitive influences.

It wasn't quite the honeymoon period I had imagined. After Míkáylà's surgeries, which included several blood transfusions and the removal of fibroids that had occupied the space in her womb as if she were carrying a six-month-old fetus, within what the surgeon had described as a 'hostile womb,' we did eventually succeed in conceiving. However, before and after our daughter's birth, Míkáylà became more distant and sorrowful. She often mourned for her past, showing less interest, leaving me with a sense of rejection that felt like a splinter piercing my soul.

Hence the weight of spoken words in the face of rejection and struggling with not having my needs met, it seemed the dark side of life had found me once again to destroy the future. In December 2009, we moved in the hope of a fresh start from North London, Enfield to North Weald, Essex to Lancaster Avenue—named so, as directly behind us was the air base that once was an important base for the Lancaster Bomber during *the Battle of Britain*, yet, amidst this historical backdrop, another battle unfolded—a clash of ideologies within the confines of our marriage, with my wife finding solace in a form of Christianity that cocooned her inner child in bubble wrap to soothe past traumas—a struggle remaining unchanged throughout.

Attending a lackluster church in Epping felt like a routine ritual—singing a song, sitting down, awaiting announcements, standing up, singing another song, sitting down again, listening to a dry sermon, singing a final song and having coffee or tea with biscuits afterward before heading home. Amidst my brokenness and quest for restoration, I earnestly sought answers to my faith. The following chapters chronicle my search for healing—trauma seeks comfort even from the depths of a pit.

# Chapter One

## The Pit of the Kings

April 2011.

I simply desired Míkáylà to be healed from all her infirmities. Despite my exposure to years of saccharine-laden God TV channels boasting miraculous tales, my experiences had been limited to the peculiar gold teeth manifestation of 1999, along with witnessing my brother's leg being healed and a man from India whom I prayed for during a night shift to ease his troubled arm. And so, my exploration into the realm of healing began— scouring online resources, immersing myself in books on fasting and the practice of speaking in tongues for hours. Yet, it was on YouTube where I stumbled upon something truly remarkable, a collection of videos uploaded by a certain gentleman hailing from Wichita, Kansas.

Pete Cabrera hails from the heartland of Wichita, Kansas. Standing at 5 feet 11 inches, his imposing presence often comes with a baseball cap perched on his Lex Luthor-esque head. A goatee beard adds character to his face, with hazel eyes complementing a shy yet welcoming smile. Over the years, I've witnessed his metamorphosis from a solid build to a sculpted, agile physique—a testament to his unwavering commitment to nurturing his spiritual and physical well-being within the Kingdom of God. Though his outward appearance offers a glimpse of his persona, it's his remarkable knack for deciphering the unspoken echoes of the Kingdom of Heaven that truly sets him apart. *[1]*

Every tattoo etched onto his skin, like the shark that graces one arm, weaves a unique tale chronicling a chapter of his extraordinary life journey. Pete's story unfolds as a triumphant narrative against adversity, a vivid example of resilience and the transformative embrace of redemption. His odyssey began with his father's untimely departure when he was just seven, plunging him into a realm marked by chaos, resentment and self-destructive inclinations. This tumultuous path led him downward into a life marked by violence, a ten-year battle with crack addiction and a spiral into a world of crime. *"I had no regard for life or anything resembling it,"* he recalls. While his mother valiantly assumed the roles of both parents, the guidance he yearned for remained elusive. This vacuum propelled him down a perilous path, spiraling into violence, a grueling decade-long wrestle with addiction and a life shadowed by criminality, where purpose seemed to elude him.

In a pivotal and haunting moment of despair, Pete found himself in the confines of a closet at 3 a.m., a noose draped around his neck, contemplating a tragic farewell. Yet, an unexpected twist of fate intervened. His mother had been praying many miles away and an intervention took place.

Galvanized by the unwavering faith of his mother, whose devotion to Jesus had become her refuge, Pete embraced a radical shift, surrendering his life to a higher calling.

As Pete opened himself to the embrace of Jesus, a profound metamorphosis overcame his perspective. The agony that once consumed him was supplanted by love and newfound purpose. Amid his voyage of healing, he embarked on an earnest exploration of Jesus' teachings, clutching tightly to the remnants of his fractured past. In this profound journey, he unearthed a reservoir of love, compassion and grace that revitalized his very essence. Overflowing with gratitude, he offered himself as an instrument of divine design.

Pete's expedition veered toward an extraordinary trajectory, as he assumed the mantle of a dedicated mentor and healer within the realm of Jesus' Kingdom. His unwavering dedication became a beacon of optimism for those yearning for spiritual enlightenment and recovery, a living testament to the unwavering tenacity of the human spirit, capable of transcending even the darkest abysses.

Pete Cabrera Jr., of Royal Family International, made things look easy. No hype, no razzmatazz, no suit, no tie and no pleas for money. He had a heart to teach people that healing is not about following a list of A-to-Z methodologies, but that we, as believers, can all do it too. Pete worked in a soup kitchen in Wichita, Kansas. The only thing I knew about Kansas was that Superman crash-landed there as a baby in the comics.

Over the years to come, after life hit me, I would eventually visit Pete three times in Kansas, spending a month in various parts of America each time. During these visits, I had the privilege and honor of being looked after by his family and witnessing how they live and learn—a genuinely loving family.

Memories of Pete praying for people on the street or handing someone at a petrol station a large amount of money, where it turned out that the person who received the money were contemplating suicide or completely broke. They would cry and be grateful, asking "What's your name?" Pete would simply reply, *'It doesn't matter.'*

In the videos, as I was then to later see in real life, Pete would place his hand on someone's shoulder, leg, foot, or face and they would be healed of all manner of infirmities. He would *command and speak* to misaligned shoulders and legs to grow out and be of equal length and sure enough, those limbs would grow out *as told*, years of toothache disappearing and cripples walking again. He even prayed for an injured dog and the animal was healed. These homemade videos were amazing—I had found a fragment to my journey of discovery and identity.

It was even more remarkable and timely that I then discovered that Pete was coming to England to teach others! I looked on Facebook to see which of Pete's friends were based in the U.K. and spoke to Rob Taylor from Bognor, who had arranged the outreach for Bognor Regis (Pit of the Kings) where Pete, brother Ruff, Jaren Barnes and evangelist Tom Fisher were to teach and demonstrate healing. I asked if I could attend and Rob said yes.

On Friday the 8th of April 2011, I packed a small rucksack, started up my silver Daewoo and made my way to Bognor Regis. Setting out under the stars to ensure an early bird's arrival, I admitted to myself that my sense of direction was about as reliable as a politician's promise. After three hours of navigating like a lost puppy, I finally stumbled upon the destination—only to realize I was so early I could have had time for a spot of tea and a gingerbread biscuit. I slept in my car overnight outside a McDonald's. It was uncomfortable and I should've planned better, but this was necessary.

## Saturday 9th of April 2011

Bognor Regis is a picturesque seaside town located on England's south coast, known for its beautiful beaches, traditional British seaside attractions and relaxed atmosphere. With its rich history and scenic surroundings, it was the perfect setting for the start of my day.

In the morning, I made my way to McDonald's, changed my clothes in the restroom, brushed my teeth and ordered some breakfast. Later, I headed to the farm and met Rob Taylor, a joyful man who, I later discovered, had paid to fly over and host the visiting evangelists out of his own pocket.

The churches in his area did not want to support him. Along with Rob, I also met Tom Fisher from Manalapan, New Jersey (who runs Cardboard Box Church). [2] Tom's boldness, confidence and tenacity were astonishing. I hadn't seen faith like this in a man since Emmanuel. Tom was expectant in his results, expecting to see people healed when he laid hands on them.

At the farm, amidst the backdrop of cow moos and sheep bleating, Pete, Jaren and brother Ruff turned up late afternoon. Jaren, a laid-back, plump hippie-looking guy from California, had forgotten his passport at the airport restaurant after he had prayed for the waiter. [3] Brother Ruff, an Afro-American gentle giant and rapper, accompanied them, adding his unique presence to the scene. [4] Despite their adventurous spirit, their geography was off-key—turns out they thought Bognor Regis was just a quirky neighborhood in London!

 Pete walked in, clapped his hands and rubbed them—part humor, part superhero mode—as he spoke in his Midwestern Wichita accent, *"What's crackin'? I haven't come here to see chickens, cows, or sheep. I've come to heal some people!—Let's have at it. Let's go heal some people!"*

He walked around and engaged in conversations with people, holding the hand of an English lady. Instantly, she experienced a surge of warmth coursing through her and she asserted that her arthritis had been healed.

I observed Jaren (in his sandals) and Tom do likewise with incredible results, back pains vanished, headaches dissipated and even depression seemed to lift. It felt like I was witnessing scenes straight out of a real-life Biblical epic!

Later in the evening, after the team had prayed for the sick in a local church, the worship singers ceased their singing as an unseen melodic choir began to fill the air. Tom shouted and pointed, 'It's angels, I hear angels singing!' I must admit, we all heard it too, the worship leaders had stopped singing and knelt and started crying in acknowledgment of what was unfolding. While I had heard of this phenomena from testimonies outside of England, there I stood, a firsthand witness to this bliss. The air seemed to shimmer with a sweet resonance, a harmonious symphony that lifted the spirits of everyone present. The sensation was as if the very atmosphere resonated with divine harmony and in that brief moment, it was as if time stood still, as all boundaries seemed to dissolve.

While some may eagerly await the reoccurrence of charismatic events, our team and I were simply hungry, prioritizing our basic needs over any mystical experiences. Shortly after, we all ate at a Chinese restaurant with about thirty of us. Many were hungry and complained that the waitress was slow. I was taken aback when the waitress asked Pete what he would like to order. He looked her in the eyes and kindly replied, "I will have anything that you recommend, I will leave it to you."

That night, after a full belly of adventure, divine music and Chow Mein, I was blessed enough to stay two nights in a spare bedroom by one of the local Christians who had also attended the gathering.

### The Wonder of Abigail.

10th of April 2011.
McDonalds.
41/43 High Street,
West Sussex.
United Kingdom.

In the morning, the team gathered for breakfast at McDonalds where one man was healed of back pain while Jaren prayed for him in the queue.

After breakfast, the team hit the streets of Bognor heading toward the town's shopping districts. I linked up with Jaren Barnes and Assiya (from Kazakhstan, whom Jaren would later marry) whilst the others stayed in the middle of the shopping precinct with a sign that Robert Taylor had made, displaying 'Free Healing' on one side and 'Words of Destiny' on the other.

Jaren, Assiya and I met some drunken people. We prayed for one gentleman. He said he was born again, but a bit messed up, but said he felt the power of God encourage him.

We then walked into a betting shop and I said to the two ladies behind the counter that we had bet our lives on one sure winner—that Jesus is coming back one day and on a horse, if that helps? That we had given Him our lives—that He loved them and we are here to share that inside information with them. Jaren asked one lady who spoke Russian if she had a dream recently and Assiya translated in Russian. It transpired that the word of knowledge Jaren gave was correct.

At lunch, we went into the Hatters pub where Jaren, Assiya and I met Rufus a guitar playing busker. This was the first time Jaren had ever been in a pub. Rufus was happy to meet us and said he was an Atheist, *"Ah, okay... that's cool... well, we're here demonstrating God's love and power... would you like to see? Have you any pain in your body?"* asked Jaren. Rufus said he had back pain. (Years ago, I remember a preacher mentioning that, according to Readers' Digest magazine, 70% of people with back problems have mismatched leg lengths).

Jaren and Assiya sat him down and just held out his leg. They said nothing, but it began to stretch out. Rufus said he felt the warmth and could not explain what had happened to him. Rufus was glowing as he went around the pub telling his friends what had just happened and how his back pain had gone. Pete turned up a few minutes later and met Rufus, then demonstrated to everyone with Rufus as he sat him on a chair with his legs on a stool his legs both growing and shrinking by command, something that was most peculiar. I filmed the demonstration and after lunch we gathered with the rest of the team and exchanged stories. One man from Norway was with me and we observed the fluffy clouds amid the blue skies, I remarked that somewhere it is written—'*the clouds are the dust of his feet.*' [1]

<u>4pm.</u>

The team hit the streets and gather outside McDonalds (Thomas Fischer, Jaren, brother Ruff, Pete, Robert and many more.) There was much commotion as specific words of knowledge began to be given to many youths that had gathered outside. These included the giving of their first names and the names of their friends and family, I had never seen this before. The youth were very excited and some cried. It was made clear by Thomas Fischer that it was Jesus Himself who was the one that was giving him the names and words of knowledge.

An older woman grabbed my arm and told me to come and talk to her while her teenage granddaughter was in a car. She asked if we were psychics, so I explained to her: "No, it's Jesus *in* us, explaining Kingdom truths." She asked to know if her granddaughter would be safe and what I could read about her. I looked at her granddaughter and the woman and intuitively, I could see clouds of white swirling mist in their eyes.

"You are concerned about your granddaughter and yet your family tree shows that you all have been involved in speaking to the dead. But they

271

need to speak to the living and not the dead. If you call on the name of Jesus, if you change the way you think, change your ways, if you come to Him, He will keep you safe, for he is alive."

She nodded her head in agreement and wanted to know if her granddaughter was pregnant. I replied, "Life is precious and God loves you and thinks you are all precious." The woman nodded again in agreement and I re-joined the rest of the group.

I was approached by a teenage girl Abby, who made a jesting remark about wanting larger breasts. I initially ignored her quips, but when she persisted, I responded politely, suggesting that she might consider engaging in swimming or exercise if she had genuine concerns. In response, Abby stormed off in a rage and began swearing and cursing, *"He just called me fat! F--king fat? F--king bleep, bleep, bleep!"*

One boy, Connor, came up to me. He was wearing a blue stripe T-shirt, sporting wavy blonde hair. Connor said he had one foot a size six and the other a size nine—which was a discomfort and expense for his Mother as she would have to buy two pairs of shoes. "Is there anything you can do about it?" It was time for me to step out and see, so I asked Connor to take his trainers off and put his heels on the kerb. He did so whilst other youth tried to distract.

I said, *'Watch this!'* I had never done this before.

I commanded his left foot to grow out and be equal in Jesus' name and it did. I had to ask another person, *'Am I seeing this for real?'* But like clockwork, his foot grew from a size six to a matching size nine. This wasn't a leg-lengthening miracle, it was a foot-stretch, something I had never heard of, let alone attempted before.

Connor was happy, the rest of the youth freaked out and when he put his trainers back on, he said it felt weird. I later asked Connor to share in his own words about his miracle. He replied, clarifying that several other things had happened to him on that day. Connor felt different, he felt safe like he didn't have to worry anymore having been born with spina bifida and having had an operation to remove the tumor. He had never been able to touch his toes, but after Pete had also prayed for him, he was able to stretch and do the thing he could not do before, touching his toes in shock.

A few minutes after the commotion, an angry Abby approached me with a freshly lit cigarette in her mouth, mockingly asking for prayer.

I replied, "Let's deal with your anger first."

Pete Cabrera Jr. was next to me and said to Abby, "Can I borrow your cigarette for a second?" Pete took it, looked at it, placed it on the cement floor, trod on it and handed it back.

Abby flipped a switch: "Are you f--king Serious? F--k! F--king f-ggot! Go back to your country! I'm gonna slap you! Why the f--k did you do that? I'm gonna punch your lights out!"

Pete's response was one of tranquility, his words soft, "You mentioned prayer, but let's address the core of your anger first."

Despite Pete's composure, Abby's outbursts persisted. Threats tumbled from her lips, along with promises of "I'm gonna slap you!" Yet, Pete stood unwavering, extending his face and cheek to her. "You want to slap me? Here's my cheek, go on."

Abby paused and then, with a resounding thunder slap that echoed through the air, Abby's hand met Pete's cheek. A collective gasp swept through the crowd, freezing the moment in a hushed, suspended silence. Tom Fischer's voice, infused with his distinct New Jersey accent, broke through, declaring, "You *don't* strike a man of God! *Lay not your hands on my anointed ones and bring no harm to my Prophets!*"

Turning to Abby, Pete's inquiry was calm, "Do you feel better now?"

Abby found herself lost in uncertainty, her response evading her grasp. As the youth watched in stunned amazement, Pete peacefully presented his other cheek, whilst a vivid, fiery handprint etched upon the other. Abby faltered, grappling for words that failed her, her friends eventually guiding her away in a muted retreat.

After a few more minutes, the team gathered to head back to The Hatters pub. As we did, Connor, whose foot had grown out, ran up the hill to meet Pete with a fresh hot chocolate, saying, "Here, I bought this for you, you didn't deserve that slap." Pete was grateful and replied, "Ah man, thank you. You didn't have to do that." When the boy ran down the hill, I could see the child like innocence of Pete come out and he began to cry and said, "Man, that ripped me."

## Power and Love

Later in the evening, after a short stop in the Hatters pub, the team gathered in the local Methodist Church. The same youth from the streets came, while worship songs were sung in Russian and English. Some jeered and joked. Pete stood up and began to give his testimony about his life in Kansas. He shared his love and encounter with Jesus, explaining that the (ecclesia) Church exists to *'Love on you.'*

Pete continued in the same heartfelt tone, seamlessly transitioning into the next part of his message:

"As a church, we must love the youth... I love you... I would die for each and every one of you," Pete's voice carried the weight of conviction and compassion. "I knew that you were going to come to the church today, I knew you were because the Holy Spirit told me he would guide you."

He locked eyes with Abby, who had come to the service and began to speak directly to her, his words infused with love and understanding:

"Abby," his voice softened, choked with emotion, "let me share some words of love and knowledge with you regarding upbringing."

Tears welled in Pete's eyes as he spoke, his sincerity touching the hearts of everyone present. Pete looked at the teens, his eyes reflecting a depth of experience and sorrow. He took a deep breath, the weight of his past hanging heavy in the air.

"Once my dad passed away, me being only seven years old at the time, my world turned upside down—full of chaos, hate and destruction," he began, his voice trembling slightly. "Ma had to shoulder the load for two parents, struggling to make ends meet for us. She couldn't rightly guide me like I needed."

He paused, glancing at the attentive faces before him. Some of the teens shifted uncomfortably, sensing the gravity of his words.

"So, I started tumbling down a dark hole, lost to violence, ten long years gripped by the devil's crack cocaine and I was neck-deep in crime. Didn't hold nothing sacred, not even life itself," Pete continued, his gaze distant as if replaying those dark days in his mind.

"My world was a pit of pain, too much to bear, 'til I reckoned the only way out was to call it quits," he said, his voice barely above a whisper. "It was 3 in the morning', I found myself in a closet, a noose 'round my neck, ready to say my goodbyes."

A few of the teens gasped their eyes widening in shock. Pete's expression softened as he remembered the turning point in his life.

275

"I rang up Ma, intending to say farewell. But things had changed, see? She'd found the Lord by then. She talked me off that ledge, told me to surrender my life to Jesus," Pete's voice grew stronger, infused with a mixture of gratitude and awe. "I cried out and He answered, swept me up with His love. I fell head over heels for that Jesus. He was the salve for all my hurt."

Pete wiped away a tear, the memory still raw and powerful. The teens watched him, some with tears in their eyes, moved by his honesty and pain.

"Then, during my spell in rehab, I hunted for Him like a hound after a scent, giving Him nothin' but the shattered pieces of a life in ruins," Pete said, his tone filled with determination. "And He showed me His love, His care, His mercy and His grace. I felt it deep, ya know? Filled me with thanks like a well that don't run dry."

He stood up straighter, his eyes meeting those of each teen, one by one. "I put myself on the altar, an offering to His plan. His purpose for my life. Teaching and healing in His Kingdom, that's what drove me, what still drives me today."

Pete's voice cracked as he spoke his final words. "And ... Abby..." He paused, tears streaming down his cheeks, the room silent and expectant. "Remember this: this same Jesus loves you too."

The room was quiet, each teen absorbing the weight and hope of Pete's testimony, their own struggles momentarily eased by his words. Suddenly, Abby stood up and took shaky steps forward, her body trembling, tears streaming down her face, until she finally embraced Pete saying "I'm so sorry, I didn't know."

Her friends, too, were overcome with emotion, their tears flowing freely. Pete, in the midst of it all, couldn't hold back his own tears as they hugged.

Amidst the countless miracles I had witnessed during those fleeting days, Abigail stood as the most profound, a symbol of such depth that even the clouds themselves seemed to weep in response.

### Connor's version *sic.*

1<sup>st</sup> May 2011, 09:53.

JOE (Types): Hi, Connor—how are you? Connor, please, could you tell me your version of what happened, your story has gone viral on parts of social media. I would like your version. Much appreciated. If you could write a little on the events of that day. Once again, thank you and God bless you.

CONNOR K (Types): Okay, which story? Because God helped me in seven different ways that day, or do you want them all?

JOE (Types): All? I had no idea there were seven ways! Be as descriptive and honest as possible, covering everything. How, what, when, where, your feelings—don't hold back. What did your friends and parents say? Be real. Spelling doesn't matter—just go for it. Thanks, Dude.

CONNOR K (Types): Well, it all happened when me and some of my friends were all in McDonalds and we saw loads of people outside and I asked someone why everyone was outside and they said some people from the Church are praying—so I said to my friends to go and get something healed that hurts to see if it works and if it does, I will go and get something on me healed and he said: 'No, you go and do it.' So, I did. I went over to one of the men and said, 'I've got a sun burn—can you heal it for me?' and the man said, 'Sure, where is it?' and I said, 'Both arms.' So, he said some words which I didn't understand and I started laughing because I thought it was all a big joke, until he said, 'How does that feel?' After he had done it (prayed), I said, 'It feels better.' Then he said, 'Do you want God in your life?' and I said, 'Okay, what do I have to do?' and he said, repeat after me, so I did and I stopped him halfway through and said, 'I feel like I'm getting married,' and he laughed and carried on. When he finished, I felt different, like I was safe and didn't have to worry, so I told one of my friends what happened to me and he said I shouldn't lie. I said, 'Come and watch me get my feet to be the same size cause one of my feet was a 6 and the other one was a 9,' so he said, 'Go on then,' so we did and I asked this man his name and he told me, but I forgot. I asked him to make my feet the same size, so he took me to the side of the path and asked me to sit down and put my knees up and feet flat and to take my shoes off, so I did and then he said some more words and it worked. I thought, if this can work, maybe he can heal my back—because I was born with spina bifida, which is a tumor that goes through your spine, although they (Doctors) cut it out, but I still feel the effects on me. I can't walk for long or run and I can't touch my toes, so I asked the same man to see if he can heal it and I said, 'I bet you can't make me touch my toes,' and there was a man who was walking by and he was like, 'this is all fake.' However, I said it's not, that it all works. So, this man who was praying for me asked his friend to help pray with him because it was too hard for just him and his friend helped him and I said, 'If it works, I will buy you a hot chocolate. I touched my toes and gave the man a BIG hug and a drink and I had said to my friend, 'If it works, you better clap,' and he did and all this made me happy—and my Mum and Dad were not really interested, but that's Mums and Dads for you and I now believe in God and He is now a part of my life, thanks for helping, guys.

xxx — Connor.

The evidence was unmistakable, etching a lasting memory within me: the teenagers, alongside Connor, had undeniably shared an encounter with angels on that remarkable day.

This encounter, this connection with Jesus, will be a precious gift, that will accompany them throughout their lifetimes. From life's depths, Christ illuminates our path, reminding us that no matter what pit we find ourselves in, royal love from above extends a hand to transform.

# Chapter Two

## Angels, Devils, Dogma and Elvis

*"When y'all lay hands on someone, it ain't just skin to skin, but spirit to spirit deep down. The Holy Spirit pours into them where there's a lack of liveliness, kickstarts them organs and sorts out them issues."*

— *Rev. Curry R. Blake.* [1]

Taking home what I had seen and learned, with the hope of bringing about Míkáylà's healing, I laid my hands on her belly and commanded life to flow. Somewhere between her sense of disappointment and familiarity lay a dogma and belief that our lives were not in order—a constant flagellation of the times in that relationship. Nevertheless, when I did place my hand on her, she said she felt a shifting, a warmth in her womb as I directed vitality.

That night, however, she bled more than usual and began to accuse me of transferring demons by quoting scriptures regarding the laying of hands and being hasty. She cussed and spewed out more disregard for the sanctity of our marriage. Undeterred, I continued my journey to look for healing throughout my undertakings. I studied the DHT (Divine Healing Technician) online with a group situated in Texas called John G. Lake Ministries.

I was able to learn many things about dominion and authority. Although I was ordained under Pete's ministry for 'Royal Family International,' I also harbored aspirations of entering the pastoral ministry, where I could further develop my skills in enforcing victories over stubborn forces and engaging in the battle between good and evil. With this newfound understanding of identity, I made the decision to put it into practice.

## Full Moon Psychics

2$^{nd of}$ August 2012
Hotel Park Inn by Radisson
Harlow Hotel,
U.K.

As I arrived at the Hotel Park Inn just after 7pm, the full moon was already visible in the sky, casting a soft silver light on everything around. Its round, glowing form hung suspended above the building, a celestial beacon drawing people toward the entrance. Greeting the organizer, As I stood at the door, Adrian, I couldn't help but glance back up at the celestial orb, its radiance seeming to infuse the air with a subtle presence. The Batman insignia could not have made it even more picture-perfect. After paying the £3.50 entry fee, I slowly walked into a stuffy, medium-sized hall where the smell of cheap perfume pulsed around the room.

To the left of me were two Reiki healers, a man and a woman, who waved their hands over another woman as she lay down in the massage position.

I whispered, "Here I am Lord, let's do this."

I felt a shift in the air as light burst forth, like a shimmer as my feet touched the parquet flooring. Counting seven psychic mediums around the room (five women and two men), I noticed each had a poster or photo of themselves (Hollywood Headshots), advertising their ability along with their media appearances on television and newspaper.

There were chairs in the middle and at the back of the room. Eighteen people were sitting down waiting to see the psychic of their choice. Six out of the seven psychics were busy speaking to those who came to sit with them. Walking slowly, not soaking but rearranging the atmosphere, taking dominion, praying and speaking softly in tongues, I looked at the people who had come to the event, they came in two by two, filling the room. They had needs, some were curious and excited and some had been to events like this many times before. I could read their mental mail by looking at them. I smiled and introduced myself to some of them.

### Arya the Medium.

One specific psychic (a young lady) sat waiting for customers. I approached her, smiled and said, "Hello. So, what do people do here?"

She replied, "Have you never been here before, then?"

"No."

"Never had your cards read?"

"No."

Her name was Arya and I asked her if I could sit down for a moment and she said yes. As I looked at her, I could feel God reaching her.

She said to me, "You are a spiritual person, I can see it."

"So how does it work?" I asked as I looked at her colored stones and star signs. A deck of tarot cards, a tape recorder and Egyptian symbolism festooned her table. Arya explained that she charges from £35.00 to £80.00 ($43 to $100) for a tarot reading or invocation.

"May I show you something?" I asked.

"Yes."

I took out my deck of self-esteem cards, a rebus-catchphrase-dingbat style of colorful visuals that I had designed for school use and asked her to randomly pick six. Arya turned them over slowly as instructed, to cut a long story short, The Holy Spirit empowered me to speak into her life and after I asked for her hand, suddenly, power surged through her.

"What was that? I've never felt anything like that before!"

I then commanded her womb pain to leave and she said she felt all tingly. I then put my hand on her head and spoke life, love and peace. "Deceiving spirits leave Arya alone. Father of lights, shine over any darkness."

Arya said she felt heat enter her head and felt lightheaded. She was thankful and said, "You are powerful. You have power, thank you. Where are you from? How do you do that?"

"My Father is the Father of Lights. My King is from the tribe of Judah and He loves you and as of tonight there will be a change in your life, some people in your family will try to keep you back and deny you your aspirations but you must remember today as you will not see me again but remember the Father of Lights loves you."


The Grays.


As I left the room to get some air, a man walked into the reception looking very agitated, wanting to buy some self-help books from the festival. The person he was looking for was not there. I looked at him and he asked me, "Whit dae ye see?" I told him he was harassed and troubled. I told him to come with me and we walked to the pub area of the hotel.

His name was Callum. He was Scottish and a crane driver. He told me that when he fell over on a table and was unconscious, he saw his spirit leave his body and he was able to float about. Yet ever since he came back to his body, he can hear spirits speak to him whenever he walks by people. The spirits even told him that the 2011 tsunami in Japan was going to happen.

"I aye hae headaches an' back pain. Ah see thae Aliens, wi' triangular faces an' big black eyes, they keep tryin' tae tak' me, they've taen me afore an' ma body freezes an' Ah cannae fend them aff."

Callum then showed me several pictures he'd taken on his phone of white orbs that followed him in his room. I sat Callum down on one armchair in the hotel and commanded his legs to realign and they did just that. Also, I placed my hands on his head and commanded, "Spirit of infirmity and lying spirits, get your claws off his mind."

Immediately, Callum said he felt something fly off.

For the next ten minutes, near the site of North Weald air base, which was once used by Lancaster bombers and Spitfire planes, I engaged in a struggle with an unseen force that seemed to come and go. It felt like there were multiple troubling entities at work. However, Callum said he saw luminous angels by our side, aiding us and he experienced a sense of calm. "What is your name?" he asked.

"Joseph," I replied.

Callum smiled and laughed and said, "Are ye serious? A' through the day, an angel telt me I'll meet a Joseph wha'll help me." Scott then said that he saw an angel nodding in agreement as I told him the Gospel of Jesus, His stripes, wounds, crucifixion, resurrection and ascension.

Callum told me that something lifted and he could see lights all around us and more angels. He then said that he felt that he had been going to the wrong places for help and that he was thinking of seeing a Priest.

"Technically, I am a Priest." [2/3]

He smiled, I prophesied over him and he left blessed and said he would read the New Testament.

JENELLE: "Interesting that he was seeing E.T.s with triangular faces *enter his trauma...* the white orbs were angels trying to fight for him, but they are limited by our free will. My pastor says that sometimes people in meetings see orbs or silver and gold sparks (I see silver sparks a lot) and sometimes there are faces in the orbs or sparks that have beards or look older. He says that sometimes what we think are small points of light or orbs look that way because in the spirit they are far away and we are seeing them at a distance. Then, they can come and manifest in the meetings if they choose. I have dreamt of white orbs flying across the atmosphere before and I was flying over them. I also have dreamt (was it a dream?) that I saw white orbs coming from far away.

As they approached closer to earth, they unfurled as if they had been curled up into tiny, tight circles—they unfurled their bodies and wings and these big—I mean big, muscular, perfectly formed, magnificent angels landed in the parking lot where we had a school bus full of kids going to Church services with us. Wild! It's just so much adventure! God loves those folks... the ones seeking psychic readings and giving them. They are hungry and they already believe there's a spirit realm. You don't have to persuade them it exists. That's too cool."

Impromptu Ministry

Returning to the festival, I saw people walking out to return to their cars. I managed to pray for two pregnant women and commanded truth and ministering angels over their wombs.

Walking back to the hall—it was not as hot as before, so I introduced myself to some new people who had walked in, spoke into their lives and laid hands on their heads again, while the angry Reiki man was watching me.

A woman sat next to me. She had just walked in, bringing her friend to see the tarot reader who had spoken to her previously.

So, I cut to the chase and took out my self-esteem cards, spoke into her life and then laid my hand on her head and commanded life to enter and deceiving spirits to leave. A few seconds later, the organizer, Adrian, rushed over to me angrily yelling to stop and leave.

"You are not allowed to do that, you are taking business away!"

Adrian took me outside and I explained that I was not charging or promoting, but just helping and blessing. We spoke reasonably and peacefully.

Arya came out with another medium and shared with her about what had happened when I had prayed for her earlier and that her womb pain had left.

Then her friend shared that she had arthritis in her knees, then a fourth medium came out and shared that he had serious back pain and I laid hands on him also. He felt heat in his heart and back. The only resistance and negative vibes were from the Reiki man whom I saw had a countenance of hate.

### Elvis, cigarettes and angel wings.

Wednesday 8th of August 2012.

I woke up this morning to go and see a cousin who was dying of cancer, but on my way there my Dad told me on the phone that he died yesterday. I felt that I procrastinated, that somewhere along the line I became distracted. I should have listened and gone to see him, but I can't go back now. I must go forward, I'm so sorry for what happened to him and his family—I'm angry.

What did Jesus do when he heard that John the Baptist had died?

He went on proclaiming the Kingdom. So, after walking into a white witch shop and praying blessings over the priestess and walking into another spiritualist shop, the Holy Ghost had ruffled the spirit of another (in Waltham Abbey).


### Steve *the* R&B man.


7pm. The evening was splendid, the night was warm and the window of my car was rolled down as the breeze hit my skin. I was on my way to visit the Freemasons lodge to ask questions about their little parade and to see if anyone needed any help or demonstration of power, but the Masons weren't in. The man I met the other day said they were going to be there tonight, but the gates were shut when I arrived, so I drove off, praying, 'Holy Spirit, let us do something.' I parked my car outside Asda's (similar to Ralph's in the U.S.) parking lot in Harlow and went for a walk to see what new adventures awaited.

 Away from the Asda store and five minutes later I was outside a casino shop (the types of casino shops that are used as a license to launder dirty money by criminals.)

A man (Steven) stood smoking and thinking.

I approached him, "Hello. Busy night?"

He replied, "Not tonight, but afternoons and Fridays it gets busy."

"Are you in your destiny?"

"No, but it's biding me along." He laughed.

"What do you want to do?"

"I want to get into the music scene, I'm a producer of RnB."

"Okay, well I know Jesus has some keys for you and he can open doors for you.

Stretch out your hand,"—and he held it out.

"Father, in the name of Jesus, you have given me the keys of Heaven and right now, in Jesus' Name, we speak for the musical keys of favor and doors to open, that Steven will be given the opportunity to write songs that influence a generation of artists to bring you glory, keys from Heaven and keys from Christ. I speak it to come to pass in Jesus' Name, a man of favor and a door of life—amen."

"Amen," replied Steven. He thanked me and said he and his girlfriend were expecting their first child in December. I replied that this year was going to be a big year for him, with a new job and a baby child.

<u>Jon</u>

I strolled back toward the area where I had parked my car outside Asda. There, a man caught my attention, engrossed in drinking beer amid a collection of empty cans scattered about. A pause ensued and our conversation began. The man introduced himself as Jon, mentioning that he had once appeared in television advertisements for advertisements for UK timber merchant Jewson's. Jon said he had been homeless for a while ever since his social benefits had stopped, but tomorrow his case was to be heard at the housing office and he had also now received a National Insurance number so he could be eligible for work again. I asked Jon if he was in any pain and if he needed anything. Jon said he suffered from back pain.

I placed my hand on his back and said, "Look, I'm a man of God and you're going to get healed, if I'm not a man of God, you won't get healed." As I spoke 'life' to flow into his back, warmth flowed into his body and he said *he could feel something coming out of his eyes* as I commanded his back to be healed. So, upon that note, I spoke for the scales to be washed away—addiction to leave—rejection to go and life to flow from head to toe from Father, God. After a minute, Jon said he felt better and thanked me. I put my hand on his head and said, "You shall be suited and booted and in a new home and a job—accessing the provision of the Father to manifest His kingdom into your life."

We spoke and he said he was going to sing karaoke tomorrow at The Shark pub. He invited me and said he'd buy me a beer while he sang Blue Suede Shoes!

## Asthma attack.

Walking into Asda feeling sad, I don't know why, then I saw a woman coughing, struggling to breathe, she ran to the toilet while her friend panicked. "I can help her," I said. Her friend went to look for a first aider. Then, I went to the lady and prayed over her, binding the spirit of infirmity and speaking peace over her, she eventually improved and I left her in the hands of the paramedics.

## Can you buy me some cigarettes?

8:40pm

As I drove to another location (1 Staple Tye, Harlow, UK CM18 7PJ), the gritty urban landscape of Harlow unfolded around me. Despite its challenging reputation as the most dangerous major town in Essex and ranking among the top 20 most dangerous overall out of Essex's 315 towns, villages and cities,[4] I found myself navigating through its streets. Eating some chicken along the way, I made my way into Blockbuster. A group of six teenagers sat on a wall, their presence emblematic of the town's atmosphere. Among them, two called out, 'Excuse me, can you buy us some cigarettes, please?'

"I can't do that, it's against the law—but I can give you something better," I replied.

"Which one of you is in pain right now? Any sort of pain, ailment, or asthma?" One girl, Olivia, replied, "I have a toothache right now, and it's really hurting."

"Okay, put your hand on your cheek where it hurts—watch this."

Without hesitation, she placed her hand on her cheek.

"In Jesus' Name, tooth pain, go now and tooth be healed!"

The other teenagers began to laugh.

"Okay—where's the pain now?" I asked.

"It's gone!" She replied. "I ain't joking!" She said to her group of friends.

Her friends stopped laughing.

"I have back pain," said another girl named Holly.

"Okay, sit down... look at your legs..." (one was shorter—I asked her friends to watch this as I pointed to her leg)—"In Jesus' Name, left leg grow!" It did.

"Whoa!"

"I have rib pain...," said one of the boys. (Magnus).

"I also have a hole in my heart from childbirth," said Holly.

I instructed her to place her hand on her heart and her friends *to release a prayer through their own hands*. Magnus placed his hand on his rib as instructed and God healed both ribs. Ten minutes later—"This guy is Jesus, man!" said Jay.

"No, I'm not Jesus, but he lives in me," I replied.

### Angels Flutter.

A few words of knowledge later, in their presence, and hearing me command angels to flutter around them, the teenagers shudder as the wings of the angels breeze on them.

"We felt that!"

Six teenagers outside Blockbuster said this prayer in harmony after I led them: "Jesus, we believe you died for us. Jesus, we believe you are alive. I believe and invite you into my life—amen."

I told them about the Holy Spirit and blessed them as I laid my hands on their heads. Additionally, I shared with them the concept of speaking to Jesus as a friend and explained how much God loves them as a Father. As I spoke these words to the kids, I hoped that they would enter a new age of understanding and experience the depth of God's love for them. I emphasized that while I loved them, God loved them even more than I ever could and that they shine like the stars.

"You won't see me again, but Christ is in you—always."

# Chapter Three

## Christ and the New Age

*"Then I saw a new heaven and a new earth, for the first heaven and the first earth had passed away... And I heard a loud voice from the throne saying, 'Behold, the dwelling place of God is with man. He will dwell with them and they will be his people and God himself will be with them as their God. He will wipe away every tear from their eyes and death shall be no more, neither shall there be mourning, nor crying, nor pain anymore, for the former things have passed away.' "*

*—Apostle John, 90-95AD* [1]

Sunday, 12[th of] August, 2012.

"What star sign are you?" somebody asks.

"I don't follow the stars. I follow the One who made the stars."

Check out The Abbey Church, which is the church of Holy Cross and St. Lawrence and is the parish church of Waltham Abbey—a few miles from where I lived at the time. Over a thousand years ago they had a vision of giving people the Gospel using the Zodiac.

"Wait, say what now? Heresy! Witchcraft! Oh, no-no-no!" some say.

They truly had a unique way of giving the Gospel to people who could not read in 1030 AD. How backward we have become that we dare not touch or redeem things that belong to God anyway. *All things* belong to us in Jesus.

The Church where King Harold Godwinson, famously struck in the eye with an arrow during the *Battle of Hastings*, is buried. A unique Church in the fact that if you look up at the ceiling, you will see the star signs of the Zodiac, something that many still find surprising today, but here is the reason for such vision. They signify the passage over time, the twelve signs are visible in the stars over the twelve months.

In their confidence, the Victorian Christians put them there, they knew their pagan origin, of course, but also that the Church had appropriated them, giving each one a Christian meaning. For example, Aquarius the water carrier—think of baptism, Gemini the twins—think the duality of Jesus, Human and Divine, sharing humanity and offering us hope of Heaven, the Victorians had confidence to bravely look at things secular, temporal and interpret them in terms of Heaven and eternity.

The envisaged arrival of Christ ushering in the New Age is anticipated as a moment of profound spiritual renewal and restoration, marked by the establishment of justice, peace and transformation of hearts. It is believed to herald a time when evil is defeated, humanity experiences heightened spiritual awareness and a harmonious connection with God leads to a revitalized world order.

Saturday 8[th of] September, 2012.

<u>Health & Healing Festival</u>
Harlow College,
Velizy Avenue.
Town Centre.
United Kingdom.

# DAY ONE.

It was a warm, beautiful Saturday morning. I asked Míkáylà if what I was wearing looked okay and she said, 'No!' My brown jacket did not match my blue trousers and my Avengers t-shirt with Iron Man was a no-no. So, I rushed back upstairs, changed my shirt and ditched the jacket.

Leaving home, I drove the short distance from my house to the destination of Harlow College, where the Health & Healing Festival was being held.

Two weeks prior to this, I received a message on my mobile from a friend whose phone battery was depleted but had enough power to inform me about a training event called The Jesus Deck held at St. Mary's Church in Old Harlow. They were providing training on how to use the Jesus Deck, a classic set of educational playing cards from the 1970s. These cards consist of 52 cards and 2 jokers, featuring retro illustrations depicting events in Jesus' life, from His birth and ministry to His death and resurrection. The four suits correspond to each of the Gospel writers: Matthew, Mark, Luke and John. Each picture is captioned with a relevant scripture text and reference. The back of each card bears the ancient monograms ICXC NIKA, which means 'Christ the Conqueror.' The cards are color-coded, adding another layer of meaning.

Upon hearing this news, I was delighted to discover fellow believers who used cards or imagery to create themes for investigation. I had previously crafted numerous card decks for my students, enabling them to delve into topics such as anger, self-esteem and gang affiliations.

I used these cards as icebreakers in my teaching. With great enthusiasm, I participated in the one-hour session, feeling an instant connection to the concept. When the organizer inquired about my availability for the event, I eagerly responded that I would be delighted to attend the full two days.

## Walk in the Spirit.

I arrived at the event and met the rest of the team. There were eight Christians, four of whom were from St. Mary's Church. I went on a prayer walk of the venue hall and met and smiled at the Reikis, the tarot readers, the tree huggers, the mediums, the Buddhists and the alien encounter aura photo man and other unique stall holders.

Within two minutes, I spoke to a man whom I could see was deeply stressed. He charcoaled pictures onto white canvas, whom he said he channeled with the help of spirit guides. I listened to him as he told me he worked for the *Daily Mail* newspaper as a columnist there.

Looking at one of his pictures of a tree, I told him exactly what it meant to him, that he was going through a blurred time and that he kept coming back in circles. He acknowledged that it was true and I asked if I could sit down and he agreed. I introduced myself to him and told him I also was a creative person and took out my cards. His interest garnered, he picked the gold dust self-esteem and identity pack. He selected six cards and as he flipped them over one by one, I was sensitive and he listened intensely. He then opened up to me and said that there was a major decision in his life to be made within two weeks and that he may have to move to America and that things were very traumatizing. Then he told me he knew Jesus 2,000 years ago and that he himself was *Judas Iscariot*. (Complete deception).

We spoke a little more and then, he showed me a picture of the Jesus he had drawn. I blessed the man and told him I would speak to him later. He came to our stall a while later encouraged by our earlier encounter and he gave me a print copy of the gloomy counterfeit Jesus he had painted. This columnist later received more ministry from another Christian team *(Lumina and Fountain of Life) and* I saw him cry as he was impacted by The Holy Spirit.

<u>Divine Touches</u>

Patrick, a bald man in a white oriental suit from Yorkshire, showed me an amber sphere containing a prehistoric bee, which he claimed was thirty-five million years old. Patrick was a lovely, cheerful fellow who had a deep interest in Buddha and had created numerous jewelry designs inspired by that theme. He spoke about his healing abilities and mentioned that his wife was a Reiki Master Healer who also had knowledge of ancient Greek. I listened attentively as he shared his experiences. In return, I shared a story of how Christ had healed a lady from arthritis just last year. I asked for his hand and invoked the presence of the Holy Spirit within him while explaining how I had come to know Christ as my Savior. I emphasized that Jesus didn't possess the 'gift' of healing, rather, He walked in the fullness of God and the anointing of the Holy Spirit. This is a significant distinction. [2-5]

Meanwhile, a medium was listening as I ministered to Patrick. When I introduced myself and asked her about her profession, she replied in a sheepish voice, almost as if in shame, "I am a medium, but I know many Christians don't approve of it."

I looked at her and felt love in my heart, so I said to her, "I am not here to judge you, I'm here to love people." I then spoke to her about the photograph behind her, mentioning that it seemed to have been taken during a sad time. She confided that she had lost her parents during that period. I felt the love of God embracing her and I shared with her the loving feelings of God the Father towards her. She smiled and received those words with joy and I left her. A few hours later, I approached her again and said, "I am a married man, so please don't misunderstand me. However, I genuinely feel a deep sense of God's love for you and I wanted to tell you that." I also asked if she was thirsty and she said yes. I then took out a kiwi juice drink I had just bought and gave it to her, to which she expressed that kiwi drink was her favorite.

*It reminded me that God is in the details.*

I then approached a woman who had plastic, colored hand templates on her table. 'Hello, give me a high five!' And she did. We spoke, and I asked her what she does. She explained that each color puts you back in balance with the spectrum of one's inner self. She had made them, and we discussed creativity. I took out my cards and told her how it works and that they are not tarot or magic—she loved the concept. She then asked if I would like to pick some colored hand templates and as I picked them, I thought of colors mentioned in the Bible. She then tried to decipher why I picked the colors— saying that I needed grounding, but I replied, "I'm seated in Heavenly places." (Ephesians 2:6)

## Sonic Boom.

Tony and his wife, Rita, had some type of electrical machine that apparently heals the body through vibrations and sonic radar. Rita commanded her somewhat hen-pecked husband to place the headphones on his head for a demonstration.

Noticing that Tony had some skin rash, I said to Rita, "If I command life to flow into him, watch what happens to your machine." Rita replied, "Even Jesus cannot heal what he has." Nevertheless, I prayed for Tony and he said he felt warmth, but their machine suddenly stopped working as it went off pitch. I left them pondering.

Approaching another tarot reader, she asked me If I wanted my cards read and as I smiled, she replied, "You don't need them anyway, you know who you are."

We spoke for a few minutes and I asked her if she had back pain, she said yes, I asked her if she wanted it to go and she quickly replied, "Yes please." So, I took her right hand which she extended and I commanded her leg to grow, her muscles to loosen and as I did, she said she felt warmth and electricity enter her lower back and the pain left.

Another woman with a crutch walked by and said, "Me next, please." I commanded her pain to leave and she said it left.

## Clairvoyant Cabaret

Sunday, 19th of August, 2012.

## SPIRIT GALA
Lynn Sport & Leisure Park.
Green Park Avenue.
Kings Lynn,
Norfolk.
United Kingdom.

Chris M of JG** UK and I made our way into the sports complex, climbed the steps to the first floor and met Andrew the Clairvoyant and organizer of *Spirit Fairs*. Andrew showed us the room with the projector and

I began to set up my presentation titled *K.O.G.nitive Recalibration*—a phrase I coined, meaning *Kingdom of God cognitive mind set change.*

A sports worker switched on the projector and prepared the computer. As he spoke, he mentioned that he had been experiencing rotator wrist pain. After two attempts of commanding the pain to leave his wrist, the pain vanished. He looked amazed at the sudden relief, his disbelief transforming into gratitude.

Outside of the projector room, a long table was set up to use in the corner for myself and Chris who had booked the event to set up our healing stall.

At the front of our stall, a banner in bold red capital font proclaimed 'Free Healing,' accompanied by several colored prayer cloths and Chris' home life group and telephone contact cards.

We were booked to do the presentation for 11am, which Andrew had reworded as 'Healing and the power of God—how you can be equipped with healing gifts yourself.'

The event was scheduled to open at 10 am, and soon, the hall buzzed with anticipation as it was joined by a handful of new age stall exhibitors. Among them, two Reiki healers and two Shamans greeted attendees at the door, adorned in tribal Indian feathers that one later waved about gracefully while chanting ancient mantras. Inside, the room teemed with activity as three tarot readers and clairvoyants offered their services, their mystical aura palpable amidst the scent of incense and the sound of tinkling bells. Two crystal stone vendors displayed their wares, their tables adorned with shimmering stones and good luck charms, while nearby, a smiling tattooed spiritualist showcased velvet blankets embroidered with intricate designs.

At 11 am, no public spectators had arrived, so we chatted with the crystal vendor and her mother. They mentioned feeling the presence of God as they spoke to us. We understood that if attendance was going to be slow, the exhibitors would be ministered to. As expected, God's love infused the room when we welcomed the Holy Spirit to enter the upstairs venue and indeed the whole building.

## New Creation Presentation.

At 11am and it was time for our presentation. One lady Chris prayed for felt tingling on her back, she had a hand reading electrical machine, which gives a printout detailing about a person's aurora. We invited her to come watch our presentation then we invited the Reiki woman too. Five minutes after I began Andrew (a famous clairvoyant) joined and watched the presentation which focused on the teaching of the new man, the New Creation and Christ restoring what we had lost.

I specifically made the point that Christ did not have the gift of healing—that He walked in the fullness of God, it was not a gift or an event, it was a lifestyle that He showed us how to walk and who we are.

I delved into the healing words found in both Hebrew and Greek, referencing 2 Corinthians 5:17, which states, *'If anyone is in Christ, he is a new creation, the old has gone and the new has come.'*

After speaking for about fifteen minutes, I asked them to reflect on what they had learned. The Reiki practitioner expressed her interest in the concept of our spirits residing in earthly vessels. The woman with an aurora-like presence shared that she had indeed experienced healing and Andrew admitted to feeling deeply moved and even frightened by the powerful words I had shared about Jesus. It was as if these words had convicted him to live more authentically.

However Andrew also disclosed that he had diabetes and requested prayer, which we offered through the laying on of hands. After the prayer, he mentioned feeling worse and observed an increase in his blood sugar levels. We reassured him, explaining that such reactions were not uncommon when confronting the spirit of infirmity, which might resist healing. We encouraged him not to be discouraged and he agreed to seek further prayer later. The Reiki practitioner also reported feeling a tingling sensation when I hovered my hand over hers.

## Live and die once.

I then went to my car and collected my Anchor-anger-management cards and it began to draw in the other exhibitors. One New Age, self-professed, re-incarnated tree worshipper (I didn't know that that was a thing) came and sat at our table. Perceiving that she had suppressed anger, I told her the format of the anger game. After she had picked the cards, God spoke into her life and she heard about the new creation and the new birth. She believed that her last life and incarnation was a sticky death one. So, I told her that the Bible says, *'It is given to man to live and die once and then to face the judgment,'* (Hebrews 9:27) but that she could be born again and all the sticky ends would end at the new creation.

## More tea, Vicar?

Immediately after, Chris and I were joined by members of the public, Fiona and Mary—Mother and daughter said they were clairvoyant tealeaf readers. I nearly asked her to get me a decaf tea but instead showed her the self-esteem cards and she was blown away by what happened next, "I have

301

never seen anything like this before, where did you get these from? This is amazing and colorful and clever and accurate."

I told her I created them for my students at school who have all manner of challenges and need to talk about things, but it was The Holy Spirit that was doing the work with the ice breaking cards. I then demonstrated that I do not need cards and spoke prophetically to both Fiona and Mary and they said they felt the presence of God fall on them as The Holy Spirit took away stress and anxiety.

## The Thief of Depression.

Immediately after Fiona and Mary left, Chris and I were joined by a family of four, Daniel, Sarah and their two young children, Samuel and Chloe. Daniel said he suffered from depression, so I took his hand and placed my hand on his head and commanded life to flush out depression. Daniel then said he felt different, his wife, Sarah, had eczema and we commanded the eczema and sleeplessness to depart. Then we blessed the daughter, Chloe. Sarah smiled and replied, "The Lord bless you." We gave them each a prayer cloth to take home. Then Daniel and his wife, Sarah, went to the clairvoyant stand with his Mother. I perceived that there was a familiar spirit, opened soul ties and doors that had led to his depression.

At the conclusion of the meeting, I felt compelled to have a conversation with Daniel's mother. I asked her a question: "Would you welcome a thief into your home if he knocked on your door?" Her initial response was that she might if she knew the person. I posed the question differently, asking if she believed she had gone to the wrong doors and places. She admitted that she had. So, I tried once more: "Would you open

302

the door if you saw a thief through the keyhole, someone who intended to steal and destroy your belongings?" This time, her answer was a firm "No."

I continued, "But sometimes, that's exactly what we do. We allow a thief to enter and wreak havoc in our lives." She stared at me, clearly affected by the analogy and then walked away in anger as I told her, "God loves you and wants to set you free." It could be argued that in future interactions, I might approach sensitive subjects with more empathy and understanding. Listen to the person's perspective and feelings and try to find common ground or shared concerns before offering guidance or advice. Building a connection based on trust and respect can often be more effective in conveying my message. But sometimes I feel that there is a sense of urgency, sometimes I wish I could go back in time and tell my younger self don't open the door. There is an answer for the emptiness in your soul.

PROF. BEATRICE: "It's like these folks are searchin' for a bond, like souls wanderin' in search of a greater belongin'. But those who've been adopted can find themselves wrestlin' with big questions 'bout life, feelin' disconnected from their roots, put in unfamiliar territories—folks' social world—, messin' up their sense of balance. Growin' up might've seemed directionless, disorganized and lackin' purpose. And so, in the mix of new age beliefs, faith and politics, we dive into the tangle of family trees and all that mess of genealogical confusion. Seekin' truth, some folks turn inward, lookin' for answers right in their own souls."

# Chapter Four

## Kingdom Truths

Chris and I sat down and a woman called Alex, whom I saw the Shaman waving feathers around sat with us. I felt led to say, "Chris and I did not go to Church today, we decided to come here, what about you?" The woman replied, "I usually attend a Methodist Church, but I'm a Pentecostal." I asked her if she believed that Jesus died for her sins and if she believed He rose again and she replied, "Yes."

I asked Alex if there was a conflict of interest as a Christian in consulting clairvoyants and tarot cards. She (rightly) replied that Jesus would say it's her personal choice whether she uses tarot cards. She also mentioned that she might let the thief in, depending on her mood at the time and that the Bible is a book of principles and guidelines. Offended, she promptly stood up and left the room.

So many things happened during and after the event. The last thing I remember was calling over a woman who had spent all day with the Reikis trying to mend her back. Her name was Carolyn and I told her that God had told me to call her over. I told her she worked in education as a welfare officer and she confirmed she did. I told her that she has been having dreams of flying and she agreed.

"The dream means that you are called by a higher power, the Father of Lights, to come into the fullness of truth and the knowledge of Christ the ascended King, He is calling you to come to Him and no more wrong door knocking." As Chris spoke, she felt a tingling sensation and sensed the presence of The Holy Spirit. Remarkably, she shared that her shorter right leg stretched out, aligning with her other leg and her back pain left. So much was done in such a short time. Andrew (the famous Clairvoyant) approached us again and asked for more prayer and as we cast out the spirit of infirmity he was shaken up, yet expectant. "GO NOW in Jesus' Name!"

We then hit the streets of Kings Lynn where we met a couple whom God spoke into their lives accurately and both left visibly impacted. One was a former author whom God told she would pick up the pen again as a new creation and the other woman had a broken heart.

K.O.G-native Recalibration PowerPoint slides.

**Slide 1:** Experience the transformative power of God's healing touch in your own hands. Discover how you can be equipped with healing gifts directly from Our Father.

**Slide 2:** Today, we gather as seekers of spiritual truth, drawn together by a shared journey. I transitioned from selling Paranormal Insurance to finding profound truth. Join me as we move beyond mere words to tangible demonstrations that could alter the course of your life forever. Are you ready?

**Slide 3:** Our journey begins with a deep dive into the roots of healing, exploring ancient Greek and Hebrew texts. [1] Unlock the mysteries of the Spirit's (pneuma) emanation and delve into profound spiritual truths about humanity's purpose and potential. Prepare for a transformative experience, including live demonstrations and insightful Q&A.

**Slide 4:** Let's dissect the title, exploring its Greek and Hebrew origins to uncover layers of meaning and significance.

Let's explore the rich meanings of the Hebrew word *'Rapha,'*

*'Rapha' (7495)* encompasses various dimensions of healing:

(A) Healing and restoration to health.

(B) Healing of nations, bringing about restored favor and reconciliation.

(C) Healing of individual distress or personal wounds.

(D) Renewal and rejuvenation, becoming fresh and vibrant.

(E) Complete and thorough healing, leaving no trace of ailment.

(F) Purification and cleansing.

(G) Restoration and repair of what is broken.

**Slide 5:** Now, let's turn our attention to the Greek concordance for healing. Two key terms stand out:

*'Therapeia' (2322)* emphasizes healing focused on the reversal of physical conditions. Think of it as restoring the body to its natural state of health.

*'Sodzo' (1982)* is a multifaceted term that means to save, deliver, protect, heal, preserve and make whole. It appears eighty times in the Bible, highlighting the comprehensive nature of salvation. In some contexts, it refers to the saving of the soul, while in others, it denotes the healing of the body from sickness.

*'Dia-sodzo' (1295)* intensifies the concept of healing, signifying thorough salvation and complete restoration of wholeness, particularly concerning physical healing.

**Slide 6:** Let's explore the Greek term *'Dynamis' (1411)*, meaning power, as it relates to healing:

(A) Inherent prayer: Power that is innate and activated through prayer.

(B) Inherent power: Power that resides in a thing by virtue of its nature.

(C) Power for miracles: The power exerted by a person to perform miracles and marvelous works.

(D) Powerful deeds: Actions that demonstrate power and bring about miraculous results.

**Slide 7:** Now, take a moment to reflect silently on your own thoughts and feelings. Are you interested in being equipped with healing gifts? Consider your motives and intentions behind this desire. What drives your interest and what do you hope to achieve through it? Reflecting on these questions can help clarify your purpose and intention.

**Slide 8.** Healing and the power of God through your hands.

**Slide 9.** *Elohiym*—Hebrew 430 (plural) meaning (A) Rulers, judges. (B) Divine One(s) (C) Works of special possessions of God. (D) The (true) God.

**Slide 10.** *Theos*—Greek 2316. The Godhead Trinity. Speaking of the one and only true God. His counsels, interests and things that are due to Him.

**Slide 11.** Spirit as a vessel. Our body is a vessel, an earth suit designed to contain our spirit.

**Slide 12.** A musical creation of emanation. The Spirit of God hovered—*Rachaph* 7363 meaning *fluttered, move, shake, vibrate, hummed, brood.*

**Slide 13.** God made Adam and Eve in *His IMAGE*. Adam and Eve had a body, soul and spirit and they were created to emanate the glory of the Creator on earth. In His image, they had immortality, dominion and authority, but they lost it—we lost it. Then sickness, disease and death invaded the earth. (Genesis 3:1-13; Ezekiel 28:12-14; Romans 5:12; 1 Timothy 2:14). I personally believe that Adam and Eve were interdimensional beings, capable of transcending movement at the speed of thought. What we might consider supernatural, to them would simply be natural!

**Slide 14.** MEANING OF LIFE! A fish was meant to swim, a bird was meant to fly and we were meant to walk with God and never die. Christ showed us what it meant to live life on earth and to walk with God as Sons of God.

**Slide 15.** Jesus paid the price to redeem and reconcile us and to restore what humanity lost. *'Therefore, if any man (be) in Christ (he is) a new creature: old things are passed away: behold, all things have become new.'* 2 Corinthians 5:17

**Slide 16.** Acts 10:18 Let us ask questions of the text. (A) God anointed Jesus of Nazareth (B) with The Holy Spirit and power (C) He went around doing good and healing *all* (D) who were under the power of the devil because God was with Him.

**Slide 17.** 1 Corinthians 15: 47-49 *'The first man was of the earth, made of dust, the second Man is the Lord from Heaven. As was the man of dust, so also are those who are of the dust and as is the man of Heaven, so also are those who are of Heaven. And just as we have borne the image of the earthly man, so shall we bear the image of the heavenly man.'*

**Slide 18.** You can reach a point where you speak and command healing and it will happen. How? By knowing your God-given identity, being reconciled to your Creator through Christ and fulfilling the purpose you were made for. Let us guide you.

The Translocated and Grand Master Santiago.


DAY TWO.

Sunday 9<sup>th of</sup> September 2012.

Health & Healing Festival.

Harlow College,

Velizy Avenue, Town Centre.

United Kingdom.

9:15am—11:30am.

It was another beautiful, sunny day with a blue sky that lasted into the evening. I returned to the health and healing event and met my friend, Rob Taylor, who had traveled over two hours and more than a hundred miles from Bognor Regis to support me. I had shared with him the previous day's activities and Rob came to fellowship, learn and participate. On one occasion, Rob and I had traveled to Manchester, where we prayed for a woman on crutches and she was healed outside a coffee place.

At our stall, I encountered two fellow Christians, one of whom I knew and another Christian lady who didn't introduce herself and appeared out of sync. Her presence made me feel uneasy, therefore, I guarded my feelings and introduced Rob to the team. Rob was enthusiastic about how the Jesus deck cards tell the Gospel story. However, when I mentioned that we had a customer as a warm-up, the discourteous lady scorned and did not greet him, refusing to show him the Bible resource. Rob picked up on her negative energy and attitude, asking, 'She's supposed to be on our side?' So, another Christian on the team showed him how it worked instead.

For the next two hours, I just couldn't get into the spirit of things, it seemed there was a block in the atmosphere of the stall. I inquired with the same rude Christian lady about her conversation with one of the girls I had directed to speak to her, but she coldly replied, "I'm not saying."

After, I walked around meeting and greeting all visitors like old friends. I tried to shake off the feeling and thought to myself it must be me, I must be imagining things and judging wrongly.

Time flew. Rob also met with the medium, Alison, who now claimed she could talk to the spirits of cats as Rob listened to her with patience and love.

Rob and I returned to the conference and it was my turn to use the Jesus deck. While waiting for others to finish, I struck up a conversation with a man waiting in line named Santiago, of Ecuadorian descent. I prophesied to him that God had been calling him since he was young, but he hadn't been running the race properly. Santiago boasted about being trained by the world's best Reiki Masters and claimed that he didn't need a Bible to hear God's Word. He quoted random scriptures and angelic doctrines and said he didn't want to 'bother' God, stating, "God must be a busy Man, if I need to speak to Him, I can channel Him through my friends."

I read Santiago the following passage.

*'In the past, God spoke to our ancestors through the prophets at many times and in various ways, but in these last days, He has spoken to us by His Son, whom He appointed heir of all things and through whom also He made the universe. The Son is the radiance of God's glory and the exact representation of His being, sustaining all things by His powerful word.'* [2]

I explained to Santiago that in the last days, God has spoken to us through Jesus. I asked Santiago to stretch out his hand and as I prayed over him, he mentioned feeling power and warmth.

He talked about how the spirits of deceased individuals had taken his lost son to the police station and emphasized his sense of power. As he continued speaking for about twenty minutes, he turned to me and said, "I have a story for you—something you'll appreciate." He came over to sit at my table and began, "I've seen smiling cats appear in my room. I've seen aliens and objects materialize and move. Even Jesus appeared to me, sitting with crossed legs and reaching out to me."

Santiago then took out his phone and showed me a picture of himself as an Elvis impersonator, shaking hands with the U.K. Prime Minister, David Cameron, at an event. Not only was he a Grand Master Reiki Lord, but he was also an Elvis impersonator! He continued by sharing stories of how he channels energy, power and healing. He recounted an incident when he almost had a car accident but was suddenly stopped by an invisible force as he passed a lorry with the image of a sword with the word 'Excalibur' on it during his journey to Glastonbury.

He paused and looked at me as I nodded and listened. "Santiago," I said, "You may be a Grand Master Reiki Lord and you unquestionably have had visitations. I believe you have seen tangible manifestations. However, I also know that there are spirits that can enter the wrong mindset and open minds to let in the wrong things. May I share with you what I see today? May I speak?"

"Yes."

"It sounds like the sword that you saw is the sword of the Spirit, which is the Word of God that is sharper than any double-edged sword. It cuts through bone and marrow and divides between soul and spirit—yet you are not using the sword of the Spirit or reading the Word to grow—you see, Santiago, in your flesh and your countenance, you are a good-looking, gifted, charismatic strong man, but in your spirit, I see a man in diapers rattling his toys whilst crawling and sucking on dummies.

When we met, I told you what God was saying to you—that He has called you to maturity, called you to grow. I know you have dreams of flying and that means that God is calling you to a higher level of truth and not to wallow in artificial light anymore. You may boast of your gifts and your status, but I will let you know something today, Jesus did not have the *gift* of healing. Jesus did not have the *gift* of prophecy. Jesus walked in the fullness of God, in the fullness of His identity in God through The Holy Spirit in Him, gifts are for children and fullness of God is for those who are mature and know who they are in Christ. You have been called to grow up, son... and the only way you can nurture your spirit is to read the milk and meat of the Word and then you will understand because your spirit will soak it in—because the words in here are spirit and life."

Santiago looked at me silently for ten seconds. I thought he was going to punch me at first, but I could see that he was pondering on the words spoken and he thanked me. I handed Santiago a Bible to keep and another book titled *Maze of Deception* by Beverley Risdon. [3] I told him I loved him and that the Father of Lights is calling him to truth and love. Santiago said that he felt God's love and thanked me again, having received the rebuke with grace.

Bow and Arrow.

Five minutes later, the rude Christian lady next to me who did not greet Rob came to my table and showed me an angel card that she was given by the tarot lady. I asked her what she would do with it and she said she would meditate about angels and that I shouldn't be a worrier. "God can use anything," she said, "I will go to *any* healer." When I asked her about Reiki healers, she said she had no problem with the way they heal but she suddenly stopped midway through the conversation when she made no sense and began to randomly speak about socks, toes and massages! When I asked her how mediums and tarot people operate, she said, "God can speak through them too. It's not up to us. It's up to God," and "Everything is a fruit of the Spirit."

I softly replied, "God works with those who allow Him to work through them through His Holy Spirit."

"That, that is so arrogant! How can you say that? That is just arrogant." She repeated the word 'gentle' three times. I asked her if she was implying that I was not being gentle. She nodded and I replied, "I can read you scripture if you want me to."

"You are angry and anxious!" she blurted—so, I ignored her. I anticipated religious fire, but I wasn't prepared for gaslighting from within the camp. This misfit had labeled me as arrogant, angry and a worrier, questioning my identity. Though I sensed her desire to argue, I chose to ignore her. I didn't want to disrupt the unity she sought.

I didn't like conflict ever since my early childhood and teenage life. I wanted to focus on the Kingdom job at hand. So, I went to the *Lumina* stall where I met with Kelly. R and her team. I shared briefly what had happened and they prayed over me. A Christian brother, Dan P., had a picture of the Lord removing the arrows from my heart and placing His arrow of love in its place that would allow me to minister to others who were wounded, he saw a picture of a bucket of gold dust being poured upon me and I was given a bow and arrow like Cupid to go and spread the love of Christ. Promptly encouraged, I did so.

Dan is an extraordinary son of God. He shares a testimony and later explains he did not know why he went into the shop because he had no money.

"I met a lovely lady called Sally today in Harlow, who ran this shop in the college. She said she has severe OCD, as you can see." *(Photo of an immaculate order of items in the shop, coordinated and displayed)* "Sally told me all about the things she feels she has to do, a constantly busy mind. So, I asked if I could pray for her and she agreed, I'm glad she did because God gave me the most beautiful word for her, which left her teary but encouraged as she said, 'Thank you, I feel so much better.' Want to know what God said? Well, He said this,

'I (God) don't like the term OCD because the D means *disorder*. You (Sally) don't have a disorder and I don't view you as having one, but I have given you a gift of organization and I pray that one day you see the beauty in Me—that I (Christ) see in your store!' "

<br>

The Translocator.

<br>

Rob and I met a man named Kevin who ran an aurora photograph stall. Kevin, also a Reiki healer, mentioned that he spoke in tongues and demonstrated uttering the sounds of glossolalia with words he claimed were Egyptian. Not only had I never encountered a Reiki tongue speaker, but what Kevin proceeded to share was also unique to my ears. He said, "I am... a time slipper *(time traveler)*." Kevin claimed that he had experienced translocations (the concept of an individual with the supernatural ability to teleport or move instantaneously from one location to another, or through time) to various parts of the world, including a time slip back two thousand years to witness Jesus walking on Earth and even claimed to have been present at His crucifixion.

I listened and said, "Kevin, hold on. Hold on. *Translocation?* Yes, I know of similar stories, but let me ask you a question because I am learning something here. You speak in tongues, your time slipped and saw Jesus on the cross, yes? So, did He die for your sins?"

"No," he replied.

"Did Jesus rise from the dead?"

"I'm not sure because the manuscripts have been changed, but I believe his bloodline exists today."

Rob and I looked at each other, silently acknowledging the uncertainty in his response. We would later ponder and assess the potential impact of how Kevin had somehow gained illegitimate access or vision to the spiritual realm of deception. We left Kevin with love, respect and the story of our own experiences. We did not argue with him. Instead, when we returned to our base, we prayed for him, hoping that his eyes might be opened.

PROF. BERNARD: "Engaging with individuals who have endured trauma can result in experiencing vicarious traumatization. We become depleted by the fatigue of trauma when we continually encounter stories of abuse, you know?"


PETE CABRERA JR: "Demonology, ghostbustin' and deliverance, it's wearing on ya and folks often put too much emphasis on the dark stuff, losing sight of the light.

The biggest sin humanity ever committed was when we took down the very one who created us, the Creator. Man killed God. But Jesus, the Lamb of God, He was destined to be sacrificed from the start and even when they traumatized him, marred him beyond recognition, bones and flesh exposed as he hung naked on a cross, he said, *'Father, forgive 'em, they don't know what they're doin'.'* That moment changed everything for good. Now we have a resurrected Christ with scars on his hands and feet—the healer with his wounds, the truly wonderful counselor."

# Chapter Five

## The Wonderful Counselor

*'For unto us a child is born,*

*unto us a son is given:*

*and the government shall be upon his shoulder:*

*and his name shall be called.*

*Wonderful, Counsellor .'* [1]

*— Isaiah (740-686 BCE)*

Friday, 12[th of] October, 2012.

JENELLE: "Joe, never underestimate how cheeky God is and how He will insert Himself into situations that seem restricted to your eyes. If you are in a place where you are unsure (and I am lots of times), begin to worship within and change the atmosphere. Automatically, doors will open in the most unlikely places, and people will start asking you questions that open the door to walk right in and bring light to them. It's quite amusing to watch the light overtake the darkness in places where they adamantly insist, 'You cannot do that!'—as if they are speaking to a customer who is opening a can of Budweiser in an NYC convenience store!"

September 2012 *Year 1*, NLM University.

Rejection was something that took years to recover from.

In early 2012, my position as a learning mentor at the secondary school was slated to be eliminated and I had to reapply for a new role as a counselor, which required me to attend university. I applied and secured the position in September of the same year, commencing my training as a counselor at NLM University.

12 Voices, 1 Classroom.

I'm one of two men amid ten women and three women teachers who will facilitate the counseling terms. All my cohorts sat down and introduced themselves and then they gave the reason why they had joined the counseling class. We discussed the definition of counseling and referral agencies. During break, the class decided to stay in the classroom as the teachers went to their offices. Ben (a music producer) was complaining about his back. He had been in a traumatic car accident years ago and had to relearn how to walk again and his back was always in pain. I told him to sit still as I examined his posture. He then told me he had one leg shorter than the other. The ten students looked on as I blew on his leg, within a few seconds, his leg grew out. Then I placed my hand on his lower back. Heat and life were commanded to flow into him. Ben felt the power of God flow into him and then felt lightheaded and drunk after he was healed in front of everyone. Straightaway, the teacher came back and it was time for sharing how week two went.

A lady spoke first and then Ben was asked by the teacher how his day went. He replied, "I'm having a great session and a mixed week. My Granddad died last week and an ex-girlfriend came to say goodbye to him as she left the country for Spain and then today, just a few minutes ago, actually,

Joe just healed me." Everyone and the teachers looked at me and feeling like a rabbit in a headlight, I replied, "I didn't do anything, it wasn't me. It was Jesus." The other students who had returned from lunch asked, "How did you heal him? How do you do that?" I gave the same reply in truth, '*Through Christ* and *His* love.'

The Professor then asked me, "Are you a Conduit?"

"What is a conduit?" I asked. She replied that a conduit is someone who channels power. "I guess I am, but it's natural, I see a lot of this in my life, it's real and it's who I am, who *we* are supposed to be. It's love in action. It's Christ in me."

Another student said, "I don't know what it is, but you have something different. It is as if when you look at me and us, it is as if you are looking into us, not in a scary way, but you see something."

I replied, "I just want to love, that's all... I am not psychic..."

The professor asked, "What was that last part?"

I replied again, "I just want to love."

The other students then felt something rest on them and the professor felt to look away as I looked at her, sensing her story.

One lady paused to cry and then, the teacher, slightly taken aback, said, "Okay, let us not put the spotlight on one person, let us keep to the rules and move on." I agreed.

Ben said he had never felt such power or tingling in his body in his whole life and felt drunk and messaged me later that night:

*Hey Joe,*

*Beautiful! Thanks for saying God is a Father who loves me, I appreciate it.*

*Thank you for today, what you have is very special, it's difficult to express with words how you made me feel. I noticed you the moment I walked into the room last week and it's been an absolute pleasure to meet you.*

*See you next week,*

*Ben. X.*

The Sword and the Psychic.

Saturday the 24th of November, 2012.

It had been a long, yet edifying drive with Chris. M, who came from Norfolk to see me and then we drove from North London and arrived at the B&B at 1:30am (Earlham Road, Norwich, NR2 3DB, U.K.)

As I settled into my stay in Norwich, a city brimming with medieval charm and cultural richness, I encountered an unexpected twist. Opting for a budget-friendly hotel near the ministry trip's location, I soon found myself facing a peculiar situation. Norwich, known for its historic cathedral, cobbled streets and ancient markets, provided the backdrop for this memorable experience. Upon arriving at my room, I discovered it already occupied by a young couple who had stumbled upon the door code and decided to indulge in some impromptu enjoyment of the amenities. Sensing the need to address the situation promptly, I contacted the on-duty manager, José, a character straight out of 'Fawlty Towers.' Despite the initial hiccup, José's easygoing demeanor and irreverent sense of humor added an unexpected layer of amusement to my stay. "What's that? There's someone in your room? You're kidding! I tell you what, mate, I don't allow people to do it, but you can do it, why don't you just punch him in the face? I would but if I do it, I'd get fired."

José later came to the room and by that time the couple had mounted their one bike, which had been left in the corridor. I met José in his office.

"What if they come back? Can you not give me another room?" I asked.

"No, mate. We're all booked up tonight. I'll tell you what to do—you put the furniture by the door, so they won't be able to come in... okay? Now, I come and I take the batteries out of the keypad for you!"

On my way to the car to collect my possessions, a woman screaming ran away from her boyfriend and opened the passenger seat and jumped in a stationed cab passenger seat. The cab driver appeared shocked and bewildered as her boyfriend caught up with her and fell on his knees begging her to stay. Another couple who knew him intervened and the cab drove off. The boyfriend was left crying and screaming in rage. What a weird start. Returning to my room where José was removing the batteries from the lock.

"Hey! You want me to change the bed sheets?"

Eventually, José gave me a key to open and lock the door on the condition that if I lost the key, "It would cost you five-hundred pounds."

I sheepishly went to sleep. Dan N* (who was on a short stay to England from Slovakia had come to meet me and Chris on this mission) also had unexpected visitors in his room, but this being the fact because he had accidently booked for December 24$^{th}$ instead of November, but by the grace of God he was given the last bigger room. Morning came quickly and Chris, Dan and myself hopped into my car and we drove to our destination.

Habitation not visitation.

*'Y'see, any form of angelic contact, well, that's 'bout the lowest form of spiritual contact a man can have. But above all impartation or visitation,*

*above knowledge and understanding, it's habitation that God's aimin' for: habitation of the human heart and spirit through his son Jesus Christ. When we let the Holy Spirit set up camp in us, it's a permanent thing and ain't nobody above us 'cept God himself. We bring him glory, sure, but that ain't why we were made. We were made for dominion, to reign over the works of His hands, not be at the mercy of fallen creation or its angelic subjects.'*

— Rev. Curry R. Blake.

MIND, BODY & SOUL EXPO

City of Norwich School.

Eaton Road.

Norwich,

Norfolk.

Norfolk, nestled in the East of England, boasts scenic countryside, picturesque coastline and serene waterways, all harmonizing with historic market towns, quaint villages and sprawling farmland. Meanwhile, within the City of Norwich Secondary School, an unsettling ambiance stirs—the sports hall serves as a gateway for unseen demons. Is it any wonder that students and teachers returning to school are plagued by headaches, tension and confusion, reflecting the ominous energy lurking within the premises?

Chris, Dan and I set up our table with two signs: 'God is light and in Him, there is no darkness' and 'free healing.' We also displayed my picture catchphrase icebreaker cards.

So much could be written but time will not permit. We were united in spirit and purpose. Dan, Chris and I knew what we had come to this place for. We had the sword of the Spirit in our hands and we came to proclaim the light to the darkness, liberty to those imprisoned and enslaved to bondage

321

and to enforce the Kingdom of God upon the places, wherever we set our feet.

After seven intense hours of ministry at the Mind, Body & Soul Exhibition event in Norwich, we ministered to numerous psychics, mediums, spiritualists, clairvoyants and customers. Several of them shed tears after experiencing healing, including individuals who had been suffering from arthritis and back pain related to uneven leg lengths. In total, we delivered thirty prophecies, proclaiming Jesus as the crucified and risen King, alive and reigning in His Kingdom power. That day, many people accepted Christ as their Lord and Savior.

We utilized the anger management and Gold Dust self-esteem identity cards that I had created for such a time as this. The mediums who experienced them were astonished by the impact, recognizing the power of my Father, the Father of Lights, speaking through us.

I struck up a conversation with a Reiki healing couple, discussing the event and its progress. They inquired if I had a stall and I confirmed that I did. Upon asking the man if he had any physical discomfort, he mentioned shoulder pain. I commanded the pain to leave his shoulder and after three attempts, he reported that the pain had vanished.

At that moment, I sensed in my spirit that the couple might be facing challenges related to fertility. I gently told the woman that I believed she might be experiencing some difficulties in her womb. I requested her husband to place his hand on her womb, while I placed my hand on his and I spoke a command for life to flow into her body. She mentioned feeling a swirling and tingling sensation in her womb. While I saw a vision of her holding a child, I chose not to reveal it explicitly. Instead, I told her that things would change from now on and I believe she understood the significance.

A young couple, both twenty-one years of age, were the first to approach our stall. They came seeking healing for stomach and ear issues. I conveyed to them that God's grace had led them to our stall as their first stop.

I received a word of knowledge for the young man and we led them in a simple prayer as they gave their lives to Jesus. To ensure their commitment, I asked if they believed in Jesus' death and resurrection, to which they affirmed and mentioned having friends who attended a church and had invited them as well. I encouraged them to heed their friends' advice and attend the church, reminding them that God's grace had guided them here.

However, I also cautioned them about the dangers of venturing into the wrong doors of the occult. I emphasized that such choices could lead to distractions and the embrace of falsehoods, ultimately polluting their spiritual journey's pure stream.

One customer did not like it when I told her that, "The lowest form of spiritual contact is contact with angels, but the highest form of spiritual contact is with God through Jesus Christ, His Son."

We also met one young man (Nigel) who was a sword maker and he suffered from chronic backache. Chris and I commanded his leg to grow and it did. He both felt and witnessed it and was then prophesied over.

## Hover.

Approaching a Buddhist man named Daniel and his wife, who had a collection of bongs and copper pots they used to create music throughout the day with gongs and chimes, I shared my belief that music possesses a unique language and frequency that can penetrate the body and spirit. They expressed their appreciation for my understanding.

323

I then asked if they were familiar with the Hebrew opening of Genesis 1:1, which reads בְּרֵאשִׁית בָּרָא אֱלֹהִים אֵת הַשָּׁמַיִם וְאֵת הָאָרֶץ, 'In the beginning, God hovered...'—the only verse I can speak in Hebrew. I went on to explain that when the Spirit of God hovered over the water, the word 'hover' encompasses meanings like flutter, brood, emanate and vibrate, signifying a musical aspect to creation.

I also gestured toward the copper vials and ceremonial pots they had and shared, 'The prayers of the Saints are collected in golden bowls and then poured out onto people by God.' [2]

So, I asked Daniel if he had ever had a Holy Ghost bong. I had never used this terminology before, but that's my sense of humor and using it in this moment felt oddly fitting. He shook his head to say no and I said, "You have been pouring into people all day, now, let me pour into you." His wife was pleased. "Go on, Daniel!"

I then hovered my hand above his stomach because he said he had pain there then I spoke in tongues and that tongue became a diversity of tongues. I then clapped my hand at his belly and blew on him and suddenly, his wife, Joanne, was in unstoppable tears, she said that was the most beautiful thing she had ever experienced.

Holding both their hands I said, "This is the God I serve. This is Jesus. Every area of darkness and trauma that masquerades as light, I command to leave now in Jesus' name." She and her husband were deeply impacted and cried and hugged me.

At the last hour, Chris, Dan and I were told by the organizer to leave because we were 'casting out demons, telling people not to go to mediums and opening wrong spiritual doors.' We did not deny or dispute this charge, guided by the unction of the Holy Spirit. We left and blessed her before making our way while praising God.

I've had enough of dealing with the enemy and his devices. Today, we showed pure love to people without compromising the message at our ministry event. This elevated our ministry, making it the most powerful one we've attended so far. As a result, the enemy was displeased. One prayer that came from my mouth was unlike any I had ever uttered before, but the Holy Spirit gave me the words to declare to those we ministered to. They felt God's love so deeply that tears of joy and relief flowed freely.

"Every area of darkness that masquerades as light, I command you to leave NOW in the Name of Jesus! Every lying, deceiving spirit, you know who I am and in the Name of Jesus, be muzzled!"

"… and his name shall be called Wonderful, Counsellor, Mighty God, Everlasting Father, Prince of Peace." [3]

# Chapter Six

## Edge of Tomorrow

*'If I ascend into heaven, you are there, if I make my bed in Sheol, behold you are there' – King David, 11th century BCE*

Despite my involvement in ministry and my attempts to exercise authority, power and dominion as a believer, my marriage showed no signs of improvement. Míkáylà's health deteriorated, leading to increased medication and infirmities. It felt like an invisible force took advantage of opportunities to belittle and provoke me, constantly reminding me of my past failings, mistakes and irregular church attendance.

I adamantly refused to attend those lifeless déjà vu meetings that resembled a game of Simon Says, complete with its monotonous lectures: 'Sit down.' 'Stand up.' 'Sing this song and raise your hands.' 'Beg God for revival.' 'Dress accordingly and enjoy a rich tea biscuit to dunk in your coffee as the meeting concludes.'

PROF. BERNARD: "No gingerbread men, right?"

JOE: "Exactly. At least gingerbread men don't dissolve when you dip them in!"

I also felt as if my identity as a man was under siege and the marriage had devolved into a hollow shell of unrecognition. Nevertheless, my ministry missions continued, providing me with slight respite and hope to reach out to others who were hurting or engaged in their search for meaning and life exploration.

From September 2012 to early January 2013, during my time at the university, I initially enjoyed the counseling sessions. There was much beauty to learn and share and in many respects, I found a parallel between my understanding of spirituality and therapy.

Before stepping into the role of a counselor, or even before delving into its study at university, I stumbled upon the realization that I had been intuitively employing techniques.

For instance, when faced with a silent teenager who would hide under a desk and refuse to speak to anyone, I would simply become the narrator, describing what I saw and felt as though I were dubbing a movie.

"'Once, there was a teenager, who found herself under a desk, away from everyone else and she wouldn't say a word. Can you imagine that? It was like she had built a fortress around herself, protecting herself from the outside world...'

'Then, the girl turned to hear the voice of the counselor. She smiled and then she laughed. As he turned away to look at the blue sky from the window, she joined him from her cave to look at the birds singing. 'Where are the birds singing?' she replied.'"

It was a bit like watching a movie. I could see her there, in her own little world, with all her thoughts and feelings swirling around her like characters in a story. Little did I know that this approach aligned with 'Narrative Therapy', an established therapeutic framework that focuses on reframing personal narratives and challenges by externalizing the issue and gaining fresh perspectives

Some counselors mentioned experiences of 'intuition,' where they seemed to tap into a client's unspoken thoughts and emotions. 'Synchronicity' was also suggested, indicating meaningful coincidences or events that appeared to be connected.

Instances where we tap into unspoken thoughts and experience meaningful coincidences are key. Concepts such as 'co-presence,' 'relational congruence,' and 'advanced empathy' also come into play, creating a deep understanding akin to telepathy. Some counselors, like me, feel closely attuned to clients' energy, using practices like 'attunement' and 'empathic resonance.'

The psychodynamic perspective introduces 'projective identification' and 'countertransference,' where emotions flow between therapist and client, reflecting the intricate dynamics of therapeutic relationships.

However, while grappling with pride, ego and past trauma, I found it challenging to embrace group counseling, especially when there was just one other man among thirteen women in the class. They openly discussed their marriages, lives and families, which made me realize I wasn't alone.

This process of sharing emotions and feelings was foreign to me, partly due to the teachings I had absorbed from the Texan spiritual paths I followed. I don't know why they call it the Bible Belt, but sometimes it feels so tight that it constricts the flow of blood to the brain and libido. These teachings, although filled with signs and wonders, had instilled a certain rigidity that hindered my ability to connect. My mindset was steeped in dualism and I held skepticism toward people, fostering a theological separation between body and spirit that often-attributed explanations to angels and demons thus denying my humanity.

Yet, despite these influences, my conviction was that Jesus himself never required a counselor. Mentally, I wrestled vehemently, ensnared in a web of self-proclaimed spiritual expertise. My home life had been a tumultuous landscape for nearly a decade, further solidifying my defensive and disconnected state of mind. Breaking down the fortified walls of defense and unraveling the layers of cognitive dissonance would ultimately demand seismic shockwaves to initiate the process of detoxifying and reawakening my awareness.

The presence of my cohort of counselors would become an essential lifeline, a fact that became profoundly evident in January 2013. Returning home, I was met with an eerie emptiness.

## Man in Black

A moment later, a man in a somber black suit materialized from the shadows, as if he had been waiting for my return and he handed me court papers. His seasoned eyes recognized the shock etched on my face—a scene he undoubtedly encountered daily in his profession. Taking a seat beside me, he locked eyes and compassionately guided me through the unwelcome process that lay ahead. In that instant, I sensed a shared understanding, a resonance born of his own life's trials.

As the weight of Míkáylà's irrational divorce proceedings sank in, a torrent of memories surged forth like an emotional tsunami, recalling the echoes of Eleanor and Lucas, the last relationship I took full responsibility for as a man without Christ. But this one left me speechless, I was seeking physical healing for the woman I loved.

Prophesy 20ᵗʰ February 2013.

"Brother Joe,

I see that you are a very creative man. You can see the high places in God. You have a very deep, spiritual vision. God loves that you see without limits and He wants to bring you to that higher plane.

There is also a bit of a cloud that has hung around your life, however and I believe that this situation you are facing may have something to do with breaking that cloud.

I believe even though you have been a believer for a while, there is some darkness in your life and it's been a process for God to unwind that completely. God wants to break this cloud of despair that's been around you.

Your Father wants to speak a word of peace into your life. Although there are serious implications to the decisions you are making, God wants to remind you that it is from the place of eternal peace that the correct decisions are made.

As you seat yourself again in the eternal perspective of God, the correct path is going to become clear to you. The peace of The Holy Spirit is your guide.

About your situation. I believe that it concerns a family member (maybe your Mum?) who is in need and this is placing a significant burden on your heart, even clouding your emotions. I believe you may be considering a relocation as part of this.

This is causing you to have to face some things from the past that are very difficult for you to face, throwing you into turmoil. God reminds you of His ever-presence in a deeper way. He says that it is in the valley of despair that you will know Him more intimately than you have ever known Him before.

Joe, you should not fear to take the step, because He is with you. God bless."

*— Prophet Will Riddle.*

<u>April 4<sup>th</sup>, 2020.</u>

PROF. BEATRICE: "What do you see Joe?"

JOE: "I see my five-year-old self is holding my mother's hand. I see her silhouette glowing in the sun's golden embrace, radiating youth and beauty. This is… this is… my first memory of her, we are at the park, so green... The breeze is blowing the back of her jet-black hair and… she's turning slowly towards me..."

As she turned towards me, I instinctively shifted my gaze away. Beatrice, perceptive as ever, inquired, "What's he (you) doing?"

July 2013.

Courts, solicitor letters, irrational requests and unheeded pleas led me to stay with my parents for a season.

Limping to complete my first stage of the BACP Diploma Level one to three in counseling, I eventually qualified on the 16<sup>th of</sup> July 2013, utilizing the wonderful counselors around me in university. Their love, their journey, their story and the support of the three wonderful therapy professors (one who was also from Kansas) was a blessing beyond time and space. Such love and growth.

<u>Therapeutic Constellations</u>

*'If I take the wings of the morning and dwell in the uttermost parts of the sea, even your hand shall lead me and your right hand shall hold me.'*
*– King David*

The earth is indeed an expansive playground, brimming with anticipation for the discovery of new friendships. On August 1st, 2013, I took a daring leap into more adventures and arrived in the iconic city. 'San Francisco,' or 'Saint Francis' in Spanish, a tribute to the mystic Saint Francis of Assisi. Within a day, my plans shifted, prompting me to set off on a Greyhound bus expedition to Redding. A week unfolded there before my return to catch a flight from this energetic city to Dallas Fort Worth, spanning from August 8th to August 14th.

Subsequently, I attended the JGLM conference from August 14th to the 18th and then spent the period from August 19th to the 31st in Kansas, before unenthusiastically returning to the U.K. These experiences profoundly shaped me in many good ways, fostering personal growth and broadening my perspective in unexpected ways.

## Adventures.

### Travel Itinerary

August 1, 2013
Departure: Heathrow, Terminal 1 at 10:05
Arrival: Douglas at 14:10
Flight: US 71 - US Airways
Booking Reference: D9*3XN

August 1, 2013
Departure: Douglas at 16:40
Arrival: San Francisco Intl, Terminal 1 at 19:28
Flight: US 77 - US Airways
Booking Reference: D9*3XN

August 8, 2013

Departure: San Francisco Intl, Terminal 1 at 15:40

Arrival: Sky Harbor Intl, Terminal 4 at 17:33

Flight: US 29 - US Airways

Booking Reference: D9*3XN


August 8, 2013

Departure: Sky Harbor Intl, Terminal 4 at 18:45

Arrival: Dallas Ft Worth Intl, Terminal E at 22:58

Flight: US 54 - US Airways

Booking Reference: D9*3XN


September 1, 2013

Departure: Dallas Ft Worth Intl, Terminal E at 15:00

Arrival: Philadelphia Intl, Terminal B at 19:02

Flight: US 172 - US Airways

Booking Reference: D9*3XN


September 1, 2013

Departure: Philadelphia Intl, Terminal A at 21:50

Arrival: Heathrow, Terminal 1 at 10:00 (September 2, 2013)

Flight: US 72 - US Airways

Booking Reference: D9*3XN


Canticle of the Sun.


On the 1st of August, 2013, I arrived in San Francisco, California, feeling like I had stepped into a movie. The city's larger-than-life fire trucks, neon signs and funky traffic lights created a surreal and vibrant atmosphere.

Despite the city's allure, I found myself spending the night in a run-down hostel, an experience that reminded me of the contrasts and unexpected twists of life. From there, in the morning, I took a greyhound to Redding.

From California to Redding, Texas to Plano and Kansas to Wichita

Journal, 4<sup>th</sup> of August 2013:

I strongly felt the urge to be baptized (again) last night. The meaning, purpose and gravity of it struck me—the shedding of the remnants of religion, a rejected relationship and my past with its control and dogma. The default button was firmly pressed, marking a new life forever more. The pastor's sermon on purity resonated deeply. The opportunity to be submerged arose and as the last to take the plunge, I willingly embraced it. The past 48 hours had been a whirlwind of supernatural occurrences, making the thought of returning home undesirable.

After spending a week there, I took a Greyhound back to San Francisco to catch my flight to Dallas. I spent another week in Texas, specifically Plano. Reflecting on the recent whirlwind of supernatural occurrences, the thought of returning home became undesirable, as I sought to carry forward the newfound clarity and purpose from my baptismal experience.

14<sup>th of</sup> August, 2013: Journal (Irving, Texas)

*'If I say, surely the darkness shall cover me, even the night shall be light about me.' – King David*

Last night, I dreamt of a wounded angel who summoned me to join him at a prayer table. His countenance was stern and warlike yet kind. As he beckoned, his suit's sleeves revealed hidden feathers, a testament to the battles he had endured. Coincidentally, my friend in Redding, CA phoned me this morning, asking, 'What happened last night? Did you have a dream?' Unbeknownst to me, she had a friend pray for me long-distance.

So, this morning after her disclosure and encouragement I went to Wal-Mart to minister life. 'Holy Spirit, I want to be sensitive, lead me,' I prayed.

It began to rain in the sweltering heat of Irving, a sudden and refreshing downpour that felt like walking into a warm shower that washed the tears away. The water cascaded down, offering a welcome contrast to the heat and my clothes clung damply, drying rapidly in the humid air.

As I walked, I felt my right arm brush and tingle to take a right turn. As soon as I did, a Wal-Mart employee said, "How are you doing today?"

I replied, "Fine. How are you? Are you in good health?" She mentioned that she was apart from diabetes. I looked at her name badge and it read Felicia. I told her that her name means joy and happiness and that it was the joy of The Lord to heal her. She nodded upon acknowledgment that she was a believer. I asked her to stretch out her hand and as I held it, I commanded the diabetes to go. I spoke life into her from head to toe. I felt power come out and I laughed as I told her, "Whoa, there it goes." As I re-enforced, the joy of the Lord was strengthening her. Felicia said she felt a heat and tingle in her right hand and she was taken aback of what was happening to her. I told her she was healed and I laughed and blessed her in the Name of the Lord. She said she still felt tingly all over. I laughed and said it was the joy of the Lord, her namesake!

I then went for a coffee at a diner where I prophesied over a man. I told him he had a servant's heart and that God wanted to take him to a new place. I held out a concertina of scripture cards to pick and he randomly picked, 'Come to me, all ye who are weary and I will give you rest for your soul.' I prayed for him before I left. A minute later, he ran out of the shop to ask me more. His name was Alexandro of Italian descent—one of the co-managers of Wal-Mart.

"No one has ever told me this before. It makes sense, but if I'm to get with Jesus, how could he want me? My life is a mess. I have a boyfriend. I'm not right, but this thing you told me makes sense. What do I need to do? This is beautiful?"

This time, I was taken aback. I felt the presence of the Holy Spirit upon me as I looked at him, sensing the love of the Lord emanating toward him.

"My brother, we all need help. We all have inclinations of the heart that need remedy, that's why Jesus came. We understand right from wrong. He didn't come for the perfect, He came for you and me. If we allow Him in, if you speak to Him and ask Him to reveal Himself to you, He will show Himself and remove what blocks you from knowing Him. That's why I told you earlier that you have a servant's heart and God desires to draw you closer to Himself."

I put my hand on his heart and told him of his childhood and spoke the Fatherly heart of God upon him and he replied, "What you say is true. This is true." I pointed him to Jesus as he prayed and said, "Your life from today will not be the same. Speak to Him and you will see." I hugged Alexandro and walked out with a ham and cheese roll the size of a baseball bat.

Upon my return to the hotel, one of the receptionists had an epileptic seizure and split her head open. A young trainee soldier took charge of the situation and I provided oversight and offered a few basic suggestions. Eventually, an ambulance was called and while they attended to the lady, I held her elbow and commanded life to enter her.

I then prayed for the hotel manager, who was in shock, speaking peace into her soul and mind. The young man who took control, Mitch and ten other cadet soldiers had been stranded in the hotel, delayed on their way to Oklahoma for basic army training. Mitch suggested that it might have been divine intervention that led them to be there to help the receptionist. I took the opportunity to speak over his life, giving him the word, 'The good shepherd lays down his life for the sheep.' (John 10:11)

I prayed over him and his squadron, asking for divine intervention and protection and prophesying that he is a leader with Jesus as his Captain. I then gave scripture cards to the other cadets, emphasizing that their delay was not accidental. They responded, 'Yes, Sir! Thank you, Sir!' as if I were a General. Shortly after, their shuttle arrived to take them on the first leg of their journey to basic training in Oklahoma.

Wednesday August 14th, 2013, at 7:00 PM CDT-to-Sunday August 18th, 2013, at 12:00 PM CDT. Holiday Inn. 1655 N. Central Expressway, Richardson. TX. 75080.

I was blessed to be collected by a brother on route to the JG** conference. He even had booked a double room for us to stay in.

JOE: "This Mexican man's humor was gold. Picture this: He shared about the days when he and his buddies used to playfully toss pretend grenades at each other, asking, 'Can ju feel dat? Can ju feel dat?' Then, 'kaboom' they'd act like the grenade exploded and holler 'Love grenade!' And that's not all – imagine them shooting invisible arrows at each other, aiming for the heart and shouting 'Healing balm of Gilead!' I was in hysterics."

PROF. VIRGIL: "A servant heart and a sense of humor—risata, laughter—is indeed like medicine."

It was at this event that I had the pleasure of hearing Rev. Curry Blake share and exposit many wonderful sermons. Even his daughters took the stage to share their thoughts. Following four days of personal growth, I approached Curry and requested if he could inquire whether anyone was headed to Kansas. As the event concluded, a young man kindly offered to buy me a flight ticket to Kansas, a gesture that truly humbled me. Seizing the opportunity, I boarded a flight to Kansas right around the time the decree absolute was finalized. Traveling undeniably broadens one's horizons and in Kansas, I discovered a renewed sense of life and forged new friendships.

PROF. BEATRICE: "I see in the film *The Wizard of Oz*, the Tinman wanted a heart, the Scarecrow wanted a brain, and the Cowardly Lion wanted courage. Dorothy, of course, wanted to go home. Yet, as you've so eloquently expressed, to be lost indicates that we have a home to go to. What that looks and feels like is something that client and therapist explore together through the yellow brick road of love. Tell me 'bout your time in Kansas and spill the beans 'bout that road trip of yours."

JOE: "Spill the beans, more like take the kryptonite out of my blood…18th of August, 2013. My Kansas Soundtrack: *'Sent Here for a Reason', from 'Man of Steel' by Hans Zimmer.*"

Pete Cabrera Jr picked me up from the airport along with his family and right from the start, he embraced me like a brother. Staying at their house for the following three weeks was both an honor and a much-needed healing retreat.

As I journeyed through the heart of Kansas, the landscape unfolded like a painting of Americana dreams. Flour mills stood like proud sentinels, their weathered facades carrying the stories of generations past. Against the canvas of endless blue skies, their presence lent an air of nostalgic charm to the scene.

Vast expanses of green fields stretched out in every direction, with bright, vibrant sunflowers as far as the eye could see. Their yellow petals were outstretched like sunlit crowns, a testament to the fertile earth's abundance. The sunlight played upon the rolling waves of grass, creating a dance of emerald hues that seemed to sway in rhythm with the calm breeze.

Amid this tapestry, windmills stood as graceful guardians of the land. Their slender arms reached out to the heavens, harnessing the power of the wind to shape the destiny of the landscape. Scattered across the horizon like silent companions, they added a touch of whimsy to the grandeur of the scene and my soul felt like I was flying. That night, I slept like a soul embraced by the divine, cradled in the serenity of dreams.

20<sup>th</sup> August 2013 Journal entry 'The Freeze Canister'

*'For thou hast possessed my reins, though hast covered me in my mother's womb.'*

*– King David*

So, the air conditioning in Pete Cabrera Jr.'s car needed fixing because the freeze canister he inserted into the air conditioning unit caused a malfunction. So, we pulled to the nearest garage. As the mechanic popped open the hood and went to work with his tools, I prayed for one man whose discs were out of sync, laid my hand on his back and with intent I *'thought commanded'* them to shift. He said he felt heat and felt giddy. Then Pete asked him to touch his toes and he was able to do that.

"*Holy sh--! What the f--k?* I haven't been able to do that in years!" I explained that I did this in Jesus' Name. I then prophesied to a young man who was watching 'Ray.' (The story of the life and career of the legendary rhythm and blues musician Ray Charles). Next was Tanya, a young Mother holding her toddler, who suffered poor eyesight and could not afford to go to the doctors. I placed my hand on her eyes and commanded her pupils to be made whole and her lenses at the back of her eyes to grow. I told her to read the sign at the end of the road and she marveled as she could now see perfectly. "Isn't that cool?" I said. Her husband (Dave) came out and he told me he had a hernia. Naturally, I placed my hand on his upper thigh and held his hand with the other. I commanded the tear in the muscle to be repaired and he felt heat enter. He said the pain went. In *all* things God works together for the good of those who love Him.

### The Bride.

### 23$^{rd\ of}$ August 2013.

Journal Entry: Day Twenty-Three in the Land of Stars and Stripes

I find myself immersed in the rich tapestry of ecclesiastical life as I journey through different facets of the bride of Christ across several states.

Week One: The body of Christ comes alive, dancing, praising and pouring forth perfume at the feet of Jesus, as Heaven touches Earth.

Week Two: I encounter a different facet—a bride seemingly mechanized and mail-ordered, donning layers of makeup to grace the pages of Vogue.

Week Three: Here, the bride wields a brilliant Kingdom saber, cutting through the darkness with one hand, yet harboring a paradoxical distrust of its own.

Weeks Four, Five and Six: I witness the bride in the nurturing role of a mother, tenderly caring for her own, much like the Psalmist in Psalm 131:2: "I have calmed and quieted myself, I am like a weaned child with its mother, like a weaned child, I am content."

As the body of Christ, we are on a collective journey, resembling a bride, seeking deeper knowledge and understanding of our identity in Him. We are a united family, pursuing the fullness of our identity, embracing both our strengths and weaknesses.

# Chapter Seven

# I Know a Man

*'How precious also are thy thoughts unto me, O God! How great is the sum of them! If I should count them, they are more in number than the sand. When I awake, I am still with thee.' – King David*

September 1st, 2013 – Journal entry.

I know a man whose journey through the year 2013 was a tapestry woven with threads of discovery and transformation. This man came to a profound realization: no matter how arduously one endeavors to compel another's affection, true love remains elusive. He was brought to his knees, tenderly broken when confronted with papers that carried the stark black ink of this reality. It was a pivotal moment that shattered the veneer of perfection, exposing the fractures in his dreams. A man who longed for the embrace of family, only to see it slip through his grasp.

In this year, a vivid vision of the underworld unfurled—a realm of ensnared souls and haunting cries, an eerie dance with the infernal. Amid the fires and debris, he glimpsed Hades' realm, a nightmarish journey. Yet, within this torment, he encountered God's presence, a glimmer of hope in the abyss of rejection.

I know a man who was deserted and abandoned by those he considered to be Godly people in the U.K. They didn't extend their hands to help because they were reluctant to get involved, preoccupied with their own lives. This man is now grateful, recognizing that God often separates the wheat from the chaff.

I know a man who almost didn't board the plane from Heathrow to America, where he hoped to visit his role models. Yet, at the last minute, he decided to take the flight. As soon as he landed in San Francisco, he found himself on a path marked by emptiness and abandonment. Even amid this pain, amid rejection and self-soothing, he encountered God.

From the depths of despair, he embarked on a journey that carried him across the ocean to America and into what some call the 'breadbasket' of the nation. It was a spontaneous decision to fly out, but within the anguish of rejection, he discovered solace in God's presence. Guided by an unseen hand, he boarded a bus bound for Redding, California. It was there that he encountered an angelic figure—a gentle Asian woman—who offered guidance and clarity for his future.

I know a man who woke up one morning and bought breakfast for a grateful homeless man. Afterward, he embarked on a three-mile, two-hour journey with a heavy rucksack on his back to climb a hill at Bethel. When he reached the summit, a remarkable encounter awaited him. The Holy Spirit had guided a lady, whom he had never met before, to drive that way and pick him up at the exact moment he completed his ascent. She took him to Twin Peaks, where he was granted instant access to a prayer team for ministry and healing.

This man was then picked up by another compassionate church member who provided accommodation, food and fellowship for a whole week. He felt as if he had been adopted and cherished like a son, a brother and a father.

He was loved, cared for, nurtured and found healing through the bride of Christ, manifesting in various shapes and forms. He witnessed brothers and sisters in Redding dancing in worship, pouring forth the ointment of praise and love at the feet of Jesus and celebrating freedom.

I know a man who was so inspired by these experiences that he chose to be baptized, washing away the burdens of religion and the dross of his past. As he emerged from the waters, he felt like a renewed virgin, baptized as the last man kneeling, with his hand raised victoriously. To his surprise, his brother and sister-in-law watched the live service from 5,187 miles away and saw him on God TV, emerging from the waters, a testament to a phoenix rising from the flames.

I know a man who, after spending a week in Redding, took a Greyhound bus back to San Francisco before flying to Texas. While sleeping in Irving, Texas, he had a vision of a kind warrior angel with tattered feathers. This angel beckoned him to a table for prayer and revealed glimpses of the future. When he woke up, he discovered that hundreds of miles away back in Redding, California, sisters had prayed for him that very night.

This man was then picked up and cared for by a compassionate couple in another part of Texas, who hosted him for a conference. There, he met one of his role models and encountered more loving individuals who inspired him to run the race with a spirit of determination.

I know a man who needed a ride to Wichita, Kansas, but instead, a stranger purchased an airline ticket for him to fly there. Upon arriving at Wichita airport, he was greeted by a role model who hadn't missed a church service in over ten years. This man was taken to a restaurant with his newfound Christian family and then stayed at their house for over three weeks. It was there that he experienced the best sleep he had had in over fifteen years, all within the same family of God's house.

I know a man who, while meeting and learning from others, journeyed with God to Kansas and experienced a form of translocation, arriving at his destination fifteen minutes early, despite being miles behind on the road, with the car in front never stopping.

He encountered a large family of believers at the conference, each with differing theological perspectives. However, they all demonstrated love and shared a common desire for the coming of Christ's Kingdom. While at the conference, this man was overcome, falling to the floor as if electrified, with tears streaming down his face.

I know a man who was given a ride back to Texas from Wichita and had his last night in America paid for by a wonderful family. This man stumbled upon an abandoned circus filled with statues and paintings of grotesque goblins and demons. He commanded them to leave and filmed the eerie atmosphere on his iPhone (because disposable cameras from Boots are so last century). This man almost didn't board the plane back to England, he was tempted to stay. However, he chose to carry a piece of America with him.

Upon his return to work in a place where Christ is banned, this man began to sing in tongues in front of the teenagers and they miraculously translated the tongues into, "God loves you, turn the journey around—peace is yours."

I know a man who expressed his desire to demonstrate and speak about his aspirations for the future, although he wasn't allowed to. When the teenagers asked him, his thoughts transformed into words and a teenager's wounded arm was healed before their eyes.

This man visited churches in the U.K., seeking a spiritual family to fellowship with and a place to settle. Instead, he encountered religious language, questions about the circumcision of his heart and doubts about whether he truly belonged to the promise of Abraham. Each visit to church left him grieved as he found perpetual legalism in place of genuine fellowship.        This is a man whose mind is being renewed day by day, walking in his identity and desiring the same for the body of believers, all while navigating the sacred cow called doctrine. I know of this man who, upon his return to England, started asking people to randomly open any book and look at the first thing their eyes fell upon. The words they landed on were the very things they needed to hear, including the word 'Gospel.'

Such a man had a broken-hearted start to the year, yet he came to the experiential realization that the only love that will never forsake us is the love of an eternal Father, the love of Christ.

This is a man who, at the end of this year, is fully convinced that he is loved and accepted for who he is—a son of God. I know a man who eagerly anticipates 2014 and beyond as years of abounding love and the fulfillment of heart desires.


## Sapphire firmament.


Upon returning from the Breadbasket of America, I had to settle my court case, representing myself in court and proposing a deal to my ex-wife. The deal required her to sell the house in North Weald to pay off one of the two other houses we jointly owned. This would allow her to live mortgage-free in one of them. The alternative was financial bankruptcy for all parties, with the banks being the sole beneficiaries. I was grateful to be released from all covenants and joint mortgage names with her. However, all involved learned that freedom, like anything else, comes at a price and sometimes life doesn't go as planned.

I moved back in with my parents until April 2014. On Easter day, I returned to Ingvar Road, embracing all the memories it held. I rented out my two rooms while fully immersing myself in Bible School and leading a therapeutic life group. Simultaneously, I grappled with cognitive dissonance, not wanting those I spoke to and disciplined to experience the same loneliness I had felt. This was despite witnessing signs and wonders and holding onto the belief in an abundant life.

Life isn't always filled with blue skies and rainbows, sometimes, the dog bites and the bee stings. I've both fallen and soared, learning valuable lessons and finding a touch of grace and peace along the way. Yet, through every trial and tribulation, I've discovered the resilience of the human spirit and the power of perseverance.

The race is ongoing. I've witnessed miracles, experienced wonders, encountered angels and caught glimpses of Heaven. Yet, one undeniable truth remains: until I truly understand and find rest within myself, my actions, regardless of the names they bear, may be blind, mechanical, militant and devoid of melody. In the midst of chaos, I search for the symphony, the harmony that binds the universe and resonates within my soul, guiding me through the tumultuous seas of life towards the shores of serenity and fulfillment.

Year 2 September 2015.

I did return to Kansas and Texas in August 2015 to visit and stay with my American family.

Following a gap year, I resumed NLM University in September 2015, despite having a broken collarbone from playing paintball. During the same week, I was scheduled to teach people about divine healing at a Church in Tottenham, North London. I'd love to tell you it's a picturesque village where Princess Di strolled with the Queen's corgis, but it exudes a bit more of a gangster vibe instead. This marked my second year at the university after taking a year off to refocus. I found myself surrounded by a new group of peers, predominantly women. I found myself in the unique position of being the only man among my cohort for two years.

From third-wave feminists to the white privilege shamers, our group included a diverse mix—a sensitive LGBTQ evangelical, a social worker, a learning mentor, a Christian, a Buddhist, an orthodox Jew, a Black Panther enthusiast and myself. — The bartender looks up and says, 'Is this the start of a joke or a support group meeting? —Sounds like the start of a joke right?

I soon discovered that I, too, felt foreign to myself at times. There were moments when it seemed prudent to remain silent and adjust my schoolwork to align with acceptable opinions, all in pursuit of a better grade.

Our interactions were like sparks igniting ideologies, dogma and belief systems, sharpening us for our future roles as counselors who would navigate constellations of traumatic personalities. These two years felt like a process of dismantling my dogmas, challenging cognitive dissonances and learning to accept people for who they were. After all, isn't that what unconditional positive regard is all about?

It was a beautiful time, a period of bonding where, undoubtedly, the occasional miracle still unfolded. One woman who had struggled to conceive was prayed for and shortly after, she became pregnant with twins. Another lady had a dream of Christ. My fundamentalist tendencies were gradually replaced with a greater acceptance of people as they were—just as they had accepted me. I was no longer an alien among them, I was an equal. Every week, we delved into the exploration of our identities, our motivations and our beliefs.

As I sat in the lecture hall, learning to accept that I live in a world with different outlooks shaped by beliefs and experiences, I felt like I was drowning in the suffocating grip of my own fundamentalism, where my perception and perspective needed to shift. Perspective influences how we see the world, but perception is the cognitive process of making sense of sensory inputs. But then, in a moment of overwhelming clarity, I heard the soft voice of the Holy Spirit and everything changed.

"I didn't come to rescue you," the voice said, "I came to show you who you are."

"Who am I?" I asked.

"You are love," the inner voice replied and suddenly I was filled with a sense of peace and understanding that I had once felt before. It was like I was born again once more.

Tears welled up in my eyes as I shared my experience with my peers. They felt it too, the presence of God, the truth of the words that had been spoken. It was a moment of pure connection and realization.

September 2016 Year 3 NLM University.

In September 2016, during my third year at the university, I returned after spending the entire month of August back in the Sunflower State for the third time.

I had been carrying a hernia for nearly a year, a result of doing some sit-ups on a steep incline at home. I underwent surgery for an inguinal hernia on November $2^{nd}$, during which time I had put on three stone in weight (32lbs) due to my inability to exercise. This weight gain brought with it some mental fatigue and feelings of stress, compounded by work pressures. I returned to counseling after missing a week due to the double surgery. The stitches were removed recently, but half of them burst open. So, as I tune in, I feel held together by what seems like packed seaweed.

At the family home, my Mother was very ill and she would later be diagnosed with cancer in December. I am aware that my intellectual side seeks to reconcile with the assassin using logic and rationale as justification for not reaching out and fellowshipping, which in turn numbs my feelings. My peacemaker side may have a voice urging me to build connections and help them, believing that by allowing them to help me, I am also helping them.

However, I find the voice of trust handcuffed and bound in a corner, taken hostage by the wayside of disappearing and disappointing friendships, this is how my configurations feel. I'm scheduled for a hospital scan soon to determine the possibility of further surgery. Maybe the scan will scan all my configurations of self. I couldn't help but laugh as I shared this with my peers at the end of the day.

Thursday 17<sup>th of</sup> November 2016 — Journal entry

*'The therapist is the catalyst, not so much the healer.'*
— *Mick Cooper.*

The walk to the university was a picturesque sight. The autumn leaves in shades of orange, brown and red blanketed the gray pavements, creating a refreshingly colorful scene. Pigeons dove off the roofs, seemingly bungee jumping, to engulf themselves in the smoke of marijuana.

To begin with, I was far from feeling present or connected to my peers. I had yet to share with them the news from the clinic yesterday. The Doctor had said that had my stitches not come open, the scan would never have picked up a marble-sized foreign object in my left scrotum, he said that it was a 'serendipitous moment' and the nurse said it was a blessing in disguise to have something like that spotted early. They are suggesting that I may need surgery to remove the foreign object. I find myself less than pleased and slightly annoyed by the inconvenience of potentially undergoing surgery either before or after Christmas. Meanwhile, my colleagues at work have not sent me any messages or notes expressing 'get well soon' sentiments or even acknowledging the situation. My sense of humor (despite these unexpected developments) coupled with the contemplation of being somewhat diminished from my former self, falls under the category of Gallows humor — a concept Professor Bernard introduced me to when I eventually shared a few concise details of the revelation. Gallows humor serves as a defense mechanism.

How many therapists does it take to change a light bulb? One, but the light bulb must want to change.


## What triggers my configurations?


Now, concerning configurations of self, I am keenly aware that each morning brings a familiar sensation: the urge to push everyone away. There's this lingering belief that they won't truly comprehend me on a profound level, that there's a depth missing in our interactions. It's as if we're all destined to part ways come June 2017, never to cross paths again.

I've come to accept that friends come and go and the assassin part within me is awakened by feelings of distrust and recent health scares. These configurations of self, influenced by past experiences and emotions, shape my reluctance to forge or pursue peer connections.

# Great Balls of fire

Journal of Thursday 19<sup>th of</sup> January 2017.

I returned to the university two days after surgery at The Royal Free Hospital in London (NW3 2QG). A part of me now resides in a jar in a hospital ward, serving as a specimen for medical students to study. The surgery had its share of complications, my body appeared to reject the silicone implant. As a result, I woke up from surgery a few hours later to find that my remaining part had swollen to the size of a basketball—no exaggeration could capture the extent of the pain I felt.

Amid my moans and alarmingly high blood pressure, doctors rushed to provide medication and insert a tube to alleviate the fluid buildup. They presented me with two options: to wait for the fluid in my swelling to naturally subside, a process that would take three weeks, or to undergo another operation to manually remove the excess fluid. I opted for the latter.

While encouraged to use the restroom, I walked with my legs akimbo. One nurse, seemingly unaware of my situation, asked why I was walking that way. Under the influence of medication and frustration at her lack of empathy, I replied, "Because I want to be John Wayne riding a horse. Why do you think I'm walking like this? Look at what I'm carrying ... I'm just a hunk, a hunk of burning love!" On another occasion, some nurses nearly administered an overdose of medication, but I managed to stay alert and prevent it.

Two days later, after the surgery to remove the excess fluid, I returned to the university, having lost track of time and space, the effects of medication still lingering in my body. I hobble in with a walking stick, I just want to complete this course. It feels like I have had sniper shots taken at me from all around. I feel that I haven't the energy to speak or sit. I briefly share about my stint in the hospital and how what should have been a straightforward 'in and out' operation ended up with complications, blood clots, scars and a secondary operation. The decision was left to me due to what seems like the incompetence of rookie doctors and surgeons who are practicing on humans to further their academic careers. I shared how some nurses treat patients like cattle and are stressed and I did not feel safe on the night shift of the ward.

Yet, I wore a silent mask, for my mother's battle with cancer had become my own shadow, concealed behind my steely resolve. A secret whispered between life's threads, all while I tread the path of surgery unshared, a choice made to shield my beloved mother from needless worry.

I managed to present my absent Father PowerPoint presentation and after I'd taken pain medication, I had to lie down and promptly fell asleep, snoring through Professor Virgil's presentation on Autism.


February 2017.


The Mystery Revealed - A presentation to my cohorts:
'What I believe and how it affects me as a counselor.'


I want to let you briefly into my world. I want to share with you a mystery hidden for thousands of years. I hope you will be empathic as you allow me to walk tentatively into the garden of your imagination. I hope we can make psychological contact.

*For God, who embodies unconditional agape love, positively regarded humanity's birthplace and sent His only begotten Son to become one of us, to put on flesh and bones. Through this act, Jesus made psychological contact with us and empathically entered our frame of reference, even amid our incongruence and distortion of our true calling. He shows me that I am the righteousness of God despite this distortion, which existed between our experiences and awareness of who we were called to be and who we truly are as an organismic self, capable of becoming the version we are called to be in this world—nurtured in an environment of agape-love.*

*By revealing and reflecting His Son, we can perceive ourselves as a congruent and genuine representation of the reality of His Son, who demonstrated and manifested life as a way of being. We forget who we are because we have forgotten who He is. He is life, He is love and whoever believes and actualizes their faith in Him will not perish in incongruence or distortion but will have a fully functioning perpetual Zoë life. He has shown us our original calling: that we are life, we are love.*

I attained my university qualification in June 2017, earning my foundation degree. Subsequently, I triumphantly secured my BA degree in the fourth year of my journey, marking 2018 as a milestone. Oh, the joy of that moment when my cohorts and I flung our university hats skyward and there I stood, holding a mock degree aloft like a cigar of accomplishment.

22<sup>nd of</sup> April 2017.

PROF. BEATRICE: "What do you see, Joe?"

JOE: "She's dying… and I don't know what to say. I don't know what to do. Yet, in her weakness and without words, she's leaning into me, tucking her head against my belly... I cannot bring myself to look at her, I don't know what to do or what to say... I..."

My mother passed away at the hospital, losing her battle with cancer on April 22$^{nd}$, 2017, which happened to be her younger son's 40$^{th}$ birthday.

Her last words were, 'Praise the Lord,' as she closed her eyes, only to open them and find herself greeted by Christ, her parents and saints from ages past welcoming her home.

April 4$^{th}$, 2020

PROF. BEATRICE: "What do you see Joe?"

JOE: "I see my five-year-old self is holding my mother's hand. I see her silhouette glowing in the sun's golden embrace, radiating youth and beauty. This is my first memory of her, we are at the park, so green... The breeze is blowing the back of her jet-black hair and she's... she's turning slowly towards me..."

As she turned towards me, I instinctively shifted my gaze away. Beatrice, perceptive as ever, inquired, "What's he doing?"

JOE: "He has turned around and is asking... (pause) he is asking me... (pause) he is asking me... to…"

# July 2024 +. In the Ghetto

The present—I now reside and practice as a Psychotherapist in the dynamic embrace of Asia. Each day gifts me with the splendor of countless exquisite encounters. I am enveloped by beauty, a dance of life's hues that nourishes my soul and fills me with a sense of being fully alive, much like a blossom reaching its zenith of blooming.

This journey is especially poignant, having emerged from the ghettos of Edmonton and Enfield in North London, where I witnessed the struggles of the disenfranchised and worked with gangs, seeing teenagers stabbed on a weekly basis. Now, in reference to paradise, I see a different end of the spectrum. I've encountered anxious, lonely children from wealthy backgrounds who are medicated by zealous doctors peddling Valium, beta blockers and other suppressants to children as young as eight, as if these were sweets.

I witness a lot of affluent neglect in a world where beauty often masks various problems. My role is to offer solace and healing to those in need. This is what I love, this is what I do. It's not without its challenges, as there are snakes in suits and mosquitoes in pencil skirts at the top of the food chain, with egos and nepotism burying the truth to maintain profit. But amidst it all, there are flowers in the dirt.

# Chapter Eight

## Flower

PROF. BEATRICE: "Well, now, while we're all caught up in our minds, wishin' for that love and hopin' folks 'round us would change, we plumb forget 'bout ourselves. The hitch in our step, that quiet buzz of jitters under the surface and them tender feelings begging for a mite of our loving care. Take a turn within, darlin', meet your own self with a heapin' spoonful of kindness and warmth. Watch the magic unfold right before your eyes— suddenly, you're hitched up, alive and kickin', real as a Kansas sunrise and wrapped up in a blanket of peace like a cozy evening breeze."

3$^{rd \, of}$ October 2017, Letter to Jenelle in New Braunfels, Texas.

Dear Jenelle, to be Intimately militant or militantly intimate?

*"Intimately militant. Joe, it is to be intimately militant."*

— *Jenelle Eickelberg.*

I denied my humanity for a long time, yes. I know I'm not from here [1-2], but the human experience is a wonderful one. Not just in spirit, but in skin too. The joys of life—pain, love, coffee, spaghetti, sticky mango and rice, Som Tum (green papaya salad) and sunshine—freedom from missions and results. And besides, people are amazing.

Nothing exposes how deeply some people have been programmed since early childhood as when religion, politics, or race issues are brought up in conversations.

Whatever triggers, offends, or challenges us, making us uncomfortable, is precisely what we must acknowledge, embrace and learn from if we truly wish to break free from our mental prison. Our mental programming, though invisible to us, is our master, controlling our feelings and actions for years.

If we genuinely desire freedom from our mental programming, we must be willing to step outside our comfort zone, for comfort is what binds us mentally. We must also venture into the realm of the unknown without fearing it.

Our mental liberation from the programming ingrained since childhood lies 'beyond the world of comfort' and 'within the realm of the unknown'.

The thing that is helping me still to cultivate love and undergo a paradigm shift is asking myself, grounding myself and being aware: Am I fostering unity? Am I contributing positively? Am I actively building the body, the bride of Christ? And if, by some chance, I found myself in a challenging situation with individuals I might not naturally get along with, we hopefully would discover a way to extend love to one another.

'Why?' The religious may ask.

Because of Christ dwelling within us, the Hope of glory resides in our hearts. I may not be in a literal prison, nor do I seek to become a martyr. Instead, let me extend my love to you wherever you may be. This perspective is illuminating my vision.

I'm not passively waiting for the second coming of Jesus. I'm eagerly anticipating the arrival of the mature bride of Christ, embodying the essence of the first coming. The latter heralds the former, not the other way around, as we wield the transformative power of love and compassion to bring about the kingdom of God on earth.

## All those powers

When my mother died, I felt like the scene in 'Superman: The Movie' [3] as he screamed to the heavens when the love of his life died and then he flew and spun around the world backwards. In that iconic film moment, Superman, with his incredible power, reversed time to save Lois Lane from a tragic fate. But in my own life, I was powerless to change what had happened. *'All those things I can do, all those powers and I couldn't even save HER.'*

As a child, I watched that scene in awe, imagining the possibility of altering the course of events with a single act. Yet, when reality struck and I faced the loss of my mother, I realized the painful truth: I couldn't rewind time or rewrite the script of her life. Instead, I grappled with the raw emotions, the grief and the profound sense of loss from the rapture of my disconnect with her.

In my anguish, I did something unexpected. I screamed and burned all my testimonies, my healing books, my ordinations and my affiliations. It wasn't a rational response, but it was a release of pent-up emotions, a mutiny against the doctrines that had defined my life for that chapter. In that moment, I shed the weight of expectations, the burden of theology and the confines of tradition.

'Where's the power? Where's the healing? Where's the promise of His stripes?' I asked. Seems like smoke and mirrors—hits and misses mixed with beg and hope, command and demand, yet there seems to be no consistency. When I read all these books and watched all these sermons, a part of me became uncertain and disillusioned in seeking power to do the job to help the ones I loved. Besides, healing is just a pause button anyway. All will enter the door to the other side one day.

I don't know how it works and don't let anyone tell you otherwise that they know it all—*nobody does*. So far, what I know is this: He's with me while I drink this coffee, eat this gingerbread man and live my life through this fleeting journey.

It wasn't a turning back time, it was a turning point in my journey, a recognition that life's complexities couldn't be unraveled by a superhero's or a Son of God's healing spin around the Earth. It was the beginning of my detox, a process of shedding old beliefs and rediscovering my faith in a way that felt genuine and authentic. And so, my story continues, like the echoes of that scene, a reminder of the power of acceptance and transformation in the face of life's mystery.

# Out of the Mire.

*"Behold, thou desirest truth in the inward parts:*
*and in the hidden part thou shalt make me to know wisdom." —*
*Psalm 51:6*

I cringe, yet I must forgive myself. Having once sipped from the institutionalized Church's milk, I also played a role in what I'll coin as the birth of 'Frank-Christ-steins'—a breed of Fatherless, militant and charismatic individuals who navigate through the murky waters of legalism, tribalism and the fear of judgment. They do all this while singing cheesy love songs that convey, 'Am I good enough? I don't truly understand who you are, or who I am, but did I perform well? Please, come to me and spare the people I love from eternal damnation.'

I regurgitated the spiritual system that produces orphans through doctrines of fear, which has now become the staple recipe for disconnection and discord.

I sincerely hope this culture of 'us versus them,' with its view of a schizoid bi polar God who loves us but seemingly condemns people to eternal suffering unless they interpret the scriptures the same way, does not spread to the East. It's a belief in 'losing salvation if you go astray' and a 'go out into the world and persuade everyone to believe and choose salvation' approach, all under the threat of consequences. Even within many camps of the charismatic circus, where those who perform signs and wonders believe it validates their doctrine, there is a tendency towards militancy and conformity. Many join in, driven by a mental delusion that never truly addresses their trauma. Instead, it fosters cognitive dissonance that hinders intimacy and genuine connections with both the Father and humanity itself. Well, at least that was my experience.

Well, thanks be to God, my eyes are now more open. The eyes of my heart have been ignited by the state of many peculiar ecclesial bricks that have been 'Sanctus skubalon,' perpetuating anti-Christ tendencies, all allegedly done in the Name of love. In reality, it's been done out of limerence, lip service, law and a fear of judgment, all wrapped in dogma-wrapped trauma.

I see many who are now burnt out, confused, deluded, power-hungry, lingering in a conflicting mental state, imprisoned under a fortress of left-hemisphere thinkers. Many have spent their lives working diligently in hospitable circumstances, yet unable to fully discern their purpose due to low self-esteem, the influence of their leaders, elders and doctrine hindering growth.

There was a time when perhaps they thought like I did: 'I don't know why I'm doing this,' but code silenced them. It's quite hard to accept new ideas, thus becoming immune and numbed within, the burnout of going through the motions when my soul has departed.

### Denial

A lot of defensiveness occurs, along with denial, which is also a hallmark of left hemisphere thinking—resembling a form of *witchcraft* in its purest form, intellectualized with a seductive allure to power and gain. This left hemisphere often controls the right hand, which grasps and then handcuffs another unfortunate soul, making them a prisoner of boredom. [4]

Yet, without the balance of the right brain, where emotions, social-emotional intelligence, intuition, love and meaning reside, the current system remains abstract. It's challenging for suppressed emotions to express subtleties, contradictions and the implicit nature found in dogma and so-called worship. [5]

Unfortunately, the institutional Church has led people to become ensnared in a view of God and life that is utterly perplexing and to be frank, as lifeless as the Dodo. It remains stagnant, rigid and certain, isolated in its competition with other denominations and demonization. It exists in a detached, apathetic world, where its only blurred value lies in its utility—to be used, to be profitable, to be beneficial for a God who, in their eyes, seeks to revive a Pentecostal revival of old, filled with stories of the past. This perception describes a deity that uses people as if they were indebted to Him because they have now attained royalty, rather than one who promotes a glorious Kingdom of love and peace, spreading through the knowledge of intimacy and oneness with Him. It's a relationship in which both parties are one yet separate, a dance of newfound, unending union—forever together in life and eternity. In this relationship, all things are seen as seamlessly interconnected, constantly flowing and perpetually changing, fostering a connection based on care and love.

The cradle of humanity is born into love in one form or another. However, there were times I felt it preferable to remain in utero and within the so-called worldly confines than to be shaped into the image of a stillborn hemisphere [6] by an anti-Christ establishment. This establishment sings the songs of beggars or militant dualism, proclaiming that God doesn't pour His spirit out on all flesh. Instead, it presents God as capricious, playing a cruel game of hide and seek with malicious intent. It's comparable to Father Christmas checking off a naughty list or the Greek god Zeus, always ready to unleash a thunderbolt.

Where is the mystery? Where is the hope? Where is the Christ? Has he even been revealed? Yes, the Kingdom is here and the hope of Glory, the Rose of Sharon and Lily of the Valley, is in us. *This* is the good news, the Gospel, simple. It's time we stop intellectualizing and feel the freedom to embrace and experience love. [7] I want out of this concrete.

### Prophecy.

February 25th, 2014, at Vineyard Church, St. Albans, England.

Midway through his sermon a visiting Pastor Robbie Dawkins stopped and looked at me.

Robbie: "What's your name, sir?"

Joe: "Joseph."

Robbie: "Joseph, I just looked over at you during worship earlier and I heard the Lord say how blessed He was by your worship. I saw it like a plant pushing its way up from the earth. You know how most plants come up through the dirt, but yours was emerging from the middle of the rock. I saw you pushing through and pushing through, like some flowers and roses do. It's pretty amazing. I heard the Lord say, 'Your worship has been like that— pushing through a lot of hard stuff, coming through some real difficulties.' But I hear the Lord saying, 'Well done, well done,' just for that expression of worship and persevering through. The Lord is pleased with you.

I just feel like, God's going to begin to release some things to you. Some things that have been blocked up or hidden, the Lord is going to start releasing them. I hear the Lord saying, 'Be encouraged, there's a breakthrough coming for you.' Does that make sense? I mean, don't be nice, if that doesn't make sense, tell me."

Joe: "It does, thank you."

Robbie (in prayer): "Father, we bless Joseph and thank you for his faith and perseverance in worship and breakthrough. We thank you for him, Father. Thank you that he's here and we bless him in Jesus' name …" Robbie (continuing with his sermon) "... Now, where were we? Oh yes, we were talking about taking risks and how it ties into our faith..."

Flower.

มะลิวัลย์

Dear Jenelle,

I miss you all and think of your family with such great affection and honor. Texas, New Braunfels has left joy in my heart. Thanks for your encouragement that Father wants me to have an adventure. You've inspired me to write again.

Everyone has a story to tell. This is mine so far, or at least a vignette thereof. "Stars twinkle but planets shine," said your daughter, Amelia, whom I'm convinced will be an amazing author.

Planet Joe had been under the shadow of a dualistic eclipse for a significant part of his life. After my encounter with Christ in 1998, the modern-day institution known as the Church robbed me of that tangible, simple, loving encounter and ensnared me in the limerence of spiritual delusion, making me jump through hoops in search of a place where I truly belonged.

I had been seeking answers and peace in the shadows of those who appeared to have it all figured out when in truth, no one really does. Mysteries and secrets will always exist, as:

'The secret things belong to the Lord our God, but the things revealed belong to us and our children forever.' [8]

Unfortunately, scripture is often used to comfort or distract us when words fail to adequately express our inner emotions. What we truly need are experiential encounters—moments of silence or companionship, experiences like witnessing a breathtaking view or receiving a loving smile without hidden motives—to rekindle our awareness of God's ever-present presence. These encounters help us embrace our God-given humanity. After all, Jesus loved His body so much that He took it home with Him.

I'm still in the process of reflecting on my recent forty-eight-month journey. Each month has been so rich in discoveries within me that writing a chapter about each could be a possibility. However, I can confidently and experientially affirm that the Father has been with me every step of the way since I departed from the charismatic circus and embarked on this new expedition.

I once heard it said, though nobody knows exactly who said it (although it is often attributed to Albert Einstein), that 'Insanity is doing the same thing over and over again and expecting different results.'

I radically needed to do something different. I rewrote my entire plan, selling everything and moving home, returning to university to finish my degree, embracing cultures and loving people, envisaging a future with Heaven's atmosphere a thousand miles from the U.K.

I'd once experienced peace and tranquility in a market in Texas, New Braunfels, sipping on beautiful cold brew coffee. Those moments of staying with a loving family who embraced and accepted me imprinted hope and love like fresh snow footprints in my soul and I will treasure them forever.

I am not conformist, nor orthodox, though may be at this phase of life, some may consider me a mystic, but I'm long done with labels. Everything changes when you see how the cross is looked at in early Christendom. And seeing it once is to never go back to the fear-based, 'small g' god of Evangelicalism.

There is no comparing the internal landscape of the heart under these premises about the character of Father God. The Westernized god can turn insiders into salesmen, laboring under a very weak concept of grace as some unfinished work that humans need to complete. I was an evangelistic, blanket insurance salesman of sorts.

In Acts 10:9-16 Peter had a vision of a blanket come down to him in the form of animals, yet the vision meant *don't call unclean that which I have cleansed.* He was to go to a people who hadn't yet heard about Christ, yet God called them pure and clean, present-perfect, not future.

We are enveloped in a love so profound, mirroring the very bond between the Father and the eternal Son. "As the Father has loved me, so have I loved you..." [9]

Yet, should we conceive of Jesus as a victim of His own legalistic, self-absorbed Father... this notion of 'love' offers scant solace. It not only strains belief in the Father's benevolence but renders the phrase 'Jesus loves you' almost disingenuous.

The Father surrendered His Son so that through Him, all the Father's children might find deliverance. Not from the Father's hand, but from their self-inflicted ruin. Our misdeeds, our fury—not the Father's wrath—are what led to Jesus' crucifixion.

Father doesn't see people as insiders and outsiders. That's the Gospel—the call to break that image and reveal the God in us who doesn't desire sacrifice and whose love doesn't even remember or keep account of sin, let alone send dissenters to burn and roast forever. Christ came for the lost in the houses of religion. Countering the concept of blood sacrifice as a character aspect of God was a significant factor in what led to His being killed. Jesus not only foresaw the attempts on His life by adversaries but also their inevitable success. Prior to His final journey to Jerusalem, He forewarned His disciples, predicting, 'They will condemn him to death and will hand him over to the Gentiles to be mocked and flogged and crucified' (Matthew 20:18-19). Yet, contrary to conventional expectations, Jesus proceeded undeterred for a singular purpose: He understood it to be the divine will for Him to undergo death. He was the only person ever born whose destiny was to die and be resurrected.

This conviction stemmed from His recognition that His death would serve as the ultimate atonement for the sins of humanity, fulfilling God's grand plan for redemption In Hebrews, it says *'according to the law'* [10] there is no forgiveness without the shedding of blood. Yet, people leave off this part and therefore cannot know God. The passage goes on to explain the better way. Where the law is not in force, there cannot be transgression. Most of Christendom has no idea about the most basic aspects of God. My years of healing have only just begun.

Earlier that year, I had been battling cancer myself, just like my mum, but I kept it a secret from my parents. Anchored by the promises of Christian language, I found myself surrounded by well-meaning charismatic individuals who, strictly adhering to sola scriptura, spoke life and met all the expected criteria.

Yet, it felt like decaf. Then, like the addition of sour milk to my mental espresso, came the blame game. Each facet of my faith — Frank, Christ and Tien — began attributing the suffering either to a lack of faith, God's affliction towards Job, the thorn in Paul's flesh, or my fault due to sin or the accumulated stress and trauma throughout my life. Bullcrap! God does not give sickness to his children, he does not use Munchausen syndrome by proxy.

The various facets of my identity and the ecclesiastical camps I encountered all sought answers and assigned blame, rather than having the humility to say, 'We don't know why your Mum passed away. We don't know why your cancer wasn't healed.'

Death, trauma, or even Eros can be transformative in life. However, it's the love of a Father God, as depicted in the parable of the prodigal son in Luke Chapter 15, that should be described as the prodigal father—an outlandishly forgiving Father who eagerly runs to welcome his wayward son back despite his mistakes. It's remarkable because it's the first time we see mention of God running to us! This highlights the theme of grace and unconditional love.

As a result, I embarked on a journey of detoxing from dogma, examining why I believe what I do and clarifying my intentions. I pondered why I believe that Christ is greater than Adam. The remarkable thing was that once I stepped off the tumultuous ride of healing, identity, lifestyle proclamations, expectations, commands, canine obedience, charismatic agendas and proselytism, I began to perceive and experience more of the Father's love than ever before.

The by-product of this newfound freedom, however, led some to label me as a heretic, a wanderer, a prodigal son, or a deserter—particularly within so-called friendship groups and even some close family circles. I am grateful I didn't choose to chase storms in Texas. When I learned of hurricanes spinning at hundreds of miles per hour, capable of hurling blades of grass and tree twigs like bullets, my bucket list took a swift turn. I've had my fair share of being shredded, thank you very much!

### God's Hand in Every Detail.

From mid and late 2017 to 2018, I decided to go on something a little calmer, after riding the high hills of Thailand on a hired motorbike soaking up the views and having a sensory overload of new neural sensations, through sights, sounds, therapeutic massage, incense, citronella and the smiles of the Thai people. Listening to the stories of expats and how they had found hope, life and love in Asia inspired me to see that God is in every detail of people's lives, He is waiting to be discovered in all.

One August night in 2018, during an Asian summer, as I lay in bed, I eagerly remembered that I had promised myself to continue expanding my ever-growing bucket list of life. It was time to truly start living—to share, experience, love, savor and taste, with the warm sun-kissed wind on my skin. I envisioned motorbikes high up on hills, the wind in my hair, basking in the sun's warmth, sipping fresh coconut water and relishing sticky rice and mango.

God revealed to me that He resides within all people, whether we are aware of it or not. I had always wanted a special type of tattoo, one that integrated the artwork so that my hand became an extension of Jesus' hand, with the artwork flowing seamlessly onto my wrist. In this design, the nail and blood colors would cleverly conceal an accidental scar I had acquired years earlier while removing a metal staple from a canvas. It was strategically positioned on the side with my vein.

My tattoo artist, who bore a striking resemblance to actor Jackie Chan, meticulously worked on my tattoo for seven hours. The finished tattoo looked stunning. Almost as if on cue, a South African woman entered the shop and admired the artwork on my wrist. She mentioned that, as believers, we are taught about the God of Abraham, Isaac and Jacob, but what about the God of our names? What about the God of our journeys? What about the God of Joe?

The following day, after much more exploring and experiencing, I decided I would have a trilogy of tattoos on my right arm that would tell a story pertinent to me. The second tattoo would be the resurrected (Chinese-looking) Christ, adorned on my right forearm as a warrior who had overcome death with the scripture of Revelation 22:2 etched under, *'the leaves of the tree are for the healing of the nations.'*

This verse is found in the final chapter of the Book of Revelation, where a vision of the end times and the creation of a new heaven and earth is described. In this profound vision, the Tree of Life assumes a central role, symbolizing eternal life and nourishment for all who are saved through God's grace. The depiction of the tree of life bearing twelve fruits, with each tree yielding its fruit every month, conveys a sense of abundance and continuous provision.

Moreover, the leaves of this tree are described as having the power to heal the nations, underscoring the idea that the restoration and reconciliation of all people will be integral to the new creation. Revelation 22:2, in its entirety, presents a vivid portrayal of God's ultimate plan for humanity. In this divine plan, all individuals will experience full reconciliation with God and with one another and a state of abundance and healing will prevail as the norm.

The leaves were to fall upon the final third envisioned tattoo. Eight hours later, a resurrected Chinese-looking Christ was adorned on my right shoulder.

The next day, the final tattoo would be of an Asian married couple symbolizing the wedding, the union of Christ and His bride. It was to be embellished with the finishing touches of the healing leaves turning to flowers falling upon the married couple of Christ and the bride. I loved the trilogy of my tattoos, however, the final flowers would take time to grow on me.

*'Father, why wasn't your hand in the etching of the final flowers?'* I asked.

*'My child,'* God replied, *'the beauty of creation is found not just in its completion but in its growth and journey. The flowers you see are a reflection of the divine hand at work, even if not etched in the final detail you envision. Just as the Kingdom of God grows within you, so too does the beauty of the world continue to unfold, shaped by love and faith. Trust in the process, for every petal and bloom, even those unfinished, hold purpose and meaning in the grand design.'*

The following night on August 7th, 2018, I went for a walk and told Papa it would be nice to meet someone and kind of settle down as my motorbike explorations were a little lonely.

That night, I saw someone who I felt didn't belong where she was, accordingly, floating back and forth as to whether to talk to her or not, but like a butterfly I was drawn to her. We chatted, we laughed. I was smitten.

'What's your name?' I ask.

'Maliwan.' มะลิวัลย์

'Has that name a meaning?' I asked.

'Flower,' she replied.

*'... and the leaves/flowers are for the healing of the nations.'*

Jenelle, it is indeed *Love* that moves the sun and stars.

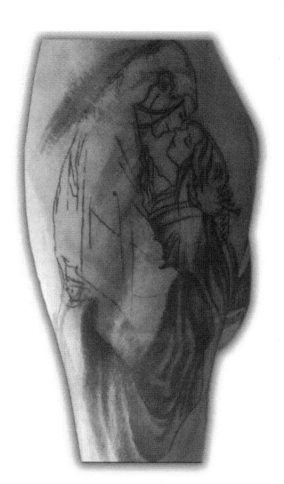

# Chapter Nine

## Boundaries and Wandering Stars

*'Boundaries define us. They define what is me and what is not me. A boundary shows me where I end and someone else begins, leading me to a sense of ownership. Knowing what I am to own and take responsibility for gives me freedom.'*—Henry Cloud [1]

In the therapeutic alliance between therapist and client, we are encouraged to say, 'Let's look at this together.' To explore themes, to be congruent, open and transparent as well as not colluding with diversions, we also need to acknowledge boundaries.

In therapy, there are no circumstances where romantic or erotic love between a therapist and a client is ethical or acceptable, it is a blatant violation of the client's trust in the therapist. Such behavior is neither benevolent nor ethical, it borders on narcissism.

Therapists should maintain deep respect and genuine care for their clients throughout the therapeutic process. This love should stem from a sincere desire to assist the individuals they work with, understanding that clients seek therapy to improve their lives and develop a stronger sense of self for optimal living.

Any therapist (or angel) who operates without appropriate boundaries, in my opinion, may metaphorically be in need of a kind of 'spiritual castration,' which perhaps echoes the idea of angels being cast out of heaven for their transgressions. This serves as a symbolic way to illustrate the consequences of their actions.

That being explicitly said, all therapists need to be aware of 'Adverse Idealizing Transference,' in addition to Freudian object transference, where the client makes the therapist the new object of their emotional attachment. This phenomenon is observed not only in therapy but also in cults, ideologies, businesses and media partnerships that manipulate fear, control and legalism, resulting in a distorted form of affection.

This negative form of Philautia (self-love) seeks selfish pleasure and often involves a desire for fame and wealth beyond necessity. It mirrors the behavior of Dominus Therapeutae Narcissus (Mr. Therapist Narcissus), who, like the mythological character Narcissus, falls in love with his own reflection. As Freud aptly stated, 'If someone's need for love is not entirely satisfied by reality, he is bound to approach every new person he meets with libidinal anticipatory ideas.' [2]

In an interview with Terence Clarke, Irvin D. Yalom explains that virtually every patient he sees has come to him because of something he has written, and that does have a significant impact on the course of therapy. He states, "It makes me into a bit of a larger-than-life figure for the people I see, and maybe potentially it even gives me more power to do good, as long as ultimately I can get past their need to see me as a special sort of figure. I don't want to be idealized by a patient because of what I've written." [3]

In an article by Dawn Devereux, former Director of public support for boundaries studies based on the accounts of people who have experienced Adverse Idealizing Transference (AIT). The most common feelings and beliefs that clients describe when AIT is developing are:

*"Believing that a 'real' relationship with the therapist would result in deep contentment, feeling that other aspects of life are diminishing in*

*importance, including relationships with friends, a partner or children, feeling that the problems that brought the person into therapy in the first place are no longer important, feeling panic or depression at the thought of the therapy ending. A transference of **this kind** clearly affects a person's judgment and interferes with their autonomy, leaving them vulnerable to sexual, emotional and financial exploitation."* [4]

Carl Jung, concerning love—*"A human being who does not know that he has enkindled love in you does not feel loved but humiliated because he is simply subjected or exposed to your own psychic state in which he himself has no part."* [5]

As a counselor, I do not want to become the object or target of my clients' libido or cathexis; this form of transference would need to be addressed and explored. Yes, it is a common occupational hazard that clients may develop feelings of being in love with their therapist, but such occurrences are thoroughly explored to understand their significance and are managed within appropriate boundaries.

<u>Even angels long to investigate these things.</u>

What connection do I see here?

Regarding aliens or UFOs, my understanding is that the aLIEn message 'the majority' of this purported, biological mixture of expressed technology, spirit and flesh bring is one of confusion, which in turn indicates how confused they may be. [6]

PROF. VIRGIL: "Sounds like they and the media want to troll the soul. In the words of Dante, 'Considerate la vostra semenza: fatti non foste a viver come bruti, ma per seguir virtute e conoscenza.'—'Consider your

376

origin, you were not born to live like brutes, but to pursue virtue and knowledge.'"

I am convinced, that these things are spooked by us, that they see an image of something that they want to be, that they know what we are, in respect to identity, but that we as humans do not know who or what we represent.

Is it possible that both malevolent and benevolent entities, even those who have maintained their domains, are still not allowed to reveal our true identity to us? [7]

However, the corrupt among them push the boundaries and masquerade as otherworldly, thus granting themselves greater access.

There always seems to be a smoking gun. Incantations and invocations serve as a calling card to these wanderers among the stars, disguised as space lizards, mutilating cows, darting in and out of inter-dimensional realms (as eternity transcends time), leaving their mark across the ages through occultic invitations. [7]

I contemplate the notion of a subconscious synchronic invitation, a concept coined by Swiss psychologist Carl Jung to explain meaningful coincidences beyond mere cause and effect. [8] This leads me to speculate on a profound connection, perhaps a spiritual link, between the founders of Ariel School or a hidden esoteric parent acting as a catalyst for the UFO encounter through synchronicity. I strongly suspect that someone within the leadership had their encounter when they were young, or other dark invitations are afoot.

My perspective suggests that the Ariel School UFO encounter was not random. It was not a profound message from the universe or a sign, but rather a narcissistic imprint left by fallen beings seeking attachment to a new generation by way of invitation. Drawing from my experience in the ministry to the new age, it's as if someone had erected a billboard to communicate with these entities, resulting in a trail of hitchhiked consciousness transferring to another generation.

Some may say that my interpretations delve into the realm of subjectivity and metaphysical concepts and that my perspective may be influenced by my own confirmation bias, viewed through a Biblical lens, but I am happy to view it through the truth of the Holy Spirit.

I am convinced that fallen deities have their own media company called 'skubalon' (excrement) where they rain down filth to pollute the minds of people.

In my research on so called extraterrestrial encounters and their impact on the human consciousness, I had the opportunity to interact with journalists on the field and conduct interviews with adults who had experienced such encounters during their childhood. Through these interactions, it became apparent that the boundaries of our understanding of reality had been challenged and in some cases, broken. The accounts shared by these individuals, of encounters with silver saucers and entities, as well as their experiences within the new age community, painted a picture of a world far more complex and mysterious than what we may have previously thought. It was clear that further exploration and examination of this topic was necessary to gain a deeper understanding of the nature of these encounters and their impact on the human experience.

Jim Semivan, a former senior intelligence service member of the Central Intelligence Agency (CIA), has issued a warning about the potential danger of discussing the UFO phenomenon with children. As a co-founder of the To the Stars Academy of Arts and Science, which seeks to advance space exploration and scientific discovery, Semivan believes that there is a force out there capable of controlling our environment and manipulating our thoughts. He warns that disclosing such information to young children could have lasting psychological effects. According to Semivan, the issue of UFOs goes much deeper than what is commonly known and there is much more to discover about this phenomenon.

*"There is a force out there that can control our environment, that can put thoughts in our heads."*

*"I had some friends who were like, 'Oh, my daughter wants to know all about UFOs. Can we talk to you about that?'"*

*"And I said no. I'm not going to talk to you about that. What am I going to tell her or him, these 10, 11-year-olds? Could such a reality kill them psychologically for the rest of their lives?"* *"Yes, that there is a force out there that can control our environment and put thoughts into our heads. That they can lie to you, deceive you and that you are not in control of your life. Tell this to a 12-year-old,"* *'... the rabbit hole goes much deeper' when it comes to the UFO phenomenon."* — *Former CIA Officer Jim Semivan.* [9]

### You look like an angel, walk like an angel

As a counselor, I believe that many genuine individuals who claim to have had an abduction or extra-terrestrial encounter experience are reliving a psychic imprint of the fall of the Adamic race at a subconscious level, influenced by their culture's interpretation of that inherited or ancestral unconsciousness, to some extent.

Carl Jung believed that myths and dreams were expressions of the collective unconscious, in that they express core ideas that are part of the human species. In other words, myths express wisdom that has been encoded in all humans, perhaps using evolution or through some spiritual process.

In 'The Significance of Constitution and Heredity in Psychology' (November 1929), Jung wrote:

"And the essential thing, psychologically, is that in dreams, fantasies and other exceptional states of mind the most far-fetched mythological motifs and symbols can appear autochthonously *(naturally and spontaneously, without external influence)* at any time, often, apparently, as the result of influences, traditions and excitations working on the individual, but more often without any sign of them. These 'primordial images' or 'archetypes,' as I have called them, belong to the basic stock of the unconscious psyche and cannot be explained as personal acquisitions. Together they make up that psychic stratum which has been called the collective unconscious."

"The existence of the collective unconscious means that individual consciousness is anything but a tabula rasa *(a philosophical concept that refers to the belief that individuals are born with a blank slate and that their character and abilities are shaped entirely by experiences and environmental factors).* and is not immune to predetermining influences.

On the contrary, it is in the highest degree influenced by inherited presuppositions, quite apart from the unavoidable influences exerted upon it by the environment. *The collective unconscious* comprises the psychic life of our ancestors right back to its earliest beginnings. It is the matrix of all conscious psychic occurrences and hence it exerts an influence that compromises the freedom of consciousness in the highest degree since it is continually striving to lead all conscious processes back into the old paths."
*10*


Genetically inherited unconscious

In his writings, it seems to me that even Jung's subconscious might be hinting at the existence of a genetically inherited unconscious, reminiscent of the Biblical story of the fall from grace in the Garden of Eden. This narrative conveys the notion that death was imprinted within all of humankind and the memory of the initial transgression involving an alien presence in the Garden continues to linger within many individuals, manifesting in various forms. The concept of a shared and enduring unconscious, carrying the echoes of ancestral experiences, holds a central place in Jungian psychology.

## Untherapeutic Alien Presence.

Regarding the Ariel school event, I posed a previously unasked question to one witness, now an adult. As context, when no teachers were present in the playground, the children were instructed not to venture into the bushy areas beyond the boundary lines that separated each field. It was within one of these untamed sections that more than 150 children witnessed a brief manifestation of a silver, levitating disc, distorting their perception of time. (Such time distortion is believed to occur due to heightened amygdala activity during moments of fear, resulting in the brain creating an additional set of memories to supplement those managed by other brain regions.) These manifestations seemed to convey a message about the impending ecological disaster facing the world.

The question I presented to the witness was straightforward: *"Did either group cross over into the other's territory?"*

*"No."*

*"What do you believe the boundary symbolized?"*

*"I've pondered that for years.* (LONG PAUSE) *Perhaps from a legal perspective, it signifies an acknowledgment of rules, but I'm still in the process of refining and expanding my thoughts on this matter."*

She then cryptically explained that the episodes of *'Black Mirror Season 1 and 2'* felt frighteningly true to her, resonating with something deep within. This prompted me to investigate and I discovered the following themes in Seasons 1 and 2. [11]

**Season 1:**

*"Fifteen Million Merits":* Set in a future where people pedal stationary bikes to generate energy, this episode focuses on a man who becomes disillusioned with the shallow entertainment culture and seeks to rebel against it.

*"The Entire History of You":* In a world where people have implants allowing them to record and replay their memories, a man becomes obsessed with his wife's past.

**Season 2:**

*"Be Right Back":* After her boyfriend dies, a woman uses a service that allows her to communicate with a digital version of him, leading to emotional complexity.

*"White Bear":* A woman with amnesia wakes up in a strange world where people record her with their phones and seem intent on harming her.

Each episode of Black Mirror explores different aspects of technology, society and human behavior, often with dark and thought-provoking themes. The series is known for its social commentary and its ability to depict the potential consequences of technological advancements.

I asked another witness who was eight at the time, now also an adult.

"What do you think the boundary represented?"

*"The logs were considered the boundary line to us and they came right up to the logs and appeared right in front of us, at about a log distance. The boundary would represent a threshold, something that would have been considered a set of rules, not to break. They did appear in front of us and communicated telepathically through what I believe was communication through their eyes. I don't recall being scared, but I recall feelings of fear and hope, it was like **I was frozen and that time had slightly slowed down during that period. Then they just disappeared when the school bell rang and everyone was in a panic on the field.**"*

"What do you think they were?"

*"Something from out of this world, but I guess my best answer would be something that we have been **misrepresenting** for a long time. Some might say aliens, some might say, angels, star people… it really for me goes with what culture I believe that they land in and communicate. Some might even think they are demonic… but I don't think so, they caused no harm and didn't want to hurt us and only left with messages of environmental concern and the use of technology on this planet and our harm. I'm glad that **the Ariel story can touch and reach people all over the world… this means it's doing what it should be doing and reaching and touching people with a positive message.** I did a lot of artwork that came out of me after I started talking about the experience. I liken it to art therapy, expressionism."*

(Authors Note: As I looked at the artwork in question, I couldn't help but notice the striking resemblance it bore to the new-age artwork I had encountered in my past experiences. The themes depicted were esoteric and dystopian, with strong undertones of trauma. This observation led me to consider the implications on the human brain, specifically the hippocampus, which is responsible for memory storage and filtering. It became clear to me that this artwork, with its dark emotions and imagery, did not promote a life of free ritual and instead seemed to suggest that the individual's memory center had been commandeered. This realization further solidified my belief in the importance of examining the cultural impact of these encounters on the human consciousness.)

*"Another time outside of that event, I saw that the creatures changed from the head of a lion to a being, it was kind of morphing. It changed back and forth between "being" Lion and yes, some human qualities. The experience was very spiritual for me... but I have had a few experiences that have been different in nature other than Ruwa with the E.T.s, I just don't talk about them as Ruwa is big enough as it is and the others are personal outside of the Ruwa event. This experience led me down a biblical path and I found out that the Bible talks about 'aliens' and 'angels' and mentions the name Ariel, all of which were of great fascination to me. It led me down a more spiritual connection to the aliens and experiences."*

## But I got wise, you're the devil in disguise

It is my opinion that one of the children, now an adult, whose parents were Salvation Army missionaries, had sufficient prayer cover that sparked awareness from the entities to briefly retreat. However, my concern arises from the spiritual experience described above. Jesus himself warned, *'For there shall arise false Christs and false prophets and shall show great signs and wonders, insomuch that, if it were possible, they shall deceive the very elect.'* [12]

In many cases, the experience undergoes a transformation, involving a different entity. This new entity often appears more angelic or introduces higher spiritual motives to the encounter. What we observe in such cases is increased communication between the entities and the experiencer, originating from the second entity that becomes involved in the experience. Despite some witnesses exploring scriptures, there is no consensus, connection, or reference to Christ as the Savior. Instead, a clever magical diversion seems to be at play.

I refrain from critiquing or judging the witness. However, drawing from my experiences as a child and from previous investigations, I discern underlying trauma within these encounters and distractions. Furthermore, I sense that these occurrences may serve as precursors to larger events.

Once young minds are enveloped by apocalyptic scenes, what remains?

<u>Taken.</u>

Furthermore, in the passage of Matthew 4:1-11, it mentions that Jesus was tempted three times, but was also '*taken*' by the first fallen angel twice. Here's a breakdown of the instances where Jesus was '*taken*':

The diábolos *took* Jesus to the highest point of the temple to tempt him to jump off and have angels save him (Matthew 4:5).

The diábolos *took* Jesus to a very high mountain to show him the kingdoms of the world and offer them to him in exchange for worship (Matthew 4:8).

The Greek word for *took* used here is *Paralambanō* (Strong's Concordance G3880), which signifies "to take to, to take with one's self, to join to one's self." Its outline of Biblical usage includes:

- Serving as an associate or companion.

- Metaphorically, accepting or acknowledging someone to be as they profess to be.
- Not rejecting or withholding obedience.
- Receiving something transmitted or discharging an office.
- Receiving with the mind, whether through oral transmission or instruction by teachers, as seen with disciples.

Now, regarding the guise or shape in which 'it' appeared, we do not know, nor do I care. It is evident to me that if we draw parallel connections between these witness statements of encounter or indeed others from the world, this 'taking' and 'showing' was not a physical or literal transportation but rather a spiritual and symbolic representation of the Adversary's attempt to engage with Jesus.

This event was a spiritual confrontation and encounter, where the light bearer approached Jesus in the wilderness, either in a vision or a heightened state of spiritual awareness. In this interpretation, the Tempter 'took' Jesus into various scenarios within their encounter to present temptations and test His faithfulness.

This perspective aligns with the understanding that the Prince of Darkness's influence is primarily spiritual and the encounter between Jesus and the Deceiver in the wilderness was a symbolic representation of a spiritual battle rather than a physical relocation. This interpretation emphasizes the moral and theological significance of the event rather than its physical mechanics.

The slanderer aimed to occupy and colonize Jesus' mind, abducting it with deceitful temptations to divert him from his divine mission and compromise his allegiance to God. Just as the temptations of Jesus in the Gospel of Matthew targeted his senses and human vulnerabilities, the accounts of alien and UFO encounters also involve the manipulation of human sensory experiences. Witnesses often describe encounters where their senses are stimulated or altered, such as vivid lights, strange sounds and altered perceptions of time and space. These sensory provocations could be seen as attempts to disrupt human understanding and challenge our perceptions of reality, paralleling the way Jesus was tested in his own human experience. In both cases, these encounters prompt individuals to confront the boundaries of their beliefs, resilience and understanding of the world around them.

When I asked both witnesses if they felt a sense of love from these beings, they remained silent, choosing not to speak.


## Stockholm Syndrome


What I am suspicious of here, particularly as the experience evolves, is a dimension of Stockholm Syndrome in the encounters of those who initially undergo profoundly traumatic close encounters. Somewhere along the line, however, a realization dawns that these experiences have transformed into messengers for the entities themselves. It's at this juncture that a secondary level of experience infiltrates their lives, leading them, in essence, to align with the purveyors of false narratives and fake news.

That's what Stockholm Syndrome refers to, a condition in which hostages develop a psychological bond with their captors during captivity. An imagination is held captive, resulting from a rather specific set of circumstances, namely the power imbalances contained in hostage-taking—kidnapping. Emotional bonds may be formed between captors and captives, during intimate time together, eventually the captives say the same thing their captors were saying. [13]

In my therapeutic understanding of the person's interaction with these mind invaders, there seems to have been a mental hijacking. I'm not talking about a physical beam-me-up abduction, which I suspect is some kind of neuro-spiritual-cerebral-projection-matrix. I see an esoteric *'colonization of consciousness'* [14] taking place. The experiencers and many of their listeners begin to collude with the ideology of their spiritual hijacker. This process represents a subtle yet pervasive infiltration of certain ideologies or beliefs into individuals' minds or psyches, often without their full awareness or consent.

This esoteric 'colonization of consciousness' is no longer confined to the realm of spiritual experiences. It is now becoming a technological reality. An article by Wired concerning thought decoders issues a warning about new technology about to be released. The development of AI-powered 'thought decoders' raises significant concerns about privacy and the broader implications for human cognition. These neural decoders can reconstruct thoughts from brain activity, potentially making our innermost thoughts accessible. Although current technologies require extensive training and cooperation from subjects, their potential misuse is alarming. Critics argue that this could mark the end of privacy, as these tools could be used to manipulate and shape thoughts rather than merely read them. The article emphasizes the need for thoughtful oversight and ethical considerations in the development and deployment of such technologies to prevent potential abuses and ensure they are used beneficially. [15]

## Colonization of consciousness

Researcher and Scientist, Dr. Jacques Vallée came to his conclusion in his research.

*"UFOs can project images or fabricated scenes designed to change our belief systems... human belief is being controlled and conditioned. Man's concepts are being rearranged and we may be headed toward a massive change of human attitudes toward paranormal abilities and extra-terrestrial life."* [16]

Psychiatrists and psychologists who observe Stockholm syndrome recognize that it's a form of brainwashing. Individuals who develop Stockholm syndrome often exhibit symptoms of posttraumatic stress, including nightmares, insomnia, flashbacks, heightened startle responses, confusion and difficulty trusting others.

We can draw parallels between these symptoms and what many encounter experiencers report. Despite the traumatic nature of their initial experiences, it appears that there is an agenda at play to elevate them to a different level, essentially turning them into disciples or messengers on Earth. This seems to be their primary goal—to transform individuals into specific testimonies for their cause. We can draw a similar comparison to people who become involved in various cults or deceptive groups, as they often undergo a form of brainwashing. It's a false intimacy intertwined with eco-system-danger-babble amid humanity's subconscious traumas.

PROF. BERNARD: "Stockholm Syndrome, trauma and addiction are linked through psychological vulnerability. Trauma can erode mental defenses, leaving individuals prone to bonding with captors or, in their pursuit of comfort, developing harmful habits like addiction. These responses are like coping strategies for enduring distressing situations. To provide effective support and treatment for those affected, understanding this connection becomes crucial. It's as if it inscribes itself in the very psyche of who we are.

As Gabor Maté once said, '*Trauma is a psychic wound that hardens you psychologically, interfering with your growth and development. It causes pain, leading you to act from that pain. It instills fear, prompting actions based on fear. Trauma isn't just what happened to you, it's what occurs within you as a result of what happened to you.*'" [17]

## Dissociation And Spiritual Prostitution.

Pornography, derived from the Greek words 'pornographos' (ΠΟΡΝΟΓΡΑΦΙΑ), essentially means 'the writings of prostitutes,' where 'graphy' stands for 'writing' and 'porne' for 'prostitutes.' In ancient Roman times, customers could purchase various forms of erotic assistance by visiting brothels and selecting from a stone menu—a relic of the world's oldest profession. [18]

Fast-forward to the present and the era of the metaverse, where digital porn addiction has evolved into a pathological relationship with mood-altering experiences, further imprinting itself upon the mind.

## Cyber Love.

'*Somewhere between right and wrong, there is a garden. I will meet you there.*'—Rumi. [19]

It has been beautifully said by author Bruce Sterling that 'Cyberspace' is the place where telephone conversation appears to occur - not inside your actual phone (the plastic device on your desk) or inside the other person's phone, in some other city, but rather, the place between the phones - *the indefinite place out there*, where the two human beings can actually meet and communicate.' [20] .

PROF. BERNARD: "As a therapist, I often explain addiction as a strong pull towards *a certain activity* or substance. Our minds are incredibly adaptable and it's easy for a habit to quickly turn into a compulsion. When this happens, we may find ourselves unable to stop, constantly seeking the same thing and becoming more and more compartmentalized. As a result, we may start to rationalize that our behavior is not harmful, or that we are not fully engaged in the behavior. This can lead to dissociation, automatic brain functions and altered states of consciousness."

JOE: "So how do people in addiction or trauma overcome their thorn in the flesh?"

PROF. BERNARD: "In a nutshell, to walk a good path, we need to address addiction and regain control. To speak and taste freedom, one must raise awareness of the compulsion's presence, seek support through a community, network, or professional, replace addictive behaviors with healthier alternatives, practice mindfulness and staying present, consider necessary lifestyle changes, and embrace self-compassion throughout the journey. When needed, enter the realm of speaking to a counselor where you can be seen and heard. A professional's job is not to collude with the darkness but to lean into it so that whatever is there may come to light."

## Salvation

Hence, back to the question of angels, what is their job? My understanding of the scriptures states that the Holy angels (with boundaries) are ministering spirits, sent to those who are to inherit salvation.

Salvation, *sōtēria*, in the Greek language, means deliverance, preservation, safety, salvation: deliverance from the molestation of enemies, inferring and meaning finding a healthy relationship and healing in addition to physical. Another Greek word for salvation is *sōzō*, meaning to make well, heal, restore to health, to preserve one who is in danger of destruction, to save or rescue, to point them to Christ. [21/22]

Thus, the angels that keep the boundary are in one sense a type of therapist, but they don't expect interaction or worship. When I carried the lamps in the night and an angel opened a door for me, I simply said, 'Thank you' and carried on with my life, I didn't pitch a tent of worship or exultation there, I didn't feed into it.

St. Paul elaborates to the Hebrews, "And God never said to any of the angels, 'Sit in the place of honor at My right hand until I humble your enemies, making them a footstool under your feet.' Are not all angels ministering spirits sent to serve those who will inherit salvation? We must pay the most careful attention, therefore, to what we have heard, so that we do not drift away. For since *the message spoken through angels was binding* and every violation and disobedience received its just punishment, how shall we escape if we ignore so great a salvation? This salvation, which was first announced by the Lord, was confirmed to us by those who heard Him … wherefore He is able also to save them to the uttermost that come unto God by Him, seeing He ever liveth to make intercession for them." [23]

In my training as a Person-Centered Therapist at NLM University, we were taught not to adopt a fixer mentality or develop a savior complex. Instead, our goal was to facilitate autonomy through the therapeutic alliance. Becoming the client's attachment figure was discouraged, as the answer to self-actualization is innate. However, achieving self-actualization often necessitates self-awareness, effort and conducive circumstances. It's

392

important to acknowledge that while some individuals actively strive for self-actualization, others may not prioritize it or may face barriers that impede their journey. [24]

This perspective aligns with what St. Paul conveyed to the Athenians, a motley crew that believed in everything except for the unknown god. Paul stated, 'For in him we live and move and exist.' As some of your own poets have said, '*We are his offspring.*' [25]

Self-actualization is an ongoing, lifelong process in which an individual's self-concept is nurtured and enhanced through reflection and the reinterpretation of various life experiences. [26/27]

The Bible encourages us to renew our minds:

Romans 12:2: "And be not conformed to this world: but be ye transformed by the renewing of your mind, that ye may prove what is that good and acceptable and perfect, will of God."

2 Corinthians 5:17: "Therefore if any man is in Christ, he is a new creature: old things are passed away, behold, all things have become new."

Ephesians 4:22-24: "That ye put off concerning the former conversation the old man, which is corrupt according to the deceitful lusts; And be renewed in the spirit of your mind; And that ye put on the new man, which after God is created in righteousness and true holiness."

Colossians 3:10: "And have put on the new man, which is renewed in knowledge after the image of him that created him."

In essence, we become a new species in Christ. Additionally, the words 'In Christ,' 'In Him,' 'In whom,' and 'In the beloved' appear over 130 times in the Bible. Every time we encounter these words in Scripture, it emphasizes the blessings and benefits we have as Christians because we are identified with Christ in His death, burial and resurrection, beyond a world that is not our home.

The world we inhabit is profoundly transient and unstable. Everything we perceive is impermanent, including the desires and passions of those entangled in earthly matters, which will eventually fade away. As Professor Virgil succinctly puts it, "Inna 70 years a time, we will alla be worm food."

Our world is subject to the influence of potent spiritual and material forces, beyond our control. We are like specks adrift in the current of a river amid the spiritual chaos and instability of this realm. Therefore, it becomes imperative to develop effective strategies for regulating our emotions, enabling us to maintain inner peace and stability. Without such strategies, we risk being carried away by the currents of life, succumbing to negative influences that seek to deceive and corrupt us.

PROF. BERNARD: "You are questioning whether both malevolent and benevolent entities, including those who have retained their authority or domains, are prohibited from disclosing humanity's true identity to us. Some entities may adhere to this restriction, while corrupt ones may exploit loopholes by posing as otherworldly beings, thereby gaining increased influence or access. Certain entities may manipulate their perceived roles or identities to exert control or influence over humanity.

JOE: "I guess that's what I'm saying."

PROF. BERNARD: "Joe, this topic used to be important for you to discuss, how does it affect your life now?"

JOE: "I just needed to get it off my chest. I don't want anyone else to be deceived. It no longer deludes me, but perhaps someone reading this, or maybe the inner child of those who witnessed the events at Ruwa or other events, can see the truth."

PROF. BERNARD: "Joe, remember, it's not our job to rescue anyone! It's crucial not to fall into the trap of rescuing individuals in distress.

Instead, aim to empower them to navigate their challenges and develop their own coping skills, just like lifeguards guide swimmers to safety without carrying them ashore."

JOE: "For me, I want others to know that the key to resisting not just these influences but the lies of life, is to remain firmly rooted in a relationship with Christ and to stay vigilant in our efforts to discern truth from falsehood."

By doing so, we can actively shape our surroundings and strive for a future grounded in love, peace and justice. I suspect that in this current generation, malevolent forces are shamelessly increasing their efforts to spiritually prostitute reality, deceiving humanity. We become what we behold, but what is humanity beholding?

# Chapter Ten

## Affect Regulation

$W$e become what we behold, so what is humanity beholding? We witness fear, hate and every form of 'ism' and 'schism.' Earthly beings are so disconnected from themselves that there's a rupture [1] within humanity that needs healing. Meanwhile, the other half of humanity, particularly the Christians who are not dealing with their trauma, are waiting for a rapture— 'harpazō' [2]—a carrying away into a new dimension, akin to the rib of Adam being snatched up, (Genesis 2:21) or the full bodies of Enoch, Elijah (Genesis 5:24; 2 Kings 2:11) and a resurrected Jesus, (Luke 24:51; Acts 1:9-11) who were taken to that divine realm.

However, healing, by God's design, is supposed to be the Father, Mother, primary caregivers and community, authentically repairing our brokenness, which creates an increase in the capacity for regulation, called our *window of tolerance.* [3] The best state of arousal or stimulation in which we can function and thrive in everyday life. When we exist within this window, we can learn effectively, play and relate well to others and ourselves. The mind is constructed out of what's happening in the body and in relation to others, but when we don't have that kind of regulation, that attunement, that contingent communication, we are going to get a system that cannot regulate itself.

*Affect Regulation*, refers to the mechanism by which our emotions, moods, feelings and their expressions are modulated in pursuit of an affective equilibrium or homeostasis. [4]    How we are feeling in our body, how I'm feeling emotionally. Am I feeling secure, am I feeling joyful, am I feeling at peace versus am I feeling anxious, threatened, fearful?

Thus, the phenomenon of fallen angels, discussed at length, is one in which the mind is usurped and the body keeps the traumatic score. This can be triggered by images, sights and sounds without ever finding resolution until the spell is broken. Of course, this doesn't limit itself to the study of alien deception, all forms of corrupt ideology, government abuse and media agendas employ mind games to disrupt our homeostasis.

We need one another. I needed a human and healthy belief system to help me regulate and remind me that I'm not a bad person, that there is hope and that I am loved. It's okay to get lost along the way, we are simply currently unaware of our location. Because that means we have a home to go to and what that looks and feels like is what we want to explore. But if we're not accustomed to relying on other people for that, then what smart children and creative individuals, like my younger self, figure out is this: 'Forget this, I hate this planet, the loneliness of never fitting in, I'm going to go and work it all out myself.'

For example, many people in their childhood, like my younger self read comic books, finding comfort in immersing themselves in the worlds of Boom! Studios, Dark Horse Comics, DC, IDW Publishing, Manga or Marvel. Some bury themselves in perpetual study, some strive for unending qualifications and PhDs, while others seek new, confusing identities as a way to regulate their anxiety.

Similarly, the metaverse served the same purpose for a COVID generation, especially during what felt like an ongoing 'p*l*andemic' with draconian measures.

I witnessed this in Beijing, where young children, confined for weeks and months on end, heavily relied on their devices, their brains marinating in dopamine, to cope with fear. Not to mention those children who were prescribed puberty blockers and anti-depressants from the age of six!

How could anyone self-regulate when there was a lack of emotional connection and strict lockdown policies that metaphorically tried to catch the wind in a cage? In reference to the stringent, restrictive measures placed upon a nation to combat COVID-19, my former Beijing headmaster, Dr. G. Carter, aptly stated, 'They are chasing a ghost.'

Devices are amoral, but their overuse became examples of using fantasy as a form of self-regulation. If a person can't self-regulate as a child, they may learn to tune out as adults. There is nothing inherently wrong with comic books, movies, video games, spirituality, church, or the metaverse. However, if they become the sole source of reality and one's identity is solely based on them, it can lead to a disconnect from one's authenticity.

Prof. Beatrice added her perspective, acknowledging the struggle to self-regulate in the face of external pressures and societal expectations. She noted that individuals may find themselves caught in a loop.

PROF. BEATRICE: "Well, ya see, what happens is we kinda struggle with dealing in the here and now. We're always tryin' to be saviors for everyone else, but ain't nobody there to save us. It's like a loop we get caught in, tryin' to regulate ourselves."

### Elon Musk and Helium-3.

In the prodigious game of life and consciousness, Elon Musk could be considered a wildcard, yet I see a sleeping Christ in his eyes, a soul that was sent here to save humanity even when humanity was unkind to him, who in his childhood of trauma and bullying picked up the encyclopedia [5] and read science books on ion engines and learned how to program computers. His vision now speaks for itself. Self-awareness at an early age is a powerfully transformative thing. Young Elon's spirit was like an internal ion engine, his drive and actualizing tendency, not only asking but then being solution-focused, 'How can I make the world a better place? How can I make my situation in this world one where I can make it improve and become a better place for all of us?' Elon speaks of endless ideas exploding in his mind, which is reflected in his ability to juggle many companies and people simultaneously. I expect his childhood memories of bullying and constant transitioning from school to school have shaped his analysis of people. Being thrown into new groups of people to make friends repeatedly is probably why he has a low tolerance for bullies in the workplace. It's the only way to live with a brain that functions like his. He must work relentlessly. It's an inner quest for integrative regulation and connection to heal and fix the world, even one day venturing forth to colonize the expanses of the universe.

*"It's very important to have reasons to be excited in life, like when you wake up in the morning, it just can't be about problems—everyone in this room deals with problems, but it's got to be more than that ... there's going to be a future out there, a base on the moon, a city on mars, the moons of Jupiter."* [6]

In one interview, Musk becomes vulnerable and candid and reveals his heart, "I'm looking for a serious companion or soul mate, that kind of thing."

*"If I'm not in love, if I'm not with a long-term companion, I cannot be happy."* That led to Musk's great fear: of being alone, as he recalled saying as a child: *"I never want to be alone. I don't want to be alone."* [7]

*'It takes a village to raise a child.'*

*— African Proverb.*


Born in South Africa, Elon Musk's vision extends far beyond a spacefaring civilization, transcending the boundaries of Earth to venture into the stars. His vision encompasses the establishment of future space settlements, where a new generation can thrive, explore and uncover the hidden wonders of distant planets. Notably, he envisions the potential for lunar mining and helium-3 (H3) harvesting to fuel advanced nuclear technologies. To put this into perspective, as of 2022, helium-3 is valued at $140 million for a 220-pound quantity. Extrapolating this to lunar resources, the estimated value of helium-3 on the Moon would reach a staggering $1.543 quadrillion. [8]

Elon Musk is known for his cryptic humor, as demonstrated in a tweet he shared on September 14, 2021. In response to a discussion about Tesla's Full Self-Driving (FSD) system, Musk stated, "I'm not saying there are UFOs... but there are UFOs." This comment emerged in the context of FSD 10's (Full Self-Driving System) ability to predict height using video pixels, eliminating the need to categorize *pixel* groups into objects. Musk humorously suggested that even if a UFO were to crash on the road ahead, the system would navigate around the debris. While his words drew the attention of a diverse audience, SpaceX CEO Elon Musk's vision remains steadfast in his unique approach to saving Earth through innovative technologies and sustainable practices, advocating for Earth's regulation, preservation, and interactive regulation.

Interactive regulation refers to the dynamic process through which individuals regulate their emotions and behaviors in response to interactions with others. This involves reciprocal influences, where the emotions, actions, and reactions of one person affect and are affected by those of another, fostering a mutual adjustment and coordination of emotional states.

## Interactive Regulation.

Ideally, it's through interactive regulation, the Father—Mother—Infant Dyad, that we learn self-regulation. In addition, later, an entire community of people must provide for and interact positively with children for those children to experience and grow in a safe and healthy environment. This is where education plays a key role in facilitating the understanding of self-regulation and awareness at an early age. People wrongly assume that young children won't grasp key concepts about these themes or well-being, but I assure them that this is fundamental, if children as young as six can memorize all the names of their football players, Ultraman or Pokémon cards, then they can easily grasp fifty-four visual concepts on self-regulation, for as I mentioned earlier, self-awareness at an early age is a powerfully transformative thing.

We can renew our minds and explore our fears when we feel that we can't breathe at this moment or when anxiety rises, causing us to feel overwhelmed. We can tell ourselves to call a friend, go for a walk, have a cup of tea, sing words of freedom, learn a new language, dance, swim, paint, or join a drama group.

We need interfacing and interaction with humans, meanwhile, there are self-regulatory things we do all day long to take care of ourselves. But many people that come from deprivation don't know how to soothe themselves when they're under duress, so we see a combination of self-comforting actions, be it alcohol, smoking, cannabis, concubines, looking at porn, or looking to the sky for cosmic redemption. Some forms of autoregulation make sense and we all engage in them, but it's possible to go too far (as with everything else in life) even with religion, or signs and wonders, or folk thinking they are doing God a favor by holding religious placards and provoking others. This is what bugs me about the whole topic of these so-called cosmic visitors, which is so prevalent in the USA but is spreading in different ways worldwide. Although I understand and empathize, having come out of that system, I wanted healing and then ended up lost in space without a satellite, mainly because I distrusted people, which then bred hate and ultimately became a beacon to draw in more animosity.

Yet, in the words of Canadian author Paul Young, *"I suppose that since most of our hurts come through relationships so will our healing and I know that grace rarely makes sense for those looking in from the outside."* [9]

My healing, *our* healing needs anthropocentric intervention. God's creation is anthropocentric, in that the purpose of creation was to produce mankind in His image, to have eternal fellowship with Him and to produce a healthy, loving union, a bride for Christ. To have fellowship and connection with one another and to walk in love.

My sagacious professor at the university, who would later earn my affectionate nickname 'St. Bernard,' gently cautioned me during my period of fundamentalism, which preceded my eventual embrace of a more balanced perspective. After all, there's little joy to be found in rigid fundamentalism. During my journey, I yearned for something or someone to alleviate the emotional anguish I was experiencing. With unwavering conviction, I proclaimed to my cohort that as therapists, it was within our purview and duty to alleviate the sorrow and pain people felt when they mourned the loss of a loved one.

PROF. BERNARD: *"Grief is a hole where love belongs, their grief is associated with their love, so why would you want to take their grief away?"*

Grief is a necessary part of the healing process. It's a testament to the love and connection that existed and trying to eliminate or suppress grief might also diminish the significance of that love. *'Blessed are those that mourn for they will be comforted.'* [10]

Mourning and comfort are part of life on this roller coaster of perpetual animation.

PROF. BEATRICE: "Joe, as you mull over the path you've traveled in life, you'll come to realize that almost every soul you've reached out to has faced deep-seated solitude. Sure, a few of those mental struggles might have their origins in the physical realm, but most of the time, it's that feeling of being alone that gets things goin'."

The greatest disease facing humanity right now is our profound and painful sense of dissociation and disconnection. A disconnection from God, our bodies, each other, our world and ourselves. A world system in which humanity structures reality, which is always opposed to the mystery of peace and love. Yet now my eyes are open to see that humanity's fascination with the themes of fallen angels who masquerade as saviors, is one where what is being played out is *the manifestation of dissociation with themselves.*

The rock group Queen sang a song from one of my favorite top-ten films, *Highlander.* Freddie Mercury delivered a poignant line, *'Who wants to live forever... when love must die?'* [11]

This song resonates with me. I'm very visual and in the context of a fallen race, I see Adam and Eve naked in a garden. They had eaten from the Tree of Knowledge of Good and Evil and paradise was now invaded by unseen hostile forces. Once immortal, they now had to face their slow exit from glory as they realized they had been deceived into decay and death. However, God in His mercy and burning loving gaze placed a cherubim [12] holding a flaming sword (the first lightsaber) to block their access to the Tree of Life.

Why? *'Lest he reach out and take also from the tree of life and eat and live forever.'* [13]

Who would want to live forever without love? It would be a lonely, traumatic, mechanical, alien and drone-like existence.


<u>April 4th, 2020.</u>


PROF. BEATRICE: "What do you see, Joe?"

JOE: "He is asking... (pause) he is asking me... (pause) he is asking me... (sob) to... to... look... to look at her."

PROF. BEATRICE: "Take a breath and let it unfold."


<u>1975 Interview: Sylvia's Fourth Discussion with Carl Rogers.</u>


In a recorded therapy session titled 'The Struggle for Self-Acceptance' between Carl Rogers and his client Sylvia, Sylvia requested to hold Carl Rogers' hands. She sought to move away from intellectualizing and delve into the realm of experiencing. Rogers provided commentary on the purpose of this request, recalling an unnamed friend who coined the term *'Did Eye therapy.'"* [14]

*"Sylvia's eyes were very much in contact and I think as much was going on in a non-verbal way as in a global way, it was a close relationship and we both experienced it that way."*

The therapist and client looked silently at each other for a minute and then continued in healthy dialogue.

*"It seems clear that the reason Sylvia wants to hold my hand is to experience something frightening to her, namely, to drop her competent, reasonable strong self and let herself feel some of her weaknesses and vulnerabilities."*

Sylvia responds, *"I think it helps to touch you, to let go, to feel contact. I don't have to be strong. I can let go."* Sylvia wants to let go of her rationalizing and at that point, she did not know how to do that, except to be silent. *"I have a desire to sit and not talk and look in your eyes as I have a desire to not be the way I am all the time."* [15]

PROF. BEATRICE: "Take a breath Joe and let it unfold..."

## Synchronized Sight, Unified Touch

In this moment of *'Eye therapy'* and the holding of hands, Sylvia appears to find a pronounced deal of security and seems to profit a great deal. The therapy indicates that just the fact of the boundary and therapeutic alliance and relationship more than the content is bringing about her discovery of self and to be able to feel.

Rogers' use of the words 'Eye therapy' reminds me of a scripture that can be easily overlooked, yet it holds profound power for me. It's something that Mark saw and wrote in Mark 10:21: "Then Jesus, beholding him, loved him." The word 'behold' means to see, observe, or look at something with attention, often with a sense of wonder or amazement. It's an old-fashioned or poetic way of saying 'to see' or 'to gaze upon.' When it says "Jesus, beholding him, loved him," it means that Jesus looked at the young man and felt a deep and compassionate love for him.

Rogers' interaction with Sylvia, using eye contact, demonstrated the creation of an empathic experience that could have initially been denied, walled up in defense, or wrapped in intellectualization. Here, we see the therapist's empathy at play—a crucial process, much like the role of a caregiver in an infant's early development, where it becomes a direct part of the infant's experience.

Daniel Stern who specializes in infant development *states "...one can contribute to the infant the capacity for psychic intimacy-the openness to disclosure, the permeability or inter-penetrability that occurs between two people. Psychic intimacy as well as physical intimacy is now possible. The desire to know and be known in this sense of mutually revealing subjective experience is great. In fact, it can be a powerful motive and can be felt as a need state."* [16]

About eye contact, Allan Schore's research shows—*"The infant's right brain is tuned to dynamically self-organize upon perceiving certain patterns of facially expressed exteroceptive senses (senses that perceive the body's position, motion and state, known as proprioceptive senses information), namely the visual and auditory stimuli emanating from the smiling and laughing joyful face of a loving Mother."* [17/18]

Picture if you will a therapist and client together in a safe therapeutic environment of attunement in the form of maternal or fraternal re-enactment. Does the following statement by Alexander Katehakis (Founder and Clinical Director of Centre for Healthy Sex in Los Angeles) sound familiar?—*"The Mother's job, is to attune by way of reciprocity: the musical sound of the voice, eye contact, gesture, touch, all the non-verbal communication that takes place within the mother/infant dyad are in a dance that is non-verbal* but highly communicative, wherein she is amplifying joy states and down-regulating sympathetic arousal when it's appropriate." [19]

Neuroscientists state that babies have three fears, loud noises, the dark and falling sensations. Israeli Psychologist Ayala Malach Pines, author of *Falling In Love* writes: "*Love doesn't last forever because we need the opportunity for growth and healing, being with a partner who pushes your buttons is good. The buttons point to the place that is most important for us to work on.*" [20]

From a therapeutic perspective of client and counselor, being able to love from a place of love itself, without it being impersonal, not falling in love with patients, for love is essential for these systems that are down in the right brain to be evoked, because of uncoupled systems and for them to kindle and to ignite again, they need novelty, they need this kind of human connection. Clients need a therapist who can push their buttons of growth, not stunt them into idealization.

*'The counselor who has a mindset of unconditional positive regard does not allow the self-protection shields of his client to cause deflection, but patiently endures and shows worth to his client and thereby earns the right to be given access behind those self-protective shields. In essence, Unconditional Positive Regard removes self-protective shields.'* [21]

## Fig leaves.

Many people, including high-ranking officials, [22] have promoted the idea that disclosure is imminent, aiming to prepare mankind for a connection to our non-anthropomorphic, idealized space daddies.

The sad reality is that if we haven't touched and united with the vulnerable place within us, we often project an image of seeming invulnerability outward. Humanity is well-versed in wearing figurative fig leaves and masks, concealing and self-protecting, unwilling to reveal all our cards. In contrast, *God seems to operate in total disclosure*, always has and always will. Mankind is continually asked to look upward, but *the answer lies within.* [23] But why?

# Chapter Eleven

## Your Eyes Follow Your Ears

*"All infants appear to have the ability to recognize perfect pitch at eight months of age. They lose this talent sometime before they reach adulthood."* [1] *— Jenny Saffran.*

'Your eyes follow your ears,' remarked Gordon, a music teacher in China, who circumnavigated Beijing with a group called *The Beatles Remastered* as we spoke regarding resonance and attentiveness and the essence of 'all you need is love.' Sounds draw our attention and stimulate our minds. Sound helps in establishing space, defining the environment and the setting, intensifying action and adding meaning or providing a counterpoint and our eyes will follow our ears. So, what are we listening to?

The three main monothetic religions all center around a man formerly known as Abram, meaning *Exalted Father* before it was later changed to Abraham, meaning *Father of a multitude.*

*Abram* before his *encounter with God*, it seemed, paid homage to the moon, stars and other heavenly objects and deities. *(Joshua 24:2-3)* So, the language that was used to reach him, was the object of his desire. He was simply oriented to the correct perspective and alignment of his being.

*"Then He (God) brought him outside and said, 'Look at the stars if you are able to number them ... so shall your descendants be.'"* [2]

It would later be his Grandson, Jacob, who wrestled and *held a materialized angel captive*, but that's another story. [3]

In the realm of imagination, all manner of things can materialize from eternity. Take, for instance, the Mona Lisa, displayed in the Louvre Museum and painted by Leonardo Da Vinci in 1503. It's not the original, it's a copy. The true original resided in the heart and imagination of Leonardo before he even touched paint to canvas. This exemplifies the notion that what you can conceive and imagine has the potential to manifest in reality. Consider Boeing's groundbreaking 777X airplane or the Lockheed Martin X-59 QueSST, which, if we had possessed the knowledge, could have taken flight 200 years ago. There remain undiscovered elements waiting to be created and found. The sky is never the limit; rather, it is the boundless imagination of humanity.

When we look at the night sky, we are filled with a feeling of awe. It's the reaction to the magnificence of the ultimate unknown and so we project eternity into the sky and that becomes the place of the ideal.

Why do we need something like that? I think that there is something within us that is constantly compelling us to look for and work toward an ideal. Like it or not, it is built into us extraordinarily deeply. It's an instinct, a fundamental structure of underlying reality. We can see the manifestation of that instinct in all sorts of ways once we start to look at where our eyes are following our ears.

Humanity's deep desire to identify an ideal and to pursue it is perhaps what Jung [4] was pointing out to some degree when he talked about UFOs as symbols and sounds of redemptive redemption from the sky. In science fiction stories, aliens are often there to save us or judge us. They're the projection of heavenly beings and that's our association, our tendency to associate the ideal with what's transcendent and above us.

The Greek root for 'metaphor,' μεταφορά (metaphorá), [5] means to carry across a meaning, to move from one place to another. Yet these meta-messengers are weaving themselves into the fabric of young minds more frequently without a formal or informal invitation on the landing or runway of life.

Ultimately, these phenomena, if we permit them, can become a distraction, a deity, a Delilah to woo you to lose your hair and vision, or a door of perspective and self-awareness to remain on purpose of destiny. Ironically, any researcher worth his salt would see that these deceptions point to God in their futile attempts to deceive, revealing a higher meaning behind even the attempts to deceive. - '… for this cause God shall send them strong delusion, that they should believe a lie.' [6]

## Clouds Without Rain.

I won't cite the thousands of books, research and theories (many of which abound, distract and consume one's life in the quest for answers). These theories include the existence of interdimensional or time-traveling vessels, secret government aircraft or technology, cryptological creatures capable of flight, vehicles piloted by advanced civilizations or ancient entities with a penchant for beef burgers and probing experiments, or the notion that they are CIA operatives in custom-made Hollywood alien costumes. Some even suggest they could be biological drones on a reconnaissance mission, or, more alarmingly, biogenetically engineered humans who have been convinced that they are not human. Additionally, Annie Jacobsen, an investigative journalist, implicates Joseph Stalin in a black propaganda hoax involving a crashed UFO in 1947, revealing the presence of deformed bodies surgically altered to resemble aliens within the craft. [7]

In conclusion, while drones may be part of the equation, spiritually, they resemble clouds without rain, blown along by the wind, unable to quench your thirst. They are like autumn trees without fruit, uprooted and twice dead. They are the wild waves of the sea, foaming with shame and wandering stars [8] with an operating system designed to colonize consciousness with ancient lies. Alternatively, according to the polar terrestrial hypotheses, they may have been here before humanity, producing meta-materials in exotic ways on Earth, or they could be evolved time travelers operating with future physics—a theory advocated by magic mushroom evangelist Joe Rogan on his podcast, which boasts over twelve million listeners. [9]

I suspect that Rogan's childhood trauma leads him to seek comfort, limerence and spiritual connection using psilocybin.

Meanwhile, other schools of thought maintain that these experiences are remnants of Hitler's side projects, technologies from the golden age of Atlantis and Noah's time, or that they involve Nephilim. Some theorists have even suggested that these are demonic technological projections. Saint Paul wrote to the Corinthians that Satan can 'transform' into an angel of light (2 Corinthians 11:14).

I note that these experiences can fracture people's sense of reality and can take on many different forms, photoshopping time and space with demonic and addictive special effects. This is a perplexing mystery that can be highly distracting if one is not grounded in the truth of our identity. To a degree, all the above play with a measure of so-called truths, excluding the Alien from another planet part. Regarding the time travel component, there seems to be an element of eternal interdimensional space-time at play, specifically not involving future humans.

Either way, it is evident to me that humanity is dealing with an intent to hack minds and consciousness. We live in a world with a history of τραύμα—Trávma, meaning wound in Greek. Many people with unresolved trauma or issues in their past can become vulnerable to all forms of distractions in the subconscious plea for healing.

Essentially, their tantalizing message enters the faculty and image upon an already imprinted psyche and narrative of a traumatized humanity. It is one of ecological impending doom, that 'technology is bad' and 'the world is in trouble.' 'We are you, you are us, we made you from our DNA, we helped you to evolve, we are your space daddies, we can show you a better way. Reconnect with us and we will give you all that you need while you remain disoriented.' There is nothing new under the sun, it is directed panspermia.

## Directed Panspermia.

The concept that Aliens brought life to Earth is called Directed Panspermia. The term was first coined by the co-discoverer of the structure of DNA, *Francis Crick* and *Leslie Orgel* in 1973. [10] They postulated that since Earth is relatively young compared to the rest of the universe, it was therefore conceivable that a technologically advanced society in outer space developed even before Earth existed.

The concept of Directed Panspermia is still advocated by many scientists today. In the movie, *Expelled.* [11] Ben Stein asked Richard Dawkins (a prominent evolutionary biologist) the question, "What do you think is the possibility that intelligent design might turn out to be the answer to some issues in genetics or evolution?"

Dawkins's reply: "Well, it could come about in the following way: it could be that at some earlier time somewhere in the universe a civilization evolved by, probably by, some kind of Darwinian means to a very, very high level of technology and designed a form of life that they seeded onto perhaps this, this [sic] planet. Now, that is a possibility and an intriguing possibility. And I suppose it's possible that you might find evidence for that if you look at the, at the detail … details of our chemistry molecular biology, you might find a signature of some sort of Designer."

But *who* made *them?*

The answer by these experts is usually *evolution*.

A question may then be asked where did God come from?

Dr. Kent Hovind's response to the questions, 'Where did God come from?' and 'Can you also tell me how a spiritual force can have an impact on a material universe to create it?'

Response: "Your question demonstrates that you're thinking of the wrong god. The God of the Bible is not affected by time, space, or matter. If God is affected by time, space, or matter then He is not God.

Time, space and matter are what's called a continuum, all of them must come into existence at the same instant, because if there was matter but no space, where would you put it? If there were matter and space but no time, when would you put it?

You cannot have time, space, or matter independently—they require a form of co-existence, to exist simultaneously. The Bible answers that in ten words, 'In the beginning (there's time), God created the heavens (there's space) and the earth (there's matter).' Hence, you have time, space and matter created—a trinity of trinities so to speak.

Time is past, present and future. Space has length, width and height. Matter is solid, liquid and gas. The God who created them needs to be outside of them. If He's limited by time, He's not God.

The guy who created this computer (points to a computer) is not the computer. He is not running around in there changing the numbers on the screen. The God who created this universe is outside of the universe: He's above it, beyond it, in it and through it—He's not affected by it.

So (in response to) the concept that a spiritual force cannot have any effect on a material body, you would have to explain to me (the effects of) emotions like love, hatred, envy, jealousy and rationality. If your brain is just a random collection of chemicals that formed by chance over billions of years, how on earth can you trust your reasoning processes and the thoughts that you think?

So, your question, 'Where did God come from?' is assuming a limited god and that's *your* problem. The God that I worship is not limited by time, space, or matter. If I could fit the infinite God in my three-pound brain, He would not be worth worshipping, that's for certain." [12]

— Kent Hovind.

## Piercing the Cosmic Veil

It is my opinion that any messenger further perpetuating the defamation of humanity's image is rooted in futility and desperation, aiming to advance deception among already gullible and media-manipulated mankind. These so-called entities claim to have traveled billions of miles or to have crashed and hidden themselves, mischievously recruiting the traumatized and disconnected to spread their message: the New Age is imminent, disclosure is at hand and the world is being prepared for an all-inclusive invitation to an intergalactic community.

So, what is their message and how are we expected to respond? They compel us to prepare for their multi-faceted spectrum of messages, taking advantage of a traumatized Earth that has relinquished its dominion by granting non-human creatures human agency. Many people fall prey to these intergalactic observers, projecting their thoughts and hopes onto them. Instead of appreciating the beauty of swaying flowers in the field and listening to the voices of hope and love, our eyes are drawn to consumerism, our ears to distractions and we unwittingly traverse a minefield of rescue by following an ancient, descended Pied Piper of lost thoughts. One who claims to have traveled millions of miles creates beef burgers through cow mutilation, gets lonely and commits unspeakable acts before fleeing in the name of Christ.

Joseph G. Jordan and MUFON.

Intriguing insights emerged during my interview with Joseph Jordan, a dedicated State Section Director and Field Investigator of the esteemed Mutual UFO Network (MUFON), as well as the leading figure behind CE4 Research, a group deeply engrossed in twenty-seven years of Alien Abduction research and investigation. What stood out was that whenever individuals found themselves in frequent contact with these entities—these enigmatic alien beings—the mere mention of the name 'Jesus' or its invocation was met with strong aversion.

Remarkably, these beings would swiftly depart when confronted with the Name above all names. Jordan and his colleagues uncovered a consistent pattern: the unwavering faith in Jesus Christ emerged as the sole and reliable means to halt alien intrusions. This fact finds solid support in more than 600 verified cases documented by CE4 Research, a remarkable 200 of which were openly shared by those willing to testify.

These cases were investigated and confirmed by CE4's investigative researchers using the rigorous investigative protocols learned from their training as MUFON Field Investigators. Where utilizing the scientific method, data gathering and logical thinking was the standard for operation. Jordan was a non-Christian at the time of the founding of CE4 Research but became a sola scriptura, Bible-believing Christian upon the discovery of the truth behind the UFO phenomenon.

*'I'm not sure how to answer this question concerning their limits. I do not know for certain that there are limits they can go to when dealing with human beings. I do see that some people are affected in very horrible ways when others are not; I feel that may be due to how involved with them we become. My personal view is that they do not outright cause death, but instead go to every effort to convince us that God is not real, or He didn't really say what He has said, or mean what He has said. They want to cheat us out of God's gift, the ultimate gift of eternal life through His Son, Jesus Christ.        As for the factor of authority, let me try and explain. In the beginning of my research, I too questioned the "authority" that the testimonies showed, of terminating the experience. I looked for the answer in God's Word for quite a while, but I just could not put my finger on it. I finally said, "Lord, help me, I think this is very important to the research." My understanding was that the sixth chapter of Ephesians was the Spiritual Warfare chapter for dealing with the lies and temptations of the enemy in our lives. I understood that verse twelve identified whom we were fighting against. Those who follow Jesus Christ are Christians and Christians have*

*access to the power in the Name and authority of Jesus Christ. The Name above all names. What gives Christians that access? The answer is found in a mystery, a once-secret mystery, but later revealed. The mystery goes like this: the demonic realm has been running this world for quite some time. Then, Jesus is born into the world. They knew who He was (God manifest in the flesh on earth) and they knew there was going to be trouble. They knew the prophecies and they were seeing them being fulfilled. During His time on Earth, Jesus did give the demonic realm a hard time, putting them in their place.'*

"Then Jesus came to them and said, 'All authority in heaven and on earth has been given to me.' " Matthew 28:18

*'So, the demonic realm planned to turn the people against Him, to have Him eliminated. They thought that once He was gone, things would return to normal. So, they influenced the minds of the people and they had Him crucified.*

*But He rose from the grave on the third day. He defeated death, but He didn't stay. He rose to the right hand of the Father (God) in Heaven. The demonic realm thought they had won since He was gone. But wait, Jesus had told His disciples something before He rose to Heaven, found in Acts 1:4 (NIV): On one occasion, while He was eating with them, He gave them this command:'*

"Do not leave Jerusalem, but wait for the gift my Father promised, which you have heard me speak about."

*'On the day of Pentecost, in the Upper Room where they were gathered together, they received the promised gift from the Father, the indwelling of the Holy Spirit. From that day forward, believers in the Lord*

*Jesus Christ would all receive the indwelling of the Holy Spirit. Christ in you. This was the mystery revealed. Because every believer in the Lord Jesus Christ would have access to the power in the Name and authority of Jesus Christ through the indwelling of the Holy Spirit. The power to defeat the demonic entities that come against them. And the testimonies that you will read in this book, will show just that.*

*This can be best seen, in the sixth chapter of Ephesians, the spiritual warfare chapter. Verse 12 identifies who we war against.'*

"For our struggle is not against flesh and blood, but against the rulers, against the authorities, against the powers of this dark world and the spiritual forces of evil in the heavenly realms." Ephesians 6:12

*'Verses 13 through 17 are about protecting yourself by putting on the whole armor of God in your daily life.'*

"Therefore, put on the full armor of God, so that when the day of evil comes, you may be able to stand your ground and after you have done everything, to stand. Stand firm then, with the belt of truth buckled around your waist, with the breastplate of righteousness in place and with your feet fitted with the readiness that comes from the gospel of peace. In addition to all this, take up the shield of faith, with which you can extinguish all the flaming arrows of the evil one. Take the helmet of salvation and the sword of the Spirit, which is the word of God." Ephesians 6:13-17

*'But you as human beings will tire; you will let down your defenses. Because of that, you have an offensive weapon that will put the demonic realm in its place. The most powerful weapon in the Universe.*

*Those are verses 18 through 20:*

419

"And pray in the Spirit on all occasions with all kinds of prayers and requests. With this in mind, be alert and always keep on praying for all the Lord's people. Pray also for me, that whenever I speak, words may be given me so that I will fearlessly make known the mystery of the gospel, for which I am an ambassador in chains. Pray that I may declare it fearlessly, as I should." Ephesians 6:18-20

*'Let me break it down in simple terms for you. Prayer is a powerful weapon, especially silent prayer (in the spirit) to God the Father. Why silent prayer? Because the demonic realm cannot read your thoughts, but they will make you think they can. I do believe they can influence your thoughts though. This is warfare, don't give anything away to them. Now look at verse 19, it says, "that whenever I speak," but speak to who? Remember, this is the spiritual warfare chapter dealing with the demonic realm. You are speaking, out loud, to the demonic realm. Why? Because they can't read your thoughts. But they can hear your voice.'*

*"Words may be given me."*

*By who? The Holy Spirit, that dwells in the believer of Jesus Christ.*

*"So that I will fearlessly make known the mystery of the gospel."* *What mystery? The mystery I shared with you earlier.* **That we have Christ in us, through the indwelling of the Holy Spirit and access to call on the power in the name and authority of Jesus Christ, the name above all names, the power over all the Universe and the earth.'** [13]

# It's A Kind of Magic.

*'As a magician, I promise never to reveal the secret of any illusion to a nonmagician, unless that one swears to uphold the Magician's Oath in turn.*

*I promise never to perform any illusion for any non-magician without first practicing the effect until I can perform it well enough to maintain the illusion of magic.' — The Magician's Oath.* [14]

In *The Matrix Reloaded,* [15] written by the Wachowski brothers, the character of the Oracle offers a thought-provoking statement. She explains, in essence, that every instance of someone claiming to have encountered a ghost, angel, or mythical creature, such as a vampire or werewolf, can be attributed to a rogue program operating outside of its intended function in the system!    Magicians, illusionists, tricksters, swindlers, deserters—masters of psychological warfare and special effects—spiritually manifesting, photoshopping, projecting and manipulating the elements and realm around. Yes, manipulating the CIA, MI5, Discordian societies—these fallen angels, authorities are mostly rogue and not what they purport to be.

Even the famous French researcher, Jacques Vallee questioned this observation:

*"I will stress once again that we do not know the source from which the UFOs or the Alien beings come. Whether or not, for example, they originate in the physical universe as modern astrophysics have described it, they manifest in the physical world and bring about definable consequences in that domain. We are dealing with a yet unrecognized level of consciousness, independent of man but closely linked to the earth. I do not*

421

*believe anymore that UFOs are simply the spacecraft of some race of extra-terrestrial visitors. This notion is too simplistic to explain their appearance, the frequency of their manifestations through recorded history and the structure of the information exchanged with them during contact.*

*Human beings are under the control of a strange force that bends them in absurd ways, forcing them to play a role in a bizarre game of deception. The symbolic display seen by the abductees is identical to the type of initiation ritual or astral voyage that is embedded in the occult traditions of every culture.*

*If they are not an advanced race from the future, are we dealing instead with a parallel universe, another dimension where there are other human races living and where we may go at our expense, never to return to the present? From that mysterious universe, are higher beings projecting objects that can materialize and dematerialize at will? Are UFOs windows rather than objects? The 'medical examination' to which abductees are said to be subjected ... is reminiscent of the medieval tales of encounters with demons. It makes no sense in a sophisticated or technical framework; any intelligent being equipped with the scientific marvels that UFOs possess would be in a position to achieve any of these alleged scientific objectives in a shorter time and with fewer risks."* [16]

"The symbolic display seen by the abductees is identical to the type of initiation ritual or astral voyage that is imbedded in the [occult] traditions of every culture... the structure of abduction stories is identical to that of occult initiation rituals... the UFO beings of today belong to the same class of manifestation as the [occult] entities that were described in centuries past." [17]

# Mulder and Scully

(JOE: "Why are you asking me if I work for the CIA?"

DELOIR—*UFO investigator, Concordia University*: "Do you realize what you've done? You've essentially done the Government's work for them. They should be paying you for this.")

In the Biblical account of the interactions between Moses and the occult leaders of Egypt, Jannes and Jambres, [18] there is a striking moment of power and authority demonstrated through the use of a rod.

As recorded in Exodus 4:3, before Moses returned to Egypt, he cast his rod on the ground and it transformed into a nâchâsh (H5175) נָחָשׁ, or serpent. This event caused Moses to flee in fear. However, in Exodus 7:10-11, a significant shift occurs. Moses and Aaron approach Pharaoh and as commanded by the Lord, Aaron casts down his rod before Pharaoh and his servants. This time, the rod transforms into a tannîyn (H8577) תַּנִּין, a dragon or sea monster. [19]

In response, Pharaoh summons his own wise men and sorcerers, who through their secret arts, also transform their rods into serpents.

But, with a powerful display of divine authority, Aaron's dragon rod consumes their rods. This event illustrates the stark contrast between the power of God and the power of man and serves as a reminder of who holds ultimate authority.

Though the occult leaders also demonstrated their ability to manipulate time, space and matter, their creations were ultimately consumed by *Aaron's dragon*, a manifestation of the power of God.

This event serves as a reminder of the dangers of deception through the manipulation of evidence. In a modern-day context, it begs the question, what if an investigation such as that of the FBI. were to analyze the DNA remnants of such an occurrence? Would it be able to distinguish between the supernatural and the occult? This serves as a cautionary tale to not be deceived by appearances, as even evidence can be manipulated to deceive a nation.

John DeSouza, a former FBI Special Agent who investigated UFOs, paranormal phenomena and extraterrestrial life, discusses the hypothesis that UFOs and their occupants are not physical beings as we understand physicality. DeSouza suggests that during abduction experiences, the beings have a dreamlike, ethereal quality, which implies that the experience is *a conversion into another reality*, rather than a physical one. DeSouza proposes that UFOs and their occupants exist in a different dimension or reality and abduction experiences involve a conversion into that reality, rather than physical transportation. [20/21]

## Abductive Deductive.

I will close this chapter with some wise words from J. Brian Huffling, Ph. D the Director of the Ph.D. Program and Associate Professor of Philosophy and Theology at SES. Southern Evangelical Seminary.

"The investigation into what UFOs and aliens are is not a deductive one. In other words, it is not going to be proven beyond any doubt in this lifetime. Rather it is, no pun intended, an abductive one. That is, the truth about the phenomena will likely be what accounts for the data the best, namely, what has the most explanatory power (how well the data is explained) and explanatory scope (how much of the data is explained) and what less ad hoc (made up without evidence). I agree with Vallée that the ETH does not possess the greatest explanatory power or scope. It does not seem to account for the history, the physical problems, or the anti-Christian themes. The data is well-accounted for with the demonic view. Such a view answers the material problems since the UFOs/aliens are not physical, but can, as Hynek suggests, cause physical effects. This also accounts for the anti-Christian teachings that are ubiquitous in the phenomena.

Apart from the UFO phenomena being interesting, it is also important. More than just a possible national security threat, there is an existential threat. If the demonic view is correct, then there is, indeed, a cosmic and spiritual battle for our entire belief systems and *thus our souls*. Statistically, given the number of sightings and experiences, many people who go to Christian churches have had an experience (although, it can be argued that if people in the church dabble in the occult and new age less, then they won't have as many doors open).

Often, people turn to new age, occultic, or otherwise anti-Christian sources either for answers to their questions, being lured by their curiosity of the paranormal, or simply being drawn in by our culture pushing it on us.

I agree with Vallée, Hynek and Ross that the alien view does not do the best job of explaining the data. Given the spiritual nature of UFOs and especially 'aliens,' there is a strong argument that such activity is demonic. If it is the case that the paranormal, occult and new age are doors to such activity, *it is imperative that Christians understand this and that it is taught in our churches and homes.* The Bible gives several commands to avoid involvement in such activity. Unfortunately, Christians and churches are easily caught up in the flow of our culture, rather than standing firm in the faith. This is indeed an important issue that deserves attention in the Church as well as in other ministries that teach the truth and importance of the faith."
[22]

# Chapter Twelve

## Where The Light Gets In

*'There's a crack in everything. That's where the light gets in.'*
*— Leonard Cohen.* [1]

On April 4th, 2020, amidst my personal inner child therapy, a profound vision unfolded.

PROF. BEATRICE: "What can you see, Joe?"

At this moment, I witnessed a glimpse of my five-year-old self, clutching my Mother's hand. Her silhouette glowed in the sun's golden embrace, radiating youth and beauty. The breeze tousled the back of her jet-black hair as she turned towards me. Instinctively, I shifted my gaze away.

Beatrice, perceptive as ever, inquired, "What's he doing?"

"He (me) turned around and is asking... (pause) he is asking me... (pause) he is asking me... (sob) to... to... look... to look at her," I shared, with hot tears from the depths of my childhood streaming down my cheeks. As my younger self held her hand, I felt the weight of his words, "See how she loves you, how proud she is of you."

Then my younger self, tenderly, placed my hand into hers, an act filled with empathy and boundless affection. With unwavering tenderness, he whispered, "Look, here is your Mother."

I looked into her eyes... Such love. Overwhelmed, I unraveled, a tempest of tears and emotion...

"Mum, I never told you I loved you...

… I love you mum."

A mending had begun, a gentle stitching of time, a gentle repairing of the rupture.

Minutes elapsed before my younger self explored my aging countenance, his young hand tracing my beard, curiosity tingling from his voice, "What happened?"

"We grew older," I sighed, a reflection laden with the weight of time. Later, as the hours unfurled, I savored pizza and my younger self requested a slice. I ventured to the restroom and as I relieved myself, his echo followed suit. In the delicate symphony of this moment, compassion flowed both ways, weaving an intricate tapestry between us across time. The compassion of the young for the older and of the older for the young.

Even now, the events of 4.4.20 remain a journey of contemplation, a narrative yet to be fully grasped.

## Belonging.

As a child, my alternative comfort was the partial belonging and rejection within my attachment, which served "as a centerpiece of my neurobiological and psychological needs." (Bowlby, 1988, 2008) [2]

Back then, I was drawn to off-world comfort. Certain ruptures and vicarious sensitivity made my younger, broken self feel that my parents' love was inconsistent and conditional, wrapped up in their own insecurities. Their own traumatic imprints left an indelible mark on my soul. Could it be that I felt denied the opportunity to feel loved or belong to any group?

My view of the world from a Bowlby theory of attachment perspective suggests that there is a lean toward attachment to a significant other and that, along with the family interaction, these patterns of behavior should provide the "secure base." [3/4]

PROF. BEATRICE: "Joe, in Melanie Klein's perspective from the 'object relations' school of thought, folks are kind of wired to yearn for emotional closeness and that sense of being linked with others." *"An innate yearning to recreate the sense of oneness with mother."* [5]

Therefore, my conversation points for further exploration in sessions would center on those times. I felt a sense of transcendence or connection to something beyond myself to better understand my intrinsic resources for flourishing. Some may feel a connection while engaging in meditation, whilst exploring primary attachment figures and how we lived with our biological parents or primary caregivers. Others feel a connection in the acceptance of their human experiencing during therapy. Carl Rogers noted that there was an inexpressible, spiritual dimension to his contact with clients during moments of significant depth:

*"At those moments it seems that my inner spirit has reached out and touched the inner spirit of the other. Our relationship transcends itself and becomes a part of something larger. Profound growth and healing and energy are present."* [6]

PROF. BEATRICE: "Rogers went and told us 'Bout those fancy stories he had during counseling, tryin' to show that there's a lot of spiritual magic in those talks, no matter what kinda chat's goin' on in that therapy room. Those meetings, they're like a cool breeze blowin' in, got nothin' to do with the fancy words they use or the big plans they make for people's lives. It's 'cause they're a real hangout with the whole shebang of life, a real taste of the big ol' world right there in front of you.'

Brian Thorne, Co-founder of the Norwich Centre for Personal, Professional and Spiritual Development, a retired counselor and psychotherapist, as well as Emeritus Professor of Counselling at the University of East Anglia in Norwich and a former Professor of Education in the College of Teachers and member of the Anglican Church, compares his experiences to Rogers' presence. However, he labels it as tenderness and like me, he believes it's a therapeutic element crucial for recovery. Thorne (1998) also delves into the therapist's internal state during moments of change: *'Magic moments signify a particular intensity of relating, where a new level of understanding is reached and a sense of validating freedom is experienced by both client and counselor. The surge of well-being that follows such moments is nearly indescribable'* (Thorne 1998: 46).[7] Thorne, a Christian Therapist and Anglican Church member, asserts that these encounters unfold in the presence of God, arising from openness, acceptance and mutual love for personal vulnerability in the client-professional interaction.

It would take a group of trainee counselors and my therapy to grasp the flow of God's love through people, unravel my journey and clear my heart, revealing that the dragons were defeated two thousand years ago at the cross; *"And you, being dead in your sins and the uncircumcision of your flesh, hath he quickened together with him, having forgiven you all trespasses; Blotting out the handwriting of ordinances that was against us, which was contrary to us and took it out of the way, nailing it to his cross; And having spoiled principalities and powers, he made a shew of them openly, triumphing over them in it."* Colossians 2: 13-14—and my true identity emerged.

To undo childhood and teenage trauma, where my insecure attachments and ambivalence strayed from my Catholic upbringing to explore New Age teachings, a genuine encounter with the living Christ occurred at age twenty-five. Things were fine until I joined the well-intentioned Pentecostal circus, with its demon hunts and body-spirit division. This literal and dualistic approach—separating natural and supernatural realms—didn't bode well with me. 'A view incorporating the idea that there can be two kinds of reality, one natural, material, or physical and the other immaterial, supernatural or metaphysical "A view incorporating the idea that there can be two kinds of reality, one natural, material, or physical and the other immaterial, supernatural or metaphysical." —Uttal, W. [8]

## I set aside childish ways.

When I was a child, I thought like a child, I talked like a child, I reasoned like a child. When I became a man, I put the ways of childhood behind me. As a man there is no more separation, no division, no enmity, no wall, no disconnect between the God of love I've come to know as Abba (Father) through Christ, my experience in my late thirties would discover the simple truth that love never leaves us on the shelf.

In the words of St. Paul, 'Can anything ever separate us from Christ's love? Does it mean He no longer loves us if we have trouble or calamity, or are persecuted, or hungry, or destitute, or in danger, or threatened with death? No, despite all these things, overwhelming victory is ours through Christ who loved us. And I am convinced that nothing can ever separate us from God's love. Neither death nor life, neither angels nor demons, neither our fears for today nor our worries about tomorrow, nor any other creature can separate us from God's love. No power in the sky above or in the earth below—indeed nothing in all creation will ever separate us from the love of God that is revealed in Christ Jesus, our Lord.'—Romans 8: 35-39 (NLT)

'God is something that needs rescuing from religion.' — Sinead O'Connor [9]

In conclusion, as a society, there is a need for a better understanding and attitudes toward clients with faith. However, the trap with some religions and even therapeutic theory is that they can be taken too literally as a formula to treat problems that don't exist for our clients. Counselors shouldn't assume that followers of Christian, Jewish, Muslim, or ethnic-centered faiths will know and live out all the elements of their faith's belief systems and rituals. Adolescence is a challenging biological and social developmental process for us all and must be understood by the counselor to support the young person and their individualized and idiosyncratic religious context, which has affected their intrapsychic worlds. Furthermore, there are key psychological changes that occur during this period "which involves the formation of a new identity."—Geldard & Geldard. [10]

Reading about a person's faith is no substitute for listening to how our clients live out and experience their faith — many in joy and bliss, others often in confusion, contradiction and fear of some of their core belief structures. Attention needs to be given to the ways organized religion and faith-based systems may originate or perpetuate mental illness by discouraging needed prescriptions or therapy. Moreover, to begin to understand this client group, we must consider the extent to which a client's spiritual and religious beliefs and values are pertinent to the client's issues. Therefore, they deserve the same respectful, ethical and skillful attention as any other personal value, a collaborative therapeutic alliance is crucial for clients to take ownership of their own lives and healing, regardless of the counselor's faith or lack of.

As a person-centered counselor in therapy, I have been presented with the "Core conditions" (Rogers, 1957) of empathy (unconditional, positive regard and congruence, empowering me to explore and support my humanity, which enabled my integration amid spirituality to remain intact, whilst remaining client led).

Beatrice, Bernard and Virgil my therapists, facilitated a place for religion and spirituality in our psychoanalytic work. Using techniques such as free association, interpretation and analysis of transference to help me gain insight into my relationships and current difficulties. This would later help me to take seriously a client's views and relationship and to use these concepts and experiences as windows into their intrapsychic distress.

Neither Fairbairn nor Klein devoted much of their attention to religion, their contribution to 'object relations theory' places emphasis on relationships, thus allowing for a more positive stance toward relation and enabling some genuine insight into the area of religion.


Innate yearning


Klein's perspective suggested that human beings are drawn to seek emotional closeness and a sense of belonging to others. "An innate yearning to recreate the sense of oneness with Mother." (Tuckwell, 2002) [11]

As an adult, exploring my psychological birthing process via my encounter with the Holy Spirit, therapy later involved internalizing or *taking in* the relationship with external objects to form the internal structures of my personality. Exploring my human personality meant exploring the history of my relationships with significant people.

PROF. BERNARD: "Fairbairn believed (as I do) that the human heart is primarily hungry to be in a relationship, acceptance and emotional closeness. This is a neurobiological need."

JOE: "Amen to that!"

PROF. BEATRICE: "Joe, ya know, when we're kinda unsure 'bout what lies ahead, it's possible we're on the brink of our true purpose. And when the path ahead looks a tad hazy, that's when we're kickin' off our real journey."

## Journey Of A Star Sailor.

In July 1996, as a young man, I embarked on an experiment to gauge the media's reaction to a certificate I had created, one that purported to offer insurance against alien abduction. My intention was to initiate discussions about UFOs, combining both seriousness and humor in the conversation. However, I had underestimated the response this endeavor would generate, leading to a campaign aimed at expanding the public's openness to the possibility of extraterrestrial life.

My journey into the paranormal began as I interviewed and engaged with individuals who had either witnessed or extensively researched the subject. Their stories left a deep impression on me, especially those of Canadian psychologist M. Deloir, photographer Alvarez and his Brazilian investigations and Sylvia from Swindon. I also had the opportunity to converse with an abductee who had made a live TV appearance in 1996, claiming ongoing contact with ETs. Despite her apparent disdain for these entities, she refused offers of assistance to investigate and confront her abductors. Her case was just one among many that involved interactions with these emancipated beings.

I also delved into the work of war journalist Tim Leach and the Ariel School incident, which remains one of the most intriguing UFO sightings in history for those who are unaware of spiritual truths.

It seemed that the pieces of the puzzle were falling into place, yet I still found no inner peace. The underlying issue is that I, like millions of others, yearned to believe in the existence of extraterrestrial life because we sought a savior, someone or something to rescue us, mend Earth's troubles and safeguard humanity. Thank God, my own transformative experiences ultimately brought closure to this chapter.

Even though some journalists were hoodwinked into writing stories that were often complete fantasy, journalist and Ikea cuddly bear hugger Bill Sebastian's book 'False Claims' also illustrates the integrity of most of the press, particularly those in the UK. It demonstrates how overwhelmingly they fulfill their core function of keeping the public's fleeting attention, while informing them by breaking hard-core news stories and meeting the growing social and commercial pressures in order to deliver light entertainment. However, it's an inordinate distraction technique to further pollute the minds of a generation under the new norms of the COVID-19 pandemic with inconsistent and deliberate division tactics. Non-stop news featuring masks and injections purporting to stop the prevention of germs is a fallacy, which only further devalues the image and glory of man.

Fake news stories still recur to this day. For example, in 2005, The Guardian ran a news story on alien abduction insurance. 'It does exist!' asserted the headline. Many other such instances of this and other ludicrous stories I propagated have appeared in print and broadcast media since then. For instance, the BBC TV show QI twice presented as fact the same fake news about alien insurance, first by Stephen Fry in 2016 and then by Sandi Toksvig in the Christmas 2020 edition of the show. Like so many unoriginal British comedies, these false claims are forever being repeated.

I quit media hoaxing in 1997. Although Johnny Cradock invited me to continue our media escapades, I decided to part ways, leaving him with the idea for the abominable snowman quest. Consequently, our paths diverged. Today, I am in Asia, where I regularly encounter various forms of trauma, with young and old frozen in their wounds. Ironically, I find myself in Nepal as I complete this volume.

## Mind Games.

For now, I am observing the psychological mind games added to the press releases (June 2021) by the Pentagon. In addition to that, an official U.S. Government video of a 2004 UAP (Unexplained Ariel Phenomena) chase encounter taken aboard a Navy fighter jet from the nuclear aircraft carrier USS Nimitz was released. The video was recorded by a U.S. Navy F-18 thermal imaging camera off the coast of Baja, California during maneuvers in 2004. Astrophysicist Eric W. Davis, who had spent years working as a consultant for the Pentagon UFO program and is now a defense contractor, gave a classified briefing to the Defense Department in March 2020. In that briefing, he referred to 'off-world vehicles not made on this earth.' [12/13]

Our world is ridden with mental pollution and a breeding ground for hate, fear and deception. The disinformation of COVID-19 and falsified statistics led to a divided humanity, with the masked versus unmasked, vaccinated versus unvaccinated and even the vilification of those who refuse to be mandated to be vaccinated. As Peter Venkman from Ghostbusters would say, 'Human sacrifice! Dogs and cats living together... mass hysteria!' [14]

Generation Alpha is growing up in homes with smart speakers and devices everywhere. Technology, built into everyday items, broadcasts the ever-shaping events of delusion with no end in sight. Humanity seeks escape, distraction, or a perpetual orgasm to change neurochemistry. This has been clouded by the whims and dictates of bad-breathed media puppeteers who sow seeds of bondage, ensuring we stay muzzled and housed inside a cranium of uninterrupted deceitful rhetoric.

Animals in the wild have highly effective methods of dealing with their everyday submergence of the fight or flight response. Despite their inundation with chronic survival responses, they remain resolute and un-traumatized. Animals in the wild do not get PTSD, despite being under routine threats. On the other hand, humans are readily overwhelmed and often subject to long-lasting traumatic symptoms of hyper-arousal and shutdown long after the threats have passed. The vagal tone, which is correlated with the capacity to regulate stress responses, can be influenced by breathing. Increasing it through meditation and exercise can contribute to resilience and the mitigation of mood and anxiety symptoms.

# Chapter Thirteen

## From Hound Dog to Enlightenment: The Neurochemistry of Elvis and Spiritual Seers

What happens in Vegas stays in Vegas. I only lasted one day before flying to Texas after staying in Las Vegas in August 2015. I'm not a gambling man, but I observed the multitude of players on roulette wheels and slot machines. The pavement smelled like melted cheese. The sun was so intense that I felt like I was walking into a hair dryer. Somebody once said that only mad dogs and Englishmen go out in the midday sun,[1] while I met a multitude of various Elvis impersonators busking 'Hound Dog' on the streets. Overall, I loved Elvis, but Vegas wasn't my thing. As a child, I loved the music of Elvis. I'd watched some of his films at my Nonna's house. I also loved Evil Knievel. The two seemed symbolic of a safer time. In 1967, Elvis, while looking into the mirror and probably not liking what he saw, fell and hit his head hard on a porcelain bathtub and was knocked unconscious. After these incidents, as is common with even mild traumatic brain injuries, Elvis' behavior changed. He became erratic and irrational. [2]

### The Vegas nerve

The Vegas nerve, aptly named for its connection to Las Vegas and the saying, 'What happens in Vegas, stays in Vegas,' [3] bears a resemblance to its Sin City counterpart in terms of discretion. The same can be said for 'What happens in the Vagus nerve, stays in the Vagus nerve.'

Now, let's delve into the Vagus nerve's importance. This vital component of the Parasympathetic Nervous System oversees a wide range of essential bodily functions, including mood regulation, immune responses, digestion and heart rate. It acts as a messenger between the brain and the gastrointestinal tract, relaying crucial information about our internal organs' status.

Vagal tone, closely tied to stress response regulation, can be influenced by something as simple as our breath. Activities like meditation and exercise (which boost vagal tone) contribute to our resilience and help alleviate symptoms of mood disorders and anxiety.

The Vagus nerve plays a pivotal role in shifting our body from the sympathetic nervous system, which kicks in during times of stress and danger, to the parasympathetic nervous system, allowing us to focus on relaxation and recovery. However, when our emotional responses don't align with the situation at hand, it could indicate a malfunction in the Vagus nerve.

At times, the Vagus nerve can become hypersensitive to certain stress triggers, such as extreme heat, fear, loud voices, or even routine activities like standing for extended periods. Stimulating the Vagus nerve sends a signal to the body, urging it to unwind and destress. This can lead to long-lasting improvements in mood, overall well-being and our ability to leap back from adversity.

Similar to the catchy lyrics of Elvis Presley's "Hound Dog," where he sings, *'You ain't never caught a rabbit and you ain't no friend of mine,'* we can find a quirky comparison in our own internal guide - the Vagus nerve. When life presents its emotional challenges, symbolized by rabbits, our Vagus nerve becomes our steadfast companion. It acts as our body's personal whisperer, helping us navigate these emotions with grace and move through life's highs and lows with a charming blend of strength and balance.

438

PROF. VIRGIL: "The Vagus nerve, cari studenti, it's like the Grand Canal of the autonomic nervous system—our guardian angel, if you will. This nerve, it's like a messenger, a cable with many threads of connection. 80% of these threads carry news from our body up to our brain, like a diligent informant keeping headquarters in the loop—we call this bottom-up, capisce? —Now, the remaining 20% do a reverse dance, sending signals from the brain to the body, orchestrating the whole symphony—that's our top-down maestro.

Now, here's the intriguing part, whenever our body's stuck in a defensive tango, our brain, bless its little neurons, starts spinning tales to make sense of the commotion. But fear not! If we can hush the turmoil in our body and remind it that all's well in the here and now, our mind will find its chill. It's like nurturing a delicate garden to flourish, it needs the right soil, sunlight and water. Our mind, too, finds solace in healthy relationships, those havens of safety and support.

Think about our young ones, the Bambini and Ragazzi—they need these bonds like tender saplings need care. Parents, teachers and folks like me – we play our part in building strong bridges of connection, nurturing secure attachments and polishing those interpersonal skills. But alas, life can toss a curveball, a traumatic twist that sets us in defense mode, ready to protect our precious selves.

Ah and in these times, we must remember the delicate dance between body and mind, like the sacred rhythm of life itself. As we tread this path of understanding, let us cultivate a garden of serenity and balance, where the breeze of tranquility rustles through our being, soothing the wounds of our souls.

For it is in this harmonious blend that we find our sanctuary, nurturing the seeds of resilience and growth."

## Who would we be without trauma?

According to Dr. Richard Swartz, "Beneath the surface of the protective parts of trauma survivors there exists an undamaged essence, the Self that is confident, curious and calm, Self that has been sheltered from destruction by the various protectors that have emerged in their efforts to ensure survival. Once these protectors trust that it is safe to separate, the Self-will spontaneously emerge and the parts can be enlisted in the healing process. Rather than being a passive observer, this mindful Self can help reorganize the inner system and communicate with the parts in ways that help those parts trust that there is someone inside who can handle things."

— Dr. Richard Swartz. [4]

PROF. BEATRICE: "How would you gaze into the mirror of your past and share this with your eight-year-old self?"

JOE: "Have you ever felt that overwhelming sadness when something really hurts you? It's like a heavy weight on your heart and you just wish you could hide from it all. But you know what? Deep inside, there are these incredible protectors, like Luke Skywalker. And there's something even more special there, called the Self. It's like the mightiest Knight, but it stays hidden to keep you safe. When your protectors see that everything's going to be okay, the Self comes out to comfort you. It speaks to your protectors, assuring them that you'll be alright. It reveals the beautiful person you are, just like a true friend who holds you when you're scared, like a comforting embrace that wipes away your tears."

PROF. BEATRICE: "Well, Joe, it's right somethin' how you've laid out that fancy dance between them protectors and that their hidden Self, kind of like a reflection in the mirror of the psyche. Your words sure do paint a clear picture of grit and tenderness. Now, let's go ahead and flip that mirror back to the past and we'll give your 8-year-old self some of that same comfort and assurance you've been talkin' about."

## Smoke and Mirrors.

*"Beware of unearned wisdom and of virtue, given that these beget pride and a fall. In order to have an influence on others, the psyche itself must undergo a change and become infected with the same thing we want to produce in others."* [5]

Jung used this quote to emphasize the importance of personal growth and development as a prerequisite for being able to help and influence others. He cautioned against blindly accepting ideas or beliefs without critical examination or personal experience and stressed the need for inner work in order to effect positive change in oneself and others.

Amidst this celestial symphony, where stars wage their cosmic battles and the mysteries of the universe unfold, there exists a connection to the inner realms of our existence – the Vagus nerve, our very own cosmic conductor. Just as the heavens above hold their secrets, so too does this intricate neural pathway within us.

The same darkness that shrouds distant galaxies and cosmic phenomena finds its reflection in the human experience. Here on this fragile, blue and green orb, we grapple with the complexities of good and evil, often hidden from plain sight. It's as if the universe itself echoes the struggles and dichotomies we face as individuals and as a collective. [6]

Imagine for a moment, if we could cradle this spinning Earth in our hands, gently like a needle on a vinyl record and listen closely. We might hear the laughter of children, the echoes of joy and the reverberations of pain within a traumatized race seeking purpose and understanding. Perhaps, amid our cosmic ponderings, we also find ourselves asking, 'Are we alone?' Not just in the vastness of the universe but in our connection to our true selves and in our deepest fears of abandonment.

The colonization of consciousness teeters on the brink amid an ongoing cognitive invasion and an unseen war waged within the realms of strange phenomena and burgeoning ideologies. The way younger generations are told to think and perceive reality is at a critical point due to continuous and pervasive influences on their minds. These influences come from various sources, particularly the media, unconventional events, emerging belief systems, and advancing AI technology, all of which are becoming increasingly popular. There is a struggle or conflict within young minds enveloped in a world of traumatic ripples, influenced by these new and strange ideas, potentially altering their understanding of and interaction with the world. Recent claims, some of which purportedly unmask extraterrestrials, have made sensational headlines. Even statements emanating from the Headquarters of the United States Department of Defense—a formidable agency entrusted with a staggering budget of $715 billion in the fiscal year of 2022, bolstered by an additional $38 billion allocation for Overseas Contingency Operations, defense initiatives and clandestine endeavors, all designed to safeguard a nation. [7]

As these narratives unfold, they trigger a profound response within us, one that resonates deep within our very beings. War and the relentless bombardment of our minds through media can lead to an overactive sympathetic nervous system (the fight-or-flight response) and an underactive parasympathetic nervous system (which includes the vagus nerve, responsible for relaxation). This imbalance can result in reduced vagal tone, which, in turn, contributes to heightened stress, decreased emotional resilience and a compromised ability to cope with the challenges of a rapidly changing world. There is no love in war, only new orphans on a planet run by orphans. Yet, who are these defense agencies mirroring?

PROF. VIRGIL: "Allow me to paint a picture of mirror neurons, a wonder birthed in the realm of Italia. In the enchanting epoch of the 1990s, a fellowship of devoted scholars, guided by the wise Giacomo Rizzolatti,[8] embarked on a journey of enlightenment. Their chosen companions? The contemplative macaque monkeys. Amidst the cerebral tapestry, a revelation unfurled like delicate lotus petals. Within the monkeys' premotor realm, certain neurons ignited not only with their actions but also in harmony with the dance of a human researcher, revealing the profound unity woven through the fabric of existence."

Temporal Reflection.


Mirror neurons, a type of brain cell, are activated both when an individual performs an action and when they observe someone else performing the same action. These neurons were first discovered in monkeys, where they were found to fire when the monkey performed an action, such as reaching for a piece of food and also when the monkey observed another monkey or human performing the same action.

Mirror neurons are believed to play a role in empathy, imitation and social learning. They are thought to be involved in understanding the actions and intentions of others, as well as in learning new skills through observation and imitation. Some researchers also suggest that mirror neurons may be involved in the development of language, as they may help to link the sounds of words with their meanings by mapping the movements of the mouth and tongue when speaking onto the listener's own motor system.

The researchers published their findings on mirror neurons in a series of papers, including 'Premotor Cortex and the Recognition of Motor Actions' in Cognitive Brain Research in 1992 and 'Mirror neurons and the simulation theory of mind-reading' in Trends in Cognitive Sciences in 1999. [9] These studies helped establish the existence of mirror neurons and their potential role in *understanding the actions and intentions of others*. Since their discovery, mirror neurons have been studied in a wide range of contexts, including social cognition, language development and motor learning and are now considered an important area of research in neuroscience, psychology and philosophy.

Mirrors have long been used as symbols of deception and illusion and war often involves deception and misdirection. Soldiers might use mirrors to signal each other or catch glimpses of an enemy's movements without being seen themselves. Mirrors have also been used in warfare to create optical illusions, such as making an army appear larger than it is. In literature and art, mirrors are sometimes used to represent the psychological toll of war. For instance, in Shakespeare's play Macbeth, Lady Macbeth famously tells her husband to "look like the innocent flower but be the serpent under it" [10] — a sentiment that suggests the use of deception and misdirection to achieve one's goals. Similarly, the phrase 'smoke and mirrors' is often used to describe political or military tactics designed to confuse or mislead. [11]

Transitioning to historical accounts, Archimedes' war-faring inventions are both vivid and possibly embellished. Among his creations were catapult launchers that hurled heavy beams and stones at Roman ships, along with burning glasses that harnessed the sun's rays to set ships ablaze. It is recounted that Archimedes thwarted a Roman attack on the ancient Greek city-state of Syracuse, located on the eastern coast of Sicily, Italy, by employing an array of mirrors (possibly polished shields) to reflect sunlight onto the enemy ships, igniting them. [12]

When it comes to the use of mirrors in literature and art to depict the psychological toll of war, Tim O'Brien's protagonist in the novel 'The Things They Carried' [13] employs a mirror to confront his reflection and the stark reality of his experiences during the Vietnam War. Similarly, in Pablo Picasso's painting 'Guernica,' broken mirrors are utilized as symbols of shattered reality and the profound psychological trauma inflicted by war.

PROF. VIRGIL: "'Ora vediamo come in uno specchio, in modo oscuro, ma allora vedremo a faccia a faccia. Ora conosco in parte, ma allora conoscerò come sono stato conosciuto.'—'Now we see through a mirror, dimly, but then we will see face to face. Now I know in part, but then I shall know just as I also am known.'" [14]

The connection between mirrors, neurons and spirituality can be seen in Jesus' words in John 5:19. 'Most assuredly, I say to you, the Son can do nothing of Himself, but what He sees the Father do, for whatever He does, the Son also does in like manner.'

Mirrors have always held a powerful symbolic role for humanity, reflecting experiences and inner selves, whether in times of peace or war. In the case of the Hebrew prophet Ezekiel, he conveys a profound message from the Holy Spirit to the exiled, rejected and orphaned child, reaching out to the entire nation of Israel and beyond.

It's worth noting that some have misinterpreted and misapplied the prophet's message, drawing parallels to UFO encounters and similar theories, as explored in Erich von Däniken's work, where the question 'Was God an astronaut?' [15] is raised. Nevertheless, Ezekiel's message remains clear and poignant, he imparts a message from the Holy Spirit, urging us to gaze into the mirror of God's truth.

"No one cared enough for you to do even one of these things out of compassion for you. Instead, you were thrown out into the open field because you were despised on the day of your birth. Then I passed by you and saw you squirming in your blood and as you lay there in your blood I said to you, 'Live!' I made you thrive like a plant of the field. You grew up and matured and became very beautiful … you were naked and bare. Then, I passed by you and saw you and you were indeed old enough for love. So, I spread my cloak over you and covered your nakedness. I pledged myself to you, entered into a covenant with you." [16]

The Bible makes no promise of technology and rescue from 'space daddies' or 'chariots of the gods' in silver saucers, concepts that many provocative studios and science fiction authors attempt to use in explaining the universe's most so-called intriguing mysteries. Instead, its essence lies in reconnection, healing, restoration, reconciliation and covenant with the creator of the universe.

Ezekiel's message serves as a powerful reminder that even in our darkest moments, hope for redemption and renewal always exists, provided we open ourselves to the possibility offered by the mirror of God's love. It's not about entering an unholy covenant or engaging in a demonic communion, as some have done, but rather about forging a meaningful relationship with the divine.

## Connection.

Connection is all about establishing an empathic, emotional bond by making a connection between the right hemispheres of the brain in both individuals. According to Iain McGilchrist, a psychiatrist, writer and former Oxford literary scholar, the nature of the therapeutic alliance between a therapist and a patient is the most important factor in any form of psychotherapy. To develop this alliance, therapists need to be trained to form a connection with patients who may be depressed, hyperactive, or fearful, for example. By establishing a connection with the patient, the therapist enables them to reveal their overwhelming experiences, which can then be processed and regulated. It's about establishing an empathic, emotional bond between the right hemispheres of the brain in both individuals.

Iain McGilchrist et al (2010) stated that the most important factor in any form of psychotherapy is the *'nature of the relationship itself,'* the therapeutic alliance – so more training should be on how to develop the therapeutic alliance with a patient, Take (for example) the depressed, the hyperactive or the fearful client. It is about forming that connection with the other human being in which the other human being can start to reveal some of these overwhelming experiences because the only way they can be regulated is they first have to be taken out of their defensive mindset. The pain has to be felt and it must be communicated to another human being. [17]

I often find myself pondering a question: What if a therapist establishes a connection with their client through God, who is Love itself? In ancient texts, the God of love, agápe, represents feelings for one's children and spouse. For Christians, the concept of pre- and post-resurrection expresses the unconditional love of God for His children.

According to Dr. Ironson, a leading mind—body medicine researcher and Professor of Psychology at the University of Miami, the most significant factor contributing to the healing of patients with HIV was their choice to believe in a 'benevolent and loving God.' This effect was even more pronounced if the patient chose to cultivate a personal relationship with the God of love.

The resilience of Therapeia was ultimately based on the decrease in viral load and an increased concentration of helper T-cells after four years of study. Helper T-cells play a crucial role in aiding the body's fight against disease and those with a higher concentration experienced a better outcome concerning their health. Conversely, those who did not believe in God's love had a three times faster loss of helper T-cells, a three times faster increase in viral loads and higher levels of damaging cortisol. Dr. Ironson (2006) summarizes her research by stating, "If you believe that God loves you, it becomes an enormously protective factor, even more protective than scoring low for depression or high for optimism." [18]

The power of belief in love is further highlighted by this phenomenological study. Whenever there is a feeling or belief that we are loved, whether, from a higher power or a therapist emanating genuine care and compassion, it seems to have the ability to rewire the mind and body, triggering a chain reaction of internal healing that science is only beginning to understand.

## The Barrators.

Now, after being raised to the heavens, this next section brings me to some earthbound research conducted by Nick Duffell, a psychotherapy trainer, psycho-historian and author of *Wounded Leaders: British Elitism and the Entitlement Illusion*—a psychohistory (2014) [19] concerning boarding schools that personally remind me of a Roman Empire system where Governments headed by Emperors (with large territorial holdings) continue to produce hardened soldiers. Or maybe it reminds me more of an ancient Spartan/Greek social system and constitution, configuring their entire society to maximize military proficiency at all costs.

PROF. VIRGIL: "In Dante's 'The Divine Comedy,' those Barrators, oh how they sway in the fiery rhythm of the eighth circle of Hell! These crafty politicians find themselves dipping their toes (and more) into a bubbling brew of pitch, a sort of infernal fondue of their shady deeds. What mirror of celestial influences stirred their ambitions and pushed them onto this wicked stage of corruption? Ah, the timeless puzzle of their tainted dance!"

In the UK, the enduring legacy of the colonial British Empire has left a lasting psychological imprint, which continues to influence the institutions and hierarchies of our government today. The rank dissociation and objectification that served as the driving force behind colonialism, often manned by young men from elite boarding schools, have given rise to a loveless mechanism that perpetuates a cycle of abandonment and insecurity.

Children who are fashioned into authors of abandonment by this system often struggle with issues that inhibit their ability to form healthy relationships or rely on their sense of self-worth. This reflection echoes the very practices that once shaped the British Empire's imperial pursuits.

This intricate interplay between past and present underscores the extent to which historical legacies continue to reverberate within contemporary societal structures, perpetuating the same cycle of institutionalized dysfunction that is seen in the Barrators of Dante's vision of Hell.

Duffell's research and his own experiences as a boarder give insight into the boarding child's imperative to survive, thus, creating a new persona that involves betraying himself and his values:

"The boarding child's dilemma is that he or she is prematurely separated from home and family and must speedily reinvent themselves as self-reliant pseudo-adults. Hence the *false* Self is apparent when we develop the psychological eyes to notice it. The child survives boarding by attaching to this Self instead of to a parent, but the ex-boarder often retains permanent unconscious anxiety, reinforced by strong internal double binds and rarely develops emotional intelligence. 'They told you they were doing it because they loved you, but it left you bereft of love,' one survivor told me."

Duffell continues that boarding school survivors tend to operate strategically, tied to rigid timetables in rule-bound institutions, "... they are ever alert to staying out of trouble... they must not look unhappy, childish or foolish – in any way vulnerable – or they'll be bullied by their peers. So, they dissociate from all these qualities, project them out onto others and develop duplicitous personalities that are constantly on the run." – And in relation to politicians and those that run our state, Duffell emphasizes, "... this sense of entitlement cannot easily be given up, it is compensation for all those years without love, touch and family, for the stress within the personality and the lack of emotional, relational and sexual maturity." [20]

## Time Traveling Therapist.

In the midst of it all, we find ourselves among distressed, inhibited and concealed inner children, confined within the bureaucratic confines of politicians governing a fallen empire. These leaders, it seems, are driven by the logical left hemisphere of their brains, yet they remain disconnected from their primal love and the essence of true meaning.

Amid this complex tapestry of emotions and unresolved childhood experiences, a therapeutic journey begins. It's reminiscent of a form of time travel, a matrix of transference, where therapist and client unite to explore the inner child's world. This union provides the inner child a chance to be heard, seen and felt—an essential element in opening the door to expression, meaning and love, all while fearlessly confronting the truth of their childhood.

Swiss psychologist Alice Miller believed that most politicians, *"... are two-year-old children who were never loved and respected as the persons they were with their feelings and needs, even if some of them were admired for their skills. They deny their frustrations of the past and are looking for loving parents in the persons of their voters. The more money they get for the election campaign, the more they feel loved. But, as this love can never make up for the absence of love the child of a strict, cold, demanding and resentful Mother had to suffer, the struggle for love can never stop. And thousands of people will pay the price."* [21]

451

Freud believed that children could become fixated or stuck in the latent phase of a child's psychosexual stage. Fixation at this stage can result in immaturity and an inability to form fulfilling relationships as an adult. [22]

This scenario mirrors the dynamics of British politics marked by racism and colonialism—a left hemisphere existence, static, conditioned and isolated in competition with others. Such a hemisphere remains detached and apathetic in an unflowing world, where the sole value is utility. For individuals in this state, being useful, profitable, or beneficial is their primary inclination, while their egos engage in a charade of outdoing one another.

In contrast, a world that views things as seamlessly interconnected appreciates the essence of therapeutic work, which is deeply rooted in relationships and connections.

Frantz Fanon who wrote and campaigned on the human, social and cultural consequences of decolonization said in his book *Black Skin, White Masks*, "Today, I believe in the possibility of love, that is why I endeavor to trace its imperfections, its perversions." [23]

What's the result of self-preservation politicians or a purely left-brain hemisphere that is out of touch with love and attachment? Well, according to Ian McGilchrist (2010), "It gives power, it's about getting. The left hemisphere controls the right hand in which we grasp, though it controls some language in which define things and pin them down... it is a neurological fact that denial is a fortress of the left hemisphere."

McGilchrist doesn't stop at observing U.K. politics. He gives an example called the 'Berlusconi of the brain' (Italian media tycoon and politician who has served as Prime Minister of Italy in four Governments)—"... the brain that controls the media, the one that does all the talking and constructs the arguments ... a piece of cake to makes its point ... it is difficult for the right hemisphere to express things that are subtle often contradictory and implicit ..." [24]

However, I won't stop to highlight the politician. What about the gang member? The one that contributes to the highest crime statistics in London's present history. Is he or she roaming the street full of hate because he never knew a dad or had a connection?

According to the NSPCC (National Society for the Prevention of Cruelty to Children) people join gangs because some might be victims of violence and are scared, they might be pressured into doing things and for lots of young people, being part of a gang makes them feel part of a family so they might not want to leave. [25] Even if they do, leaving or attempting to leave can be a scary idea. They might be frightened about what will happen to them, their friends, or their family if they leave.

It seems that the hooded teenage gangbanger and the whistle and flute boarding school politicians have something in common.

McGilchrist—"... instead of spending much of his early years engaged with his Mother's face—which is how children crucially develop the sense of a secure self, distinct from, but not entirely separate from others,—a child now is likely to spend more time interacting with a piece of equipment ... constantly distracted and over-stimulated and in due course to watch scenes of violence with calm detachment. All that is true. But then this virtuality and emphasis on technology is also in itself a reflection of a world dominated by the left hemisphere." [26]


What about the abandoned and those starved of love?


A twelve-year study by Harvard University and Boston Children's Hospital in the U.S. found that the brains of the orphans stopped developing properly after they were abandoned in the Bucharest institutions. Their *white matter* – the part of the brain that helps neurons communicate – was significantly damaged by their ordeal leading to poor language skills and decreased mental ability. Researchers also discovered that those children fortunate enough to find loving foster homes were able to regrow the missing connections and restore lost function. [27]

Alan Schore, an American clinical psychologist, researcher and author renowned for his contributions to neuropsychology and attachment theory, sheds light on an intriguing aspect of human development. In collaboration with others in 2017, Schore's work underscores a fascinating connection between a mother's early perceptions of her baby and long-term structural changes in the midbrain region. This includes areas like the hypothalamus, substantia nigra, globus pallidus and amygdala. Remarkably, the positivity of a mother's feelings towards her infant within the first month postpartum may contribute to an increase in gray matter. (The limbic system gray matter refers to the gray matter or neural tissue within the limbic system of the brain. The limbic system is associated with emotions, memory and motivation and its gray matter plays a role in processing these functions.) "Thus, the mother's positive feelings for her baby may facilitate increased levels of gray matter. Mutual love increases limbic system gray matter on both sides of any loving dyad, whether it's a parent-infant relationship, adult romantic connection, or intimate friendships and so on." [28/29]

These dimensions and perceptions of love are essential aspects to teach, understand, grow into and experience from a spiritual, psychological and human perspective.

# Chapter Fourteen
## <u>Love Me Tender</u>

*"Amor, ch'a nullo amato amar perdona"*
*"Love, which permits no one to love who loves in return." — Inferno,*
*Canto V*

So, what is it that therapists and clients search for? I like to think of myself as a treasure seeker, guiding clients in exploring the depths of their brains and bodies. It's a parallel journey where we work together to unearth their true selves, a precious treasure hidden beneath layers of conformity to a demanding superego. This superego can sometimes drown out their fragile ego, leaving them with a cacophony of internal voices, all urging them to stay silent.

How can I express therapeutic love to a client who feels adrift at sea without attempting to rescue them or provide quick solutions? The remnants of my star sailor expedition have left me with the insight that love is often the only enduring element. It's a force that, in its healthiest forms, aids us all, including clients, in finding our way home. To say that someone is lost implies they have a home to return to and as I once told one client's inner child, 'You are not lost, you are just temporarily unaware of your location.'

The remarkable byproduct of facilitating this journey is that I have the privilege of learning about myself while resonating with our shared humanity as my clients navigate the emotions, they've encountered on this blue orb we call the cradle of humanity.

The Shorter Oxford English Dictionary defines love as *a state or feeling / deep affection / strong emotional attachment.* [1]

St. Paul wrote 'Love *agapē.* is patient Love is kind. It does not envy. It does not boast. It is not proud. It does not dishonor others. It is not self-seeking. It is not easily angered. It keeps no record of wrongs. Love does not delight in evil but rejoices with the truth. It always protects, always trusts, always hopes and always perseveres. Love *never* fails.' [2]

In his speech on Toxic Culture, Dr. Gabor Maté [3] emphasizes that if we or others feel alienated, we can still reconnect with ourselves. He underscores that empathy is a genuine human quality wired within us and 'we are wired for connection, love and compassion.' To progress, we must return to our true nature, echoing the concept of **Philautia,** which represents healthy self-love or self-regard. It involves caring for and valuing oneself without becoming self-centered or narcissistic.

In cases where the absence of **Storge,** meaning 'love and affection' typically found in familial or family-related relationships, is observed, evidence from a Canadian study [4] reveals that a group of two-to-four-year-old children, who had spent their infancy in overcrowded institutions with too few caretakers, experienced a positive transformation when enrolled in regular play sessions with adults and children for two years. Over time, their initial apathy and indifference were lifted and they began to exhibit the typical vitality of four-year-old children. It appears that they developed self-regulation skills through socializing with others who had experienced Storge.

**Philia,** signifying 'affectionate regard' or 'friendship,' often expressed as loyalty to friends, specifically 'brotherly love,' family and community, necessitates virtues, equality and familiarity.

Drawing a parallel, we can compare this to the BACP ethical framework to understand what their interpretation of therapeutic love might entail. Currently, the framework emphasizes that members and registrants should aspire to key personal qualities, including candor, benevolence, courage, diligence, empathy, fairness, humility, identity, integrity, resilience, respect, sincerity and wisdom. [5]

This seems like a solid foundation for understanding what love entails within the therapeutic relationship. However, outside of this context, I posed a question to my counselors: 'Why do we express love by saying, 'I love you?'

Their responses were beautiful, heartfelt and genuine.

PROF. BEATRICE: "Well, I've been thinkin' 'bout that question quite a bit lately and I reckon I could ponder on it for a good while longer. You know, when I tell someone 'I love you,' it's like we're connectin' deep down, like roots of a big ol' tree. I care 'bout how they're doin' and what's goin' on with 'em and I trust they'll care right back, maybe even stronger. Your question's been takin' me on a nice little journey of thoughts and I sure do appreciate the chance to share 'em."

PROF. VIRGIL: "When I hear those words 'Ti amo'—I love you, a wave of security washes over me, a reminder that this person is there, by my side, unswayed by my moods or the trials life throws at us. And when I respond with 'Anch'io ti amo' (I love you too), it's my way of saying I'm dedicated to standing by them, no matter the challenges life brings. Love is a steady flame in moments of joy, but its true essence shines when it remains unshaken in the face of life's storms."

I find myself contemplating whether, as therapists, we desire care, love, or respect from our clients. What if they don't respect us?

PROF. BERNARD offered his perspective: "In my experience, it's not so much that they initially lack respect for the process, but rather, as they witness positive changes, their respect grows. It's a journey we embark on together, gradually building the client-therapist relationship and earning their respect. As my grandma used to say, 'Mi deyah'—which means 'I am here.'"

## Chemical Love

Love is a topic that has inspired countless love songs and love itself serves as a universal language, transcending time and space. Ultimately, we exist because of a form of love. Can love be measured? Can it be quantified, manufactured, bottled and sold? Are we merely the sum of cerebral frontal cortex activity, influenced by dopamine and endorphins that trigger moments of joy and passion?

Louis Cozolino (professor of psychology at Pepperdine University) reminds us that therapy is, *"... a safe emergency because of the supportive structure in which emotional learning takes place. A client's sense of safety is enhanced by the therapist's skill, knowledge and confidence, which support emotional regulation and maintain moderate states of arousal. It is quite possible that the caring, encouragement and enthusiasm of the therapist also reinforce learning, neural growth and plasticity through the enhanced production of dopamine, serotonin and other neurochemicals."* [6]

What's at the core of what therapists and clients seek? It seems that we are biologically predisposed to love. According to neuroscientist Alan Schore, in all humans and animals, the right brain is the first part to come online. [7] It regulates our bodily functions, emotional states and connections with one another. The right brain functions include humor, empathy, compassion, intuition, creativity and meaning. If things don't unfold favorably in the early stages of life in terms of connections, certain forms of personality, such as an insecure, dismissive personality, may develop. This individual essentially attempts to function within the realm of the left brain, striving to decipher how to navigate the world with other human beings in a social, logical and analytical manner, but something crucial may be missing.

Dr. Allan N. Schore (in an interview with Journal Play) defines, *"Love can be a noun denoting deep affection or a verb ... that describes the feeling of tenderness and passion that one lover communicates to another. The contrast in these two usages mirrors the ongoing shift from a one-person, intrapsychic to a two-person, interpersonal perspective in psychology, including the most prominent theory in developmental psychology, attachment theory."*

Dr. Schore uses data from neuroscience to shed light on the ability of humans to love one another. The paradigmatic expression of this strongest of all emotions is forged in an attachment bond of mutual love between a Mother and her infant and this right brain-to-right brain, growth-promoting, emotional experience acts as a relational matrix for the emergence of the capacity to share a loving relationship with a valued other at later stages of life. [8]

He explains that love operates as an emotional communication system deeply ingrained in a fundamental mechanism situated within the early developing emotion-processing right brain.

The mutual love shared between the mother and the infant plays a crucial role in optimizing this evolutionary process. Accessing and nurturing the processes of love and attachment in both hemispheres are of paramount importance. Ultimately, it is within the right hemisphere that meaning is generated, even though the basic regulation systems are predominantly located on the right side. This interplay between hemispheres is particularly relevant in the context of psychological disorders.

When we shift our focus to the emotional realm, the right hemisphere takes center stage in our conscious awareness. One hemisphere predominantly exerts inhibitory effects on the other. A key question regarding resilience revolves around how we can effectively utilize the right hemisphere for emotional aspects and the left hemisphere for more intellectual and linguistic functions.

Now, what does love mean in practical therapy? What does it look like when we apply love in a therapeutic context? I'll briefly dig into these questions without getting too academic. 'Therapeia' is the Greek word for healing and while I won't dive too deep into romantic love or erotic transfer, I'll explore love in terms of empathy and unconditional positive regard and some research findings to keep things grounded.

Regulation theory operates within a two-person dyadic system. Thus, this research holds personal significance for me. I'm bringing my whole self into this work because it can influence how people change (a notion supported by neuroscience) and resonate with fellow therapists. Self-healing is essential if we aim to facilitate the healing of others. It enables me to tap into my full human potential, allowing my patients to do the same.

I've come to realize that in the past, there were moments when I felt like I was in a thousand pieces, yearning for comfort and a supportive network. I needed a surrogate heart, a tranquil mind with stable thoughts, someone to hold me when insecurity and fear loomed large and my vision of the future seemed distant. This kind of love and comfort that I seek as a client, as a human, will it equip me to better relate to my own clients? Who will be there to support me? Who will hold my emotions as I unravel to uncover what lies beneath the saboteur within?

### Therapeutic womb

A study of Swiss children (Davis, C, 1966) born to unmarried, poorly educated immigrants, who spent their first year living in an impoverished nursery (where stimulation was minimal and caretakers changed often) were re-examined at age fourteen. Most of them had average intelligence and several friends. The few who were extremely unhappy or anxious had been physically abused or spent their post-infancy years with parents who quarreled often. Those who had gone from the depriving nursery to benevolent homes, however, did not show the same level of anxiety, suggesting that it was attributable to experiences that occurred after leaving the nursery.[9]

Therapeutic love is not a permanent matrix or womb for the client to become reliant on the counselor. For me, the end is always at the beginning, from the outset of therapy, the focus should be on the eventual conclusion or goal, rather than creating a prolonged reliance on the therapist. For some clients, the therapeutic alliance is recreating a healthy dyad, a born-again experience in a holistic safe environment *"The counselor's task is not one of actively making or even suggesting changes for a client, but one of creating a climate in which a client can come to know and accept himself."* (Rogers, 1957).[10]

### Touch.

When it comes to the way we communicate attachment through touch and gestures, Sieratzki and Woll[11] delve into the effects of touch on the developing right hemisphere. They suggest that touch has a more direct and immediate emotional impact when an infant is cradled on the left side of the body, known as left-sided cradling.

Clinical research highlights the crucial role of maternal 'affective touch' in the first year of an infant's life. This touch helps both the infant and the mother establish a system of touch synchrony, which can influence vagal tone and cortisol reactivity. Essentially, the mother-infant dyad uses interpersonal touch as a communication system, especially for conveying and regulating emotional information.

Additional studies reveal that breastfeeding involves high levels of tactile stimulation and mutual touch. During these moments, six-month-old infants exhibit increased EEG amplitude in the right posterior cortical areas, indicating the significance of somatosensory tactile contact for healthy right hemisphere development.

This research underscores the importance of affectionate touch for an infant's well-rounded development, which can be assessed through an infant-caregiver evaluation. Clinicians should not only evaluate the quality and quantity of spontaneous eye contact and auditory communication between caregiver and infant but also pay attention to the quality and quantity of sensitive interpersonal touch received and expressed by the infant.

Assessing whether the infant is cradled on the left or right side is also essential, as right cradling has been linked to maternal depression and stress. Furthermore, the choice of cradling side can provide diagnostic insights, as adults who cradle on the right tend to be more detached and less responsive to their infants compared to those who cradle on the left. [12,13,14]

## What does a Loveless Culture birth?

Swiss psychologist Alice Miller (2005) was interviewed and asked, 'One of the basic psychological truths is that persons emotionally deprived in childhood hope all their lives to receive the love denied to them. Why is it so hard to accept that we weren't important to anyone?'

*"Some prefer to commit suicide or willingly accept a chronic illness and some prefer to become dictators over whole nations, or serial murderers*

*and to show to others what they learned as children (violence, cruelty and perversion), rather than acknowledge their early deprivation. The more deprived and mistreated people were in their childhood, the more they stayed attached to their parents, waiting for them to change. They also seem to be stuck with their fear. This fear of the tormented child makes any kind of rebellion unthinkable, even if the parents are already dead."* [15]

How can we measure love on Earth? How do we quantify love? How can we compare love? What are the demands of love? Do different countries foster or exhibit therapeutic love differently? And is the absence of love linked to sociopathy? It's important to note that sociopathy is a term used to describe individuals with antisocial personality disorder (ASPD). [16] Those with ASPD often struggle to comprehend the emotions of others and may frequently break rules or make impulsive decisions without experiencing guilt for the harm they may cause.

Let's explore what we do know. Our planet is home to eight billion people, all brought into existence through a common form of love. However, they come from diverse cultures of attachment, yet share a universal need for human connection, as recognized by psychologists and therapists.

We inhabit a world that is both stunningly beautiful and occasionally fraught with violence, a quantifiable reality. Within this world, humanity faces the pressure to conform to certain norms, which can vary depending on factors such as conditions of worth, culture, core beliefs, dogma, education and philosophy.

According to the findings of the annual Global Peace Index (GPI, 2021) which measures the 'peacefulness' of nations based on levels of safety and security in society, the extent of domestic and international conflict and the degree of militarization, the most dangerous countries in the world are concentrated in Africa and the Middle East—where poverty and war create a highly unstable mix. [17]

Syria, a country plagued by a brutal seven-year-long civil war, in 2019 ranked as the most dangerous country on the planet, closely followed by other war-ravaged nations like Iraq. But now, Afghanistan is currently the most dangerous country on the planet. No doubt politics, ideologies, dogmas and religious perversion have all added to the mix in these nations that continue to breed hatred toward those who do not believe what they are told to believe. Overall, the report found that the world has become less peaceful over the last eight years with the gap between the most and least violent widening.

The updated index is released each year at events in London, Washington D.C. and the United Nations Secretariat in New York City. The 2021 GPI indicates Iceland, New Zealand, Denmark, Portugal and Slovenia to be the most peaceful countries and Afghanistan, Yemen, Syria, South Sudan and Iraq to be the least peaceful.

The safest country is Iceland. However, it's worth noting that Iceland is quite literally situated in the middle of nowhere and boasts a relatively small population of only 345,393 residents. One of the remarkable aspects of Iceland is its nearly non-existent class system. In fact, a staggering 97% of Icelanders identify themselves as middle class, rendering the presence of a class system almost negligible. This, in turn, significantly reduces issues related to jealousy and crimes often associated with poverty.

In Iceland, children enjoy equal educational opportunities and attend the same schools, fostering a sense of equity from an early age. The nation prides itself on being egalitarian, emphasizing freedom and fairness and it proudly holds the top spot globally for gender equality. Interestingly, Iceland doesn't maintain a standing army, navy, or air force. The sole group of police officers authorized to carry firearms is known as the *Viking Squad* and their deployment is a rare occurrence. [18]

Drawing a parallel to therapy, one might wonder if we need a therapeutic 'Viking Squad' of sorts to patrol the depths of our subconscious minds, clearing away the emotional debris that might be lurking under the surface. This introspective journey could be seen as a means to rekindle our capacity for love and emotional warmth. So, how do we initiate this process of thawing the frozen aspects of our inner world and rediscovering the profound capacity for love within us?

## Bridge over troubled water

Social Psychologist Erich Seligmann Fromm (1950) wrote: 'Whatever complaints the neurotic patient may have, whatever symptoms he may present are rooted in his inability to love if we mean by love a capacity for the experiences of concern, responsibility, respect and understanding of another person and the intense desire for that person's growth. Analytical therapy is essentially an attempt to help the patient gain or regain his capacity for love. If this aim is not fulfilled, nothing but surface changes can be accomplished. [19]

According to Allan Schore's regulation theory, therapeutic practice does not have a fixed protocol. While the theory provides a framework, practitioners need to utilize clinical intuition, take calculated risks and be aware of key factors to develop the necessary skills for a successful dyadic relationship with clients. This approach is preferable to the traditional one-person system, in which therapists hold all the expertise and make interpretations that clients may not fully understand, leading to ongoing feelings of anxiety, depression and neurosis.

As a therapist, I believe in bringing my whole self into my work, diving into the waters of life and embracing my humanity and emotions. However, I should be mindful of burnout, which is a real concern for many of us in the helping professions, especially when we become emotionally distant or overwhelmed. This can lead to us internalizing our clients' experiences without a healthy outlet. I witnessed this dynamic during my school years when I saw teachers who seemed disconnected and weary in the face of a mechanical and draining educational system. It's not limited to schools, we can observe similar burnout in various institutions and workplaces, including politics, where individuals become disconnected from their humanity due to the relentless pursuit of results connected with their childhood psyche.

Moreover, congruence enables us to navigate countertransference effectively. During those moments when my client and I share tears and emotions, it opens the door to honest dialogue. We discuss openly what's happening between us, acknowledging both the magical aspects and addressing any concerns that may arise. These deep and connected moments not only promote change but also cultivate more meaningful and positive therapeutic experiences for our clients. This helps in healing any ruptures and preventing a fractured mindset of escape to the rapture, whether it be a literal one or an artificial one of our makings. We need one another, we need connection.

It's incredibly vital for those in positions of influence, not just therapists, but educators, politicians, religious leaders, social workers, healthcare professionals, law enforcement officers and parents, to champion and educate others about the importance of building secure attachments between parents and their infants. These efforts can help prevent situations where psychotherapists are left to step in as a 'cleanup crew' to deal with the aftermath of insecure attachments.

A significant portion of humanity hasn't had the opportunity to experience the secure emotional connection needed during infancy, often due to instances of abuse, neglect, or the emotional unavailability of caregivers. As a result, many continue their quest for authenticity well into adulthood. Our species inherently craves relationships and connections. However, we're transforming into a high functioning but easily distracted society, marked by delayed maturity and ongoing conflicts, as reflected in the Global Peace Index (GPI).

Transference.

Transference is a powerful defense mechanism that operates both implicitly and explicitly within a traumatized race, often leading individuals to avoid exploring their experiences and instead retreat into the self. Delving into these areas can be intimidating, as it forces us to confront memories and emotions that may have remained implicit in our subconscious. When we encounter another culture, another person, or even a therapist, these implicit memories can resurface, shaping our perceptions and behaviors.

Who do I resemble in your eyes? How am I evolving in your perception, with implicit biases affecting your judgments? To whom or what do we turn for answers, whether seeking solace in substances like sex, drugs, or food, or resorting to compulsive shopping, leadership positions, binge-watching TV, gambling, cults, or something beyond our conscious awareness? What are we attuned to?

Without positive transference or healthy connections, humanity finds itself in a void.

In the words of Carl Jung, *"People will do anything, no matter how absurd, to avoid facing their own souls. One does not become enlightened by imagining figures of light, but by making the darkness conscious."* [20]

## Attunement.

It could be that from a young age, there was not enough mirroring or attunement—Greenberg, Rice and Elliot provide a definition of attunement (1959 Bowlby) which implicitly embraces empathy and empathic attunement: Attunement is the reactiveness we have to another person. It is the process by which we form relationships. [21]

When we talk about attunement, it's like tuning in to someone else's feelings and thoughts. It's somewhat like when you listen to your favorite song on the radio and the music perfectly aligns with your mood. This connection is immensely vital in close relationships. Just as babies rely on their parents to discern when they're hungry or upset, we all need someone who truly understands us, especially as we mature. In everyday life, attunement can be as straightforward as a friend recognizing that when you say, 'I'm fine,' you might not truly be fine and they take the time to uncover what's troubling you.

"In empathic attunement, one tries to respond to the client's perception of reality at that moment, as opposed to one's own or some *objective* or *external* view of what is real ... the therapist takes in and tastes the client's intentions, feelings and perceptions, developing a feel of what it is like to be the client at that moment. At the same time, he or she retains a sense of self, as opposed to being swamped by or *fusing* with the client's experience." [22/23]

Neuroscientist, Psychiatrist and Christian author Curt Thompson who provides a framework for understanding science and spirituality states, *"When each one of us comes into this world, we enter it looking for someone looking for us ... and it never stops."* [24] On the day we were born our deepest need was for another to be attuned to us and it remains our deepest need today.

Japan, which now ranks twelfth in the GPI according to the 2021 report (a drop of four from 2015), boasts the world's most aged population, with over a quarter of its citizens aged sixty-five or older. This demographic shift has strained its financial system and retail industry. According to a report by the BBC and Bloomberg, [25] in recent years, Japan has witnessed a surge in petty crimes committed by elderly people to secure a place in prison for their remaining days. Complaints and arrests involving older citizens are surpassing those of any other demographic in Japan, with the elderly crime rate quadrupling over the past few decades. In prisons, one prisoner out of every five inmates is a senior citizen. In many cases, particularly for senior women, nine out of ten incarcerated individuals are there for petty shoplifting. The number of Japanese seniors living alone surged by 600% between 1985 and 2015, as reported by Bloomberg in 2017. [26] Half of the seniors caught shoplifting reported living alone and the government discovered last year that 40% of them said they either don't have family or rarely communicate with them.

Theft, primarily shoplifting, stands out as the most prevalent crime committed by elderly offenders. They typically steal food valued at less than 3,000 yen ($20) from shops they visit regularly. Michael Newman, an Australian-born demographer affiliated with the Tokyo-based research firm Custom Products Research Group, highlights the challenge of living on the 'measly' basic state pension in Japan. In a paper published in 2016 (Newman,

2016), he calculates that the escalating costs of rent, food and healthcare could push recipients into debt if they lack other sources of income and this is before factoring in expenses for heating or clothing. In the past, it was customary for children to care for their parents, but in many provinces, a dearth of economic opportunities has driven younger people away, leaving their parents to fend for themselves. [27]

For these seniors, life in jail is preferable to the alternative. Their fundamental need for connection and attunement remains unfulfilled. Finance and retail have eroded the significance of family and human connections to the point where they scarcely exist. Consequently, these seniors are discovering a sense of connection within prison.

Paradoxically, being behind bars, while physically restrictive, offers them a sense of liberation because it assures them that they are not alone. This, for them, becomes a form of therapy, far beyond mere window shopping. The melancholy and the state of human affairs are intertwined, as they subconsciously seek positive nurture. Positive nurturing experiences lead to the hard wiring of dopamine and oxytocin, which they embrace as these seniors jump into the process of redefining their sense of connection and well-being.

Kangaroo Therapy.

Speaking of nurturing experiences, there's a remarkable example in the form of 'Kangaroo Mother Care.' This technique of newborn care, where babies are kept skin-to-skin with a parent, typically their mother, was first used in 1979 in Bogota, Colombia, by neonatologists Edgar Rey and Hector Martinez. [28] They drew inspiration from nature, particularly kangaroos, which hold their young as soon as they are born. I had a personal experience with this when my daughter was born prematurely and her mother and I took turns tucking her under our shirts to incubate her to the synchronicity of our hearts.

Mothers were instructed to hold their infants diapered but bare-chested between their breasts in an upright position as often as possible, feeding them only breast milk. What the doctors found was that this skin-to-skin contact not only allowed mothers to leave the hospitals, reducing overcrowding, but it also decreased their babies' dependency on incubators. Kangaroo Care offers several benefits, including regulating the baby's body temperature, promoting bonding between the parent and the baby and providing comfort to the infant. It has been shown to help stabilize the baby's heart rate and breathing, improve breastfeeding rates and even reduce the risk of infections. Most astonishingly, the doctors observed mortality rates plummet from 70% to 30%.

Alan Schore believes that the deeper realms of human emotion and motivation primarily operate at the unconscious level and are predominantly processed in the right hemisphere, in contrast to the left hemisphere. This communication is facilitated through the corpus callosum—a thick bundle of nerve fibers connecting the left and right cerebral hemispheres, responsible for enabling them to work together and share information.

To understand why someone behaves the way they do on the surface, it's essential to grasp the brain processes happening beneath their awareness. Over the last two decades, Dr. Schore has presented evidence demonstrating that these systems, interconnected by the corpus callosum, reside predominantly in the right hemisphere, which developed before the left hemisphere. Emphasizing the nonverbal, intuitive and holistic functions of the right brain, in collaboration with the corpus callosum, is essential, rather than relying solely on the verbal, logical and analytical left hemisphere. [29]

As we delve deeper into the intricacies of the mind, we find that even language plays a role in shaping our understanding.

For instance, consider a Jewish prayer that is often mistranslated as 'You will keep him in PERFECT PEACE, whose mind is stayed on you because he trusts in you.'

However, the Hebrew language offers a unique perspective, one that seems indicative of blessing both hemispheres of the mind:
'You will keep him in 'PEACE-PEACE,' whose mind is stayed on you.' [30]

## Battle of the Mind.

As we contemplate the idea of 'PEACE-PEACE' representing a state of perfect equilibrium, we also confront the relentless battle that rages within the mind—a battle where thousands of voices cry for attention, emanating from the realms of twisted media, pedantic ideologies, government and legalistic religion, all striving to advance their agendas. Just turn on your television, radio, or internet and within sixty seconds of news consumption, your brain is marinated and microwaved in a dopamine-fueled narrative of fear and confusion. This relentless barrage seeks to numb the senses and plant seeds of fear deep within the subconscious. It aims to desensitize your prefrontal cortex. Questions swirl: Are we the sole intelligent life in the universe? Is this the most violent planet in the cosmos? Are we truly alone? By the time you finish reading this, I aspire to reveal that we are not alone.

Many of you reading this may have had some kind of experience with the unknown. Perhaps you've seen something or felt something. For others, the contents may seem a bit 'woo-woo,' but I'll admit that sometimes ignorance truly is bliss. Take me back to an island with sun, sea and signorinas and my twenty-one-year-old self in Bermuda would agree. I'd happily gaze at palm trees, blue skies and golden sands while sipping my coconut water. No intergalactic connections on my mind. If humanity wants to colonize Mars because this planet is depleting itself, do you honestly think we'll fare better on red, dead, terraformed sand if we haven't had the revelation of the new man within?

Some of you may not have had a tangible experience and are simply browsing through this book to learn more and that's perfectly okay. We're all on this learning journey together.

Religions and governments, each with differing ideologies and even mantras, can become control structures with one lasting negative effect — they divide us.

In my experience, truth is a person and that person is the embodiment of Jesus Christ. 'Christ' meaning 'The One who saves.' But which Christ?

## The Carpenter

The Carpenter who stepped out from eternity into time itself, emerging through the veil of human existence as a newborn through the amniotic sac, which in its rupture, symbolized the profound moment of His arrival. This sacred birth, born of a virgin, was a divine revelation clothed in the flesh of humanity, walking upon this earthly realm. Like any newborn, He took His first breath, marking the transition from the divine to the earthly. Just as a baby's first breath signifies life outside the womb, His first breath signified His presence among us.

As He traversed the terrain of human experiences, as a child He knew what it was like to be an immigrant, a refugee, to have parents who fled from imperialism, He saw crucifixion, He was misunderstood by his peers, but He still had to learn how to read, write, to shape wood, He was tempted by all things and even tested by unseen entities, that is why He is able to empathize with all of humanity. He revealed His divine identity and purpose through His compassionate actions. Yet he was the only man that was born that was ever meant to die, before the foundation of earth he was slain. [31]

His journey culminated in the ultimate sacrifice: crucifixion. Nailed to a cross, He bore the weight of humanity's sins, enduring unimaginable agony and suffering. Yet, even in His darkest hour, He displayed unparalleled love and forgiveness, offering salvation to all who would believe.

Yet, my belief remains steadfast: He rose from the dead on the third day. His profound love for His earthly vessel led Him to take it home with Him, forever residing in that resurrected human body. He possesses the remarkable ability to transcend time and space in an instant, without the need for exotic technologies or newfound elements that aid levitation. The universe and its elements yield to His natural, organic power and glory, making Christ the epitome of transcendence. Within us, He blends and integrates seamlessly, creating a profound sense of oneness with His divine presence. Yet, this same transcendent being became flesh, taking on human form in the Incarnation and uniting divine and human natures. He loved his body so much that He not only inhabited it during His earthly life but also ensured its eternal significance through resurrection, taking it with Him into eternity.

"He that descended is the same also that ascended up far above all heavens, that he might fill all things." Ephesians 4:10.

"Who is the image of the invisible God, the firstborn of every creature: For by Him were all things created, that are in heaven and that are in earth, visible and invisible, whether they be thrones, or dominions, or principalities, or powers, all things were created by Him and for Him.

And He is before all things and by Him all things exist. And He is the head of the body, the church, who is the beginning, the firstborn from the dead, that in all things He might have the preeminence. For it pleased the Father that in Him should all fulness dwell; And having made peace through the blood of His cross, by Him to reconcile all things unto Himself; by Him, I say, whether they be things in Earth or things in Heaven." Colossians 1:15-20.

He is returning, people are awakening to discover life, love, light and truth within themselves as they embrace Christ. This represents the true return, the authentic redemption and the decisive resolution of our once-reluctant therapy.

This is my story of redemption and how the love of Christ rescued me. Ultimately, it's a love story. Are you still with me? I understand that if I were reading this over twenty years ago, I might have started feeling a sigh and a bubbling of rage. If I had begun with new age mantras, universal spiritual synchronism, tales of space-daddy Alien rescue and lofty ideals like unified world peace or saving the whales, I might have soaked it all in like a sponge initially. I might have tolerated it for a while. But, if I were to go along with that, I would have been lying to myself. However, the anger isn't mine to hold onto, my roots run deep.

There's another dimension, a spiritual realm, but most importantly, there is a God. He hasn't left His answering machine on while He went on a walkabout, nor has He left it to go rogue with us mere mortals to play mind games with humanity. Far from it. This God is alive and personally involved with those who choose to tune in, away from the gods of twisted administrations and perverted ideologies.

'He is the savior of ALL men, ESPECIALLY THOSE who believe.' [32]

## Freud and Yofi.

Sigmund Freud, the founder of psychoanalysis, believed that religion was a crutch for the fragile ego, which needed "a cosmic parental figure for security and protection." [33] Much of his theory was in response to his work with persons who embodied unhealthy and unresolved religious and oedipal struggles. As a child, Freud's family faced financial difficulties in Vienna after his father, Jacob, experienced financial setbacks and struggled to find steady employment.

These early experiences of poverty left a lasting impact on Freud and he carried a constant fear of financial insecurity throughout his life. Freud linked his fear of poverty to his father's perceived lack of success, but he also harbored feelings of disappointment regarding his father's response to an incident of anti-Semitic abuse.

While Freud's ideas about the cosmic parental figure still hold relevance, modern media might brand him as a 'crackhead,' overshadowing his contributions. His peers at the time may have overlooked his trauma, as Freud himself coped with personal struggles, including a reliance on cocaine. His excessive use of cocaine might have even surpassed that of several racehorses, a habit that could have impacted his therapeutic judgment and perhaps even the lineage of his beloved puppy Chow. [34]

I would love to sit and have coffee with Freud and talk with him about fathers, as I have so much to learn.

Did his past still echo in his soul? Were these early experiences of poverty and financial difficulties in Vienna, caused by his father Jacob's setbacks and employment struggles, responsible for leaving a lasting impact on Freud?

Freud carried a constant fear of financial insecurity throughout his life, linking it to his father's perceived lack of success. He also harbored feelings of disappointment regarding his father's response to an incident of anti-Semitic abuse. Freud had hoped for a more defiant reaction from his father in the face of discrimination, desiring a paternal figure who would be assertive rather than submissive. [35]

In my opinion, Freud was also unable to acknowledge that there are varying forms of religion and spirituality, some of which are healthier than others. However, spiritually competent psychotherapists should seek to assess and understand how a client's religious and spiritual worldview and values affect the client's sense of identity, lifestyle and emotional and interpersonal functioning. [36]

## Do you call yourself a Christian?

The remnants of my expedition have led me to the realization that love appears to be the only enduring presence. Love, in its healthiest forms, guides us all to find our way home. After all, to say that we are lost implies that we have a home to return to. As I often tell clients when working with their inner child, 'You are not lost, you are just temporarily unaware of your location.'

'Do you call yourself a Christian?'

'In a way that you may not yet comprehend, yes. But in the way you inquire, no.'

I am a believer if it means I embrace a loving father who is neither abusive, narcissistic, addicted to worship, nor an egotistical control freak. I am a believer if it means I reject the notion of one who came to establish religion and gave rise to thirty-three thousand Christian denominations with divergent agendas. I am a believer if it means I don't speak in Christian jargon or dwell in legalism, monotony, repetitive supplications and control. I am a believer if it means embracing freedom, grace and a departure from the familiar. I am a believer if it means recognizing that His love is unconditional. I am a believer if it means He dwells within me and we are one. I am a believer that if it means He resides in all of humanity, awaiting discovery. If this is what you mean by calling myself a Christian, then yes, I am.

Christ will meet you on the road you are on. Paul never told people to "get born again!" You couldn't even get yourself born the first time; how are you going to get it right a second time? Jesus said to Nicodemus, unless you're born from above (meaning unless you originate from above), you would have no appetite for heavenly things!—John 3:13.

### The Mystery Revealed.

As I crystallized my thoughts, considering renaming this book from 'The Reluctant Counselor,' I realized upon reflecting on my experiences that a more fitting descriptor for me would be 'The Reluctant Christian.' I'm hesitant to solely align myself with the mechanical aspects of my faith, instead, I see myself as a son of God. [37]

In John 14:16-17, during a last meal with his disciples just hours before his betrayal and death, Jesus drops a bombshell: he is going to leave his followers behind. However, Jesus assures them that he will not abandon them but will provide them with a counselor or companion. He says, "I will ask the Father, and he will give you another kinsman to help you and be with you forever—the Spirit of truth."

478

The Greek term Jesus used here, 'Paraklete,' referred to a person who comes alongside during times of legal difficulty. It has been translated variously as 'counselor' (unfortunately, sometimes as 'advocate,' implying Jesus needs to persuade the Father to like us and perhaps forgive us). The Paraklete serves as our 'comforter,' 'intercessor,' 'strengthener' and 'standby.' This promised close companion and kinsman is none other than the Holy Spirit. The Holy Spirit is my intimate connection, the counselor I identify with and whom I will follow. He is my sphere of influence. The Holy Spirit is not our sin inspector, yes he convicts us but convicts us of our innocence because innocence is essential for intimacy and joyful participation in loving relationships, which has always been the goal of the Father, Son and Holy Spirit when they made us in their image.

In the words of St. Paul:

"I am made a minister, according to the dispensation of God which is given to me for you, to fulfill the word of God, even the mystery which hath been hid from ages and from generations, but now is made manifest to his saints, to whom God would make known what is the riches of the glory of this mystery among the Gentiles, which is Christ in you, the hope of glory, whom we preach, warning every man and teaching every man in all wisdom, that we may present every man perfect in Christ Jesus." [38]

"Yea doubtless and I count all things but loss for the excellency of the knowledge of Christ Jesus my Lord: for whom I have suffered the loss of all things and do count them but skubalon, that I may win Christ." [39]

*'There are holes in the sky where the rain gets in. But they're ever so small, that's why the rain is thin.'*

*— Spike Milligan* [40]

To the religious, conservative, fundamental leaders of Jesus' day, He was considered 'New Age.' He did not come to establish Christianity. He came to reveal our true selves. Presently, I don't align with any institutional religion or dogma. I'm not interested in debating the existence of God. Instead, I reflect on how awareness of the Holy Spirit's spiritual dimensions aids in self-discovery, much like 'self-actualization.'

The only phenomenon I pursue is Unveiling the Abiding Presence, finding joy in my humanity, experiencing oneness—an eternal unity—with Christ, conscious of His paternal and maternal love within me always. I embrace life in the present, not a distant future, without seeking escape. I believe in love. And as I immerse my gingerbread man into the foamy swirl of my dusty chocolate cappuccino, ready to savor each bite, I have one final thought to share.

Author:

I didn't come to rescue you. I came to show you who you are.

Reader:

Who am I?

Author:

You are love.

*Closing sound track 街のドルフィン (Dolphin in Town) - Kingo Hamada*

# VOLUME 1 BIBLIOGRAPHY

Bibliography for Foreword

1. Debriefed FMR AATIP Director Lue Elizondo Unusual Technologies. (2021, April 3). [Video]. YouTube.
https://www.youtube.com/watch?v=ABOTk-YL82E&list=PLkDfKeSd-iDAMMvq78VNGZJcziAd6z88C&index=12
2. Steele, P., & Summerfield, D. (2012). The unseen casualties of armed conflict. The Lancet, 379(9823), 23-24.
https://doi.org/10.1016/S0140-6736(12)61655-9
3. Vallee, J. (1977). UFO's the Psychic Solution. from https://www.pdfdrive.com/ufos-the-psychic-solution-e185463209.html
4. Budd Hopkins. (n.d.). In Wikipedia. Retrieved March 7, 2023, from https://en.wikipedia.org/wiki/Budd_Hopkins#Hypnosis
5. J. Allen Hynek. (n.d.). In Wikipedia. Retrieved March 7, 2023, from
https://en.wikipedia.org/wiki/J._Allen_Hynek#UFO_origin_hypotheses
6. J. Allen Hynek. (n.d.). In Wikipedia. Retrieved March 7, 2023, from
https://en.wikipedia.org/wiki/J._Allen_Hynek#UFO_origin_hypotheses
7. Hayakawa, N. F. (1993). UFOs, the Grand Deception and the Coming New World Order. Civilian Intelligence Network
8. Bates, G. (n.d.). UFOs as spiritual phenomena. Creation Ministries International. Retrieved March 7, 2023, from
https://creation.com/ufo-spiritual-phenomena
9. Douthat, R. (n.d.). Ross Douthat. Retrieved March 7, 2023, from https://rossdouthat.com/
10. Ganapathy, S. (n.d.). Interdimensional hypothesis. In Wikipedia. Retrieved March 7, 2023, from
https://en.wikipedia.org/wiki/Interdimensional_hypothesis
11. Tagliarini, J. (2023). The Reluctant Counselor, VOL 2, Pilgrimage to the Mystery of Presence. Self-regulation. Skubalon. Space
Daddies. Love & Elvis. Oxford Seraphim Wellness Publications.

Bibliography for Preface

1. Milligan, S., & Barker, C. (1968). The Bald Twit Lion. Dennis Dobson.
2. Kolk, B. (2021). The Body Keeps the Score. La Vergne: Memories of Ages Press.

Bibliography for Chapter One

1. Young, W. P. (2008). The Shack. Hodder & Stoughton.
2. Klonsky, D., & Muehlenkamp, J. (2007). Self-injury: A research review for the practitioner. Journal of Clinical Psychology, 63(11),
1045-1056. http://dx.doi.org/10.1002/jclp.20412
3. Wikipedia contributors. (2024). Operation Barbarossa. In Wikipedia. Retrieved June 10, 2024, from
https://en.wikipedia.org/wiki/Operation_Barbarossa
4. Wikipedia contributors. (2024). Italy in World War II. In Wikipedia. Retrieved June 10, 2024, from
https://en.wikipedia.org/wiki/Military_history_of_Italy_during_World_War_II
5. Wikipedia contributors. (2024). Prisoner of war. In Wikipedia. Retrieved June 10, 2024, from
https://en.wikipedia.org/wiki/Prisoner_of_war
6. Wikipedia contributors. (2024). Italian prisoners of war in the Soviet Union. In Wikipedia. Retrieved June 10, 2024, from
https://en.wikipedia.org/wiki/Italian_prisoners_of_war_in_the_Soviet_Union
7. Wikipedia contributors. (2024). World War II casualties. In Wikipedia. Retrieved June 10, 2024, from
https://en.wikipedia.org/wiki/World_War_II_casualties
8. Améry, J. (1980). At the mind's limits: Contemplations by a survivor on Auschwitz and its realities. Indiana University Press.
9. https://en.wikipedia.org/wiki/Triskelion
10. Celentano, A. (1966). Il ragazzo della via Gluck. [Recorded by A. Celentano]. La festa [Album]. Clan Celentano.
11. Brewster, D. (2019). Memoirs of the life writings and discoveries of Sir Isaac Newton. Forgotten Books.

12. Darwin, C. (1872). The expression of the emotions in man and animals. John Murray. https://doi.org/10.1037/10001-000

13. Freud, S. (1915-1917). A child's first erotic object. In J. Strachey (Ed. & Trans.), The standard edition of the complete psychological works of Sigmund Freud (Vol. 17, pp. 189-195). Hogarth Press. (Original work published 1917)

14. Klein, M. (1988). The psychotherapy of the psychoses. In M. Klein, J. Heimann, & S. Isaacs (Eds.), Love, guilt and reparation and other works 1921-1945 (pp. 233-268). Vintage.

15. Bowlby, J. (1965). Maternal care and mental health: A report prepared on behalf of the World Health Organization as a contribution to the United Nations program for the welfare of homeless children. Penguin Books. (Original work published 1951).

Bibliography for Chapter Two

1. Miller, A., & Jesenovec, B. P. (2005). Violence Kills Love: Spanking, the Fourth Commandment and the Suppression of Authentic Emotions. Magazine ONA (Slovenia). Retrieved from https://www.alice-miller.com/en/violence-kills-love-spanking-the-fourth-commandment-and-the-suppression-of-authentic-emotions/

2. Abram, J. (1996). The Language of Winnicott: A Dictionary of Winnicott's Use of Words, Second Edition. Clunie Press. (p. 115). Retrieved from https://docslide.us/documents/the-language-of-winnicott-1996.html

3. Bőthe, B., Tóth-Király, I., Potenza, M. N., Griffiths, M. D., Orosz, G., & Demetrovics, Z. (2015). The development of the Problematic Sexual Behavior Inventory: A preliminary study with men and women. Journal of Behavioral Addictions, 4(4), 293-302. doi: 10.1556/2006.4.2015.038

4. Brubaker, M. D., & Garrett-Walker, J. (2019). Shame and sex addiction: A systematic review of the literature. Journal of Sex Research, 56(9), 1109-1121. doi: 10.1080/00224499.2018.1527253

Bibliography of Chapter Three

1. Sevison, A. (n.d.). Give me oil in my lamp [Hymn]. Hymnary.org. https://hymnary.org/text/give_me_oil_in_my_lamp_keep_me_burning

2. McClellan, S., Paculabo, J. (1946-2013), & Ryecroft, K. (b 1949). Colors Of Day.

3. The Bible. *1st Corinthians 13:11.*

4. The Bible. *Genesis 49:12*

5. Blackmore, S. (1998). Abduction by aliens or sleep paralysis? Skeptical Inquirer, 22(5). https://www.csicop.org/si/show/abduction_by_aliens_or_sleep_paralysis

6. Tiffon, C. (2018). The Impact of Nutrition and Environmental Epigenetics on Human Health and Disease. International Journal of Molecular Sciences, 19(11), 3425. https://doi.org/10.3390/ijms19113425

7. Wikipedia contributors. (n.d.). One Punch Man. In Wikipedia. Retrieved November 10, 2023, from https://en.wikipedia.org/wiki/One_(manga_artist)

8. Nietzsche, F. (1883–1892). Also sprach Zarathustra: Ein Buch für Alle und Keinen. Germany: Ernst Schmeitzner.

9. https://en.wikipedia.org/wiki/Hungry_ghost

10. Gazzaniga, M. S. (2018). The consciousness instinct: Unraveling the mystery of how the brain makes the mind. Farrar, Straus and Giroux.

11. Erikson, E. H. (1963). Childhood and Society. Vintage Digital.

12. Lewis, S., & Abell, S. (2017). Autonomy versus shame and doubt. In Encyclopedia of Personality and Individual Differences (pp. 1–4). https://doi.org/10.1007/978-3-319-28099-8_570-1

13. Orenstein, G. A., & Lewis, L. (2021). Erikson's stages of psychosocial development. PubMed; StatPearls Publishing. https://www.ncbi.nlm.nih.gov/books/NBK556096/

14. McClellan, S., Paculabo, J. (1946-2013), & Ryecroft, K. (b 1949). Colors Of Day.

Bibliography of Chapter Four

1. Hoffman Institute. (2019). Hoffman Magazine. Retrieved from https://issuu.com/hoffmaninstitute/docs/hoffman_magazine_2019

2. Hinshelwood, R. D. (1997). An introduction to object relations (Chapter 3, pp. 60-61). The Counselling Foundation.

https://www.counsellingfoundation.org/wp-content/uploads/2014/10/An-Introduction-To-Object-Relations-1997-Chap-3.pdf

3. Psychology Wiki. (n.d.). Ronald Fairbairn. Retrieved March 9, 2023, from https://psychology.wikia.org/wiki/Ronald_Fairbairn

4. The Bible. *Exodus 4:1-5*

5. Steven J. Hoekstra, Richard Jackson Harris & Angela L. Helmick (1999) Autobiographical Memories About the Experience of Seeing Frightening Movies in Childhood, Media Psychology, 1:2, 117-140, DOI: 10.1207/s1532785xmep0102_2

6. Effects of Horror Movies on Psychological Health of Youth.

https://pdfs.semanticscholar.org/1a56/14286ab561f021da51b50b7f2439abeac0fd.pdf


## Bibliography of Chapter Five


1. Edison, T. (1971). The diary of Thomas A. Edison. Chatham Press. (Original work published 1935).

2. Katehakis, A. (2016). The body, sexuality and trauma resolution. Shrink Rap Radio. https://www.shrinkrapradio.com/527.pdf

3. Maté, G. (2003). When the body says no: The cost of hidden stress. John Wiley & Sons.

4. The Bible. *Leviticus 20:6-7.*


## Bibliography of Chapter Six


1. Daily Mail. (2019, March 4). John Lennon's never-seen sketch of UFO he drew after he thought he saw one over New York. Retrieved from https://www.dailymail.co.uk/news/article-6777043/John-Lennons-never-seen-sketch-UFO-drawn-thought-saw-one-New-York.html

2. YouTube. (n.d.). John Lennon: "I saw a UFO." [Video]. Retrieved from https://www.youtube.com/watch?v=Xm1xhgB1-9E

3. Erikson, E. H. (1963). Youth: Change and challenge. Basic books.

4. Marcia, J. E. (2010). Life transitions and stress in the context of psychosocial development. In T. W. Miller (Ed.), Handbook of stressful transitions across the lifespan (pp. 19–34). Springer Science + Business Media.

5. Bisto. (n.d.). About Bisto. Retrieved from http://www.bisto.co.uk/about


## Bibliography of Chapter Seven


1. Tennov, D. (1979). Love and Limerence: The Experience of Being in Love. Scarborough House. (Psychologist Dorothy Tennov coined the term "limerence" as a state of mind which results from a romantic attraction to another person and typically includes obsessive thoughts and fantasies and a desire to form or maintain a relationship with the object of love and have one's feelings reciprocated).

2. The Bible. *Proverbs 27:8.*

3. "11 pop stars who claim to have seen UFOs." BBC Music. Retrieved from https://www.bbc.co.uk/music/articles/d09fdaf6-ca65-427d-8177-25f209ad9c3b

4. "How do I become a ufologist?" WiseGeek. Retrieved from https://www.wise-geek.com/how-do-i-become-a-ufologist.htm

5. Speigel, L. (2016). WikiLeaks Documents Reveal United Nations Interest In UFOs. HuffPost. Retrieved from https://www.huffpost.com/entry/wikileaks-ufos-united-nations_n_5813aa17e4b0390e69d0322e

6. Public Library of US Diplomacy. (Year of Publication). Diplomatic Discussions, Spacecraft, UNGA Resolutions, Unidentified Objects Detection. Retrieved from https://wikileaks.org/plusd/cables/1978USUNN05425_d.html

7. https://www.vdrsyd.com/planet/transpermia.html#:~:text=Introduction,more%20general%20concept%20of%20panspermia.

8. Schore, A. N. (2016). Modern attachment theory; the enduring impact of early right brain-brain development [Video]. YouTube. https://youtu.be/c0sKY86Qmzo

9. Schore, A. N. (2017). Interview with American Journal of Play, volume 9, number 2, 2017. Journal of Play, 9(2). https://www.journalofplay.org/sites/www.journalofplay.org/files/pdf-articles/9-2-interview.pdf

10. https://skepticalinquirer.org/1998/05/abduction-by-aliens-or-sleep-paralysis/

Bibliography of Chapter Eight

1. The Roper Poll. (1991). In 1991, the Roper Organization conducted a poll that found 2% of Americans believed they had been abducted by aliens. This equated to approximately 4 million people based on the population at the time. Retrieved from https://www.ropercenter.cornell.edu/polls/us-public-opinion-occult-spiritualism-and-paranormal-phenomena

2. The National Geographic Channel Poll. (2012). In 2012, the National Geographic Channel conducted a poll in which 36% of Americans stated that they believe in UFOs and 11% claimed to have personally seen a UFO. This poll did not specifically ask about alien abductions. Retrieved from https://www.nationalgeographic.com/news/2012/6/120619-ufos-sightings-polls-beliefs-space-science/

3. The Chapman University Survey of American Fears. (2018). In 2018, the Chapman University Survey of American Fears found that 14% of Americans believe they have been in contact with aliens, either through abduction or communication. Retrieved from https://blogs.chapman.edu/wilkinson/2018/10/16/americas-fear-of-aliens/

Bibliography of Chapter Ten

1. Freud, S. (1921). Group Psychology and the Analysis of the Ego. Standard Edition, Vol. 18, pp. 90-91.

2. Freud, S. (1976). "The Dissolution of the Oedipus Complex." In J. Strachey (Trans.), On Sexuality (Vol. 7, pp. 313-322). Penguin Freud Library, Harmondsworth, Penguin.

3. Yang, L. (1987). "Venus, the Goddess of Fertility, Numerologically 15 in Babylon and the Origin of the Chinese System of 8 Designs, Called Pa-Kua." Journal of Chinese Philosophy, 14(3), 273-282. doi:10.1142/S0192415X87000126.

Bibliography of Chapter Eleven

1. Vallee, J. F., & Davis, E. W. (1998). Physical analysis in ten cases of unexplained aerial objects with material samples. Journal of Scientific Exploration, 12(3), 359-386. Retrieved from http://www.scientificexploration.org/journal/jse_12_3_vallee_2.pdf

2. US House. Committee on National Security, the Border and Foreign Affairs. (2023). Unidentified Anomalous Phenomena: Implications on National Security. Hearing, 26 July. Washington: Government Printing Office. Available at: https://en.wikipedia.org/wiki/David_Grusch_UFO_whistleblower_claims

3. Wikipedia contributors. (n.d.). The War of the Worlds (1938 radio drama). In Wikipedia. Retrieved November 10, 2023, from https://en.wikipedia.org/wiki/The_War_of_the_Worlds_(1938_radio_drama)

Bibliography of Chapter Twelve

1. Wikipedia contributors. (n.d.). Alien autopsy. In Wikipedia. Retrieved November 10, 2023, from https://en.wikipedia.org/wiki/Alien_Autopsy

2. The Bible. *Genesis 32:22-32*

3. Alighieri, D., & Musa, M. (1985). The divine comedy. New York: Penguin Books.

Bibliography of Chapter Thirteen

1. The Bible. *2nd Thessalonians 2:9-11.*

2. https://www.theguardian.com/science/shortcuts/2014/may/14/pope-francis-baptise-martian-would-they-want-our-religions

Bibliography of Chapter Fourteen

1. Alighieri, D. (1308-1320). The Divine Comedy.

2. https://en.wikipedia.org/wiki/Discordianism

3. Nolan, C. (Director). (2008). The Dark Knight [Film]. Warner Bros. Pictures. Legendary Pictures, Syncopy. *Based on Characters appearing in comic books published by DC Comics*

4. https://www.investopedia.com/stock-analysis/021815/worlds-top-ten-news-companies-nws-gci-trco-nyt.aspx

5. Law Insider. (n.d.). Closed Claim. Retrieved from https://www.lawinsider.com/dictionary/closed-claim

6. The Bible. *2nd Corinthians 4:2.*

7. Holy Joys. (n.d.). John Wesley's Ritual for Infant Baptism. Holy Joys. From https://holyjoys.org/ritual-infant-baptism/

8. Alighieri, D. (1308-1320). The Divine Comedy.


Bibliography of Chapter Fifteen


1. Alighieri, D. and Ciardi, J. (2003) The divine comedy: The Inferno, the Purgatorio, and the paradiso. New York: New American Library.

2. The Bible. *Acts 19:18-19.*

3. Mate, Dr. Gabor. (2018). In the Realm of Hungry Ghosts. Vermilion.

4. Lawrence, B. (2008) The brother lawrence collection: Practice and presence of god - spiritual maxims - the life of brother lawrence. Radford: Wilder Publications.

5. The Bible. *Galatians 1:15.*

6. McClellan, S., Paculabo, J. (1946-2013), & Ryecroft, K. (b 1949). Colors Of Day.

7. McClellan, S., Paculabo, J. (1946-2013), & Ryecroft, K. (b 1949). Colors Of Day.

8. The Bible. *Acts 10:44.*

9. Worthington, E. (2006). Forgiveness and Reconciliation. Routledge.

10. Tongues of the mind. (2018). Science Magazine. Retrieved from https://www.science.org/content/article/tongues-mind

11. Somatic experiencing. (n.d.). Positive Psychology. Retrieved from https://positivepsychology.com/somatic-experiencing/

12. The Bible. *Ecclesiastes 1:9*


Bibliography of Chapter Sixteen


1. Laurent. (1981). The practice of the presence of God. London: Hodder & Stoughton.

2. Wikipedia. (n.d.). Brian Eno. Retrieved from https://en.wikipedia.org/wiki/Brian_Eno#cite_note-89

3. Selvin, J. (2 June 1996). Q and A With Brian Eno. San Francisco Chronicle. Retrieved from https://www.sfgate.com/music/popquiz/article/q-and-a-with-brian-eno-2979740.php

4. The Bible. *John 6:63.*

5. Rogers, C., Kirschenbaum, H., & Henderson, V. (1989). The Carl Rogers reader. Boston: Houghton Mifflin. pp. 137.

6. Rogers, C., Kirschenbaum, H., & Henderson, V. (1989). The Carl Rogers reader. Boston: Houghton Mifflin. pp. 137.

7. Uttal, W. R. (2013). Dualism: The original sin of cognitivism. New York: Psychology Press.

8. The Bible. *John 10:30.*

9. The Bible. *John 17:11.*

10. The Bible. *John 14:16-20.*

11. Geldard, K., & Geldard, D. (2010). Counseling adolescents: The proactive approach for young people. (3rd ed.). London: Sage. pp. 9.

12. https://www.tramwaycf.com/

13. The Bible. *Isaiah 60:17.*

14. The Bible. *Mark 16:17-20.*

15. The Bible. *Colossians 1:27*

16. The Bible. *John 9:6*


Bibliography of Chapter Seventeen


1. Rogers, C. (1951). *Client-centered Therapy: Its Current Practice, Implications and Theory.* Constable.

2. Rogers, C. R. (1995). *A way of being.* Mariner Books.

3. Maté, G. (2014). *Scattered minds.* Plume.

4. https://www.youtube.com/watch?v=edslpDKzdxc Environmentalist rips Ocasio-Cortez, Green New Deal

5. https://www.science.org/content/article/us-supreme-court-upholds-monsanto-soybean-patents-rejects-blame-bean-defense#:~:text=The%20court%20ruled%20that%20Monsanto's,environment%20that%20contain%20Monsanto's%20genes

6. *United States Census Bureau*. (n.d.). QuickFacts: Texas. Retrieved from https://www.census.gov/quickfacts/TX.

7. *World Population Review*. (n.d.). Countries. Retrieved from https://worldpopulationreview.com/countries.

8. UK National Ecosystem Assessment. (2011). Retrieved from https://uknea.unep-wcmc.org/Resources/tabid/82/Default.aspx.

9. Office for National Statistics. (2021). Population estimates for the UK, England and Wales, Scotland and Northern Ireland: mid-2021. Retrieved from https://www.ons.gov.uk/peoplepopulationandcommunity/populationandmigration/populationestimates.

10. Alcorn, R.C. (2007). Heaven. Carol Stream, Illinois: Tyndale House Publishers.

11. The Bible. KJV. Galatians 3:2

12. Schore, A. N. (1998b). Early shame experiences and infant brain development. In P. Gilbert & B. Andrews, Shame: interpersonal behavior, psychopathology, and culture (pp. 57–77). New York: Oxford University Press.

13. Schore, A. N. (2000). Foreword to the reissue of Attachment and Loss, Vol. 1: Attachment by John Bowlby. New York: Basic Books

14. Schore, A. N. (in press, a). The self-organization of the right brain and the neuro- biology of emotional development. In M. D. Lewis & I. Granic (Eds), Emotion,

development, and self-organization. New York: Cambridge University Press

15. Dante Alighieri. (Circa 1308–1321). The Divine Comedy (Italian: La divina commedia; original name: La commedia).

# VOLUME 2 BIBLIOGRAPHY

Bibliography of Interlude

1. Young, W. P. (2008). The Shack. Hodder & Stoughton.
2. The Bible. *Luke 19:10*
3. The Bible. *John 10:10*
4. The Bible. *John 12:46*
5. The Bible. *John 19:7*
6. The Bible. *Galatians 4:4*
7. The Bible. *1st Timothy 4:10*
8. The Bible. *John 8:36*

Bibliography of Chapter One

1. https://www.youtube.com/@PeteCabreraJr
2. https://www.youtube.com/@ThomasFischer1964/videos
3. https://www.youtube.com/@landmavericks/videos
4. https://www.youtube.com/@RoyalFamilyNetwork/videos
5. The Bible. *Nahum 1:3*

Bibliography of Chapter Two

1. https://www.youtube.com/@JohnGLakeMinistries
2. The Bible. *1st Peter 2:9*
3. The Bible. *Revelation 5:10*
4. "Crime and Safety in Harlow." (n.d.). crimerate.co.uk. Retrieved from https://crimerate.co.uk/essex/harlow#:~:text=Crime%20and%20Safety%20in%20Harlow&text=Harlow%20is%20the%20most%20dangerous,towns%2C%20villages%2C%20and%20cities.

Bibliography of Chapter Three

1. The Bible. *Revelation 21:1-5*
2. The Bible. *Acts 10:38,*
3. The Bible. Ephesians 3:19
4. The Bible. *Ephesian 5:18-20*
5. The Bible. *Colossians 1:19*
6. The Bible. *2 Peter 1:4*

Bibliography of Chapter Four

1. https://www.blueletterbible.org/
2. The Bible. *Hebrews 1:1-3*
3. Risdon, B. (2022). Maze of Deception. Dundurn Press.

Bibliography of Chapter Five

1.The Bible. *Isaiah 9:6*
2 .The Bible. *Revelation 5:8*
3. The Bible. *Isaiah 9:6*

Bibliography of Chapter Eight

1. The Bible. *Philippians 3:20*
2. The Bible. *John 17:16*
3. Donner, R. (Director). (1978). Superman [Motion picture]. Warner Bros
4. Schore, A. N. (2003). Affect Dysregulation and Disorders of the Self. W.W. Norton & Company.
5. McGilchrist, I. (2009). The Master and His Emissary: The Divided Brain and the Making of the Western World. Yale University Press.
6. The Bible. *Ecclesiastes 6:4-6*
7. The Bible. Deuteronomy 29:29
8. The Bible. *Ephesians 5:14*
9. The Bible. *John 15:9*
10. The Bible. *Hebrews 9:22*

Bibliography of Chapter Nine

1. Cloud, H., & Townsend, J. S. (2017). Boundaries: When to Say Yes, How to Say No to Take Control of Your Life. Zondervan.
2. Freud, S., Breuer, J., Strachey, J., Freud, A. and Richards, A. (2001). The Standard Edition of the Complete Psychological Works of Sigmund Freud. London: Vintage. [Dynamics of Transference] Freud, S., 1912:100.
3. Clarke, T. (2015). Irvin D. Yalom: A Conversation. Retrieved from https://terenceclarke.org/2015/05/12/irvin-d-yalom-a-conversation/
4. Devereux, D. (2016). Transference Love and Harm. Therapy Today for Counseling and Psychotherapy Professionals, 27(7).
5. Jung, C. G. (1978). Psychological Reflections. Routledge. (Original work published 1961).
6. The Bible. *1st Peter 1:12*
7. The Bible. *Jude 1:6*
8. Jung, C. G. (1960). Synchronicity: An Acausal Connecting Principle. In C. G. Jung & R. F. C. Hull (Trans.), The Collected Works of C. G. Jung (Vol. 8, pp. 417-519). Princeton University Press. (Original work published 1952).
9. Semivan, J. (2019, April 18). To The Stars*, UFO Legacy Programs and Experiencers [Video]. YouTube. https://www.youtube.com/watch?v=KxtL-sBhe30
10. Jung, C. G. (1960). The Significance of Constitution and Heredity in Psychology (Vol. 8). Routledge & Kegan Paul.
11. Brooker, C. (2011). Black Mirror. Zeppotron (2011–2013), House of Tomorrow (2014–2019), Broke & Bones (2023–present).

487

12. The Bible. *Matthew 24:24*

13. Essay Sauce. (n.d.). Does Stockholm Syndrome Affect All Abductees' Minds? Retrieved March 2, 2022, from https://www.essaysauce.com/philosophy-essays/does-stockholm-syndrome-affect-all-abductees-minds/.

14. Frederiks, M., & Nagy, D. (2021). Critical Readings in the History of Christian Mission (Vol. 3). Koninklijke Brill NV. ("To colonize their consciousness with the signs and practices, the axioms and aesthetics, of an alien culture")

15. Kim, L., 2023. AI-powered 'thought decoders' won't just read your mind—they'll change it. *Wired*, 12 September. Available at: https://www.wired.com/story/ai-thought-decoder-mind-philosophy/#:~:text=11%3A02%20AM-,AI%2DPowered%20'Thought%20Decoders'%20Won't%20Just%20Read,technology%20are%20even%20more%20concerning [Accessed 22 May 2024].

16. Vallée, J. (2008). Confrontations: A Scientist's Search for Alien Contact. Anomalist Books. (Original work published 1990).

17. Human Window. (n.d.). Dr Gabor Maté Interview: Childhood Trauma, Anxiety & Culture. Retrieved from https://humanwindow.com/dr-gabor-mate-interview-childhood-trauma-anxiety-culture/?fbclid=IwAR1Y1fD-snlU4yohgkL6csBZ_Nec_oPsMEhH4iwyObn9qeY86gbDza_AltU

18. Levin-Richardson, S. (2019). The Brothel of Pompeii: Sex, Class and Gender at the Margins of Roman Society. Cambridge University Press.

19. Rumi, J. al-D., Star, J., & Shiva, S. (1992). A Garden Beyond Paradise. Bantam Books.

20. Sterling, B. (1992). The Hacker Crackdown: Law and Disorder On the Electronic Frontier. Spectra Books. (p. 6)

21. Blue Letter Bible. (n.d.). Lexicon :: Strong's G4991 - sōtēria. Retrieved from https://www.blueletterbible.org/lexicon/g4991/kjv/tr/0-1/

22. Blue Letter Bible. (n.d.). Lexicon :: Strong's G4982 - sōzō. Retrieved from https://www.blueletterbible.org/lexicon/g4982/kjv/tr/0-1/

23. The Bible. *Hebrews 1:13-14, Hebrews 2:1-3, Hebrews 7:25.*

24. Maslow, A. H. (1954). Motivation and Personality. Harper & Row.

25. The Bible. *Acts 17:28.*

26. Rogers, C. (1951). Client-Centered Therapy. 515-520.

27. Rogers, C. (1963). The Actualizing Tendency in Relation to "Motives" and to Consciousness. In M.R. Jones (Ed.), Nebraska Symposium on Motivation (pp. 1-24). University of Nebraska Press.

Bibliography of Chapter Ten

1. Jacobshendel, H. (n.d.). Rupture and repair part 1: Infancy. Retrieved from https://www.hilaryjacobshendel.com/post/rupture-repair-part-1-infancy

2. Blue Letter Bible. (n.d.). Lexicon:Strong's G726 - harpagē. Retrieved from https://www.blueletterbible.org/lexicon/g726/kjv/tr/0-1/

3. Ogden, P. (2009). Emotion, mindfulness and movement: Expanding the regulatory boundaries of the window of affect tolerance. In D. Fosha, D. Siegal, & M. Solomon (Eds.), The healing power of emotion: Affective neuroscience development and clinical practice (pp. 77-94). New York: W.W. Norton.

4. Schore, A. N. (1994). Affect regulation and the origin of the self: The neurobiology of emotional development. Mahweh, NJ: Erlbaum.

5. CNBC Television. (2017, November 2). "They ABUSED Me For Years! I Need To Make This Public" - Elon Musk REVEALS His Abuse & Bullying! [Video]. YouTube. https://www.youtube.com/watch?v=n3ovMIuYcSw

6. Solving The Money Problem. Elon Musk: The Future Of Humanity, Mars, AI, Ending Aging [Video]. YouTube. https://www.youtube.com/watch?v=U-wgVLVj_AY

7. MarketWatch. (2017, November 15). Elon Musk opens up on love life, traumatic childhood, Tesla goals. https://www.marketwatch.com/story/elon-musk-opens-up-on-love-life-traumatic-childhood-tesla-goals-2017-11-15

8. Kudriavtsev, D. (2018, February 2). It's Time to Mine the Moon for Helium-3. China Is Already Planning on It. International Policy Digest. https://intpolicydigest.org/it-s-time-to-mine-the-moon-for-helium-3-china-is-already-planning-on-it/#:~:text=The%20current%20price%20for%20helium,%24140%20million%20for%20220%20pounds.

9. Young, W. P. (2008). The Shack. Hodder & Stoughton.

10. The Bible. *Matthew 5:4.*

11. May, B. (1986). Who Wants to Live Forever [Recorded by Queen]. On A Kind of Magic [Album]. EMI.

12. The Bible. *Ezekiel 1:5-11.*

13. The Bible. *Genesis 3:22.*

14. Saybrook University. (2017, September 14). Sylvia: The Struggle for Self-Acceptance | Saybrook University [Video]. YouTube. https://www.youtube.com/watch?v=l-ZdeOYwjgY

15. Rogers, C. R. (n.d.). Carl Rogers therapy session transcripts. Retrieved from https://anamartinspsicoterapiaacp.files.wordpress.com/2016/04/brodley-transcripts-of-carl-rogers-therapy-sessions.pdf

16. https://www.acpfrance.fr/wp-content/uploads/2019/04/Interview-Rogers-Sylvia5.Eng_.pdf

17. Stern, D. N. (2001). The interpersonal world of the infant. New York: BasicBooks.

18. Schore, A. N. (2001). The effects of early relational trauma on right brain development, affect regulation and infant mental health. Infant Mental Health Journal, 22(1-2), 201-269. https://doi.org/10.1002/1097-0355(200101/04)22:1%3C201::AID-IMHJ8%3E3.0.CO;2-9

19. Katehakis, A. (2016). Sex addiction as affect dysregulation: Alexandra Katehakis, Ph.D. [Interview transcript]. Shrink Rap Radio. Retrieved from https://shrinkrapradio.com/527-sex-addiction-as-affect-dysregulation-with-alexandra-katehakis/

20. Pines, A. M. (2004, July). Relationships: Love ain't enough. Psychology Today. Retrieved from https://www.psychologytoday.com/us/articles/200407/relationships-love-aint-enough

21. Mearns, D., Thorne, B., & McLeod, J. (2013). Person-Centered Counseling in Action (4th ed.). Sage.

22. Elizondo, L. (2021). The sky is not the limit: An insider's look at the UFO phenomenon. HarperCollins.

23. The Bible. *Colossians 1:26-27*

Bibliography of Chapter Eleven

1. Moulton, K. (2015, February 5). Born with the Perfect Pitch. University of Wisconsin-Madison News. https://news.wisc.edu/born-with-the-perfect-pitch/.

2. The Bible. *Genesis 15:5*

3. The Bible. *Genesis 32:26*

4. Jung, C. and Hull, R. (1978). Flying Saucers. MJF Books.

5. Harper, D. (2023). Etymology of Metaphor. Online Etymology Dictionary. https://www.etymonline.com/word/metaphor.

6. The Bible. *2 Thessalonians 2:11*

7. Jacobsen, A. (2021). Annie Jacobsen: Nuclear War, CIA, KGB, Aliens, Area 51, Roswell & Secrecy [Audio podcast episode]. In Lex Fridman Podcast (No. 420). Retrieved from https://www.youtube.com/watch?v=GXgGR8KxFao

8. The Bible. *Jude 6-12*

9. Flagrant 2 with Andrew Schulz & Akaash Singh. (2021, May 7). Episode #1314 w/Charlamagne tha God & Andrew Schulz [Audio podcast episode]. In Apple Podcasts. https://podcasts.apple.com/us/podcast/flagrant-2-with-andrew-schulz-akaash-singh/id1357019725?i=1000520019745.

10. Crick, F.H.C. and Orgel, L.E. (1973). Directed Panspermia. Icarus, 19, 341-346. Burchell, M.J. (2004). Panspermia Today. Astronomy and Geophysics, 45(1), 1.18-1.24. https://doi.org/10.1046/j.1468-4004.2003.45118.x

11. Frankwski, N. (Director). (2008). Expelled [DVD]. Premise Media.

12. Hovind, K. (2018, January 4). The Garden of Eden. YouTube. https://youtu.be/8_OC2t7mIWE.

13. Jordan, J.G. and Dezember, J. (2020). Piercing the Cosmic Veil: You Shall Not Be Afraid of the Terror by Night. Seekye1 USA.

14. Anderson, J.D. (2018). The Science of Magic. Teacher Created Material.

15. Wachowski, A. (Director/Writer), & Wachowski, L. (Director/Writer). (2003). The Matrix Reloaded [Motion picture]. United States: Warner Bros.

16. AZ Quotes. (n.d.). Jacques Vallee Quotes. Retrieved from https://www.azquotes.com/author/33226-Jacques_Vallee Vallee, J. (1990, 2008). Confrontations: A Scientist's search for Alien Contact. Anomalist Books.

17. Vallee, J. (1990, 2008). Confrontations: A Scientist's search for Alien Contact. Anomalist Books. Meheust, B. (1978). Science-Fiction et Soucoupes Volantes. Paris; Meheust, B. (1985). Soucoupes Volantes et Folklore. Paris. Cited in Vallee, J. (1990, 2008). Confrontations, 146, 159-161.

18. The Bible. *2nd Timothy 3:8.*

19. Senter, P., Robson, H., & Snyder, K. (2016). Snake to Monster: Conrad Gessner's Schlangenbuch and the Evolution of the Dragon in the Literature of Natural History. Journal of Folklore Research, 53(1), 67-124. doi:10.2979/jfolkrese.53.1-4.67 https://muse.jhu.edu/article/610975/pdf

20. DeSouza, J. (2021, August 28). The Extra-Dimensionals: True Tales And Concepts of Alien Visitors | John DeSouza. [Video]. YouTube. https://www.youtube.com/clip/Ugkx0AbF0hQIVv9KBYdtgGWphgXw_Y9ufgus

21. https://vault.fbi.gov/unexplained-phenomenon

22. Huffling, B. (2022, September 6). UFOs, Aliens and Christianity? Retrieved from http://brianhuffling.com/2022/09/06/ufos-aliens-and-christianity/?fbclid=IwAR0l30YonnLhkLfS3T3YEO_g-mUzZ8-pJMEYR_nvAZm5xTZE9Hv_ubeUvtE#comments

.

Bibliography of Chapter Twelve

1. Cohen, L. (1992). Anthem [Recorded by Leonard Cohen]. On The Future [Album]. Columbia Records.

2. Bowlby, J. (1988). A secure base: Parent-child attachment and healthy human development. Basic Books.

3. Bowlby, J. (1988). A secure base: Parent-child attachment and healthy human development. Basic Books.

4. Bowlby, J. (2005). A secure base. Routledge.

5. Klein, M. (1921). Development of conscience in the child. Love, guilt and reparation, 252. Klein, M. (1923). The development of a child. International Journal of Psychoanalysis, 4, 419-474. Bowlby, J. (2008). Attachment: Volume one of the Attachment and Loss Trilogy: Attachment Vol 1 (Attachment & Loss) (Revised edition). Vintage Digital.

6. Rogers, C. (1980). A way of being. Constable.

7. Thorne, B. (1998). Person-centered counseling and Christian spirituality: The secular and the holy. Whurr.

8. Uttal, W. (2013). Dualism the original sin of cognitivism. Psychology Press.

9. Rolling Stone Magazine, Issue 642, October 1992, Sinead O'Connor Cover.

10. Geldard, K., & Geldard, D. (2010). Counselling adolescents: The proactive approach for young people (3rd ed.). Sage.

11. Tuckwell, G. (2002). Racial identity, white counsellors and therapists. Open University Press.

12. The New York Times. (2020, July 23). Navy UFO footage: Pentagon finally confirms leaked 'real' videos are genuine. https://www.nytimes.com/2020/07/23/us/politics/pentagon-ufo-harry-reid-navy.html

13. Esquire. (2020, July 24). The Pentagon released new information about UFOs. Here's what we know. https://www.esquire.com/news-politics/politics/a33413711/pentagon-ufo-program-information-release/

14. Reitman, I. (1984). Ghostbusters. Columbia Pictures.

Bibliography of Chapter Thirteen

1. https://en.wikipedia.org/wiki/Mad_Dogs_and_Englishmen_(song)

2. Practical Pain Management. (n.d.). Elvis Presley: Head Trauma, Autoimmunity, Pain and Early Death. Retrieved from https://www.practicalpainmanagement.com/pain/other/brain-injury/elvis-presley-head-trauma-autoimmunity-pain-early-death#:~:text=The%20most%20serious%20head%20trauma,an%20indeterminate%20amount%20of%20time.

3. Kleinman, M. (2015). The unlikely story of "What happens in Vegas, stays in Vegas." The New Yorker. Retrieved from https://www.newyorker.com/business/currency/the-unlikely-story-of-what-happens-in-vegas-stays-in-vegas

4. Kolk, B. (2021). The Body Keeps the Score. Memories of Ages Press.

5. Jung, C. G. (1954). The structure and dynamics of the psyche (2nd ed.). Routledge.

6. The Bible. *Romans 8:19*

7. Office of the Under Secretary of Defense (Comptroller). (n.d.). Budget Materials. Retrieved from https://comptroller.defense.gov/Budget-Materials/

8. Rizzolatti, G., Fadiga, L., Gallese, V., & Fogassi, L. (1996). Premotor cortex and the recognition of motor actions. Cognitive Brain Research, 3(2), 131-141. doi: 10.1016/0926-6410(95)00038-0

9. Gallese, V., & Goldman, A. (1998). Mirror neurons and the simulation theory of mind-reading. Trends in Cognitive Sciences, 2(12), 493-501. doi: 10.1016/S1364-6613(98)01262-5

11. Shakespeare, W. (1606). Macbeth.

11. Breslin, J. (1975). How the Good Guys Finally Won: Notes from an Impeachment Summer. Viking Press.

12. The Mirror Weapon in Archimedes Era.A.S. Papadogiannis, N.S. Papadogianni, A. Carabelas, S. Tsitomeneas, P. Kyraggelos & T.G. Chondros. https://link.springer.com/chapter/10.1007/978-1-4020-8915-2_4

13. O'Brien, T. (1990). The things they carried. Houghton Mifflin.

14. The Bible. 1 Corinzi 13:12

15. Däniken, E., & Heron, M. (2017). Chariots of the Gods? Souvenir.

16. The Bible. *Ezekiel 16:5-8*

17. McGilchrist, I. (2010). The Master and His Emissary: The Divided Brain and the Making of the Western World. Yale University Press.

18. Ironson, G. (2006). An Increase in Religiousness/Spirituality Occurs after HIV Diagnosis and Predicts Slower Disease Progression over Four Years in People with HIV. Journal of General Internal Medicine, 21, 62-68. https://doi.org/10.1111/j.1525-1497.2005.00302.x

19. Duffell, N. (2014). Wounded Leaders: British Elitism and the Entitlement Illusion - A Psychohistory. Lone Arrow Press.

20. Duffell, N. (2014). The Making of Them: The British Attitude to Children and the Boarding School System. Therapy Today, 25(6), 14-18.

21. Miller, A., & Jesenovec, B. P. (2005). Violence Kills Love: Spanking, the Fourth Commandment and the Suppression of Authentic Emotions. ONA Magazine. Retrieved from https://www.alice-miller.com/en/violence-kills-love-spanking-the-fourth-commandment-and-the-suppression-of-authentic-emotions/

22. Freud, S., Person, E., Hagelin, A., & Fonagy, P. (1993). On Freud's "Observations on Transference-Love". In D. Stern (Ed.), Acting Versus Remembering in Transference-Love and Infantile Love, - Freud's "Observations on Transference-Love." (pp. 67-85). Yale University Press.

23. Fanon, F. (2008). Black Skin, White Masks (New Edition). Pluto Press.

24. The RSA. (2018). The Divided Brain and the Making of the Western World. Retrieved from https://www.thersa.org/globalassets/pdfs/blogs/rsa-divided-brain-divided-world.pdf

25. NSPCC. (2019). Gangs and Young People. Retrieved from https://www.nspcc.org.uk/preventing-abuse/keeping-children-safe/staying-safe-away-from-home/gangs-young-people/

26. The RSA. (2018). The Divided Brain and the Making of the Western World. Retrieved from https://www.thersa.org/globalassets/pdfs/blogs/rsa-divided-brain-divided-world.pdf

27. The Telegraph. (2014, January 22). Loving foster homes repaired brain damage of Romanian orphans. https://www.telegraph.co.uk/news/science/science-news/11370571/Loving-foster-homes-repaired-brain-damage-of-Romanian-orphans.html

28. Schore, A. N. (2016). Modern attachment theory; the enduring impact of early right brain-brain development [Video]. YouTube. https://youtu.be/c0sKY86Qmzo

29. Schore, A. N. (2017). Interview with American Journal of Play, volume 9, number 2, 2017. Journal of Play, 9(2). http://www.journalofplay.org/sites/www.journalofplay.org/files/pdf-articles/9-2-interview.pdf

Bibliography of Chapter Fourteen

1. Stevenson, A., Brown, L., & Hole, G. (2007). *Shorter Oxford English dictionary on historical principles*. Oxford: Oxford University Press.

2. The Bible. *1 Corinthians 13:4-8*

3. Mate, G. (n.d.). Toxic Culture [Video]. YouTube. Retrieved from https://www.youtube.com/results?search_query=toxic+culture+gabor+mate

4. Winick, M., Meyer, K. K., & Harris, R. C. (1975). *Malnutrition and environmental enrichment by early adoption*. Science, 190, 1173-1175. doi: 10.1126/science.1188366

5. British Association for Counselling and Psychotherapy. (2018). *Ethical framework for the counselling professions*. Retrieved from https://www.bacp.co.uk/media/3103/bacp-ethical-framework-for-the-counselling-professions-2018.pdf

6. Cozolino, L. (2002). *The neuroscience of psychotherapy: Building and rebuilding the human brain*. New York: Norton.

7. Schore, A.N. (2003). Affect Regulation and the Repair of the Self. W. W. Norton & Company

8. Brown, S. R. (2017). *The case for play.* The Strong National Museum of Play. Retrieved from http://www.journalofplay.org/sites/www.journalofplay.org/files/pdf-articles/9-2-interview.pdf

9. Davis, C. (1966). *Room to grow: A study of parent-child relationships*. Toronto: University of Toronto Press.

10. Tolan, J. (2012). *Skills in person-centered counseling and psychotherapy*. London: Sage.

11. Sieratzki, J. S., & Woll, B. (1996). *Why do mothers cradle their babies on the left?* Lancet, 347, 1746-1748. doi: 10.1016/S0140-6736(96)90813-2 Schore, A. N. (2013). Regulation theory and the early assessment of attachment and autistic spectrum disorders: A response to Voran's clinical case. Journal of Infant, Child and Adolescent Psychotherapy, 12, 164-189. doi: 10.1080/15289168.2013.822741

12. Malatesta, G., Marzoli, D., Rapino, M., & Tommasi, L. (2019). The left-cradling bias and its relationship with empathy and depression. Scientific Reports, 9, 6141.

13. Todd, B. K., & Banerjee, R. (2015). Lateralization of infant holding by mothers: a longitudinal evaluation of variations over the first 12 weeks. Laterality, 21, 12–33.

14. Almerigi, J. B., Carbary, T. J., & Harris, L. J. (2002). Most adults show opposite-side biases in the imagined holding of infants and objects. Brain and Cognition, 48, 258–263.

15. Miller, A., & Jesenovec, B. P. (2005). *Violence kills love: Spanking, the fourth commandment and the suppression of authentic emotions.* Magazine ONA (Slovenia). Retrieved from https://www.alice-miller.com/en/violence-kills-love-spanking-the-fourth-commandment-and-the-suppression-of-authentic-emotions/

16. Healthline. (n.d.). Sociopath. Retrieved from https://www.healthline.com/health/mental-health/sociopath

17. Institute for Economics and Peace. (n.d.). *Global Peace Index.* Retrieved from https://www.visionofhumanity.org/maps/#/

18. https://en.wikipedia.org/wiki/Viking_Squad

19. Fromm, E. (1978). *Psychoanalysis and religion.* New Haven: Yale University Press.

20. Jung, C. G. (1966). *The collected works of C. G. Jung* (Vols. 12-14). Princeton, NJ: Princeton University Press.

21. Greenberg, L. S., Rice, L. N., & Elliott, R. (1993). *Facilitating emotional change.* New York: Guilford Press.

22. Greenberg, L. S., Rice, L. N., & Elliott, R. (1993). *Facilitating emotional change* (p. 104). New York: Guilford Press.

23. Greenberg, L., Rice, L. and Elliott, R. (1993). *Facilitating Emotional Change: The Moment-by-Moment Process.* New York: Guilford Press.

24. Thompson, C. (2015). *The Soul of Shame: Retelling the Stories We Believe About Ourselves.* Illinois: InterVarsity Press.

25. BBC News. (2019, January 31). *Japan's Prisons are a Haven for Elderly Women.* https://www.bbc.com/news/stories-47033704

26. Bloomberg. (2017, August 3). *More elderly Japanese are committing petty crimes to go to prison.* The Japan Times. https://www.japantimes.co.jp/news/2017/08/03/national/crime-legal/elderly-japanese-committing-petty-crimes-go-prison/#.YVzEmC9KjIU

27. Newman, M. (2016). *Poverty among senior citizens in Japan.* Journal of Population Ageing, 9(2), 97-109. https://doi.org/10.1007/s12062-016-9141-6Grayson, C. E. (2018).

28. *Kangaroo Care Is Effective in Diminishing Pain Response in Preterm Neonates.* Embryo Project Encyclopedia. http://embryo.asu.edu/handle/10776/13072

29. *The Science of Psychotherapy.* (2016, August 29). An Interview with Allan Schore. https://www.thescienceofpsychotherapy.com/an-interview-with-allan-schore/

30. The Bible. *Isaiah 26:3.*

31. The Bible. *Revelation 13:8*

32. The Bible. *1 Timothy 4:10.*

33. Armstrong, K. (1993). *The History of God.* New York: Alfred A. Knopf.

34. History of Yesterday. (2018, December 5). *Sigmund Freud: A Brief Introduction to His Life and Work.* https://historyofyesterday.com/sigmund-freud-8465463ac204

35. https://en.wikipedia.org/wiki/Jacob_Freud#cite_note-11

36. Richards, P. S., & Bergin, A. E. (2014). *Handbook of Psychotherapy and Religious Diversity.* Washington, DC: American Psychological Association.

37. The Bible: *John 1:12*

38. The Bible: *Colossians 1:25-28.*

39. The Bible: *Philippians 3:8*

40. Milligan, S. and Games, A. (2003) *The Essential Spike Milligan.* London: Fourth Estate.

# ABOUT THE AUTHOR

As an international counselor, content writer, Life Skills teacher and recent cow-whisperer tending to the cows on his field in Asia, Joe brings extensive experience in therapeutic practice and mentoring to diverse communities. With a background encompassing locations like Bangkok, Beijing, Lebanon, London, New York, Nepal and various parts of Asia, Joe possesses a genuine passion for connecting with new people and embracing their stories and adventures.

Joe's qualifications from and membership in the BACP underscore his dedication to aiding individuals who have encountered trauma, assisting them on their journey toward love and emotional fulfillment. He is renowned for pioneering innovative Therapeutic Self-regulation, mindfulness and compact rebus resources, employed across schools and clinics worldwide to benefit people of all ages.

Outside of his professional pursuits, Joe takes pleasure in exploring the hills of Asia on his Honda Rebel 500, actively meeting people and listening to their stories

This is *his* story.